MW00624885

"In this accessible and engaging work, John Peckham outlines and engages with many of the ongoing debates in philosophical theology about God's attributes, exploring the *biblical* warrant for many of classical theism's claims about what God must be like if he is indeed maximally great. What emerges from Peckham's own biblically rooted approach is an immensely attractive picture of a God who is 'great' in terms of his capacity for, and commitment to, relationships of love. This book covers a tremendous amount of ground in a short space and is very useful as a resource for ongoing discussions of perfect being theology. The book also serves as a penetrating challenge to rethink the question of whether our starting point for a doctrine of God should be philosophical ideas of perfection or biblical themes of covenant. Thoughtful, informative, and highly recommended."

—**Kevin Kinghorn**, Asbury Seminary

"This book provides an excellent exposition and defense of moderate classical theism. Peckham displays vast knowledge of a wide range of biblical, philosophical, historical, and contemporary sources. He offers sagacious evaluation of controversial issues, and his covenantal approach is a significant contribution. After reading this book one feels a deep sense of gratitude for gaining a better understanding of the God whom we worship."

—**Andrew T. Loke**, Hong Kong Baptist University

"Peckham's *Divine Attributes* offers a much-needed voice in contemporary debates over the nature of God. For quite some time, the debates seem to be between those who wish to maintain a strict classical conception of God and those who affirm an open and relational model of God. What Peckham offers is a genuine middle ground between these two views that affirms traditional understandings of divine foreknowledge but also offers a relational and covenantal God with the rich emotional life that Scripture proclaims. *Divine Attributes* will be a game changer for debates about the nature of God. Strict classical theists and open theists must deal with the powerful biblical case that Peckham presents. If you are looking for a theology text that is faithful to the biblical witness and sensitive to the philosophical challenges that arise from thinking about the nature of God, then *Divine Attributes* is the book for you."

—**R. T. Mullins**, Helsinki Collegium for Advanced Studies

Divine Attributes

Knowing
the Covenantal God
of Scripture

JOHN C. PECKHAM

B
Baker Academic
a division of Baker Publishing Group
Grand Rapids, Michigan

© 2021 by John C. Peckham

Published by Baker Academic
a division of Baker Publishing Group
PO Box 6287, Grand Rapids, MI 49516-6287
www.bakeracademic.com

Printed in the United States of America

All rights reserved. No part of this publication may be reproduced, stored in a retrieval system, or transmitted in any form or by any means—for example, electronic, photocopy, recording—without the prior written permission of the publisher. The only exception is brief quotations in printed reviews.

Library of Congress Cataloging-in-Publication Data
Names: Peckham, John, 1981– author.
Title: Divine attributes : knowing the covenantal God of scripture / John C. Peckham.
Description: Grand Rapids, Michigan : Baker Academic, a division of Baker Publishing Group, [2021] | Includes bibliographical references and index.
Identifiers: LCCN 2020033260 | ISBN 9781540961259 (paperback) | ISBN 9781540964120 (casebound)
Subjects: LCSH: God (Christianity)—Attributes.
Classification: LCC BT130 .P36 2021 | DDC 231/.4—dc23
LC record available at https://lccn.loc.gov/2020033260

Unless otherwise indicated, Scripture quotations are from the New Revised Standard Version of the Bible, copyright © 1989 National Council of the Churches of Christ in the United States of America. Used by permission. All rights reserved.

Scripture quotations labeled JPS are from the Jewish Publication Society Version.

Scripture quotations labeled KJV are from the King James Version of the Bible.

Scripture quotations labeled NASB are from the New American Standard Bible® (NASB), copyright © 1960, 1962, 1963, 1968, 1971, 1972, 1973, 1975, 1977, 1995 by The Lockman Foundation. Used by permission. www.Lockman.org

Scripture quotations labeled NKJV are from the New King James Version®. Copyright © 1982 by Thomas Nelson. Used by permission. All rights reserved.

Baker Publishing Group publications use paper produced from sustainable forestry practices and post-consumer waste whenever possible.

To Fernando Canale,
my Doktorvater

Contents

Acknowledgments

Without the help and support of many people, I could not have written this book. First, I'd like to thank Dave Nelson at Baker Academic for his interest in this project and for his great support and guidance throughout the process. I am also grateful to Melisa Blok, who did a fantastic job guiding this project through the editing process. Many thanks are also due to the rest of the Baker Academic team, with whom it has been a joy and a privilege to work on this book.

I'd also like to thank my colleagues in the Theology and Christian Philosophy department of the seminary of Andrews University. It is my privilege to work with such great colleagues and friends. Thanks are also due to those who read part or all of this work and provided feedback and encouragement and to my students who have shown interest in the doctrine of God and encouraged me along the way.

I am also deeply grateful to my family. I cannot thank my parents, Ernest and Karen, enough for their untiring and constant support in so many ways. I am thankful to my nine-year-old son, Joel, for providing so much joy in my life. Thank you for being my best buddy. I am so glad you are my son. Last, but certainly not least, there are no words to express my love, gratitude, and appreciation for my amazing wife, Brenda, my best friend and the most wonderful wife and mother anyone could hope for.

Abbreviations

General

ANE   ancient Near Eastern
chap(s).   chapter(s)
DSS   Dead Sea Scrolls
LXX   Septuagint
MT   Masoretic Text
NT   New Testament
OT   Old Testament
v(v).   verse(s)

Scripture Versions

JPS   Jewish Publication Society
           Version
KJV   King James Version
NASB   New American Standard Bible
NIV   New International Version
NKJV   New King James Version
NRSV   New Revised Standard Version

Secondary Sources

ABD   *The Anchor Bible Dictio-
           nary*. Edited by David Noel
           Freedman. 6 vols. New York:
           Doubleday, 1992.
ACCS   Ancient Christian Commen-
           tary on Scripture
ANF   *Ante-Nicene Fathers*

AUSS   *Andrews University Sem-
           inary Studies*
BDAG   Bauer, Walter, Frederick W.
           Danker, William F. Arndt,
           and F. Wilbur Gingrich. *A
           Greek-English Lexicon of
           the New Testament and
           Other Early Christian Lit-
           erature*. 2nd ed. Chicago:
           University of Chicago Press,
           1979.
BDB   Brown, Francis, S. R. Driver,
           and Charles A. Briggs.
           *Brown-Driver-Briggs He-
           brew and English Lexicon*.
           Oxford: Clarendon, 1977.
BSac   *Bibliotheca Sacra*
CD   Karl Barth. *Church Dogmat-
           ics*. Edited by Geoffrey W.
           Bromiley and T. F. Torrance.
           14 vols. Edinburgh: T&T
           Clark, 1936–69.
EDNT   *Exegetical Dictionary of
           the New Testament*. Edited
           by Horst Balz and Gerhard
           Schneider. 3 vols. Grand
           Rapids: Eerdmans, 1990–93.
ERT   *Evangelical Review of
           Theology*

HALOT	Koehler, Ludwig, Walter Baumgartner, and Johann Jakob Stamm. *The Hebrew and Aramaic Lexicon of the Old Testament*. Translated and edited under the supervision of Mervyn E. J. Richardson. 4 vols. Leiden: Brill, 1994–99.		*Theology and Exegesis*. Edited by Willem A. VanGemeren. 5 vols. Grand Rapids: Zondervan, 1997.
		NPNF	*Nicene and Post-Nicene Fathers*. Edited by Philip Schaff. 14 vols. Buffalo: Christian Literature Company, 1885–87.
HBT	*Horizons in Biblical Theology*	*NTS*	*New Testament Studies*
HTR	*Harvard Theological Review*	*TDNT*	*Theological Dictionary of the New Testament*. Edited by Gerhard Kittel and Gerhard Friedrich. Translated by Geoffrey W. Bromiley. 10 vols. Grand Rapids: Eerdmans, 1964–76.
IJST	*International Journal of Systematic Theology*		
JATS	*Journal of the Adventist Theological Society*		
JBL	*Journal of Biblical Literature*		
JBTM	*Journal for Baptist Theology and Ministry*	*TDOT*	*Theological Dictionary of the Old Testament*. Edited by G. Johannes Botterweck and Helmer Ringgren. Translated by John T. Willis, G. W. Bromiley, and D. E. Green. 15 vols. Grand Rapids: Eerdmans, 1974–2006.
JETS	*Journal of the Evangelical Theological Society*		
JSNT	*Journal for the Study of the New Testament*		
JSOT	*Journal for the Study of the Old Testament*		
L&N	Louw, Johannes P., and Eugene A. Nida, eds. *Greek-English Lexicon of the New Testament: Based on Semantic Domains*. 2nd ed. New York: United Bible Societies, 1989.	*TLNT*	*Theological Lexicon of the New Testament*. C. Spicq. Translated and edited by J. D. Ernest. 3 vols. Peabody, MA: Hendrickson, 1994.
		TLOT	*Theological Lexicon of the Old Testament*. Edited by Ernst Jenni and Claus Westermann. Translated by Mark E. Biddle. 3 vols. Peabody, MA: Hendrickson, 1997.
LCL	Loeb Classical Library		
NIB	*The New Interpreter's Bible*. Edited by Leander E. Keck. 12 vols. Nashville: Abingdon, 1994–2004.		
NIDNTT	*New International Dictionary of New Testament Theology*. Edited by Colin Brown. 4 vols. Grand Rapids: Zondervan, 1975–78.	*TWOT*	*Theological Wordbook of the Old Testament*. Edited by R. Laird Harris, Gleason L. Archer Jr., and Bruce K. Waltke. 2 vols. Chicago: Moody, 1980.
NIDOTTE	*New International Dictionary of Old Testament*		

Introduction

The Covenantal God of Scripture

This book addresses some core questions about the nature and attributes of God, focusing on what we have biblical warrant to affirm with respect to such questions, in order to better understand the living God whom Christians worship and to whom Christians pray. These questions include: Does God change? Does God have emotions? Does God know everything, including the future? Is God all-powerful? Does everything occur as God wills? Is God entirely good and loving? How can God be one God and three persons?

To set the stage for the following chapters, this introduction offers an overview of some significant portrayals of and claims about God that repeatedly appear in Scripture and that are important to keep in mind throughout this book.[1] In short, Scripture depicts God as a covenantal God who

creates, sustains, and creates anew;

speaks, hears, and responds;

sees, provides, delivers/saves, and rules;

knows, plans, wills, calls, and chooses but has unfulfilled desires;

judges, acts justly, *and* mercifully and graciously forgives;

loves compassionately, passionately, and steadfastly;

grieves, suffers, laments, and relents;

---

1. While many other biblical depictions could be surveyed here, I have selected these because of their prominence throughout Scripture and because of their significance to the questions considered in this book.

1

promises, covenants, and engages in covenant relationship;
engages in court proceedings and defeats evil; and
dwells with us and makes holy.

The God of Scripture Creates, Sustains, and Creates Anew

From beginning to end, Scripture emphasizes that God is the only Creator
(e.g., Isa. 45:18). "In the beginning God created the heavens and the earth"
(Gen. 1:1 NASB), and "God saw all that He had made, and behold, it was very
good" (1:31 NASB).[2] Indeed, "everything created by God is good" (1 Tim. 4:4
NASB). God is "before all things" (Col. 1:17 NASB) and "created all things,"
for "because of [God's] will they existed, and were created" (Rev. 4:11 NASB;
cf. Ps. 33:6; Col. 1:16; Heb. 11:3).

As Creator of all, God transcends creation. The God of Scripture not only
creates all but "upholds all things by the word of His power" (Heb. 1:3 NASB).
Amazingly, God *freely* sustains creatures even after they egregiously rebel (see,
e.g., Hosea 14:4). Everything depends on God for its existence, but as Creator,
God exists of himself (*a se*). There is an absolute distinction between God and
creatures, the Creator-creature distinction. As Creator, God is utterly unique:
"I am God, and there is no other; / I am God, and there is no one like Me"
(Isa. 46:9 NASB; cf. Exod. 8:10; 9:14; Ps. 86:8). Yet given that "God created
humankind in his image" (Gen. 1:27), there is *some* likeness between God and
humans, though far greater unlikeness.

Because God "created all things" by his "will," God is uniquely praiseworthy (Rev. 4:11 NASB). Creatures are to "worship Him [and him alone] who
made the heaven and the earth and sea and springs of waters" (14:7 NASB;
cf. Exod. 20:11; Pss. 33:8; 95:1–6). Moreover, in the end, the Creator will
make "all things new," including "a new heaven and a new earth" (Rev. 21:1,
5 NASB; cf. Isa. 65:17; 66:22), "according to His promise" (2 Pet. 3:13 NASB).

The God of Scripture Speaks, Hears, and Responds

In the act of creation, God spoke. "God said, 'Let there be light'; and there
was light" (Gen. 1:3 NASB). "By the word of the LORD the heavens were
made" (Ps. 33:6 NASB), for God "spoke, and it was done; / He commanded,
and it stood fast" (33:9 NASB). Yes, "the worlds were prepared by the word
of God" (Heb. 11:3 NASB).

---

2. Unless otherwise noted, all biblical quotations are from the NRSV.

The God of Scripture also repeatedly speaks *to* creatures. In the garden of Eden, God speaks to Adam, Eve, and even the serpent. Then God speaks to Cain, Noah, Job, Abraham, Hagar, Isaac, Jacob, Joseph, Moses, Aaron, Miriam, Pharaoh, the nation of Israel, judges, prophets, kings, apostles, and many others. In speech and other manners, the God of Scripture is a God of revelation (see Heb. 1:1–2).

The God of Scripture not only speaks but also hears and responds. Throughout Scripture, God repeatedly engages in *back-and-forth* dialogue with creatures. When God tells Abraham about impending judgment on Sodom, Abraham repeatedly asks God to spare the city for the sake of even a small number of righteous in it, and God responds that he will not destroy the city if even ten righteous people may be found there (Gen. 18:26, 32; cf. Gen. 15). Later, Jacob prays to God for deliverance on the basis of his covenant promises (32:9–12), then wrestles with a "man" who turns out to be divine—clinging to him until the "man" agrees to bless him (32:24–30; cf. Hosea 12:3–4). Elsewhere God directly responds to Job's pointed questions about his undeserved suffering (Job 38–41) and engages in back-and-forth dialogue with (the) Satan before the heavenly council (1:6–12; 2:1–6).

After the golden calf rebellion, Moses persistently petitions God to relent and continue to dwell with Israel in covenant relationship (Exod. 32:11–14, 30–34). Via multiple rounds of back-and-forth dialogue, God assures Moses he will remain with Israel in covenant relationship and "make all [his] goodness pass" before Moses and "proclaim the name of the LORD before" him (33:19 NASB; see 33:14, 17; cf. 34:6–7). Indeed, "the LORD used to speak to Moses face to face, as one speaks to a friend" (33:11). Later, Hezekiah prays and God replies, "I have heard your prayer, I have seen your tears; behold, I will heal you," and "I will add fifteen years to your life" and "deliver you and this city" (2 Kings 20:5–6 NASB). Still later, Daniel prays for his people in exile (Dan. 9), and God responds. A host of other examples appear in Scripture.

God is sometimes moved by prayer, entreaty, and lament (see, e.g., Gen. 21:17; Exod. 2:24; 2 Chron. 7:14; Isa. 30:19; Jer. 33:3). God was "moved to pity by" his people's groaning (Judg. 2:18 NASB), "could bear the misery of Israel no longer" (10:16 NASB), and was "moved by prayer for the land" (2 Sam. 21:14; 24:25 NASB). Further, Jesus is repeatedly moved by seeing people in distress (e.g., John 11:33; cf. Matt. 14:14; Mark 6:34; Luke 7:13) and models a life of petitionary prayer (e.g., Matt. 26:39; Luke 22:32; 23:34; cf. Heb. 7:25). He declares, "Ask, and it will be given to you; seek, and you will find; knock, and it will be opened to you" (Matt. 7:7 NASB; cf. Luke 11:5–13; John 16:23; Rev. 3:20). In these ways (and others), the God of Scripture responds to creatures such that the course of divine action is affected by human activity (cf. Ps. 81:13–14; Jer. 18:7–10).

The God of Scripture Sees, Provides, Delivers/Saves, and Rules

Scripture repeatedly teaches that God "sees." God repeatedly "saw that" what he created "was good" (Gen. 1:4, 10, 18, 21, 25; cf. 1:31). Later, however, "God saw that the earth was corrupt; for all flesh had corrupted its ways upon the earth" (6:12; cf. Jer. 7:11). Here and elsewhere God sees in the sense of moral evaluation. Yet "God sees not as man sees, for man looks at the outward appearance, but the Lord looks at the heart" (1 Sam. 16:7 NASB; cf. Luke 16:15).

God's "seeing" is often translated in terms of God's providing. When Isaac asks Abraham where the lamb for the sacrifice is, Abraham answers, "God will provide [*rā'â*, literally "see"] for Himself the lamb" (Gen. 22:8 NASB).[3] After God does so, "Abraham called the name of that place The Lord Will Provide [*YHWH yir'eh* (from the root *rā'â*), "YHWH sees"]" (22:14 NASB; cf. 16:13; 1 Sam. 16:1). Repeatedly, God "sees" and acts. For example, "God saw the sons of Israel [enslaved in Egypt], and God took notice of them" (Exod. 2:25 NASB) and delivered them according to his covenant promises (cf. Gen. 31:42). Much later, "when God saw" that the Ninevites "turned from their wicked way," God "relented" (Jon. 3:10 NASB).

The God of Scripture provides for and governs the entire world, often acting providentially to save. God saves "many people" in Egypt and elsewhere from famine by sending dreams of warning to Pharaoh and giving Joseph opportunity and wisdom to interpret such dreams (Gen. 50:20). The way God repeatedly delivers Israel, in the exodus and afterward (Deut. 8:14–16), demonstrates God's sovereign rule over earthly rulers and "their gods" (2 Sam. 7:23 NASB; cf. Exod. 9:14; 12:12; Num. 33:4). Despite their cycle of rebellion, God repeatedly responds to his people's cries (e.g., Neh. 9; Ps. 78), sending deliverers and prophets, miraculously rescuing his people from foreign armies (e.g., 2 Kings 6:17–18; cf. Ps. 34:7), and otherwise working to deliver and redeem his people, for the sake of all peoples (Gen. 12:3). Despite many miraculous interventions on behalf of his people, the cycle of rebellion continues. The people eventually forfeit God's covenant protection and are given over to conquest and exile. Yet even in exile, God continues to work, manifesting God's sovereign rulership such that even King Nebuchadnezzar of Babylon comes to recognize that Daniel's God is

---

3. Unless otherwise noted, I gloss the noninflected verb or noun form of Hebrew and Greek terms so readers can more easily see patterns.

"God of gods and Lord of kings" (Dan. 2:47) with "everlasting sovereignty" (4:34; cf. 4:32).

The God of Scripture is the ruler of all; he "reigns over the nations" (Ps. 47:8 NASB). Ultimately, in Christ, God delivers and saves the world and sets up his "everlasting dominion" (see Dan. 7:13–14; Luke 1:33; Heb. 1:8; 2 Pet. 1:11). Christ does so first by a demonstration of God's utter righteousness and love (Rom. 3:25–26; 5:8), including the ultimate sacrifice, and later will return to fully establish his kingdom. In the end, the cry goes forth, "Hallelujah! For the Lord our God, the Almighty, reigns" (Rev. 19:6 NASB).

The God of Scripture Knows, Plans, Wills, Calls, and Chooses but Has Unfulfilled Desires

The God of Scripture works according to his plan or purpose—willing, calling, choosing, and sending. The world exists only by God's will (Rev. 4:11), and God declares

> the end from the beginning
> and from ancient times things not yet done,
> saying, "My purpose shall stand,
> and I will fulfill my intention,"
> calling a bird of prey from the east,
> the man for my purpose from a far country.
> I have spoken, and I will bring it to pass;
> I have planned, and I will do it. (Isa. 46:10–11; cf. Rom. 8:28–30)

God "knows all things" (1 John 3:20 NASB; cf. Rom. 11:33) and "works all things after the counsel of His will" (Eph. 1:11 NASB), often doing so by calling and electing people to various missions.

God calls Abraham to father a new people, the chosen people (Isa. 41:8–9) through whom God blesses all nations (Gen. 12:3; 22:18; 26:4) and through whom Jesus comes to save the whole world, including both Jews and Gentiles in God's elect (Rom. 9:24–26). God chooses Abraham's son Isaac as the child of the promise, and, of Isaac's twin boys, God graciously elects the slightly younger brother, Jacob (cf. Rom. 9). Later, God calls and elects Moses to lead his people out of slavery, affirming that God "chose" Israel "because the LORD loved [them] and kept the oath that he swore to [their] ancestors" (Deut. 7:7–8). Still later, God raises up and elects many priests, judges, prophets, and kings.

Though always unmerited, God's election is depicted as contingent on human response. In *response* to the people wickedly "demanding a king" against God's warnings (1 Sam. 12:17), thereby "reject[ing]" God "from being king over them" (8:7; cf. 10:19; 12:12–13), God chooses Saul to be king (10:24; cf. 12:13). While God "would have established" Saul's "kingdom over Israel forever" (13:13), by repeated disobedience Saul eventually forfeits his election (13:8–14; 15:3, 9–11, 23).

To replace Saul, God chooses David, "a man after His own heart" (1 Sam. 13:14 NASB), and covenants to "establish the throne of his kingdom forever" (2 Sam. 7:13 NASB; cf. 1 Sam. 13:13). This covenant promise is extended to Solomon, contingent on faithfulness; *if* Solomon remains faithful, God will establish his "kingdom over Israel forever," but if Solomon or his children "turn away from following" God, then God "will cut off Israel" (1 Kings 9:5–7 NASB). Tragically, Solomon is unfaithful, and the kingdom is divided in the next generation (11:11–13), followed by a line that includes many rebellious kings in Israel and Judah.

Though God repeatedly wanted to deliver and restore his elect people, God explains,

> I called, but no one answered;
> I spoke, but they did not listen.
> And they did evil in My sight
> And chose that in which I did not delight. (Isa. 66:4 NASB; cf. 65:12;
>   Jer. 7:13)

Elsewhere God declares,

> My people did not listen to my voice;
>   Israel would not submit to me.
> So I gave them over to their stubborn hearts,
>   to follow their own counsels.
> O that my people would listen to me,
>   that Israel would walk in my ways! (Ps. 81:11–13)

Jesus comes as the new Israel, the perfectly elect Son of God and of David, unwaveringly faithful to God's covenantal will. As God chose the twelve tribes of Israel, Jesus chooses twelve apostles (John 15:16–17), but Judas forfeits his election. Further, Jesus teaches via his parable of the wedding feast that "many are called [or invited], but few are chosen [*eklektos*]" (Matt. 22:14 NASB); many are invited (*kaleō*, "called") to the wedding feast but decline the invitation. Only those who accept the invitation are finally elect. While God is "patient . . . , not wanting any to perish, but all to come to repentance" (2 Pet. 3:9; cf. Ezek. 33:11; John 3:16), God's desires are sometimes unfulfilled because people reject God's calling and purpose. Luke 7:30 reports, "By refusing to be baptized by [John], the Pharisees and the lawyers rejected God's purpose for themselves." Accordingly, Christ laments over Jerusalem, "How often I wanted to gather your children together, the way a hen gathers her chicks under her wings, and you were unwilling!" (Matt. 23:37 NASB; cf. Deut. 32:11).

The God of Scripture Judges, Acts Justly, *and* Mercifully and Graciously Forgives

The God of Scripture cares deeply about justice. God "loves justice" (Ps. 37:28 NASB; cf. 33:5; 99:4) but hates evil (5:4–5). "Righteousness and justice are the foundation of [God's] throne," and "steadfast love and faithfulness go before" God (89:14; cf. 85:10). God's "work is perfect, for all his ways are just; a God of faithfulness and without injustice, righteous and upright is He" (Deut. 32:4 NASB; cf. Rev. 15:3; 19:1–2). God "is righteous in all His ways / And kind in all His deeds" (Ps. 145:17 NASB). God "will do no injustice" (Zeph. 3:5 NASB); he "is upright" and "there is no unrighteousness in Him" (Ps. 92:15 NASB). "God is Light, and in Him there is no darkness at all" (1 John 1:5 NASB). God cannot even be tempted by evil (James 1:13; cf. Hab. 1:13).

God always judges righteously (see Dan. 9:14; Neh. 9:33) but also mercifully warns and compassionately forgives. God's judgment itself is frequently an act of deliverance of the oppressed from their oppressors. God executes judgment only against evil. Even then God "does not willingly afflict or grieve anyone" (Lam. 3:33), bringing judgment only as a last resort after providing a way of escape. "I have no pleasure in the death of anyone, says the Lord GOD. Turn, then, and live" (Ezek. 18:32; cf. 18:23; 33:11). Although God's people repeatedly rebelled and broke covenant relationship in a cycle of rebellion (e.g., Ps. 78; Neh. 9), God

> being compassionate,
> > forgave their iniquity,
> > and did not destroy them;
> > often he restrained his anger,
> > and did not stir up all his wrath. (Ps. 78:38)

God did everything that could be done for Judah (Isa. 5:1–7); God "sent persistently to them by his messengers, because he had compassion on his people and on his dwelling place; but they kept mocking the messengers of

God, despising his words, and scoffing at his prophets, until the wrath of the LORD against his people became so great that there was no remedy" (2 Chron. 36:15–16; cf. Jer. 7:13, 25–26).

In all this, God's grace and mercy extend far beyond any reasonable expectations. God wants to forgive and redeem; God "longs to be gracious" and "waits on high to have compassion . . . / For the LORD is a God of justice" (Isa. 30:18 NASB). The God of Scripture is

> merciful and gracious,
> slow to anger,
> and abounding in steadfast love and faithfulness,
> keeping steadfast love for the thousandth generation,
> forgiving iniquity and transgression and sin,
> yet by no means clearing the guilty. (Exod. 34:6–7; cf. Nah. 1:3)

Instead, God makes atonement so that he can forgive those who are guilty, without compromising justice (see Jer. 30:11). This atonement is modeled in the sanctuary services, which point to Christ—the one who fulfills the sanctuary services as the only sufficient sacrifice, the ultimate high priest, and the living temple of God's presence. Whereas in the OT God repeatedly looks for and calls for intercession but often finds no one to effectively intercede (Ezek. 22:30), in the NT Jesus is found worthy (Rev. 5) and "is able to save forever those who draw near to God through Him, since He always lives to make intercession" (Heb. 7:25 NASB). Through Christ and by the Spirit (Rom. 8:26–27), God himself intercedes. God himself makes atonement (2 Cor. 5:18–19). God takes on himself the consequences of evil, demonstrating his righteousness (Rom. 3:25–26) and love (5:8). All judgment is given over to Christ (John 5:22), "the righteous Judge" (2 Tim. 4:8 NASB; cf. 1 John 2:1; Rev. 19:11), who will establish and rule over an eternal kingdom of perfect justice and love.

The God of Scripture Loves Compassionately, Passionately, and Steadfastly

The God of Scripture is an exceedingly "compassionate God" (Deut. 4:31 NASB). Scripture portrays God's love as akin to the tender affection of a parent who adopts and cares for a child. "Just as a father has compassion on his children, / So the LORD has compassion on those who fear Him" (Ps. 103:13 NASB). And "as a mother comforts her child, so" God promises to lovingly "comfort" his people (Isa. 66:13). Yet God's compassion is even greater than a mother's compassion for her newborn. God declares,

> Can a woman forget her nursing child,
> and have no compassion on the son of her womb?
> Even these may forget, but I will not forget you. (49:15 NASB)

God calls his people "my dear son" and "the child I delight in," proclaiming, "I am deeply moved for him; I will surely have mercy on him" (Jer. 31:20; cf. Luke 15:20).

God also "takes pleasure in" (Ps. 149:4 NASB; cf. Zeph. 3:17) and passionately loves his people. Scripture portrays God's love as the virtuous and passionate love of a husband for his wife, though she is repeatedly unfaithful (e.g., Hosea 1–3; Isa. 62:4; Jer. 2:2; 3; Ezek. 16; 23; Zech. 8:2; cf. 2 Cor. 11:2). Among other things, God's people "provoked him to anger with their high places; they moved him to jealousy with their idols" (Ps. 78:58; cf. Deut. 32:21; 1 Kings 14:22). Yet God is also passionate in favor of his beloved people and against those who abuse and oppress them (see Isa. 26:11; Joel 2:18; Zech. 1:14–17; Heb. 10:27).

In contrast to unreliable humans, God's character of love is utterly steadfast. Closely associated in Scripture with God's goodness, faithfulness, justice, and mercy, God's steadfast love (*ḥesed*) grounds covenant relationship while consistently going far beyond all duties and reasonable expectations. "Abounding in steadfast love and faithfulness," God continues his steadfast love toward Israel even after the golden calf rebellion (Exod. 34:6; cf. Ps. 86:15). Indeed, God's "steadfast love endures forever" (Ps. 136; cf. 1 Chron. 16:34; Jer. 31:3; 33:11; Rom. 8:35, 39); his "mercies are great" (2 Sam. 24:14 NASB; 1 Chron. 21:13; cf. Luke 1:78); his "lovingkindnesses indeed never cease"; and his "compassions never fail" (Lam. 3:22 NASB).

Just as the God of Israel is moved with compassionate, passionate, and steadfast love for his people throughout the OT (e.g., Judg. 2:18; Isa. 30:18–19), in the NT Jesus is frequently moved to compassion, often by people in need (Matt. 9:36; 14:14; Mark 1:41; 6:34; Luke 7:13; cf. Mark 10:21). The incomparable passion and steadfastness of Christ's love is ultimately manifested in Christ's self-giving at the cross (John 15:13; Rom. 5:7–8). The God of the cross is "rich in mercy" and "great love" (Eph. 2:4 NASB; cf. Exod. 34:6–7; Luke 1:78; 2 Cor. 1:3). Accordingly, we can confidently cast our cares on God, "because he cares for [us]" (1 Pet. 5:7).

The God of Scripture Grieves, Suffers, Laments, and Relents

The God of Scripture grieves, suffers, and laments evil. According to Genesis 6:6, "The LORD was sorry that he had made humankind on the earth, and it grieved him to his heart." Later, "in all their affliction, He was afflicted," and though God "lifted" the people and "carried them all the days of old," God's covenant people "rebelled and grieved His Holy Spirit" (Isa. 63:9–10 NASB). Indeed, Psalm 78:40–41 proclaims,

> How often they rebelled against Him in the wilderness
> And grieved Him in the desert!
> Again and again they tempted God,
> And pained the Holy One of Israel. (NASB; cf. 1 Cor. 10:5)

After recounting extreme evils (including child sacrifice [2 Kings 21:6]), God says of his people, "They have done evil in My sight, and have been provoking Me to anger since the day their fathers came from Egypt, even to this day" (21:15 NASB; cf. Deut. 4:25; 32:16, 21; Judg. 2:12; 1 Kings 14:9; Ps. 78:58; Isa. 65:3; Jer. 7:18–19; Ezek. 8:17; 16:26; 20:28; Hosea 12:14[15]).[4] Elsewhere God laments,

> I reared children and brought them up,
>   but they have rebelled against me.
> . . . .
> Ah, sinful nation,
>   people laden with iniquity,
> offspring who do evil,
>   children who deal corruptly,
> who have forsaken the LORD,
>   who have despised the Holy One of Israel,
> . . . .
>   Why do you continue to rebel? (Isa. 1:2, 4–5; cf. Jer. 3)

Elsewhere, God laments, "Oh that My people would listen to Me, / That Israel would walk in My ways!" (Ps. 81:13 NASB; cf. Ezek. 33:11). And God proclaims,

> How can I give you up, O Ephraim?
> How can I surrender you, O Israel?
> How can I make you like Admah?
> How can I treat you like Zeboiim?
> My heart is turned over within Me,
> All My compassions are kindled. (Hosea 11:8 NASB; cf. Jer. 31:20)

4. In this and other cases where brackets appear in citations from the OT, the brackets include the versification from the MT.

God also relents. In response to Moses's pleas after the golden calf rebellion, "the LORD relented from the harm which He said He would do to His people" (Exod. 32:14 NKJV; cf. Jon. 3:10). While God is the sovereign potter and humans are the clay, God relents from judgment in response to repentance (Jer. 18:7–10). When Israel "put away the foreign gods from among them and worshiped the LORD," God "could no longer bear to see Israel suffer" (Judg. 10:16; cf. 2:18). God is repeatedly "moved to pity by" the "groaning" of his people (2:18 NASB). Even as God grieves and laments in the OT, in the NT Christ grieves and laments over evil (Matt. 23:37) and voluntarily suffers to defeat it.

The God of Scripture Promises, Covenants, and Engages in Covenant Relationship

The God of Scripture is a promise-making God who engages in back-and-forth covenant relationship and always keeps his promises. God covenants with Noah "and every living creature . . . for all future generations," promising "never again shall all flesh be cut off by the waters of a flood" (Gen. 9:11–12; cf. 6:18; 9:9–17). After the tower of Babel narrative, which some interpret as evidence of the people's unbelief in God's promise and their rebellion, God calls Abraham to leave his country, promising, "I will make of you a great nation, and I will bless you, and make your name great, so that you will be a blessing" and "in you all the families of the earth shall be blessed" (12:2–3; cf. 15:17–18). This covenant blessing is not for Abraham's (natural) descendants alone but extends to "all the nations of the earth" (26:4), a promise ultimately fulfilled in Christ—the desire of all nations (cf. Hag. 2:7). In Christ, "those who believe are the descendants of Abraham" (Gal. 3:7); "if you belong to Christ, then you are Abraham's descendants, heirs according to promise" (3:29 NASB; cf. 3:6–9).

God's covenant relationship with Abraham is not unilateral but requires response. God commands Abraham, "I am God Almighty; walk before Me, and be blameless. I will establish My covenant between Me and you, and will multiply you exceedingly" (Gen. 17:1–2 NASB; cf. 17:3–6). This is an "everlasting covenant" with Abraham and his offspring (17:7 NASB), but it also includes conditions. It is a grant-type covenant, which promises a faithful servant continuance of covenant blessings to future generations, but whether particular generations enjoy covenant blessings is contingent on faithfulness (17:10–11, 14). Accordingly, God says of Abraham, "I have chosen him, that he may charge his children and his household after him to keep the way of the

Lord by doing righteousness and justice; so that the Lord may bring about for Abraham what he has promised him" (18:19). Later, God tells Isaac, "I will fulfill the oath that I swore to your father Abraham . . . because Abraham obeyed my voice and kept my charge, my commandments, my statutes, and my laws" (26:3, 5; cf. 22:16–17; Heb. 11:17–19).

In Exodus, God keeps his promises to Abraham, extended in the so-called Mosaic covenant (Gen. 15:13–18; Deut. 7:7–8; 9:5; Ps. 105). God "heard" the people's "groaning" and "remembered His covenant with Abraham, Isaac, and Jacob" (Exod. 2:24 NASB). God identifies himself to Moses from the burning bush, saying, "I am the God of your father, the God of Abraham, the God of Isaac, and the God of Jacob. . . . I have surely seen the affliction of My people" and "have given heed to their cry" and "am aware of their sufferings," and I will "deliver them from the power of the Egyptians" and bring them to the land promised to Abraham (3:6–8 NASB; cf. 3:13–15).

After delivering the people in the exodus, God provides more specific covenant laws, with explicit blessings and curses contingent on covenant faithfulness. God promises, "If you obey my voice and keep my covenant, you shall be my treasured possession out of all the peoples. Indeed, the whole earth is mine, but you shall be for me a priestly kingdom and a holy nation" (Exod. 19:5–6). Further, God promises that if the people are faithful, "I will make My dwelling among you" and "walk among you and be your God, and you shall be My people" (Lev. 26:11–12 NASB). But if the people "do not obey" and "break My covenant" (26:14–15 NASB), covenant curses will follow instead (26:16–39; cf. Deut. 7:7–13; 29:9–25). For his part, God always keeps his covenant commitments, and God's mercy graciously extends far beyond all obligations, covenantal or otherwise (Exod. 32–34; Deut. 9:6–7)

Much later, God establishes the Davidic covenant—a grant-type covenant in which God promises David, "Your throne shall be established forever" (2 Sam. 7:16 NASB; cf. 1 Kings 3:6–7; Ps. 89:2–4, 26–38, 49; Acts 2:30). Yet some blessings are contingent: "If your sons are careful of their way, to walk before Me in truth with all their heart and with all their soul, you shall not lack a man on the throne of Israel" (1 Kings 2:4 NASB; cf. 9:4–7; Ps. 132:11–12). Nevertheless, God proclaims, "If any of you could break my covenant with the day and my covenant with the night, so that day and night would not come at their appointed time, only then could my covenant with my servant David be broken, so that he would not have a son to reign on his throne" (Jer. 33:20–21; cf. 31:35–37; Ps. 89:33–34; Heb. 6:17–18).

While the merely human line of David tragically fails, despite God's repeated warnings (see, e.g., 1 Kings 9:6–7; Jer. 11:5–7), in Christ—the covenantal son of David—the everlasting covenant is fulfilled (see Luke 1:68–75).

In Christ, the new covenant is established (22:20; cf. 1 Cor. 11:25; Heb. 9:15; 12:24), and Christ is "the mediator of a better covenant, which has been enacted on better promises," as God promised in the OT (Heb 8:6 NASB; see 8:8–12, quoting Jer. 31:31–34; cf. Gen. 3:15; Jer. 32:38–41; Ezek. 11:19; 18:31; 36:26; Heb. 9:15). In all this, the God of Scripture is a covenantal God who always keeps his promises and engages in back-and-forth covenant relationship.

The God of Scripture Engages in Court Proceedings and Defeats Evil

The God of Scripture also engages in back-and-forth legal proceedings, some of which biblical scholars refer to as covenant lawsuits. While there is dispute over what qualifies as a *formal* covenant lawsuit, Scripture repeatedly portrays God as the cosmic judge who brings charges (lawsuits) against the nations, their gods, and sometimes his covenant people.[5] Indeed, Scripture frequently depicts a heavenly council or court including celestial creatures, presided over by YHWH, the proceedings of which affect what takes place on earth.[6]

The book of Job depicts a back-and-forth dispute between God and (the) Satan during proceedings of the heavenly council, wherein (the) Satan brings slanderous allegations against Job and against God's positive judgment of Job (Job 1:6–12; 2:1–7; cf. Zech. 3:1–7). Another heavenly court scene appears in Daniel 7, portraying a "cosmic lawsuit."[7] After Daniel sees (in a vision) four beasts representing four successive oppressive kingdoms, Daniel sees a heavenly court:

> Thrones were set up,
> And [God] the Ancient of Days took His seat.
> . . . .
> Thousands upon thousands were attending Him,
> And myriads upon myriads were standing before Him;
> The court sat,
> And the books were opened. (7:9–10 NASB; cf. 7:26)

5. See, e.g., 1 Kings 22:19–23; 2 Chron. 18:18–22; Job 1:6–12; 2:1–7; Pss. 29:1–2; 82; 89:5–8; Isa. 6:1–13; Dan. 7:9–14; Zech. 3:1–7; cf. Isa. 24:21–23; Jer. 23:18, 22; Ezek. 1–3; Dan. 4:13, 17; Amos 3:7–8; Rev. 4:1–5:14; 7:9–17; 8:1–4; 11:15–18; 14:1–5; 15:2–8; 19:1–10; see also R. Davidson, "Divine Covenant Lawsuit Motif," 83.

6. See chap. 6.

7. Louis F. Hartman comments that this is a depiction of the "celestial court" or "celestial tribunal," a picture of the "divine judge enthroned in the assembly of his angels." Hartman and Di Lella, *Daniel*, 217.

Afterward, judgment is executed against the beasts, and the Son of Man is given an "everlasting dominion" (7:12–14 NASB; cf. Ps. 82; Rev. 12–13). This scene exhibits a common biblical pattern: "Before God executes judgment (either positively or negatively) toward an individual or a people, He first conducts legal proceedings, not for Him to know the facts, but to reveal in open court, as it were, that He is just and fair in all of His dealings."[8]

Language of a cosmic lawsuit or trial also appears in the NT. Paul speaks of his ministry as an exhibit in cosmic legal proceedings: "For, I think, God has exhibited us apostles last of all, as men condemned to death; because we have become a spectacle to the world [*kosmos*], both to angels and to men" (1 Cor. 4:9 NASB).[9] Elsewhere Paul states, "The saints will judge the world" and "we will judge angels" (6:2–3 NASB). Further, Christians are repeatedly called "witnesses" who are to "testify," alongside other legal and courtroom imagery (cf. the heavenly court scenes in Revelation). Christ himself "came into the world, to testify to the truth" (John 18:37; cf. 8:44–45; Rev. 3:14) and to demonstrate God's righteousness and love (Rom. 3:25–26; 5:8), bringing judgment against the devil and his angels (John 12:31–33; 16:11), who sow evil in the world (Matt. 13:24–30, 36–43). Indeed, "the Son of God was revealed for this purpose, to destroy the works of the devil" (1 John 3:8), and Jesus became human "so that through death he might destroy the one who has the power of death, that is, the devil" (Heb. 2:14; cf. Gen. 3:15). Accordingly, Revelation 12:10–11 links the defeat of Satan and his accusations before the heavenly court with Christ's sacrificial death, saying, "Now the salvation, and the power, and the kingdom of our God and the authority of His Christ have come, for the accuser of our brethren has been thrown down, he who accuses them before our God day and night. And they overcame him because of the blood of the Lamb and because of the word of their testimony" (NASB). Christ's victory at the cross renders a legal judgment against the devil, a requisite precursor to the final eradication of evil to come (Rev. 21). In the meantime, the devil "knows that his time is short" (12:12).

The God of Scripture Dwells with Us and Makes Holy

The God of Scripture dwells with creatures. God promises his covenant people, "I will make My dwelling among you, and My soul will not reject you. I will also walk among you and be your God, and you shall be My people" (Lev.

---

8. R. Davidson, "Divine Covenant Lawsuit Motif," 83.

9. Gordon D. Fee comments that there is "a cosmic dimension to the spectacle: He is on display before the whole universe, as it were." Fee, *First Epistle to the Corinthians*, 175.

26:11–12 NASB). God not only appears to many individuals throughout Scripture (e.g., Abraham, Isaac, Jacob, Moses) but also commands Moses, "Construct a sanctuary for Me, that I may dwell among them" (Exod. 25:8 NASB).

When the sanctuary is completed, "the cloud covered the tent of meeting, and the glory of the LORD filled the tabernacle," and "Moses was not able to enter the tent of meeting because the cloud had settled on it, and the glory of the LORD filled the tabernacle" (Exod. 40:34–35 NASB). Likewise, God's glory fills Solomon's temple after it is completed (1 Kings 8:10–11). Solomon describes the temple as a "place for [God's] dwelling forever" (8:13 NASB), while recognizing that "heaven and the highest heaven cannot contain You, how much less this house which I have built!" (8:27 NASB).

Prior to the construction of the sanctuary, God tells Moses from the burning bush, "Come no closer! Remove the sandals from your feet, for the place on which you are standing is holy ground" (Exod. 3:5; cf. Josh. 5:15). Here and elsewhere, Scripture identifies wherever God dwells as "holy" (Ps. 46:4). Scripture repeatedly refers to God's "holy mountain," where God dwells (see, e.g., Pss. 48:1; 99:9; cf. Ezek. 20:40; 28:14; Dan. 9:20; Joel 3:17; Zech. 8:3). God's throne is "His holy throne" (Ps. 47:8 NASB). God's temple is "His holy temple" (Mic. 1:2 NASB). The sanctuary/temple is holy, with a holy place and a most holy place, because God dwells there. The land in which God dwells with his covenant people is a holy land. The city God chooses for his dwelling is a holy city (see 1 Chron. 23:25; Jer. 7:12). God's covenant people, whom God will dwell with if they remain faithful to the covenant, are to be a "holy people" (Deut. 28:9; cf. 7:6; 14:2; Lev. 11:44–45; 19:2; 20:7; 1 Cor. 3:16–17). And the heavenly council is "the council of the holy ones," wherein God is "greatly feared" and recognized as "awesome above all those who are around Him" (Ps. 89:7 NASB).

Scripture repeatedly praises God as holy (see, e.g., Ps. 71:22; cf. 77:13; 99:5, 9). "There is no one holy like the LORD, indeed, there is no one besides You, nor is there any rock like our God" (1 Sam. 2:2 NASB). In Revelation 4:8, "four living creatures" around God's throne unceasingly sing, "Holy, holy, holy, is the Lord God, the Almighty, who was and who is and who is to come" (NASB). God's name is holy (see, e.g., Ezek. 20:39; 36:22; cf. Matt. 6:9), and God vindicates his holy name against being profaned among the nations (Ezek. 36:23; cf. 39:25); "the holy God will show Himself holy in righteousness" (Isa. 5:16 NASB; cf. Rom. 3:25–26).

Whereas humans may be "holy" by proximity to God, God is holy in and of himself: "I am God and not man, the Holy One in your midst" (Hosea 11:9 NASB). Absolutely holy, God is "a consuming fire" (Deut. 4:24 NASB) such that "no evil dwells with" God (Ps. 5:4 NASB). Any evil thing coming into unmediated contact with the holy God will be destroyed. Because God's unmediated presence will destroy sinful people, evil (partially) separates people from God.

> The LORD's hand is not too short to save,
>   nor his ear too dull to hear.
> Rather, your iniquities have been barriers
>   between you and your God,
> and your sins have hidden his face from you
>   so that he does not hear. (Isa. 59:1–2)

Accordingly, God warns, "Because the LORD your God travels along with your camp, to save you and to hand over your enemies to you, therefore your camp must be holy, so that he may not see anything indecent among you and turn away from you" (Deut. 23:14; cf. Num. 5:3; Jer. 7:3).

God can go "with" the people without destroying them (Exod. 33:3) only if his presence is mediated and his glory shrouded, and this is one function of the sanctuary. Although God mediates his presence to accommodate the people, "again and again" the people "tempted God, and pained the Holy One of Israel" (Ps. 78:41 NASB) so much that, eventually, God's presence departs from Solomon's temple and from Jerusalem (Ezek. 9; 10; 11:22–23). Yet God promises to "return to Zion and . . . dwell in the midst of Jerusalem. Then Jerusalem will be called the City of Truth, and the mountain of the LORD of hosts will be called the Holy Mountain" (Zech. 8:3 NASB). Later, God's glory returns to Jerusalem and the second temple in Jesus (John 1:14), who is Immanuel—"God with us" (Matt. 1:23 KJV). As the OT calls God "the Holy One of Israel" (Isa. 30:15 KJV), the NT calls Jesus "the Holy One of God" (Mark 1:24; Luke 4:34; cf. 1:35; John 6:69), and the NT explicitly reveals the Holy Spirit.

In the new covenant, the resurrected Christ enters "the greater and more perfect tabernacle [in heaven], not made with hands" (Heb. 9:11 NASB; cf. 9:12, 24), and the Holy Spirit dwells within believers. Paul writes, "You are a temple of God," "the Spirit of God dwells in you," and "the temple of God is holy, and that is what you are" (1 Cor. 3:16–17 NASB; cf. 6:19; Rom. 8:9). In the future, "the holy city, new Jerusalem" will come "down out of heaven from God, made ready as a bride adorned for her husband" (Rev. 21:2 NASB; cf. 21:10; 2 Pet. 3:13). Then "the tabernacle of God is among men, and He will dwell among them, and they shall be His people, and God Himself will be among them, and He will wipe away every tear from their eyes; and there will no longer be any death; there will no longer be any mourning, or crying, or pain; the first things have passed away" (Rev. 21:3–4 NASB).

Conclusion

This introduction has offered a brief survey of some prominent biblical depictions of the covenantal God of Scripture, which portray God as relating to creatures in striking ways—speaking, hearing, willing, covenanting, grieving, relenting, responding to prayer, dwelling with them, and otherwise engaging in back-and-forth relationship with them. If theology is to be normed by Scripture, as I believe it should be, then these and other biblical depictions of God must be adequately accounted for in one's conception of divine attributes. As shall be discussed further in the following chapter, however, just how such depictions of God should be understood theologically is a matter of some dispute, particularly given what some see as significant tension between these and other depictions of the God of Scripture and the so-called God of the philosophers depicted in at least some versions of classical theism. With this tension in mind, the following chapters offer a careful theological analysis of divine attributes that seeks to account for these and other biblical depictions of God in a way that upholds the unique normativity of Scripture, in dialogue with core issues in the contemporary discussion of classical theism.

Chapter 1 begins by introducing the contemporary discussion of classical theism and the approach this book takes to the doctrine of God, an approach to the theological interpretation of Scripture that carefully attends to biblical depictions of God, seeking to affirm all that Scripture teaches about God without conceptually reducing God to the way he is portrayed in the economy. The chapters that follow address whether God changes and has emotions (chap. 2); whether he is present in space and time (chap. 3); whether he knows everything, including the future (chap. 4); whether he has all power and always attains what he desires (chap. 5); whether he is entirely good and loving (chap. 6); how one God can be three persons (chap. 7); and how the view of covenantal theism set forth in this book relates to classical theism, the Christian tradition, perfect being theology, and the issues of worship and prayer (chap. 8).

Before turning to these chapters, however, it is appropriate to pause to worship the God of Scripture:

> Praise the LORD!
> > O give thanks to the LORD, for he is good;
> > for his steadfast love endures forever.
> . . . .
> Blessed be the LORD, the God of Israel,
> > from everlasting to everlasting.
> And let all the people say, "Amen."
> > Praise the LORD! (Ps. 106:1, 48)

One

The God of Scripture and the God of the Philosophers

> Holy, holy, holy,
> the Lord God the Almighty,
>   who was and is and is to come.

According to Revelation 4:8, this refrain is sung "day and night without ceasing." The God of Scripture is the holy one who alone is worthy of worship. Accordingly, much of Scripture highlights God's unique praiseworthiness as the covenant-making and covenant-keeping God to whom Christians should "pray without ceasing" (1 Thess. 5:17). Yet who is this covenantal God whom Christians worship and to whom Christians pray? Christians generally view God as worthy of worship because he is perfect, the one to whom it makes sense to pray because he is compassionate and responds to prayer (Dan. 9:4, 18). Yet there is quite a bit of diversity—even controversy—among Christian theologians regarding God's nature and how God relates to creation. Much of the controversy concerns whether the (so-called) God of the philosophers is compatible with the God of Scripture, "whether the so-called God of the philosophers has any real claim to being *the God of Abraham, Isaac, and Jacob, or God, the Father of Jesus, or God, the object of our ultimate concern.*"[1]

The God of Abraham, Isaac, and Jacob, the Father of Jesus, is the covenantal God whom many Christians envision when they worship and pray,

---

1. Rea and Pojman, "Concept of God," 3.

the God revealed in the story line of Scripture who creates the world, forms Adam and Eve from dust, calls Abraham, meets Moses, loves, covenants, acts, speaks, hears, responds, and saves. Yet William Alston notes a "pervasive tension in Christian thought between 'the God of the philosophers and the God of the Bible,' between God as 'wholly other' and God as a partner in interpersonal relationships, between God as the absolute, ultimate source of all being and God as the dominant actor on the stage of history."[2]

With this tension in mind, this book offers a constructive account of divine attributes, bringing biblical portrayals of God into dialogue with core questions in the contemporary discussion of classical theism, including whether God changes and has emotions, whether he is present in space and time, whether he knows everything (including the future), whether he has all power and always attains what he desires, whether he is entirely good and loving, and how one God can be three persons.[3] This chapter introduces the contemporary discussion of the (so-called) God of the philosophers and the approach this book takes to the doctrine of God, an approach to the theological interpretation of Scripture that carefully attends to the biblical portrayals of God, toward affirming what Scripture teaches about God without conceptually reducing God to the way he is portrayed in the economy (i.e., in relation to the world). Accordingly, I seek to limit my conclusions according to the standards of biblical warrant and systematic coherence while recognizing that "we see in a mirror dimly" (1 Cor. 13:12 NASB) and that God is greater than humans can conceive.

The God of the Philosophers?

Strict Classical Theism

While there are many different philosophical conceptions of God, when Christian theists speak of "the God of the philosophers," they typically have in mind an understanding of God called classical theism.[4] According to a *strict* form of classical theism, God must possess the following attributes (explained further below): divine perfection, necessity, *pure* aseity, *utter* self-sufficiency, *strict* simplicity, *timeless* eternity, *strict* immutability, *strict* impassibility,

2. Alston, *Divine Nature and Human Language*, 147.
3. For an introduction to contemporary approaches to the doctrine of God, see Peckham, *Doctrine of God*.
4. See, e.g., Rea and Pojman, "Concept of God," 3; Rogers, *Perfect Being Theology*, 6; Kenny, *God of the Philosophers*; and Stump, *God of the Bible*, 11. However, "traditional classical theism is not a single, monolithic position." J. Cooper, *Panentheism*, 322.

omnipotence, omniscience, and omnipresence.[5] To differentiate them from others who self-identify as classical theists, I refer to those who subscribe to a strict understanding of these attributes as *strict* classical theists.[6]

On this view, divine perfection means that God is the greatest possible being. God exists necessarily and is who he is entirely of himself (*a se*), without dependence on anything else relative to his existence or otherwise (*pure* aseity and *utter* self-sufficiency). God "exists independently of all causal influence from his creatures"; creatures cannot impact God or his actions.[7] This is bound up with *strict* simplicity, which means (among other things) that God is not composed of parts and that there are no genuine distinctions in God.[8]

This God is timeless. For God, there is no passing of time, no "before" or "after," no past or future, no temporal succession. Accordingly, God is *strictly* immutable and *strictly* impassible. Strict immutability, meaning God cannot change in any way, follows from timelessness because change requires the passing of time—from prior state to later state. This rules out emotional change and suffering. Instead, God is strictly impassible, meaning that God cannot be affected by anything outside himself. Creatures cannot affect God, and thus God cannot become pleased or displeased by anything creatures do.

Finally, God is omnipotent, meaning God is all-powerful. God is omniscient, meaning God knows everything (typically explained in terms of God causing everything to be as it is).[9] And God is omnipresent, meaning God's power is active everywhere, sustaining everything.

Process Theology and Open Theism

Alongside numerous other strong critics of (strict) classical theism, process theology posits an alternative "God of the philosophers," rooted in the process philosophy of Alfred North Whitehead.[10] Characterizing classical theism as (in Charles Hartshorne's words) "metaphysical snobbery toward relativity, . . . responsiveness or sensitivity" and "worship of mere absoluteness,

---

5. Subsequent chapters further discuss these attributes.

6. See Peckham, *Doctrine of God*, 4–14. Among others, Augustine, Anselm, and Thomas Aquinas are often interpreted as exemplars of strict classical theism.

7. Dolezal, "Strong Impassibility," 18.

8. Thomas Williams explains that God is "in no way a composite." God "does not have a variety of features or attributes that are distinct from God's nature and from each other" (Williams, "Introduction to Classical Theism," 96). Brian Leftow adds that God is "completely without parts. Whatever has parts depends on them for its existence and nature." Leftow, "God, Concepts of."

9. However, not all strict classical theists are determinists. See, e.g., Rogers, *Perfect Being Theology*.

10. See Whitehead, *Process and Reality*.

independence, and one-sided activity or power," process theology advocates a nearly reverse image of strict classical theism, typically denying what strict classical theism affirms and affirming what it denies.[11] Whereas the God of strict classical theism is utterly transcendent, the God of process theology is nearly entirely immanent. A form of panentheism (literally "all in God"), process theology maintains that the world (the physical universe) is *in* God such that God cannot exist without *some* world and is always in the process of changing and growing as the world changes.

While process theologians agree that God is a necessary and perfect being, many attributes that strict classical theists consider "perfections" are considered deficiencies by process theologians.[12] According to process theology, the necessary and perfect being must be (1) essentially related to some world, not self-sufficient or *a se*; (2) temporal, not timeless; (3) always changing, not strictly immutable; (4) eminently passible, not impassible; (5) the most powerful being, but not omnipotent in the sense of possessing all power, capable of "acting" only via persuasion (never coercion); and (6) all-knowing relative to the present but not omniscient in terms of possessing exhaustive foreknowledge.

Open theism, another approach that has strongly criticized (strict) classical theism in recent decades, is often confused with process theology but differs in significant respects.[13] While agreeing with process theists that God is temporal rather than timeless, neither *strictly* immutable nor impassible, and all-knowing relative to the present but lacking exhaustive foreknowledge, *most* open theists reject the view that God is essentially related to the world and affirm a more traditional concept of omnipotence.[14] Accordingly, many open theists are closer to moderate classical theism (defined below) than to process theism.

Moderate Classical Theism

Many other theists identify as classical theists (in a broad sense) but deny or qualify some tenets of *strict* classical theism. *Moderate* classical theists

11. Hartshorne, *Divine Relativity*, 50. Hartshorne contends that classical theism "made God, not an exalted being, but an empty absurdity, a love which is simply not love, a purpose which is no purpose, a will which is no will, a knowledge which is no knowledge." Hartshorne, *Omnipotence*, 31.

12. Hartshorne's view is an alternative form of perfect being theology. See Peckham, *Concept of Divine Love*, 124–68.

13. See Griffin, Cobb, and Pinnock, *Searching for an Adequate God*. See also Pinnock et al., *Openness of God*.

14. One exception is Thomas Jay Oord's essential kenosis theology, similar in many ways to process theism. See Oord, *Uncontrolling Love of God*.

affirm a common core of classical theism—divine perfection, necessity, aseity, self-sufficiency, unity, eternity, immutability (of some kind), omnipotence, and omniscience (typically understood to include exhaustive definite foreknowledge).[15] While upholding an unqualified Creator-creature distinction such that God does not depend on or need anything with respect to his existence and essential nature (aseity and self-sufficiency), moderate classical theism departs from strict classical theism by affirming that God engages in genuine relationship with creatures that makes a difference to God (contra *pure* aseity).[16] Further, moderate classical theism affirms that God experiences changing emotions (contra strict impassibility) and that God is immutable with respect to his character and essential nature but changes relationally (contra strict immutability) and therefore affirms some form of divine temporality (contra strict timelessness).[17]

The God of Greek Philosophy?

Much contemporary discussion of divine attributes revolves around the claims of strict classical theists and counterclaims of process theists, open theists, and moderate classical theists. As Eleonore Stump notes, "It is common among contemporary theologians and philosophers to suppose that the God of the Bible is radically different from the God of the philosophers," that "there is an inconsistency between the description of God given by the Bible and the characterization of God upheld by [strict] classical theism."[18] Indeed, "to many people the God of [strict] classical theism seems unresponsive" and "unengaged" and thus "seems very different from the God of the Bible."[19]

For example, Stephen T. Davis argues, "A timeless being cannot be the personal, caring, involved God we read about in the Bible. The God of the Bible is, above all, a God who cares deeply about what happens in history and who acts to bring about his will."[20] Paul Copan likewise comments, "The triune

15. Traditional theists widely agree that God is "among other things an all-powerful, all-knowing, perfectly good, eternal and transcendent being who has created our entire universe and preserves its existence moment to moment." T. Morris, *Our Idea of God*, 17.

16. I label this "moderate" because the label "modified" classical theism (J. Cooper, *Panentheism*, 321) indicates that this is not the *classical* view, which is disputed. Some use the label "neo-classical theism" to describe this category, which they affirm. See Mullins, *God and Emotions*; and R. Campbell, *Worldviews and the Problem of Evil*, 205–6.

17. Moderate classical theists also deny *strict* simplicity but *may* affirm a qualified simplicity.

18. Stump, *God of the Bible*, 11.

19. Stump, *God of the Bible*, 18. She maintains that the "God of classical theism is the engaged, personally present, responsive God of the Bible" (Stump, *God of the Bible*, 19). Similarly, Rogers, *Perfect Being Theology*, 8–10.

20. Davis, *Logic and the Nature of God*, 14.

God isn't the static, untouchable deity commonly associated with traditional Greek philosophy. He's a prayer-answering, history-engaging God."[21] Ronald Nash adds, "If God is [strictly] immutable, He cannot be the religiously available God of the Scriptures. But if God is religiously available, He cannot be the unchanging God of the philosophers."[22] Further, Sallie McFague avers that the "two images of God—one as the distant, all-powerful, perfect, immutable Lord existing in lonely isolation, and the other as the One who enters human flesh as a baby to eventually assume the alienation and oppression of all peoples in the world—do not fit together."[23] Likewise, James Cone maintains, "Unlike the God of Greek philosophy who is removed from history, the God of the Bible is involved in history, and his revelation is inseparable from the social and political affairs of Israel."[24]

Numerous critics of classical theism affirm the controversial Hellenization thesis, which claims that early Christian tradition was *corrupted* by importing a Greek philosophical framework, replacing the God of the Bible with the God of the philosophers.[25] As Colin Gunton puts it, "The impersonal attributes come from Greece, the Greek philosophical tradition; the personal ones come from the Bible and don't appear to be consistent with them."[26] While the Hellenization thesis is often traced to modern scholarship (especially the much-criticized work of Adolf von Harnack), Paul Gavrilyuk notes that "a version of this theory was not unknown to the early Fathers and had been around since Hippolytus of Rome (170–235), who argued that the heretics did not derive their doctrines from the scriptures and apostolic tradition, but rather from Greek philosophers."[27] As Tertullian put it, "What indeed has Athens to do with Jerusalem?"[28]

According to Michael Allen, modern versions of the Hellenization thesis typically include three claims: (1) "a belief in monolithic Greek philosophy," (2) "the claim that the fathers of the early church borrowed from Greek philosophy *uncritically*," and (3) the "insist[ence] that this borrowing is inherently antithetical to the material content of the gospel."[29] Framed this way,

21. Copan, *Loving Wisdom*, 94.
22. Nash, *Concept of God*, 100.
23. McFague, *Body of God*, 136.
24. Cone, *God of the Oppressed*, 62.
25. See, e.g., Moltmann, *Trinity and the Kingdom*, 22. Cf. Brunner, *Christian Doctrine of God*, 154; R. Plantinga, Thompson, and Lundberg, *Introduction to Christian Theology*, 83–91, 99–108; and J. Sanders, "Historical Considerations," 59–91.
26. Gunton, *Barth Lectures*, 94.
27. Gavrilyuk, *Suffering of the Impassible God*, 3.
28. Tertullian, *Prescription against Heretics* 7 (ANF 3:246).
29. M. Allen, "Exodus 3 after the Hellenization Thesis," 181.

the Hellenization thesis is relatively easy to falsify; one need only demonstrate that early church fathers borrowed from Greek philosophy *critically* and *selectively*. Accordingly, many classical theists identify this (exaggerated) Hellenization thesis as a caricature, contending that (1) ancient Greek philosophy was not monolithic, (2) early church fathers did not borrow from Greek philosophy "uncritically" or uniformly, and (3) what was "borrowed" from Greek philosophy is not inconsistent with the teachings of Scripture.[30]

Critics and advocates agree, however, that various streams of Greek philosophy heavily influenced early church fathers. As classical theist Gerald Bray explains, there "is no doubt that the early Christians," needing "to address their contemporaries," "were influenced by the philosophical currents surrounding them."[31] Another classical theist, Thomas Williams, refers to classical theism as "the model of God we find in Platonic, neo-Platonic, and Aristotelian philosophy and in Christian, Muslim, and Jewish thinkers who appropriate those traditions of classical Greek philosophy."[32] Likewise, Katherin Rogers adds, "Both the Neoplatonism of Augustine and Anselm and the (Neoplatonic?) Aristotelianism of Aquinas provide all-encompassing frameworks within which to make sense of God and creation."[33] Similarly, Karl Barth maintains, "The idea of God . . . was shaped by a general conception of God (that of ancient Stoicism and Neo-Platonism)."[34] The primary argument, then, is not whether the early Christian theological tradition was deeply influenced by streams of Greek philosophy but whether such influence was uncritically (or sufficiently critically) received and whether it *corrupted* Christian theology. Indeed, a minimal Hellenization thesis, claiming that *some* Christian thinkers and movements were influenced by streams of Greek philosophy in a way that amounted to or supported false theological claims, would be widely affirmed, even by many critics of the (exaggerated)

---

30. See, e.g., Gavrilyuk, *Suffering of the Impassible God*. See also Pelikan, *Emergence of the Catholic Tradition*, 45–55.

31. Bray, "Has the Christian Doctrine of God," 112. Cf. Castelo, *Apathetic God*, 64; Kärkkäinen, *Doctrine of God*, 40–41; and R. Olson, *Story of Christian Theology*, 54–57. Rob Lister adds that it "is obvious to all that the Patristic theologians borrowed Greek language and made use of Greek concepts" (R. Lister, *God Is Impassible and Impassioned*, 61). Indeed, many maintain that divine impassibility's "foundation in Christian sources is probably due to direct Greek influences." *Oxford Dictionary of the Christian Church*, s.v. "Impassibility of God," 828.

32. Williams, "Introduction to Classical Theism," 95. Leftow adds, "Classical theism's ancestry includes Plato, Aristotle, Middle Platonism and Neoplatonism," which "entered Christianity as early as Irenaeus and Clement of Alexandria and became Christian orthodoxy as the Roman Empire wound down" (Leftow, "God, Concepts of"). Cf. Rogers, *Perfect Being Theology*, 6.

33. Rogers, *Perfect Being Theology*, 6.

34. CD II/1, 329.

Hellenization thesis.[35] Yet the controversial question is, Which individuals, movements, and/or creeds were influenced in a way that "corrupted" their theology?

This question is complicated by the facts that various thinkers hold nuanced views and that competent scholars offer differing interpretations of the same theologians, movements, and creeds.[36] As such, claims that the Christian tradition has or has not been corrupted by the influence of Greek philosophy are complicated by questions like: (1) Which part(s) of the Christian tradition? and (2) Whose interpretation of those part(s) of the Christian tradition?[37] Given these and other complexities, I make no attempt to settle the debate regarding the positive or negative influence of Greek philosophies on the Christian tradition in general, nor do I intend what follows as a referendum on the Christian tradition.[38] While some theologians claim that their view is *the* traditional view of divine attributes, there are differing scholarly interpretations of just what various classical Christian writers meant by the language they used and assertions they made relative to various divine attributes such that various models of God might claim some support in the classical Christian tradition.[39]

Apart from this, whether some conclusion has been influenced by some philosophical system does not determine whether that conclusion is true.[40] Every theological perspective has been influenced by extrabiblical thought in some way. The question is not whether the Christian tradition appropriated elements of Greek philosophy but whether a given articulation of Christian theology is consistent with, and normed by, Scripture. As Jay Wesley Richards comments, "The problem is not simply that the classical theist employs extrabiblical or philosophical notions of divinity"; the problem is that the philosophical "intuitions" that are "fed by a pre-Christian concept of God can sometimes contradict what Christians believe God has revealed about himself in salvation history and the biblical narratives."[41] Daniel Castelo

---

35. While rejecting the exaggerated Hellenization thesis, Michael Horton notes, "Traces of Stoicism are evident among Christian writers in the ancient, medieval, and modern period. However, the indifferent god of Stoicism is radically different from the living God of Scripture" (Horton, *Christian Faith*, 248). Cf. Gavrilyuk, *Suffering of the Impassible God*; and Pannenberg, "Appropriation of the Philosophical Concept of God," 2:119–83.

36. See chap. 8.

37. On these two questions (which tradition? whose interpretation?), see Peckham, *Canonical Theology*.

38. Doing justice to the richness of the Christian tradition would demand dedicated attention to each thinker in their historical context, requiring multiple lengthy monographs.

39. See chap. 8.

40. To claim otherwise would exhibit the genetic fallacy.

41. Richards, *Untamed God*, 40. Cf. R. Plantinga, Thompson, and Lundberg, *Introduction to Christian Theology*, 101–2.

adds, "At some level the need for an accounting is obvious: the God-talk . . . of the Bible and that of the ancient church repeatedly sound at odds with each other."[42]

Yet how should one go about this accounting? In this regard, Peter Martens explains, "According to the aggravated version of the Hellenization of Christianity thesis, a teaching becomes heretical when it fulfills two conditions: it is simultaneously resistant to clear scriptural testimony and uncritically dependent upon Platonic [or other Greek] philosophy."[43] Given the complexities relative to determining whether a teaching might be *uncritically* dependent on a given philosophy, however, perhaps we might say that a teaching becomes problematic when it is dependent on extrabiblical thought *such that* it is "resistant to clear scriptural testimony." This applies not only to the influence of Greek thought but to the undue influence of any extrabiblical thought. The question, then, is not whether extrabiblical thought has influenced a teaching but whether the influence and/or resultant claim is "resistant to clear scriptural testimony."

The God of Scripture

Whether one views the so-called God of the philosophers and the God of Scripture as complementary or incompatible depends not only on what one means by "the God of the philosophers" but also on what one means by "the God of Scripture." At least two stages of inquiry are involved in the attempt to address the controversial question, Who is the God of Scripture? The first stage concerns identifying biblical portrayals and claims about God (what the text says), and the second stage concerns how to theologically interpret such portrayals and claims (what one says on the basis of what the text says). Regarding the first stage, I operate on the conviction that an adequate conception of the God of Scripture must carefully consider and correspond to biblical portrayals and claims about God that Scripture affirms.[44] Yet at the second stage, theologians interpret biblical portrayals and claims in vastly differing ways.

Many theologians emphasize that biblical portrayals and claims are accommodative—that is, biblical teachings are communicated in a manner that

---

42. Castelo, "Qualified Impassibility," 57. While noting that "not every bit of dehellenization is laudatory, for not everything that the Greeks said is false," Nicholas Wolterstorff claims further, "The patterns of classical Greek thought are incompatible with the pattern of biblical thought." Wolterstorff, *Inquiring about God*, 134.

43. Martens, "Embodiment, Heresy, and the Hellenization of Christianity," 620.

44. By speaking of what "Scripture affirms," I mean what Scripture teaches as true, excluding false claims that merely appear in Scripture (e.g., the theology of Job's friends).

accommodates limited human understanding. Some theologians thus maintain that, for example, biblical portrayals of God experiencing changing emotions should not be taken to mean that God actually experiences changing emotions; rather, they teach some deeper truth about God via accommodative imagery. In this and other respects, while theologians typically agree that Scripture is accommodative, there is considerable disagreement about how accommodative language should be interpreted theologically, which I will return to below.

To engage this second stage of inquiry further, however, it is important to be mindful of biblical depictions of God. As surveyed in the introduction, Scripture portrays God as (among many other things) the covenantal God who

creates, sustains, and creates anew;

speaks, hears, and responds;

sees, provides, delivers/saves, and rules;

knows, plans, wills, calls, and chooses but has unfulfilled desires;

judges, acts justly, *and* mercifully and graciously forgives;

loves compassionately, passionately, and steadfastly;

grieves, suffers, laments, and relents;

promises, covenants, and engages in covenant relationship;

engages in court proceedings and defeats evil; and

dwells with us and makes holy.[45]

In these and other ways, the God of Scripture is consistently described as a covenantal God, not only in the sense of making and keeping formal covenants with creatures but also in the broader sense of engaging in various kinds of back-and-forth relationships with creatures wherein God makes and keeps commitments and is responsive to creatures. When I refer to the covenantal God, I mean *covenantal* in this broader sense of committed, back-and-forth relationship. As Amos Yong puts it, the God of Scripture is "not only the covenant-making but also covenant-keeping God who enters into and is involved with the history of the people of God, who seeks to accomplish what is just on their behalf, and who liberates the people of God from their plight in order to reestablish—redeem or restore—the relationship between creation and the creator."[46] Michael Horton adds, "The biblical testimony to a living

45. As John Goldingay describes the OT narrative, "God began. God started over. God promised. God delivered. God sealed. God gave. God accommodated. God wrestled. God preserved." Goldingay, *Old Testament Theology*, 1:32.

46. Yong, *Spirit of Love*, 81–82. Yong draws on the work of Samuel Solivan, who notes that the OT prophets reveal a God who "is touched by our suffering . . . [and] sympathetic to our condition." Solivan, *Spirit, Pathos, and Liberation*, 74.

history with a living God in a covenant with genuine interaction resists all Stoic and Platonic conceptions of a nonrelational and nonpersonal One. In the unfolding drama there are suits and countersuits, witnesses and counterwitnesses, and God is represented as repenting, relenting, and responding to creatures."[47]

That Scripture depicts God as a covenantal God who engages in committed, back-and-forth relationship with creatures is not a matter of dispute. Disagreement typically appears at the second level: theological interpretation of such depictions. In my view, a conception of God normed by Scripture must be able to account for these (and other) biblical portrayals and claims in a way congruent with the uniquely normative authority of Scripture as canon.

Doing Theology as Canonical Theology

This returns us to discussion of theological interpretation. Rather than attempting to make a case for the soundness of my own approach here (as I have done elsewhere), I will simply outline some commitments of my canonical theological method, followed by a brief discussion of my approach to biblical language as accommodative and analogical.[48]

Canonical Theology

My approach operates on the conviction that Scripture is a unified corpus of writings that God has commissioned as the uniquely normative rule of faith and practice and the *final norm* of theological interpretation, to be understood in subjection to guidance by the Holy Spirit.[49] Canonical theology seeks to "read the Bible canonically, as one book," as "Christ's Spirit-borne

47. Horton, *Christian Faith*, 240.

48. Regarding my theological method and the rationale for my approach in conversation with potential objections, see Peckham, *Canonical Theology*. Cf. Peckham, "Rationale for Canonical Theology," 83–105.

49. I mean "canonical" in three primary ways: first, in the basic sense of the term "canon" as a rule or standard; second, relative to the concept of "canon" as a unified, but not uniform, corpus; third, understanding the biblical canon as "canonical" in virtue of being divinely commissioned. To say Scripture is "canonical," then, is to say that Scripture rules, rules as a whole, and rules because it has been commissioned to rule by the Ruler himself. I believe the biblical canon is correctly recognized as the sixty-six books of the Old and New Testaments, ratified and commissioned by Christ, the common canonical core recognized by nearly all Christians (including those who recognize more books). On the scope of the biblical canon, see Peckham, *Canonical Theology*, chaps. 1–3.

commissioned testimony to himself," with the conviction that "each part has meaning in light of the whole (and in light of its center, Jesus Christ)."[50]

Seeking to integrate biblical exegesis and systematic theology under the rule of Scripture, canonical theology aims at two overarching goals: canonical correspondence and coherence, which I hereafter refer to as the standards of biblical warrant and systematic coherence. Coinciding with the belief that Scripture is God-breathed (2 Tim. 3:16) and thus internally coherent, the standard of systematic coherence demands that theological claims be consistent with one another. Equally important, affirming the view of the vast majority of Christians that Scripture should be normative over theological claims, the standard of biblical warrant maintains that theological claims should be adequately grounded in what Scripture affirms.[51] This involves the aim of reading *all* of Scripture in a way that is consistent with the entirety of what Scripture teaches (by way of careful *and contextual* exegesis), without dismissing, contorting, divesting of meaning, or explaining away individual passages.[52]

This standard of biblical warrant is not a new standard but is consistent with Gregory of Nyssa's words, "We make the Holy Scriptures the rule and measure of every tenet; we necessarily fix our eyes upon that, and approve that alone which may be made to harmonize with the intention of those writings" such that we "adopt, as the guide of our reasoning, the Scripture."[53] Elsewhere Gregory writes, "Let the inspired Scripture, then, be our umpire, and the vote of truth will surely be given to those whose dogmas are found to agree with the Divine words."[54] In this regard, Uche Anizor notes, "Christian theologians have almost universally assumed . . . that a theological claim can be true only insofar as it is drawn from or at least coheres with Scripture."[55]

---

50. Vanhoozer, *Drama of Doctrine*, 178, 194. David Yeago writes that recognizing "the biblical canon as inspired Scripture" means approaching "the texts as the discourse of the Holy Spirit" such that "the church receives the canon, in all its diversity, as nonetheless a *single* body of discourse." Yeago, "Bible," 70.

51. Jay Wesley Richards notes, "Commitment to biblical normativity" is "the norm among Catholic and Orthodox" and Protestant theologians. Richards, *Untamed God*, 32.

52. My reading employs grammatical-historical procedures of exegesis in a way that affirms Scripture's dual authorship such that the intention *in* the text is not reduced to human authorial intent but includes the effect of the divine author's intention. I thus depart from any iterations of grammatical-historical method that foster atomism or are otherwise unduly influenced by modernistic biblical criticism, seeking instead to read the canon's parts in light of the whole canon (and vice versa) without injury to any part. See Peckham, *Canonical Theology*, 203–6; Peckham, "Rationale for Canonical Theology." Cf. Voss, "From 'Grammatical-Historical Exegesis,'" 140–52; Treier, *Introducing Theological Interpretation of Scripture*, 110–16.

53. Gregory of Nyssa, *On the Soul and the Resurrection* (NPNF 5:439).

54. Gregory of Nyssa, *On the Holy Trinity* (NPNF 5:327).

55. Anizor, *How to Read Theology*, 60.

Further, Anizor writes, "The strength and plausibility of every formulation are tied to how much they directly engage with the Bible."[56] I agree. However, whenever one engages with the Bible relative to the theological interpretation of Scripture, at least three levels of interpretation are operative: (1) the interpretation of individual biblical texts and passages (the micro-level), (2) one's doctrinal framework (the meso-level), and (3) one's philosophical framework (the macro-level).[57] The macro-level consists of one's overarching presuppositions regarding the nature of reality, particularly with respect to the nature of God and the world (one's metaphysical framework), which massively impact the way one views and interprets everything, including one's reading of Scripture and doctrinal beliefs.[58] Indeed, each of these levels impinges on the others.

If Scripture is to be theologically normative, Scripture must be normative with respect to one's doctrinal and metaphysical frameworks. One must engender self-criticism and humility that invite Scripture to rule over one's cherished presuppositions at both levels.[59] Accordingly, canonical theology engages in what Stephen Holmes calls the age-old "search for a set of concepts that would allow every text of Scripture (including the Old Testament texts) to be true in what it affirmed."[60] As I see it, this demands (among other things) that one's metaphysical and doctrinal commitments are subjected to testing and reforming by Scripture.[61] In this regard, Roger Olson echoes Edmond Cherbonnier's concern that "Christian thought has often suffered internal conflicts by reading 'into the Bible a metaphysic which has no place there'" such that "the implicit biblical metaphysic is often denied a fair hearing."[62] Canonical theology is deliberately cognizant of this possibility and attempts to guard against it, believing that (as Richards puts it)

---

56. Anizor, *How to Read Theology*, 85.

57. Fernando Canale articulates these levels as micro-, meso-, and macro-hermeneutical principles (Canale, *Back to Revelation-Inspiration*, 148–49). See also Rodrigues, *Toward a Priestly Christology*, 9–10.

58. Brevard Childs notes, "For systematic theologians the overarching categories are frequently philosophical. The same is often the case for biblical scholars even when cloaked under the guise of a theory of history" (Childs, *Biblical Theology in Crisis*, 158). Craig Bartholomew adds, "One ignores the role of philosophy in biblical interpretation at one's peril." Bartholomew, *Introducing Biblical Hermeneutics*, 131.

59. On the importance of humility and other virtues for theological interpretation, see Peckham, *Canonical Theology*, 218–21.

60. Holmes, *Quest for the Trinity*, 198.

61. As Karl Barth famously put it, "Take now my last piece of advice: Exegesis, exegesis, and once more, exegesis! If I have become a dogmatician, it is because I long before endeavored to carry on exegesis." K. Barth, *Das Evangelium in der Gegenwart*, quoted in Burnett, *Karl Barth's Theological Exegesis*, 174–75.

62. R. Olson, *Essentials of Christian Thought*, 85. Cf. Cherbonnier, "Is There a Biblical Metaphysic?," 455.

"the theologian's metaphysical and ontological commitments should emerge from, or be consistent with, Scripture" and, where necessary, be modified "to conform to biblical normativity."[63] Oliver Crisp puts it well when he affirms "with the great majority of Christian theologians down through the ages that Scripture is the norming norm in theology this side of the grave. Other theological norms, such as the canons of ecumenical councils or the confessions of particular ecclesial communities, or even the arguments of theologians, are to be understood in light of Scripture and as ancillary to Scripture."[64]

Some argue, however, that Scripture cannot effectively function as an adequate theological norm because it can be interpreted in various ways, and thus the classical tradition should be employed as the rule of theological interpretation of Scripture.[65] However, major exemplars in the classical tradition themselves instruct that their own writings should not be employed as a rule of faith. For example, Augustine writes, "Our writings . . . are not a rule of faith or practice, but only a help to edification," and "we may suppose that they contain some things falling short of the truth."[66] While writings outside Scripture offer "merely a profitable study," Augustine writes that one owes "unhesitating assent to nothing but the canonical Scriptures."[67] Moreover, the classical tradition can also be variously interpreted (as can any communication). To employ it as a rule, one must first decide which of the various mutually exclusive interpretations set forth by competent scholars is to be preferred (which interpretation?). Further, since the Christian tradition is fallible and not uniform, including positions that contradict one another, the question arises as to which part(s) of the tradition should be employed as a rule (which tradition[s]?).[68] As shall be seen in subsequent chapters, diverg-

63. Richards, *Untamed God*, 31, 42.

64. Crisp, "Desiderata for Models of the Hypostatic Union," 22.

65. For a discussion of numerous such proposals, see Peckham, *Canonical Theology*, chaps. 4–5. To take one recent example, Craig A. Carter proposes that Christian theology should be approached via the "Christian Platonism of the Great Tradition," which he states "was developed in order to express the metaphysical implications of the doctrine of God that emerged from pro-Nicene scriptural exegesis in the fourth century, and as a result the exegesis, the dogma, and the metaphysics are all intertwined together." Carter, *Interpreting Scripture with the Great Tradition*, xiii.

66. Augustine, *Against Faustus the Manichaean* 11.5 (NPNF 4:180). Cf. Thomas Aquinas, *Summa Theologiae* I.1.8. Thomas Aquinas himself wrote, "Only the canonical Scriptures are the standard of faith" (*sola canonica scriptura est regula fidei*). Thomas Aquinas, *Commentary on John*, chap. 21, lectio 6.

67. Augustine, *Against Faustus the Manichaean* 11.8 (NPNF 4:183); Augustine, *Nature and Grace* 71 (NPNF 5:146). See the discussion of these and similar statements by Cyril of Jerusalem and Basil of Caesarea in Armstrong, "From the κανὼν τῆς ἀληθείας," 46.

68. See Peckham, *Canonical Theology*, chaps. 5, 7. John Wesley cautioned, "As to the Fathers and Councils, we cannot but observe, that in an hundred instances they contradict one another" and thus cannot "be rule of faith to us." Wesley, *Works of John Wesley*, 10:144.

ing positions regarding various tenets of classical theism claim some support within the Christian tradition, hinging on how the tradition is interpreted and what parts of it are examined.

Beyond these issues, if Scripture is to function as the final norm of theological interpretation, it must be allowed to norm and potentially correct even traditional theological interpretations and metaphysical frameworks. Because *all* interpretations are fallible and influenced by some vantage point and conceptual framework, *all* theological interpretations should be continually subjected to, measured by, and tested by the infallible standard of Scripture via a continuous hermeneutical spiral. Although competent interpreters may differ, interpreters might test interpretations by the standard of Scripture, guarding against privileging and imposing philosophical and doctrinal frameworks that are the fallible products of particular social locations.[69] This calls for careful attention to Scripture and considerable humility, recognizing that our theologies are fallible and incomplete—God is greater than our understanding.

Accordingly, the definitive question this book seeks to address is, What do we have biblical warrant to (confidently) claim relative to the doctrine of God? In order to meet the standard of biblical warrant, one should be able to *demonstrate* that one's claims are adequately grounded in Scripture. While deeply committed to this standard of biblical warrant, I am also interested in engaging some perennial philosophical and systematic issues concerning divine attributes. Throughout this book, I aim to carefully attend to the way God acts in relation to the world (i.e., in the economy) as revealed in Scripture while also attending to relevant philosophical and systematic issues. In keeping with the commitments of canonical theology outlined above, this approach aims to affirm all that Scripture teaches about the nature and attributes of God in the economy without conceptually reducing God to the way he is portrayed in the economy, recognizing that "we see through a glass, darkly" (1 Cor. 13:12 KJV).

The Language of Scripture as Accommodative and Analogical

How, then, should one handle the accommodative language of Scripture? Many biblical depictions of God appear to be at odds with some tenets of strict classical theism. For example, if God cannot be causally influenced by creatures, what does it mean to say God hears, responds, and engages in covenant relationship? If God is timeless, strictly immutable, and strictly

---

69. See Sanou and Peckham, "Canonical Theology, Social Location."

impassible, how could God have changing emotions such as grief, suffering, lamenting, or relenting?

To reconcile their metaphysical framework with biblical depictions of God, strict classical theists often appeal to two claims: (1) all biblical depictions of discrete and temporal divine "acts" actually refer to the effects of one timelessly eternal divine act, and (2) biblical depictions of God are accommodative—portrayals of God in limited human language whereby God "communicates the truth about his infinite and unchanging existence under the form of what is finite and changeable."[70] The first claim, that God "does all He does in one, perfect, eternal and immutable act," faces the significant difficulty of accounting for the ways Scripture describes various divine actions over time, especially depictions of God undergoing *responsive* changes.[71] I will reserve further discussion of why I believe this claim does not meet the standard of biblical warrant for chapter 3.

The second claim is addressed further in chapter 2. For now, it is important to recognize that while biblical language is accommodative, so is *all* language that is understandable by humans. Indeed, *all* Scripture conveys revelation at a level that humans can understand and, thus, necessarily involves divine condescension. God is far greater than could be conveyed in human language, and in this sense, not only biblical language but (in Justo L. González's words) "all speech about God is anthropomorphic."[72] Accordingly, as Paul Hinlicky notes, "None of our theological models escape anthropomorphism."[73] Merely recognizing *that* biblical language is accommodative does not tell us whether and to what extent such language corresponds to God as he *truly* is. I can speak to my nine-year-old son in a way that accommodates his lesser grasp of language and concepts while also speaking *truly*. Accommodative language, then, may effectively communicate truth. Likewise, while much of the biblical language about God is figurative, figurative language still conveys meaning. Indeed, J. Scott Duvall and J. Daniel Hays claim, "There are always literal realities behind the figures of speech in the Scriptures."[74]

Upon recognition that the language of Scripture is accommodative and sometimes figurative, there remains the hard work of interpreting the biblical language about God in a way that corresponds to what Scripture actually says and affirms—in a way that "allow[s] every text of Scripture (including

70. Dolezal, "Still Impassible," 135.
71. Rogers, *Perfect Being Theology*, 54.
72. González, *Essential Theological Terms*, 9.
73. Hinlicky, *Divine Simplicity*, 200.
74. Duvall and Hays, *God's Relational Presence*, 8.

the Old Testament texts) to be true in what it affirm[s]."[75] Toward this end, I believe each instance should be considered on a case-by-case basis, with careful attention given to whether there is biblical warrant for a given theological interpretation, in accordance with proper exegesis (*at least* that which lets Scripture speak for itself without contortion) and in light of the entire biblical canon.[76] Otherwise, *any* biblical depiction of God that conflicts with one's doctrinal and/or metaphysical commitments might be explained away by simply claiming it is an accommodative depiction, thereby divesting Scripture of its function as theologically normative.

At the same time, we must be careful not to conceptually reduce God to the way he represents himself to humans in the economy of biblical revelation. It would be a mistake to take a letter I wrote to my nine-year-old son and assume on that basis that my vocabulary is fourth-grade level. God is always greater than can be revealed to creatures. For the Creator God, infinitely great and utterly distinct from creation, to *actually* relate to humans in the way Scripture depicts— appearing, speaking, hearing, responding, delivering, forgiving, compassionately loving, grieving, covenanting, dwelling—would involve massive condescension. Yet if such biblical portrayals of divine action are rightly taken as *real, historical* actions of God (as I believe they should be), then it must be that God as he is in himself (*in se*) is compatible with whatever condescension is involved in relating to humans in such ways (in the incarnation and otherwise).[77] The debate over whether such depictions correspond to discrete divine actions is addressed in chapter 3. For now, suffice it to say that if what Scripture affirms about God is unfailingly true, then we should affirm that what Scripture affirms about God (somehow) truly corresponds to God as he is (or was). I believe that whatever is *affirmed* about God via the economy of biblical revelation is compatible with God's nature—without conflating the partial and limited revelation about God in the economy with the far greater reality of God in himself.[78]

Saying that such portrayals and claims are true should not be confused with claiming that they are always to be taken literally or interpreted univocally—

---

75. Holmes, *Quest for the Trinity*, 198.

76. Rather than *allegorical interpretation* of Scripture (when the genre is not demonstrably allegorical), which may treat Scripture like a wax nose, I affirm biblical typology of the kind advocated by Richard Davidson in his book *Typology in Scripture*.

77. Glenn R. Kreider traces God's condescension for the sake of creatures throughout the biblical narratives, concluding, "That God humbles himself and interacts with his creation is the major plotline of the Bible and of each of the biblical stories." Kreider, *God with Us*, 24.

78. Though I agree with Hermann Cremer that "a proper treatment of the doctrine of the divine attributes" should "start from revelation itself" and that "what we actually come to know in revelation is *who* God is and *what kind* of God he is," I disagree with Cremer's claim that "there can be no aspect of God's being beyond his revelation." Cremer, *Christian Doctrine of Divine Attributes*, xxii, 6, 8 (emphasis original).

that such language is to be interpreted as if it applies to God and creatures in precisely the same way. Neither, however, should theological language be taken as equivocal—as if such language holds an *altogether* different meaning when applied to God than its meaning in human contexts. If biblical language is equivocal, it could not effectively communicate anything about God that humans could understand. As such, I agree with the many theologians who believe that language about God should be understood as analogical[79]—that is, there is some analogy or correspondence between language as it applies to God and language as it applies to creatures, but there is also great dissimilarity because God is the utterly unique Creator of all. As God himself stresses, "I am God and not man" (Hosea 11:9 NASB).

For example, there is *some* similarity between the meaning of the word "wise" in the phrase "Solomon is wise" and its meaning in the phrase "God is wise." Otherwise, we could have no understanding of what the word "wise" means relative to God. However, there is also great dissimilarity since God's wisdom is utterly perfect. Yet to know precisely what the extent of similarity and dissimilarity is would require an understanding of God and of language that transcends human limitations. It seems best, then, to recognize that *all* theological language accessible to humans is unavoidably analogical and that all human theological concepts are imperfect and, in turn, to attempt to understand divine revelation as faithfully as we can while recognizing that God is always greater than human language can convey.

While this recognition should prompt us to humility, recognizing our fallibility and limitations, it need not undermine confidence in the communicative efficacy of Scripture. If I am capable of speaking to my nine-year-old in a way that is incomplete (and thus imperfect) and yet remains true, how much more must God be capable of communicating to humans in a way that is incomplete (due to our innate limitations) yet remains true? While I believe the language of Scripture is accommodative and analogical, I also believe it is nevertheless sufficient to effectively communicate what God wants humans to understand through it.[80] Indeed, I believe humans have access to no better understanding or language than what is in Scripture, and I believe such language should be understood in its minimal, demonstrable, exegetical sense (in light of the whole canon), alongside the recognition that one's resulting concept of God is unavoidably analogical and imperfect (as is all

79. See Peckham, *Love of God*, 172–76.
80. On the efficacy and limits of revealed language, see Peckham, *Canonical Theology*, 222–25.

God-talk). As Mildred Bangs Wynkoop puts it, "There is no better source of information about God and Christ than the Scriptures themselves."[81]

My aim in what follows, then, is to humbly exposit and theologically interpret Scripture as faithfully as I can, attempting to limit my conclusions to what I have biblical warrant to (confidently) claim in a way that is systematically coherent, all the while remembering that my theological concepts are analogical and imperfect and thus subject to modification. Given this book's scope, the biblical analysis summarized in subsequent chapters corresponds to only a sample of the canonical investigation I conducted to write this book. There is much more to say about the biblical passages surveyed in this book and about the theological and philosophical issues involved in theological interpretation of the divine attributes. Nevertheless, while I do not expect all readers to agree with all my conclusions, I aim to set forth a case that warrants careful reflection and encourages still more sustained engagement with Scripture relative to the doctrine of God.

Conclusion

This chapter has set the stage for the remaining chapters, which take up various prominent questions relative to divine attributes, including whether God changes and has emotions, whether he is present in space and time, whether he knows everything (including the future), whether he has all power and always gets what he wants, whether he is entirely good and loving, and how one God can be three persons. The remainder of this book sets forth a constructive model of God's attributes that I call covenantal theism, descriptive of the covenantal God of Scripture envisioned in much traditional Christian worship and prayer—the God who acts in the world, intervenes, speaks, communes, and covenants with his people. Among other things, the modifier "covenantal" conveys that God enters into real back-and-forth relationship with creatures but does so voluntarily, remaining transcendent even as he condescends to be with us (immanent). In brief, covenantal theism affirms God's aseity and self-sufficiency, qualified immutability and passibility, everlasting eternity, omnipresence, omniscience, omnipotence and sovereign providence, covenantal action, omnibenevolence, and relational triunity.

In future chapters we will see (among other things) that this God of love is indomitable, all-powerful, and utterly distinct from creatures but voluntarily changes in relationship, willingly suffers with us and for us in love,

81. Wynkoop, *Theology of Love*, 219.

condescends to spend time with us as genuinely present in creation (while not reduced to or encompassed by it), knows us better than we know ourselves, knows what is best for us and lovingly plans accordingly for our good, sustains and cares for all creation, exercises his infinite power for the best good of all while granting power to others for the sake of the flourishing of love, wills only good for all, meets and defeats evil—at inestimable cost to himself—and eternally enjoys loving fellowship as the Trinity of love, but freely created others to share in the fellowship of love.

Two

The Unchanging God
Who Suffers in Love

Aseity, Immutability, and Qualified Passibility

Have you,' he cried in a dreadful voice, 'have you ever suffered?'"[1] At the conclusion of G. K. Chesterton's novel *The Man Who Was Thursday*, an undercover policeman named Syme puts this question to a character called Sunday. Syme had thought that Sunday—a massive, mysterious, and imposing figure—was the criminal mastermind of an enormous conspiracy to rain anarchy upon the world. However, Syme discovered that Sunday was not who he seemed. For reasons inscrutable to Syme, Sunday had orchestrated many occurrences—including many dangers and hardships—for the sake of goodness and peace in the end.

Syme's question is a thinly veiled accusation. Syme himself has suffered, but does the one pulling the strings feel the cost of his plans? Does he have any intimate understanding of the suffering involved? Following his question, as Syme gazed, "the great face grew to an awful size . . . larger and larger, filling the whole sky; then everything went black." In the blackness, Syme heard "a distant voice saying a commonplace text that he had heard somewhere, 'Can ye drink of the cup that I drink of?'" (Mark 10:38 KJV).[2]

1. Chesterton, *Man Who Was Thursday*, 279.
2. Chesterton, *Man Who Was Thursday*, 279.

"Have you ever suffered?" This question might be put to God by anyone acquainted with suffering. Many are troubled by the idea of a God unaffected by grief. As Dietrich Bonhoeffer writes, "Only the suffering God can help."[3] If God cannot suffer, some maintain, then God cannot love.[4] Here many point to the fact that Christ willingly suffered for us, providing the greatest demonstration of divine love (John 3:16; Rom. 5:8) and evidencing Christ's ability to "sympathize with our weaknesses" (Heb. 4:15 NASB; cf. Isa. 53:3). Understood one way, if Christ is divine and Christ suffered for us, it seems to follow that God *has indeed* suffered for us. Yet some maintain that God *cannot* suffer, reconciling this with the passion of Christ by attributing Christ's sufferings to his human nature alone such that Christ sympathized with our weaknesses in his human nature, but the divine nature remained untouched.

The question of whether God can suffer is integrally connected to questions such as whether God can change and whether God can engage in real relationships with creatures. Contrasting "the religiously available God of the Scriptures" with "the unchanging God of the philosophers," Ronald Nash asks, "If God cannot change, how can He enter into the kinds of interpersonal relations attributed to Him in Scripture? How can He love and care? How can the world and human beings make any difference at all to Him?"[5] Against this background, this chapter addresses ongoing debates over divine immutability and impassibility, alongside the closely related issue of divine aseity, seeking to answer questions such as, Does God change? Does God have emotions? Does God truly care about humans?

The Covenantal God of Love

When asked what one word describes God, most Christians would say "love." After all, "God is love" (1 John 4:8, 16). Yet divine love is variously understood and closely linked with differing conceptions of God's nature. Given this, some years ago I conducted an inductive investigation of Scripture regarding God's love, with an eye toward implications regarding God's nature. Here I can only briefly outline some elements of what I found in what turned out to be a study over seven hundred pages long that sometimes surprised me and continually moved me to worship.[6]

3. Bonhoeffer, *Letters and Papers from Prison*, 8:479.
4. See Moltmann, *Crucified God*, 222.
5. Nash, *Concept of God*, 100.
6. See Peckham, *Concept of Divine Love*.

Scripture consistently teaches that God's love is good, holy, kind, just, faithful, freely given, generous, unmerited, evaluative, warm, deeply compassionate, intensely passionate (but never irrational), long-suffering, merciful, gracious, everlastingly steadfast, relationally responsive, covenantal, and continually active for the good of all. The God of Scripture persistently draws people into relationship with himself, inviting and calling humans to freely enter into this intimate, reciprocal (but asymmetrical) love relationship. The following aspects of divine love in relation to the world are particularly prominent throughout Scripture:

1. God's love is covenantal, meaning it is steadfastly relational and (ideally) reciprocal love.
2. God's love is volitional, meaning love is freely given.
3. God's love is evaluative, meaning God may be delighted and displeased in love relationship.
4. God's love is emotional, meaning God's love includes relationally affected emotions such as compassion.[7]

The Covenantal Aspect of Divine Love

Scripture consistently portrays God as engaging in back-and-forth covenant relationship with humans, aimed at reciprocal love relationship. God is "the faithful God, who keeps His covenant and His lovingkindness to a thousandth generation with those who love Him and keep His commandments" (Deut. 7:9 NASB; cf. Exod. 20:6; 1 Kings 8:23; Dan. 9:4).[8] Love between God and humans is asymmetrical in many ways. While humans may or may not love God and the days of humans are "like grass," God is everlastingly steadfast in love (Ps. 103:15–17 NASB; cf. Ps. 136; Rom. 8:35–39). While God created humans with the capacity to love and be loved, God himself is the ground

7. These aspects appear prominently in the Torah, Prophets, Writings, Gospels and Acts, Pauline Epistles, General Epistles, and Revelation. Peckham, *Concept of Divine Love*.

8. The word translated "lovingkindness," *ḥesed*, exemplifies the covenantal aspect of divine love (and much more). *Ḥesed* expects relational responsiveness toward the goal of, or within, reciprocal relationship (often formal covenant relationship). On one hand, *ḥesed* is "characterized by permanence and reliability" (Zobel, "חֶסֶד," 5:57). On the other hand, "Numerous texts witness to at least the hypothetical possibility of losing God's חֶסֶד or of having it taken away" (Baer and Gordon, "חֶסֶד," 2:215) (see Gen. 24:27; 2 Chron. 6:42; Pss. 36:10 [11]; 77:8; 88:11; 106:45). God's *ḥesed* is extremely steadfast, reliable, and enduring. Yet Katharine D. Sakenfeld explains, "God's *ḥesed* is conditional, dependent upon the good repair of the covenant relationship that it is up to Israel to maintain" (Sakenfeld, "Love in the OT," 4:379) (see Deut. 7:9, 12; 2 Sam. 22:26; 1 Kings 8:23; 2 Chron. 6:14; Pss. 25:10; 32:10). See also Peckham, *Concept of Divine Love*, 300–319.

and source of all love (1 John 4:7, 19; cf. Jer. 31:3) and covenants to bless all peoples (Gen. 12:3; cf. Deut. 4:37).

While God's love is everlasting and God bestows love on everyone (John 3:16) prior to any response, enjoying love *relationship* with God—while *always unmerited*—is contingent on humans' response to God's love (Deut. 7:9–13; John 14:21–23; 16:27; Rom. 11:22; Jude 21; cf. Jer. 11:15; 14:10; 16:5; Hosea 9:15; John 1:12).[9] With those who respond positively, God enjoys reciprocal love relationship—a covenantal relationship wherein "the steadfast love of the LORD is from everlasting to everlasting on those who fear him . . . to those who keep his covenant" (Ps. 103:17–18; cf. Deut. 7:9–13; Matt. 18:27–33).[10] With Israel, such covenant relationship was formal and particular, but the God of Scripture invites all to intimate reciprocal love relationship, which can be characterized as "covenantal" in the broad sense of bilateral relationship, ordered by promises and corresponding expectations and conditions.

The Volitional Aspect of Divine Love

The covenantal love of God presupposes the volitional aspect of divine love. Before the foundation of the world, God enjoyed eternal love relationship within the Trinity (see John 17:24). God need not have loved creatures because God need not have created at all. God *freely* did so. As Revelation 4:11 proclaims, "Worthy are You, our Lord and our God, to receive glory and honor and power; for You created all things, and because of Your will they existed, and were created" (NASB).[11] God not only *freely* created the world but also *freely* bestows his love on creatures who have rebelled against him. Whereas humans have forfeited any claim to the continuance of God's covenantal love, God willingly sustains love relationship—just as God *freely* did in the aftermath of the golden calf rebellion (Exod. 33:19; 34:6–7; Neh. 9:31).[12] Likewise, God states of his apostate people in Hosea 14:4, "I will heal their apostasy, / I will love them freely" (NASB). The term "freely" here (*nədābâ*) connotes the "determinative . . . element of free will," what is offered

9. To describe this aspect, I coined the term "foreconditional," meaning prior to conditions but not exclusive of conditions (relative to continued relationship). See Peckham, *Love of God*, chaps. 7–8; Peckham, *Concept of Divine Love*, 300–350, 456–88.

10. Cf. the unconditionality and conditionality exhibited in grant-type covenants (e.g., Abrahamic, Davidic). See Peckham, *Concept of Divine Love*, 212–25.

11. Contrary to views wherein God is essentially related to creation, the God of Scripture existed "before" the world (Col. 1:16–17) and needs nothing (Acts 17:25).

12. On the volitional aspect of divine love, see Peckham, *Concept of Divine Love*, 204–35, 372–99, 577–82; Peckham, *Love of God*, 89–115, 257–63.

"totally voluntarily," and is thus often translated as "freewill offering" (e.g., Exod. 35:29).[13]

The Evaluative Aspect of Divine Love

Divine love is not merely volitional, however. It is also evaluative and emotional. To say God's love is evaluative is to say God's love involves rational appraisal and enjoyment of value in others. God loves goodness and justice and hates evil and injustice (Isa. 61:8; cf. Ps. 37:28; Prov. 15:8–9). God may thus become pleased or displeased with humans; God "loves one who pursues righteousness" (Prov. 15:9 NASB; cf. Ps. 146:8; 2 Cor. 9:7; Heb. 13:16). God's people are precious in his sight (Isa. 43:4; cf. Matt. 10:31), God "takes pleasure in His people" (Ps. 149:4 NASB), and God will one day "rejoice over" his people "with shouts of joy" (Zeph. 3:17 NASB). Further, God promises his covenant people, "If you obey my voice and keep my covenant, you shall be my treasured possession out of all the peoples" (Exod. 19:5; cf. Deut. 26:18). Yet humans can bring joy to God only because of God's enabling and drawing—always unmerited—prevenient love (Jer. 31:3), manifest in Christ's mediation (1 Pet. 2:5; cf. Heb. 13:16) and the Holy Spirit's ministry (Rom. 5:5; cf. 8:26–27). Though himself the source of all value and needing nothing (Acts 17:25), God delights in humans somewhat like a father delights in a gift given to him by his child, though bought with the father's own money. "We love, because He first loved us" (1 John 4:19 NASB; cf. 4:7; Jer. 31:3).

The Emotional Aspect of Divine Love

Scripture also consistently portrays God's love as profoundly emotional. God is ardently concerned with the well-being of humans, akin to—but exponentially greater than—the compassion of a mother for her infant and the passion of a loving husband for his wife (see, e.g., Isa. 49:15). Frequently depicted as a scorned and unrequited lover, the God of Scripture is repeatedly grieved and provoked by human evil while also delighting in goodness and rejoicing over every person who responds to his loving overtures (Luke 15:7). Through it all, God manifests extravagantly great compassion and passion to bring wayward humans back into (covenantal) love relationship (see, e.g., Hosea 11:8–9; cf. Jer. 31:20).[14] Altogether, then, God's love for creatures is

---

13. Conrad, "נדב," 9:220, 222.

14. On the emotional aspect of divine love, see Peckham, *Love of God*, chap. 6; Peckham, *Concept of Divine Love*, 256–300, 432–56.

volitional, evaluative, emotional, and covenantal. Yet how can the God whom
the Bible describes as unchanging (e.g., Mal. 3:6) love in this manner?

The Changing Emotions of the Unchanging God

Competing Conceptions of Divine Immutability and Impassibility

Theologians continue to debate whether God is impassible. Strict classical theists claim that God is *strictly* impassible, meaning God cannot be affected by anything. As James Dolezal puts it, "God cannot undergo emotional
changes" and "God cannot suffer." Further, Dolezal claims that this "was the
orthodox Christian consensus for nearly two millennia."[15] Yet some classical
theists claim that *qualified* impassibility is the traditional view.[16] Advocates
of *qualified* impassibility generally agree that God can be affected but never
"against his will by an outside force."[17] For some, this means that God has
emotions, but these are determined by God alone.[18]

Paul Gavrilyuk has made an influential case that there was no single, monolithic patristic view of impassibility. But "divine impassibility [was] primarily
a metaphysical term, marking God's unlikeness to everything in the created
order, not a psychological term denoting (as modern passibilists allege) God's
emotional apathy."[19] Indeed, Gavrilyuk argues, "The picture of an essentially
impassibilist account of God in patristic theology, varied only by the minority
voices that advocated divine suffering, is incorrect."[20] Rather than ruling out
divine emotions, Gavrilyuk maintains that "divine impassibility functioned
as an apophatic qualifier of all divine emotions."[21] Yet he notes that there was

---

15. Dolezal, "Still Impassible," 125. So also Thomas Weinandy, *Does God Suffer?*, 38. For
a very different form of unqualified impassibility, see Schleiermacher, *Christian Faith*, 206.

16. See Gavrilyuk, *Suffering of the Impassible God*; and R. Lister, *God Is Impassible and
Impassioned*.

17. Castelo, *Apathetic God*, 16.

18. See, e.g., R. Lister, *God Is Impassible and Impassioned*.

19. Gavrilyuk, "God's Impassible Suffering," 139.

20. Gavrilyuk, *Suffering of the Impassible God*, 20. Amaluche G. Nnamani agrees with
Gavrilyuk regarding the first two centuries of Christian theology but argues that divine impassibility has been the standard view since the fourth and fifth centuries. Nnamani, *Paradox of
a Suffering God*, 98.

21. Gavrilyuk, *Suffering of the Impassible God*, 173. In this regard, Origen maintains that
"God is altogether impassible, and is to be regarded as wholly free from all affections of that
kind" (i.e., "human affection or passion"). Accordingly, "when we read" in Scripture "of the
anger of God, we do not take such expressions literally, but seek in them a spiritual meaning,
that we may think of God as He deserves to be thought of" (Origen, *De Principiis* 2.4 [*ANF*
4:277–78]). On the other hand, Origen writes that Christ "came down to earth out of compassion for the human race. Having experienced our sufferings even before he suffered on the cross,

a diversity of patristic views on this issue and that many fathers, including some Gavrilyuk deems orthodox, employed (qualified) expressions of divine suffering.[22] Noting "'impassibilist' positions proposed by some of the Fathers that seem akin to what would, in modern theology, be termed 'passibilism,'" Anastasia Philippa Scrutton similarly concludes, "Some modern forms of passibilism may not be as much of a break from tradition as has generally been perceived."[23] If this is right, some patristic views might cohere with some kind of *qualified* passibility, wherein God is *voluntarily* possible in relation to the world in a carefully qualified sense but not essentially related to the world (as process theists and other *essential* passibilists claim).[24]

The impassibility debate closely relates to the debate over divine immutability. If God cannot change at all (strict immutability), then God cannot undergo emotional change (strict impassibility).[25] Conversely, if God undergoes emotional change, then God cannot be strictly immutable. Because change requires the passing of time, strict immutability follows from divine timelessness.[26] Strict immutability also follows from the Aristotelian-Thomist conception of God as pure act (*actus purus*), which affirms that there can be no possibility of change (potentiality) and that "God exists independently of all causal influence from his creatures" (pure aseity).[27]

However, numerous Christian theists affirm a *qualified* kind of divine immutability, meaning God's essential nature and character are changeless,

---

he condescended to assume our flesh. For if he had not suffered, he would not have come to live on the level of human life." He suffered "the suffering of love." Also, when the Father "directs human affairs he suffers human suffering" and "bears our ways, just as the Son of God bears our sufferings" (cf. Deut. 1:31). "The Father himself is not without suffering. When he is prayed to, he has pity and compassion." Origen, *Homilies 1–14 on Ezekiel* 6.6.3 (Scheck, 92–93).

22. Gavrilyuk, *Suffering of the Impassible God*, 89, 127.

23. Scrutton, *Thinking Through Feeling*, 2.

24. In Gavrilyuk's view, God is "impassible inasmuch as he is able to conquer sin, suffering, and death; and God is also passible (in a carefully qualified sense) inasmuch as in the incarnation God has chosen to enter the human condition in order to transform it." Gavrilyuk, "God's Impassible Suffering," 146.

25. In Dolezal's words, "Impassibility is simply a subset of divine immutability." Dolezal, "Still Impassible," 129.

26. According to Thomas Aquinas, "God is utterly unchangeable. . . . That which begins or ceases to live, or is subject in living, is changeable," and "succession results from change of some kind." But God is not "subject to succession in living. Therefore His life is eternal." Thomas Aquinas, *Summa Contra Gentiles* 1.99.

27. Dolezal, "Strong Impassibility," 18. As pure act, God cannot have any "passive potency," which Aquinas defines as "the principle of being acted upon by something else" (Thomas Aquinas, *Summa Theologiae* I.25.1). Steven J. Duby explains, "Divine aseity entails first that God is *actus purus*" (pure act). God is without any "capacity to be moved" and without any "passive potency" because "God is fully in act" (Duby, *Divine Simplicity*, 121). Cf. Webster, *God without Measure*, 1:120.

yet God voluntarily enters into real relationship with creatures and thus changes relationally. In Alan Padgett's words, "God is immutable relative to essential divine attributes" and "changes only in relational ways, in order to create and care for that creation."[28] While denying that God is pure act, qualified immutability affirms divine aseity and self-sufficiency, meaning God does not depend on anything with respect to his existence or essential nature.

Scripture on Divine Emotions and Change

What, however, does Scripture reveal regarding whether God changes or has changing emotions? Specifically, what do we have biblical warrant to confidently claim regarding these issues? On the one hand, Scripture teaches that God is immutable. God himself states, "I, the LORD, do not change" (Mal. 3:6 NASB). On the other hand, Scripture portrays God undergoing emotional and other change. For example, according to Judges 2:18, God was "moved to pity [*nāḥam*, niphal] by their groaning" (NASB; cf. 10:16) and was often "provoked" to anger (Ps. 78:58 NASB; cf. Deut. 32:21; Ps. 78:40–41) and other emotions. The following sections briefly survey some of what Scripture portrays in both respects.

GOD IS SELF-EXISTENT AND IMMUTABLE

Scripture identifies God as the Creator of all (Rev. 4:11; cf. Gen. 1:1; Ps. 33:6; Heb. 11:3), who needs nothing (Acts 17:25). God's existence is not dependent on anything. The Creator exists of himself (*a se*). Everything else depends on God: "For from Him and through Him and to Him are all things" (Rom. 11:36 NASB), and God has "life in Himself" (John 5:26 NASB).[29] Further, Scripture teaches that the self-existent Creator remains the same throughout all ages. Psalm 102:27 declares, "You are the same, / and Your years will not come to an end" (NASB). God's unchanging nature undergirds God's constancy toward creatures: "For I the LORD do not change; therefore you, O children of Jacob, have not perished" (Mal. 3:6). Likewise, James 1:17 states, "Every generous act of giving, with every perfect gift, is from above,

28. Padgett, "Eternity as Relative Timelessness," 109. See also Padgett, *God, Eternity, and the Nature of Time*, 131. Similarly, see Copan, *Loving Wisdom*, 93–95; Ware, *God's Greater Glory*, 28, 141; and Davis, *Logic and the Nature of God*, 24. Cf. Emil Brunner's view that God "is—in a certain sense—not unchangeable" because God "is 'affected' by what happens to His creatures" and "'reacts' to the acts of men." Yet God is not one who "becomes," but "the God of the Bible is eternally Unchangeable." Brunner, *Christian Doctrine of God*, 268–69.

29. According to Douglas J. Moo, Rom. 11:35–36 teaches that God is "the source (*ek*), sustainer (*dia*), and goal (*eis*) of all things." Moo, *Epistle to the Romans*, 743.

coming down from the Father of lights, with whom there is no variation or shadow due to change."

While some have taken God's statement "I the LORD do not change" to mean that God is immutable in every way (strictly immutable), this statement appears in the context of responsive relationship, with God going on to say, "Therefore you, O children of Jacob, have not perished" (Mal. 3:6) and in the next verse urging, "Return [*šûb*] to me, and I will return [*šûb*] to you" (3:7; cf. Jer. 15:19; Zech. 1:3). The Hebrew verb *šûb* typically means "to return or turn back," indicating a *change* of course.[30] Here it seems to indicate a relational change of the kind Scripture frequently predicates of God (cf. Jer. 18:7–10).[31] For example, God proclaims in Psalm 81:13–14,

> O that my people would listen to me,
>   that Israel would walk in my ways!
> Then I would quickly subdue their enemies,
>   and turn [*šûb*] my hand against their foes.

Read in context, Malachi 3:6–7 expresses the constancy of God's character (*moral* immutability), which undergirds God's steadfast *covenantal* faithfulness (cf. Heb. 13:8), while also portraying God as changing relationally.[32] James 1:17 likewise depicts God as *morally* changeless, describing God as unchanging relative to giving perfect gifts while not addressing whether God may change relationally.[33]

Elsewhere Scripture repeatedly emphasizes God's moral changelessness. First John 1:5 states, "God is Light, and in Him there is no darkness at all" (NASB). Deuteronomy 32:4 adds that God's

> work is perfect,
> For all His ways are just;
> A God of faithfulness and without injustice,
> Righteous and upright is He. (NASB)

---

30. Pieter Verhoef comments that this phrasing "denotes a consequence: 'in order that I may turn to you,' or 'then I will turn to you.' The transgressions of the people were the cause of God's turning away from them, the reason why he was no longer pleased with them (1:8, 10; 2:13)." Verhoef, *Books of Haggai and Malachi*, 302.

31. See Ware, "Evangelical Reexamination," 431–46. Cf. Chisholm, "Does God 'Change His Mind'?," 387–99.

32. Nicholas Wolterstorff comments that this passage affirms "covenant fidelity, not [strict] ontological immutability." Wolterstorff, *Inquiring about God*, 161. Likewise, Moreland and Craig, *Philosophical Foundations*, 526.

33. According to Wolterstorff, James 1:17 teaches "that God is unchangeable in that God is never the source of evil" but "only and always of good." Wolterstorff, *Inquiring about God*, 163.

Psalm 100:5 likewise declares,

> The LORD is good;
>   his steadfast love endures forever,
>   and his faithfulness to all generations.

Psalm 117:2 adds, "The faithfulness of the LORD endures forever." Accordingly, even "if we are faithless, He remains faithful, for He cannot deny Himself" (2 Tim. 2:13 NASB). God's promises, then, are unbreakable. Indeed, God "never lies" (Titus 1:2), and Hebrews 6:17–18 speaks of "two unchangeable things, in which it is impossible that God would prove false," "the unchangeable character of [God's] purpose," which God "guaranteed" by God's unchangeable "oath" (cf. Num. 23:19; Isa. 25:1). The God of Scripture is the unwaveringly faithful covenant-making and promise-keeping God.

Yet Scripture also repeatedly portrays God as changing relationally, including being "moved by prayer for the land" (2 Sam. 24:25 NASB; cf. 21:14) and otherwise affected by and responsive to human entreaty (e.g., Exod. 33:12–34:10; Judg. 2:18). God himself elicits intercession and responds to prayer. In Ezekiel 22:30, God states, "I sought for anyone among them who would repair the wall and stand in the breach before me on behalf of the land, so that I would not destroy it; but I found no one" (cf. Exod. 32:10–14; Isa. 30:18–19; 63:5; Jer. 33:3). Further, God promises his covenant people, "If my people who are called by my name humble themselves, pray, seek my face, and turn from their wicked ways, then I will hear from heaven, and will forgive their sin and heal their land" (2 Chron. 7:14; cf. 2 Kings 20:5).

Christ himself models a life of intercessory prayer (see, e.g., Luke 22:32; 23:34) and teaches his followers to pray that God's "will be done" (Matt. 6:10 NASB) and to "ask, and it will be given to you," for "everyone who asks receives" (7:7–8 NASB; cf. Luke 11:5–13; John 16:23). Conversely, Scripture sometimes portrays divine action as impeded by a lack of faith (e.g., Mark 6:5) or prayer (9:29). Scripture also repeatedly depicts God as moved by human suffering (Judg. 10:16; cf. Luke 19:41) and otherwise emotionally affected. In this regard, Walter Brueggemann maintains that the *strictly* "immutable God" of "scholastic theology . . . stands in deep tension with the biblical presentation of God."[34] Scripture affirms God is changeless in some respects while affirming God changes *relationally*.

---

34. Brueggemann, "Book of Exodus," 1:932.

God Relents

Similar nuance appears relative to divine relenting or "repentance." On one hand, Numbers 23:19 proclaims,

> God is not a man, that He should lie,
> Nor a son of man, that He should repent [*nāḥam*];
> Has he said, and will He not do it?
> Or has He spoken, and will He not make it good? (NASB)

Likewise, 1 Samuel 15:29 states, "The Glory of Israel will not lie or change His mind [*nāḥam*]; for He is not a man that He should change His mind [*nāḥam*]" (NASB). Yet in the same chapter, God states, "I regret [*nāḥam*, niphal] that I made Saul king" (15:11), and 1 Samuel 15:35 declares, "The Lord was sorry [*nāḥam*, niphal] that he had made Saul king over Israel." Many other passages likewise portray divine *nāḥam* (e.g., Gen. 6:6; Exod. 32:14; 2 Sam. 24:16; Ps. 106:45; Jer. 18:7–10; Joel 2:12–14; Jon. 3:9–10; 4:2). In context, 1 Samuel 15:29 indicates that God will not *nāḥam* with respect to his judgment against Saul—it is a final judgment (cf. Jer. 4:28). As John T. Willis notes, Scripture "nowhere indicates that the idea that God does not repent [*nāḥam*] is a universal principle, but always with relation to a specific event or situation."[35] Indeed, according to Daniel I. Block, the biblical data suggests that "to repent concerning [threatened/real] calamity" is "fundamental to the divine nature."[36]

Scripture repeatedly portrays God as eager to relent [*nāḥam*] from negative judgment *if* his people will repent of their evil (e.g., Jer. 18:7–8; cf. Joel 2:13). Conversely, if the people turn to evil, God will relent from the blessing he intended for them (Jer. 18:9–10).[37] In response to evil, God relents from blessing; in response to genuine human repentance, God relents from punishment. Such responsive change perfectly accords with God's moral immutability as steadfastly righteous, compassionate, and gracious. Joel 2:13 thus exhorts,

> Return to the Lord, your God,
> for he is gracious and merciful,
> slow to anger, and abounding in steadfast love,
> and relents [*nāḥam*, niphal] from punishing. (cf. Exod. 32:14;
> 34:6–7)

35. Willis, "'Repentance' of God," 168.
36. Block, *Judges, Ruth*, 131.
37. See Peckham, "Passible Potter," 130–50.

Here and elsewhere, God "relents" in accordance with his changeless character of steadfast love, always keeping and often exceeding his unbreakable covenant promises. When God "heard their cry" and "remembered His covenant for their sake," God "relented according to the greatness of His lovingkindness" (Ps. 106:44–45 NASB).[38]

Here it is worth noting that translating *nāḥam* in terms of changing one's mind might be misleading, particularly relative to omniscience (see chap. 4). The root *nāḥam* does not itself indicate a *change of mind* per se. Rather, according to H. Van Dyke Parunak, *nāḥam* (in the niphal stem) basically means "suffer emotional pain," sometimes "extended to describe the release of emotional tension" via God's relenting—that is, "retracting a declared action" such as "punishment" or "blessing."[39] It thus typically depicts divine "sorrow" but does not entail any "suggestion of regret" for God's own actions.[40] Whereas humans repent of wrongdoing, "God is never said to have committed any sin of which God needs to repent."[41] In this and other ways, divine *nāḥam* differs significantly from human *nāḥam*. God "is not a man that He should [repent or] change His mind [*nāḥam*]" (1 Sam. 15:29 NASB), but God does sorrow over many things (15:11, 35).

The constancy of God's character is highlighted in Jonah's angry response to God's relenting from judgment against Nineveh: "That is why," Jonah complains, "I fled to Tarshish at the beginning; for I knew that you are a gracious God and merciful, slow to anger, and abounding in steadfast love, and ready to relent [*nāḥam*, niphal] from punishing" (Jon. 4:2; cf. 3:10). Jonah treats this as bad news, but the constancy of God's loving character and willingness to relent is exceedingly good news. God relents, but not like unreliable humans (Num. 23:19; 1 Sam. 15:29); God relents according to his perfect nature as wholly just and loving.

38. Throughout Scripture, the phrase "God remembered" does not indicate that God had "forgotten" but has the "implication of taking appropriate action," often on the basis of God's covenant commitments. Andrew Bowling, "זָכַר," 1:241. As Stephen T. Davis notes, "To remember is to have beliefs or knowledge about what is past" but does not entail that one forgot. Davis, *Logic and the Nature of God*, 14.

39. Parunak, "Semantic Survey of NHM," 532. Similarly, H. J. Stoebe identifies two categories of *nāḥam*'s meaning in passive forms, "'be comforted' and 'be sorry' in the broadest scope" (Stoebe, "נחם," *TLOT* 2:734). With God as subject, *nāḥam* often appears in the niphal, which may denote divine sorrow and/or grief (Gen. 6:6–7; 1 Sam. 15:11, 35), being "moved to pity" or "feeling sympathy for" (Judg. 2:18; cf. Ps. 90:13), and/or relenting or changing course in action (Exod. 32:12, 14; 2 Sam. 24:16; 1 Chron. 21:15; Ps. 106:45; Isa. 57:6; Jer. 26:19; Joel 2:13–14; Jon. 3:9–10; 4:2; Amos 7:3, 6; cf. Isa. 1:24). For a full survey of this term, see Peckham, *Concept of Divine Love*, 266–68.

40. Parunak, "Semantic Survey of NHM," 532. One can be sorrowful over something without regretting one's actions relative to it.

41. Fretheim, "Repentance of God," 50. See also Fretheim, *Suffering of God*.

GOD HAS CHANGING EMOTIONS

Scripture also repeatedly portrays God as experiencing *changing* emotions in *response* to humans, though always perfectly in accord with his unchanging character. Scripture frequently depicts God as pleased or displeased in response to humans. God loves justice but hates evil: "The sacrifice of the wicked is an abomination to the LORD, / But the prayer of the upright is His delight" (Prov. 15:8 NASB; cf. 11:20; 12:22). Accordingly, humans may "please" God "in all respects" if they "walk in a manner worthy of the Lord" (Col. 1:10 NASB; cf. 3:20). While "the LORD takes pleasure in His people" (Ps. 149:4 NASB), they also repeatedly "provoked" God "to wrath in the wilderness" by being "rebellious against the LORD" (Deut. 9:7 NASB).[42] The term translated "provoked . . . to wrath" (*qāṣap*, "to be angry") is in the hiphil stem, indicating the people *caused* God to be angry. Elsewhere God is repeatedly "provoked to anger" (32:16 NASB; cf. Ps. 78:40–41, 58) or otherwise "provoked" or "moved" with respect to some emotion, such as being "moved to pity [*nāḥam*, niphal] by" his people's "groaning" (Judg. 2:18 NASB).[43] Later, responsive to the people's repenting from foreign gods, God "could no longer bear to see Israel suffer" (10:16).[44]

Elsewhere God describes himself as changing from one emotional state to another: "I am extremely angry with the nations that are at ease; for while I was only a little angry, they made the disaster worse" (Zech. 1:15). Thus, "I have returned [*šûb*] to Jerusalem with compassion" (1:16). In Hosea 11:8, God also proclaims,

> How can I give you up, O Ephraim?
> How can I surrender you, O Israel?
> How can I make you like Admah?
> How can I treat you like Zeboiim?
> My heart is turned over within Me,
> All My compassions [*niḥumîm*] are kindled [*kāmar*, niphal]. (NASB)[45]

42. See, e.g., Deut. 4:25; Judg. 2:12; 1 Kings 14:9; 2 Kings 21:6, 15; Isa. 65:3; Jer. 7:18–19; Ezek. 8:17; 16:26; 20:28; Hosea 12:14.

43. God being "moved" is often depicted with the niphal (usually passive), and God being "provoked" is often depicted via the hiphil (typically causative). Regarding Judg. 2:18, the word translated "groaning" appears with a causative *mem*, indicating causal relationship between God's "hearing" of Israel's pain and his compassionate feelings for them (*minna'ăqātām*, "because of their groaning"). See Block, *Judges, Ruth*, 130. According to Dennis T. Olson, this usage "signifies sorrow at the hurt or pain of another and a desire to come to the victim's aid." D. Olson, "Book of Judges," 2:756.

44. Translated literally, Judg. 10:16 states that God's "soul [*nepeš*] was shortened [*qāṣar*] at the trouble of Israel." See Haak, "Study and New Interpretation of *Qsr Nps*," 161–67.

45. The "heart" (*lēb*) recoiling language is an idiom of profound emotions, similar to the English idiom "gut-wrenching" (such idiomatic "body language" is discussed more later). The

Here God describes himself as experiencing intense, *changing* emotions in response to human rebellion.[46] Likewise, in Jeremiah 31:20, God calls his covenant people "my dear son," saying,

> I am deeply moved for him;
>   I will surely have mercy [*rāḥam*] on him,
>   says the LORD. (cf. Isa. 63:15)[47]

The God of Scripture not only is compassionate but also becomes righteously indignant against evil and injustice: "God is a righteous judge, / And a God who has indignation every day" (Ps. 7:11 NASB). Bruce Baloian comments that in Scripture "God is passionately concerned about the lives of human beings and whether justice takes place among them."[48] Further, Gordon Wenham notes that God exhibits "the anger of someone who loves deeply."[49] While some think that a God of love should not become angry, in Scripture love and justice are intertwined such that love requires justice (e.g., Pss. 33:5; 89:14; 119:149; Isa. 61:8; Jer. 9:24; Hosea 2:19; Mic. 6:8; Luke 11:42). Divine wrath is the appropriate response of love to evil.[50] God hates evil because evil always hurts God's creatures, even if self-inflicted. As Peter C. Craigie explains, "The behavior of the Israelites vexed God; he had a fatherly concern for them as his sons and daughters, so that to see them rejecting his

---

description of God's compassions (*niḥûm*) growing warm and tender (*kmr*, niphal) is also a striking depiction of emotions, as *kmr* elsewhere depicts intense human emotions such as in the case of the mother who was "deeply stirred [*kmr*, niphal + *raḥămîm*] over her son" before Solomon (1 Kings 3:26 NASB) and Joseph's emotions over his brothers (Gen. 43:30). Cf. Butterworth, "רחם," *NIDOTTE* 3:1093; and Stoebe, "רחם," *TLOT* 3:1226.

46. See further Peckham, "Qualified Passibility"; cf. Peckham, *Concept of Divine Love*; Peckham, *Love of God*.

47. The deeply emotional term *rāḥam* is discussed further below. The language translated "I am deeply moved for him" is a Hebrew idiom that could be literally translated "my heart yearns" (*mēʿeh* + *hāmâ*). This is idiomatic imagery of "God's stomach being churned up with longing" for his people (Thompson, *Jeremiah*, 575). Cf. Schunck, "המה," 4:464. *Mēʿeh* + *hāmâ/hāmôn*—murmur, roar—appears five times, always an idiom of intense emotional feeling, whether of God (Isa. 63:15; Jer. 31:20) or of humans (Song 5:4; Isa. 16:11; Jer. 4:19). Kazoh Kitamori makes a case that here *hāmâ* depicts the pain of God, and he argues that "'love rooted in the pain of God' concerns the entire message of the Bible." Kitamori, *Theology of the Pain of God*, 162.

48. Baloian, "Anger," 4:381.

49. Wenham, *Genesis 1–15*, 146.

50. D. C. K. Watson explains, "Unless God detests sin and evil with great loathing, He cannot be a God of Love" (Watson, *My God Is Real*, 39). However, R. T. Mullins makes a persuasive argument that divine wrath itself seems to be incompatible with strict classical theism (Mullins, *God and Emotions*). As Brunner puts it, if "there really is such a fact as the Mercy of God and the Wrath of God, then God, too, is 'affected' by what happens to His creatures." Brunner, *Christian Doctrine of God*, 268.

love caused him not only anger, but also pain" because "a loving Father finds it hard to look on while his children invite disaster by their sinful behavior."[51] In this regard, Jordan Wessling explains, "Because God loves His wayward children, He refuses merely to stand by when they hurt themselves and others."[52]

Accordingly, Christ expressed righteous indignation against those who used the temple system to take advantage of widows, orphans, and the poor (Matt. 21:12–13).[53] Both compassionate mercy *and* justice are integral to God's perfect character. If we downplay God's wrath and highlight only God's compassion, we may undermine Scripture's nearly ubiquitous emphasis on God's concern for justice.[54] Miroslav Volf writes in this regard,

> I used to think that wrath was unworthy of God. Isn't God love? Shouldn't divine love be beyond wrath? God is love, and God loves every person and every creature. That's exactly why God is wrathful against some of them. My last resistance to the idea of God's wrath was a casualty of the war in former Yugoslavia, the region from which I come. According to some estimates, 200,000 people were killed and over 3,000,000 were displaced. My villages and cities were destroyed, my people shelled day in and day out, some of them brutalized beyond imagination, and I could not imagine God not being angry. Or think of Rwanda in the last decade of the past century, where 800,000 people were hacked to death in one hundred days! How did God react to the carnage? By doting on the perpetrators in a grandparently fashion? By refusing to condemn the bloodbath but instead affirming the perpetrators' basic goodness? Wasn't God fiercely angry with them? Though I used to complain about the indecency of the idea of God's wrath, I came to think that I would have to rebel against a God who wasn't wrathful at the sight of the world's evil. God isn't wrathful in spite of being love. God is wrathful because God is love.[55]

51. Craigie, *Book of Deuteronomy*, 383.

52. Wessling, *Love Divine*.

53. Gerald Borchert comments, "Anger and judgment can in fact be the obverse side of the coin of love." Borchert, *John 1–11*, 164.

54. For a sample of the many texts that display God's concern for justice in the OT (particularly for the oppressed), see Exod. 22:25–27; Lev. 19:15; 23:22; Pss. 9:8–9; 146:7, 9; Isa. 1:17; 10:1–3; 58:6–7; Jer. 22:13, 16; Zech. 7:9–10; cf. NT texts like Matt. 23:23; Luke 11:42; Gal. 3:28; James 2:5–8; 1 John 4:20.

55. Volf, *Free of Charge*, 138–39. Cf. Dorena Williamson's piece on the juxtaposition of a black person's forgiveness of his brother's murderer going viral while the victim's mother's cries for justice went largely overlooked. She writes, "When a black person extends radical forgiveness, we see the grace of the gospel. But when we ignore a black person's call for justice, we cheapen that grace. Both are acting like the God we serve; we need to listen to both." Williamson, "Botham Jean's Brother's Offer of Forgiveness." See also the discussion of anger against injustice alongside hope for the salvation of even the oppressors in McCaulley, *Reading While Black*.

Yet wrath is not an *essential* attribute of God. Because divine wrath is the righteous response of love against evil, "where there is no sin [or evil], there is no wrath."[56] While humans become angry for illegitimate reasons, the God of Scripture becomes angry only in response to evil; God's negative emotions are never unmotivated or arbitrary. As Thomas McCall puts it, "God's righteous wrath is always portrayed in Scripture as God's antagonism toward sin. . . . It is the contingent [yet natural] expression of the holy love that is shared between Father, Son, and Holy Spirit."[57] While humans are prone to overreaction, God never overreacts. Indeed, according to Psalm 78:38, amid the cycle of rebellion by his people, God, "being compassionate," often "restrained His anger" (NASB; cf. Isa. 48:9).

Accordingly, rather than asking why God brings judgment, biblical authors tend to ask why God does not bring judgment more often and establish justice more swiftly. Even when God brings judgment, he does not want to do so. God "does not willingly afflict or grieve anyone" (Lam. 3:33; cf. Ps. 81:11–14; Hosea 11:8–9) but does so only when there is no preferable alternative available to him. God takes "no pleasure in the death of the wicked" (Ezek. 33:11 NASB; cf. 18:23) but offers warnings, consistently provides a way of escape, and delays judgment until there is "no remedy" (2 Chron. 36:16; cf. Isa. 5:1–7). As Kevin Kinghorn explains, God's wrath is a function of God's love, always motivated by God's concern for the long-term well-being of others, limited, provisional, "always a last resort," and responsive to repentance.[58] God's compassion far exceeds his wrath. God's "anger is but for a moment," while

> His favor is for a lifetime;
> Weeping may last for the night,
> But a shout of joy comes in the morning. (Ps. 30:5 NASB)[59]

The God of Scripture is both the "compassionate God" (*'ēl raḥûm*, Deut. 4:31 NASB; cf. Exod. 34:6–7) and the "jealous" or "passionate" God (*'ēl qannā'*, Deut. 4:24 NASB; cf. Exod. 34:14; Nah. 1:2). God is often portrayed as the unrequited lover of an unfaithful spouse, and God's "jealousy" is always portrayed as *righteous* passion for exclusive relationship with his people (see Isa. 62:4; Jer. 2:2; 3:1–12; Ezek. 16, 23; Hosea 1–3; Zech. 8:2; cf. 2 Cor. 11:2), which Scripture sharply differentiates from the often unrighteous passion of

---

56. Carson, *Difficult Doctrine of the Love of God*, 67.
57. McCall, *Against God and Nature*, 334.
58. Kinghorn with Travis, *But What about God's Wrath?*, 63, 82.
59. Cf. Exod. 34:6; Judg. 10:16; Isa. 54:7–10. On divine wrath, see Peckham, *Love of God*, 159–61; Peckham, *Theodicy of Love*, 154–59.

human jealousy (e.g., envy) and that of the ANE gods.[60] God's people repeatedly "made Him jealous [*qānā'*, hiphil] with strange gods; With abominations they provoked Him to anger" (Deut. 32:16 NASB). Likewise, Psalm 78:40–41 states,

> How often they rebelled against Him in the wilderness
> And grieved Him ['*āṣab*, hiphil] in the desert!
> Again and again they tempted God,
> And pained [*tāwâ*, hiphil] the Holy One of Israel. (NASB; cf. Isa.
>   63:10; 1 Cor. 10:5)

Notably, these and other instances portray human action as a cause of changing divine emotions. John Oswalt notes, "The OT returns again and again" to God's "compassion: his tenderness and his ability to be touched by the pain and grief of his people."[61]

While human compassion may fail, God's "compassions never fail" (Lam. 3:22 NASB). As God himself states in Isaiah 49:15,

> Can a woman forget her nursing child
> And have no compassion [*rāḥam*] on the son of her womb?
> Even these may forget, but I will not forget you. (NASB; cf. Ps. 103:13)

God's compassion is exceedingly greater than even a mother's love for her newborn. Believed to be based on the noun *reḥem*, meaning "womb," the verb *rāḥam* denotes compassionate love and deeply visceral emotions, a "womblike mother love."[62] Further, John Goldingay explains that *rāḥam* is a "feelings word" that "denotes strong emotion," the "strong feelings of love and concern."[63]

The NT also highlights "the tender mercy" of God (Luke 1:78 NASB), frequently using *splanchnizomai*, a Greek counterpart of the Hebrew verb *rāḥam*, to depict Christ's visceral feelings of compassion as he is moved by the sight of people in distress (e.g., Matt. 9:36; 14:14; Mark 1:41; 6:34; Luke 7:13; cf. Mark 10:21; Heb. 4:15), strikingly similar to OT language and imagery of

---

60. The ancient Near Eastern gods tended to be envious, but the gods never displayed "zeal in relation to his worshiper" (Sauer, "קנא," 3:1146). Whereas the combination of *qānā'* + *b* suggests the negative emotion of envy (e.g., Prov. 3:31), never used of God, the construction *qānā'* + *l* suggests an appropriate passion with action on behalf of its object, used of humans (e.g., 1 Kings 19:10) and of God (e.g., Zech. 8:2). See Reuter, "קנא," 13:49.

61. Oswalt, *Book of Isaiah*, 299. See further Heschel, *Prophets*, 285–337.

62. See Trible, *God and the Rhetoric of Sexuality*, 31–59. See also Stoebe, "רחם," *TLOT* 3:1226. Cf. *HALOT* 3:1217–18; Butterworth, "רחם," *NIDOTTE* 3:1093.

63. Goldingay, *Daniel*, 243, 244.

divine compassion.[64] In the parable of the prodigal son, Jesus uses *splanchni-zomai* to depict the way the father "felt compassion for" his son, whereupon he "ran and embraced him and kissed him" (Luke 15:20 NASB; cf. Matt. 18:27). Such imagery corresponds to OT portrayals of God being deeply moved by people's suffering (Judg. 10:16; Hosea 11:8–9; cf. Luke 19:41) and *voluntarily* responsive to entreaty (Exod. 33:12–34:10; Judg. 2:18; Isa. 30:18–19).

God's passion and compassion, however, are not *only* emotional responses but are also consistently portrayed as volitionally free and evaluative responses—neither automatic nor passive (Jer. 15:6; Mal. 1:9–10) nor irrational. Over and over, God *voluntarily* meets human rebellion with amazing forbearance, often restraining his anger (Ps. 78:38), *freely* continuing to love his people (Hosea 14:4), and *freely* bestowing grace and compassion (Exod. 33:19; cf. Rom. 9:15–16).

The Suffering of the Unchangeable and Self-Existent God

According to the brief survey above, Scripture affirms that God does not change, *at least* with respect to God's character. Yet Scripture also frequently portrays God as changing relationally and undergoing emotional change. The question is, How should this biblical data be interpreted theologically?

Negating Divine Emotions?

Theologians on all sides of the debate agree that Scripture depicts God experiencing changes, including changing emotions. As the qualified impassibilist Rob Lister writes, "The biblical portrayal of divine emotion is both powerful and pervasive. One cannot read Scripture and come away with the conclusion that God is affectionless."[65] Similarly, while maintaining that "God is impassible in the sense that he sustains no 'passion,' no emotion, that makes him vulnerable from the outside, over which he has no control, or which he has not foreseen," D. A. Carson adds that viewing God as "emotionless" is "profoundly unbiblical and should be repudiated."[66] He goes on to say that God's love "is clearly a vulnerable love that feels the pain and pleads for repentance."[67]

Strict impassibilists such as Dolezal, however, take a different view. Dolezal recognizes that "many passages of the Bible" do "speak of God as undergoing

64. This Greek verb, *splanchnizomai*, "literally [describes] a movement of the entrails," referring to a "visceral feeling of compassion." Spicq, "σπλάγχνα, σπλαγχνίζομαι," 3:274–75.
65. R. Lister, *God Is Impassible and Impassioned*, 195.
66. Carson, *Difficult Doctrine of the Love of God*, 60, 48.
67. Carson, *Difficult Doctrine of the Love of God*, 59.

affective changes," yet he maintains that God does not actually undergo any emotional change.[68] Rather, via accommodative language, God "communicates the truth about his infinite and unchanging existence under the form of what is finite and changeable."[69] Similarly, Paul Helm contends, "The impression we may form, reading the biblical narrative, that God changes is [an] illusion."[70] Specifically, many strict impassibilists claim that such language is anthropopathic, speaking of God *as if* he experiences changing emotions (*pathos*) like humans (*anthropos*).[71]

Dolezal argues that biblical passages attributing change to God should be interpreted according to the way of negation, "in which the theologian denies all creaturely imperfection and finitude in God's intrinsic being."[72] Specifically, Dolezal maintains that a particular understanding of the Creator-creature distinction should be employed as "a hermeneutical principle" that "precedes Scripture and is brought to the text as a lens by which we are able to make assessments about the literal or figurative quality of the Bible's varied statements about God." For Dolezal, this includes presupposing that God is pure act and thus necessarily "unmoved in his being."[73]

Without biblical warrant for the claim that God cannot experience changing emotions, however, this method *may* impose alien presuppositions about God onto Scripture. Dolezal himself affirms that "Scripture is the supreme judge in all doctrinal controversies about God's nature."[74] However, if one *presupposes* God is pure act as "a hermeneutical principle" that "precedes Scripture and is brought to the text as a lens" to assess Scripture, I do not see how Scripture can *actually function* as "the supreme judge" with respect to this and other "doctrinal controversies about God's nature." Rather than allowing Scripture to potentially reform one's metaphysical framework, such an approach seems to (unintentionally) bypass the standard of biblical warrant, presupposing the conclusion that God is strictly impassible. I agree that the Creator-creature distinction is crucial, but as Paul Hinlicky notes, "This distinction is not in the possession of any particular metaphysical articulation of it."[75]

At this juncture, the strict impassibilist might (1) argue that the view that God is pure act is itself biblically warranted, from which strict impassibility

68. Dolezal, "Still Impossible," 134.
69. Dolezal, "Still Impossible," 135.
70. Helm, "Divine Timeless Eternity," 46.
71. See, e.g., Dolezal, "Strong Impassibility," 34.
72. Dolezal, "Still Impossible," 140.
73. Dolezal, "Strong Impassibility Response," 114.
74. Dolezal, "Strong Impassibility Response," 115.
75. Hinlicky, *Divine Simplicity*, 123.

follows, and/or (2) argue that strict impassibility should be presupposed because it is the traditional view or because of some arguments of natural theology. With regard to the first option (discussed further in the next section), I do not see any biblical warrant for the claim that God is pure act; indeed, that claim seems to conflict with the teachings of Scripture.

Regarding the argument from tradition, (as noted earlier) there are competing scholarly interpretations of the Christian tradition regarding divine impassibility. Further, even if one agrees that *strict* impassibility is "the classical doctrine" with "wide ecumenical backing," Dolezal himself notes that "broad historical support by no means fixes the truth of the doctrine."[76] Regarding natural theology, it is not at all obvious that a perfect being must be impassible, and some have made rigorous arguments to the contrary.[77] Indeed, some have argued that one who lacks emotionally affected compassion for suffering creatures is deficient. In this and other regards, scholars make different value judgments regarding just what predications correspond to perfect being. In my view, if Scripture is to be finally normative in all theological matters, it must be allowed to function as finally normative regarding which predications are appropriate to God, and this points back to the standard of biblical warrant.[78]

Yet many strict impassibilists argue that if we do not presuppose some metaphysical framework as a hermeneutical lens to decide which statements about God are literal or figurative, consistency will require that we interpret anatomical imagery used of God to mean that God is a material being.[79] In other words, some suppose that if one argues that biblical passages depicting changing divine emotions are evidence that God is passible, one should also interpret passages that use language of body parts in reference to God as evidence that God is a material being.

However, there is a crucial difference between biblical language of divine emotions and "body language"—namely, that Scripture makes claims that set parameters regarding any predication(s) of divine materiality. For example, Jesus himself expressly teaches that "God is spirit" (John 4:24 NASB; cf. Luke 24:39; Rom. 1:20), and Scripture elsewhere affirms that "heaven and the highest heaven cannot contain" God (1 Kings 8:27 NASB; cf. 2 Chron. 6:18; Isa. 66:1; Acts 7:49). These and other texts (see chap. 3) indicate that,

76. Dolezal, "Strong Impassibility," 14.

77. For a rigorous argument from perfect being theology in favor of divine passibility, see Wessling, *Love Divine*. Cf. Mullins, *God and Emotions*.

78. I do not mean to dismiss the value of rigorous arguments regarding what properties are appropriate to perfect being, but I believe such arguments should themselves be subjected to the uniquely normative authority of Scripture (insofar as Scripture speaks to a given matter).

79. See, e.g., Dolezal, "Strong Impassibility," 33–35.

as "spirit," God is not *confined* to physical location or materiality. While this data is consistent with God taking on or manifesting himself in physical form, it is inconsistent with any claim that God is *essentially* corporeal (see the further discussion in chap. 3). As Bruce Ware puts it, then, "Unlike in the case of Scripture's references to God's bodily parts, where other Scriptures tell us that God transcends those bodily qualities, understood literally, in the case of emotions we have no Scripture that would lead us to think that God actually transcends the emotions Scripture ascribes to him."[80]

Further, the "body language" Scripture uses to depict divine emotions is demonstrably idiomatic; it is well-known *figurative* language that is used *of both God and humans* to convey emotion. Such language should not be taken as attributing actual body parts to God, and one can reach this conclusion exegetically without presupposing that God cannot take physical form. For example, in Hosea 11:8 God says, "My heart [*lēb*] is turned over [*hāpak*] within Me" (NASB), and in Lamentations 1:20 a human says, "My heart [*lēb*] is overturned [*hāpak*] within me" (NASB). These verses use the same demonstrably idiomatic anatomical imagery to convey emotions—of God and of a human respectively.

Other demonstrably idiomatic anatomical imagery used of both God and humans includes the following:

> using language of one's "heart" (*mēʿeh*, literally "belly" or "innards") as a description of emotions (Isa. 16:11; Jer. 31:20; Lam. 1:20)[81]
>
> inclining one's ear (2 Kings 19:16; Prov. 5:1)
>
> finding favor in someone's eyes (Gen. 6:8; 32:5)
>
> being "slow to anger" (literally "long of nose," Exod. 34:6; Prov. 14:29)
>
> hiding one's face as indicating displeasure (Deut. 31:17–18; Isa. 53:3)
>
> using "mouth" as an idiom of speech (Gen. 45:21; Deut. 8:3; 2 Sam. 14:19)
>
> referencing arm to mean strength or power (Exod. 6:6; Job 35:9)
>
> referring to hands idiomatically in various ways (Gen. 14:20; 49:24)

Such "body language" is widely understood by biblical scholars to be idiomatic, without dependence on literal body parts.[82] It is figurative and accommodative

---

80. Ware, *God's Greater Glory*, 146.

81. Elsewhere *mēʿeh* depicts intense physiological pain (Job 30:27; Ps. 22:15), but more frequently it denotes intense human emotions (Isa. 16:11; Jer. 4:19; Lam. 1:20; 2:11). Stoebe sees this as "expanded parallelism" that "approximate[s] *rahamim*." Stoebe, "רחם," *TLOT* 3:1226.

82. On the "proclivity" in Semitic languages "to utilize anatomical terms in the creation of new idioms," see J. Griffin, "Investigation of Idiomatic Expressions," 39.

language, but figurative and accommodative language nevertheless conveys meaning.[83]

While some theologians claim that emotions require corresponding anatomy, Katherine Sonderegger suggests, "Emotion might be a matter of mind or spirit, rather than flesh. It may be that emotion is largely, perhaps even predominately, an intellectual state, even in human beings."[84] Scrutton likewise argues, "An incorporeal God may experience strong and intense emotions without needing to have a body, just as humans can feel intensely sad without feeling a knot in the pit of their stomach."[85] Moreover, whereas human willing involves a physical brain, human speaking uses vocal chords, and humans act on the world via bodily movement, few theologians would deny that God somehow wills, speaks, and acts on the world (albeit analogically).[86] As Kevin Vanhoozer explains, while humans act through "bodily movement," the "concept" of acting does not require bodily movement; we can correctly, then, predicate "'being an agent' and 'being a speaker' of God analogically."[87] I agree. And it seems to me that emotions might similarly be predicated of God (analogically) without collapsing the Creator-creature distinction. In this regard, while I do not see any good reason (consistent with the standard of biblical warrant) to negate the biblical depictions of God undergoing emotional change, we should be careful not to think God experiences changing emotions in the same way as humans. Just after describing his emotions in Hosea 11:9, God proclaims, "I am God and not man, the Holy One in your midst" (NASB). Scripture portrays God not only as the immanent God of compassion but also as the transcendent Creator.

Taking Stock of the Biblical Data

Scripture repeatedly depicts God as experiencing changing emotions, and it is widely recognized that no biblical passages teach divine impassibility.[88]

83. Further, Brian C. Howell explains, "Biblical anthropomorphisms are metaphorical, but not strictly derived from the human arena. . . . It is misleading to speak of these attributes and actions as drawn from the human realm and somewhat naively applied to God. Rather, the concepts, originally understood from their employment in the human realm, are applied to God metaphorically in such a way as to 'point' to the divine attribute or action, without fully defining it." Howell, *In the Eyes of God*, 103.

84. Sonderegger, *Systematic Theology*, 491–92.

85. Scrutton, *Thinking Through Feeling*, 181.

86. Scrutton writes, "Traditionally Christians have not ascribed a physical brain to God, and yet this has not stopped them attributing intelligence, understanding and thought to God." Scrutton, *Thinking Through Feeling*, 183.

87. Vanhoozer, *Remythologizing Theology*, 58.

88. For example, Rob Lister notes, "Scripture never makes a direct assertion of a metaphysical doctrine of divine impassibility" (R. Lister, *God Is Impassible and Impassioned*, 190). Justo L.

Some impassibilists claim, however, that there is biblical warrant for strict immutability and/or (pure) aseity, either of which would entail strict impassibility. As Trent Pomplun explains, many theologians believed God "was impervious to any pathos external to his own nature" because they believed "God was immutable (Mal. 3:6) and invariable (James 1:17)."[89] However, the biblical passages typically offered as evidence of strict immutability (e.g., Num. 23:19; Mal. 3:6; James 1:17) do not indicate that God is *strictly* immutable, and I am not aware of any passages that do.[90]

Regarding the claim of *pure* aseity, Dolezal argues that viewing God as pure act follows from the biblical teaching that God is the Creator.[91] Yet there is no inconsistency in affirming that God is the Creator while denying that God is pure act, as many Christian theologians do. Indeed, many Christian theists argue that the world is contingent on God's *free* decision to create such that God being the Creator is itself a contingent property of God, contra the view that God is pure act.[92] If God can freely choose to create the world, why could God not *freely* choose to engage in back-and-forth relationship with creatures in the ways Scripture depicts?

Dolezal further appeals to Romans 11:35–36 and Acts 17:23–29.[93] Yet while I believe these passages teach that all things are from God (Rom. 11:36) and that God needs nothing (Acts 17:25) such that he must be self-existent (*a se*), I do not see anything in these or other passages that affirms *pure* aseity or teaches that God "exists independently of all causal influence from his creatures."[94] If God is pure act, God could not be pleased or displeased by humans. Human sins would "have no effect upon God," as Dolezal claims.[95] Yet Scripture repeatedly depicts God as displeased, grieved, pained, and provoked to anger and passion *in response to* human actions (e.g., Gen. 6:6–7; Deut. 9:7; 32:21; Ps. 78:40–41; 1 Cor. 10:5). God "takes pleasure in those who fear him" (Ps. 147:11; cf. 149:4), and while "the sacrifice of the wicked is an

---

González adds: "Nowhere does the Bible say that God is impassible. On the contrary, there are repeated references to divine anger, love, and even repentance!" González, *Mañana*, 92.

89. Pomplun, "Impassibility in St. Hilary of Poitiers's *De Trinitate*," 187.

90. Notably, Dolezal affirms that "passages in which God is said not to change" are "underdeterminative" relative to the issue, at least "taken in isolation." Dolezal, "Strong Impassibility Response," 115.

91. Dolezal, "Strong Impassibility Response," 116. See further Dolezal, "Strong Impassibility," 17–24.

92. See Mullins, *End of the Timeless God*, 140–43.

93. See Dolezal, "Strong Impassibility," 18–22. Dolezal also appeals to statements made by Job's interlocutors, but I think there is good reason to refrain from theological predications based on the teachings of Job's friends.

94. Dolezal, "Strong Impassibility," 18.

95. Dolezal, "Strong Impassibility," 23.

abomination to the LORD," "the prayer of the upright is his delight" (Prov. 15:8; cf. 11:20; 12:22; Col. 1:10; 3:20; Heb. 11:5). The claim that God is pure act, then, runs directly counter to the way Scripture consistently depicts God.

The situation relative to biblical warrant, then, is this. Abundant biblical data depicts God as undergoing changing emotions, but there appears to be no biblical warrant for *pure* aseity, *strict* immutability, *strict* impassibility, or the interpretive move of negating biblical depictions of changing divine emotions. In light of this and other data, I believe the view that God undergoes changing emotions is biblically warranted, and if God undergoes changing emotions, then God is neither strictly immutable nor strictly impassible. More specifically, I believe the biblical data provides biblical warrant for the following claims:

1. God is the Creator of all things and by his will they exist (Rev. 4:11).

2. As Creator, God does not depend on anything for his existence but is the source of all things (Rom. 11:36). God is thus self-existent (from himself or *a se*).

3. God needs nothing (Acts 17:25) and thus cannot depend on anything to be essentially who he is (since that would involve need).

4. God does not change morally (Mal. 3:6; James 1:17); God's character is unwaveringly constant (Deut. 32:4; 1 John 1:5).

5. God never lies but always keeps his promises (Titus 1:2). God is gracious, exceedingly compassionate, long-suffering, and abounds in steadfast love and faithfulness (Exod. 34:6).

6. God changes in relation to creatures; God does new things, enters into back-and-forth covenant relationship, and responds to prayer (2 Sam. 24:25; 2 Chron. 7:14).

7. God undergoes emotional change, such as being "moved to pity" (Judg. 2:18), "provoked" to anger (Ps. 78:58; cf. Deut. 9:7), made jealous/passionate (Deut. 32:16), and others, even describing himself as changing from one emotional state to another (e.g., Jer. 31:20; Hosea 11:8; Zech. 1:15–16).

8. God sometimes "takes pleasure in his people" (Ps. 149:4) but also suffers and is sometimes caused to grieve (Gen. 6:6; Ps. 78:40–41).

9. God's wrath is always the appropriate, holy response to evil, but God does not want to bring judgment (e.g., Lam. 3:33) and, being compassionate, often restrains his anger (Ps. 78:38).

10. While God sometimes "regrets" and "relents" (*nāham*) in response to creaturely actions (Gen. 6:6; 1 Sam. 15:11, 35; Jer. 18:7–10), God does

not relent (*nāḥam*) *like a human* (Num. 23:19; 1 Sam. 15:29). God is holy, and his emotions should not be confused or conflated with human emotions (Hosea 11:9).

While other points are also relevant, any model committed to the standard of biblical warrant should be able to consistently account for at least these points or make a compelling case that such points are not actually biblically warranted.

A Model of Qualified Immutability and Qualified Passibility

Bruce McCormack argues that theologians must choose whether to privilege texts describing God as immutable or those portraying God as "repenting" or otherwise changing. The "choice of either," he claims, "is predicated finally upon a presupposed metaphysical construct (in the one case, the metaphysics of pure being and, in the other case, the metaphysics of love)."[96] However, I do not see any conflict between the passages that indicate divine immutability and those that depict God undergoing change in relation to creatures. In my view, both sets of texts—carefully interpreted exegetically and canonically—fit together in a consistent model of the covenantal God depicted in Scripture, without privileging or negating either set of texts.

If we are to uphold the canonical commitments outlined in the previous chapter, what we affirm must be compatible with both the passages that teach divine aseity and immutability and those that depict God as engaging in back-and-forth covenant relationship, delighting in goodness but grieved and provoked by evil, being long-suffering and compassionate and often moved by prayer, relenting from judgment in response to human repentance, and otherwise responding to creatures. That is, an adequate canonical model must affirm that God is both changeless in some crucial respects and changes relationally in other respects (including emotional change).

Although inconsistent with *strict* immutability and impassibility, affirming that God undergoes emotional (and other relational) changes is perfectly consistent with affirming a qualified kind of immutability and passibility. *Qualified* immutability affirms that God's essential nature and character never change but that God changes relationally (in ways consistent with his essential nature) because he voluntarily engages in back-and-forth relationship with the world, which he *freely* created.[97] While denying *pure* aseity, this model

---

96. McCormack, "Actuality of God," 194.
97. Moreland and Craig comment, "God could have remained [utterly] changeless had he wished to; the fact that he did not is testimony to both his love and freedom." Moreland and Craig, *Philosophical Foundations*, 527.

affirms God's aseity and self-sufficiency, meaning God exists of himself and, as Creator, does not depend on anything with respect to his existence or essential nature. Contra process theology, God is *freely* rather than essentially related to the world. As Creator, God is "before all things" (Col. 1:17); God existed prior to any creation. As self-existent, God needs no creation but freely "created all things" ("and because of [his] will they existed, and were created" [Rev. 4:11 NASB]) and freely sustains all things (Heb. 1:3).

If the Creator God needs nothing (Acts 17:25), God cannot depend on anything to be who he essentially is. God's *essential* nature is thus *a se* (of himself) and changeless. As eternal—having no beginning and no end (see chap. 3)—God could not become more or less eternal. As all-knowing (see chap. 4), God always possesses knowledge of whatever can be known. As all-powerful (Jer. 32:17; Rev. 19:6; see chap. 5), God cannot become more powerful. If God always sustains the universe (Rom. 11:36; Heb. 1:3), God must always have the capacity to sustain the universe. As omnibenevolent (see chap. 6), God is always perfectly good and righteous; his character is utterly steadfast (e.g., Deut. 32:4; 1 John 1:5) and his promises unbreakable (Heb. 6:18–20).[98] Covenantal theism thus affirms that these (and any other essential attributes of God) are unchanging, while God also changes relationally.[99]

The immutability of God's essential nature and character goes hand in hand with the way God covenantally and responsively relates to the world. As Thomas Oden writes, "It is precisely because God is unchanging in the eternal character of his self-giving love that God is free in responding to changing historical circumstances, and versatile in empathy."[100] Nash explains, "God must be immutable with regard to His nature and character," yet "immutability should not exclude the possibility of God's acting and interacting with His creation in an interpersonal way. The paradigm of an impersonal immutability is Aristotle's Unmoved Mover who was incapable of doing anything other than contemplating his own perfection. The change that necessarily accompanies God's interpersonal relations with His creatures is not a sign of imperfection. On the contrary, a personal God would lack perfection if He

98. Notably, even if God's ethical immutability requires unchanging ontological foundation, as some claim (e.g., Dolezal, "Still Impassibility," 129), affirming that God's essential nature is immutable is sufficient for such foundation. As Moreland and Craig state, God "is immutable in his existence (necessity, aseity, eternity) and his being omnipresent, omniscient and omnipotent. These essential attributes are enough to safeguard God's perfection without freezing him into immobility." Moreland and Craig, *Philosophical Foundations*, 527.

99. Contrary to the view that any change must be for better or for worse, some changes are value neutral (e.g., changing the color of one's shirt).

100. Oden, *Classic Christianity*, 68.

were incapable of such relations."[101] Padgett likewise adds that while "God is immutable relative to essential divine attributes," the "ability to change in response to others is part of what makes God a perfect Being."[102]

Complementing *qualified* immutability, covenantal theism affirms *qualified* passibility, meaning God is *voluntarily* passible in relation to the world in a way that does not collapse or diminish the Creator-creature distinction. While God could have enjoyed eternal love relationship in the Trinity without any world (John 17:24), God freely chose to create (Rev. 4:11) and freely opened himself up to being affected by creation. Contrary to process theology, then, God is not essentially passible in relation to the world; no creature could affect God if God had not enabled creatures to do so. Yet because God opened himself up to being affected by creatures, God's emotions are responsive to creaturely actions such that God can be pleased by goodness and grieved by evil. As Nicholas Wolterstorff writes, "God's love for his world is a rejoicing and suffering love."[103] Claiming that "the axiom of apathy" and "the axiom of immutability" are "unsuitable axioms for the Christian concept of God," Eberhard Jüngel argues, "The God who is love must be able to suffer and does suffer beyond all limits in the giving up of what is most authentically his for the sake of mortal men."[104] Yet the God of the cross does not suffer passively—Christ willingly gave himself for us (John 10:18) in order to defeat suffering and "the power of death" (Heb. 2:14)—and the voluntarily suffering God of Scripture retains the power to finally eradicate suffering and evil forevermore and will do so in the end. Further, while God suffers *with* creatures, God also does not indiscriminately feel all the feelings of others (contra process theology). God's emotions are always perfectly rational, appropriately evaluative, and in accordance with God's perfect nature, character, and will.[105]

While some claim qualified passibility privileges God's will or power over his love, I believe God's attributes are perfectly congruent and should not be pitted against one another. God's love is free, and God always exercises

---

101. Nash, *Concept of God*, 101.

102. Padgett, "Eternity as Relative Timelessness," 109. Likewise, John Feinberg maintains that God does not change with respect to his "person [being and attributes], purposes, will, and ethical rules" but "changes in relationships" with creatures (Feinberg, *No One Like Him*, 271). Similarly, see Wolterstorff, *Inquiring about God*, 134; Davis, *Logic and the Nature of God*, 24; Ware, *God's Greater Glory*, 141.

103. Wolterstorff, *Inquiring about God*, 219.

104. Jüngel, *God as the Mystery of the World*, 374. Robert Jenson adds, "The sufferer of the Gospels is, without qualification or evasion, the second identity of God." Jenson, *Systematic Theology*, 1:144.

105. As Jüngel notes, a "love story which is only a story of suffering and wants to be only that would contradict the essence of love." Jüngel, *God as the Mystery of the World*, 374. The gospel is a story of victory over suffering.

his freedom and power in an utterly loving fashion. God's love is not merely emotional but also volitional, evaluative, and covenantal.[106] God's emotional responses to creatures are affected but not determined by creaturely actions in a way that does not override or exclude God's volition (Ps. 78:38) or God's perfectly rational, righteous, and loving evaluation.

In these and numerous other ways, the God of Scripture is *not* passible in the same way that humans are passible; divine emotions are *analogical.* Whereas humans often delight in evil, God delights only in that which is good and hates evil (Ps. 5:4). Human love is transient (Hosea 6:4), but God's steadfast love is everlasting (Ps. 100:5). While even a mother's compassion may fail (Isa. 49:15), God's "compassions never fail" (Lam. 3:22 NASB). Human compassion and passion are imperfect, but God's compassion and passion are perfect and extend beyond all reasonable expectations. Whereas human passions are often irrational and wicked, God's passions are always perfectly rational, evaluative, and just. Whereas humans are sometimes controlled by their anger, God willingly restrains his anger (Ps. 78:38) and cannot be "manipulated, overwhelmed, or surprised."[107]

Whereas humans are intrinsically susceptible to pain and suffering, God is not. Yet in a matchless expression of love, God willingly made himself "vulnerable to pain."[108] Indeed, John Stott asks, "In the real world of pain, how could one worship a God who was immune to it?"[109] Far from weakness, Alvin Plantinga suggests that "God's capacity for suffering" is "proportional to his greatness."[110] Though humans are often overcome and defeated by suffering, God is never defeated or overcome. Whereas scarcely any human is willing to die for even a righteous person, "God demonstrates His love toward us, in that while we were yet sinners, Christ died for us" (Rom. 5:7–8 NASB; cf. John 10:18; 15:13; Heb. 12:2). Humans tend to avoid suffering at all costs, but God voluntarily took on suffering and, by doing so, ultimately defeated suffering once and for all. The God who does this is unconquerable and indomitable and invincible, but not impassible. As Michael Horton puts

---

106. See Peckham, *Love of God*, 89–247.

107. R. Lister, *God Is Impassible and Impassioned*, 36.

108. Stott, *Cross of Christ*, 323. Likewise, Donald Bloesch affirms, "God in himself is indestructible, eternal, and unchangeable," yet "in his freedom he makes himself vulnerable to pain and suffering." Bloesch, *God the Almighty*, 210.

109. Stott, *Cross of Christ*, 326.

110. A. Plantinga, "Self-Profile," 36. Paul Copan agrees, concluding that the Scriptures "present a God who is able to suffer" and "God truly does suffer" (Copan, *Loving Wisdom*, 95). Similarly, while noting "serious problems with an unreflective passibilism," Charles Taliaferro argues, "Theistic passibilism is defensible insofar as we can understand God's sorrow, not as an imperfection, but an aspect of what it is for God to be supremely good." Taliaferro, *Consciousness and the Mind of God*, 323.

it, we should affirm that God "is the transcendent Lord of the covenant who is never a passive victim" and does not respond "in the same way we respond to each other," but "we must avoid the conclusion that God is untouched or unmoved by creaturely suffering."[111]

Theologians who affirm qualified impassibility might mean something like this, with some arguing the term "impassibility" should be retained as an "apophatic qualifier" and in deference to the traditional patristic language.[112] Yet as noted earlier, scholars variously interpret the traditional language on this issue. If Gavrilyuk is right, even a qualified conception of possibility might find support in the tradition, particularly given the "theopaschite expressions" of divine suffering that many fathers employ "with reference to the crucifixion."[113] It is not difficult to see how language of divine impassibility—rightly concerned with sharply distinguishing the God of Christianity from the anthropomorphic, often irrational, and immoral gods of Greco-Roman mythology—might have provided considerable explanatory value in the patristic age. The language of *apatheia* may have been quite appropriate for that goal, particularly if Gavrilyuk is right that such patristic language did not denote "emotional apathy" but "functioned as an apophatic qualifier of all divine emotions."[114] However, to contemporary ears, such language seems to negate any emotion, and I do not see how employing the language of impassibility today provides explanatory value beyond that which is already capably

---

111. Horton, *Christian Faith*, 248, 247.

112. So Castelo, *Apathetic God*, 124; Gavrilyuk, *Suffering of the Impassible God*, 173; R. Lister, *God Is Impassible and Impassioned*, 102.

113. Gavrilyuk, *Suffering of the Impassible God*, 127, 89. Cf. Scrutton, *Thinking Through Feeling*. Gavrilyuk argues that, in Cyril of Alexandria's view, "both qualified divine impassibility and qualified divine passibility were necessary for a sound theology of incarnation" (Gavrilyuk, *Suffering of the Impassible God*, 150; cf. Cyril of Alexandria, *On the Unity of Christ* 117). Further, Tertullian wrote that God has "the same emotions and sensations" as humans have but "they are not of the same kind" since "God alone" is "perfect" and has them according to his "property of incorruptibility." Tertullian, *Against Marcion* 2.16 (*ANF* 3:309). See also Lactantius, *On the Anger of God* 1–2, 21 (*ANF* 7:259–60, 277). Regarding divine anger specifically, Gavrilyuk contends that some Church Fathers offered "a purely subjectivist interpretation" claiming that God is not actually angry, but humans merely perceive him to be angry. Others (e.g., Tertullian, Lactantius, Novatian, and Cyril of Alexandria), however, claimed that God "indeed experiences anger," but "in a carefully qualified sense." Gavrilyuk, *Suffering of the Impassible God*, 58.

114. Gavrilyuk, "God's Impassible Suffering," 139; Gavrilyuk, *Suffering of the Impassible God*, 173. See also Scrutton's reappropriation of the "Augustinian-Thomist distinction between emotional experiences that are *affectiones* (voluntary, potentially rational, not inherently physiological) and *passiones* (involuntary, arational and, in Thomas, inherently physiological)" (Scrutton, *Thinking Through Feeling*, 4). She makes a thoughtful and illuminating case that "some emotional experiences, far from being incompatible with divine omnipotence, are necessary to God's omnipotence and omniscience, as well as integral to personally involved divine love." Scrutton, *Thinking Through Feeling*, 188.

conveyed by other theological concepts (such as aseity, qualified immutability, and omnipotence), for which there is abundant biblical warrant.[115] As such, I prefer to speak of qualified passibility, but one might avoid the dispute over language by speaking of divine emotions as theopathic instead.[116]

Some Questions and Implications

A number of further issues warrant consideration, but space permits only brief consideration of a few relevant issues here. First, some strict classical theists appeal to divine blessedness, claiming that "God is infinitely happy" and must therefore always be in an immutable and tranquil state of perfect bliss.[117] Yet if "God is infinitely happy and we can do nothing to lessen it," as Rogers argues, then God cannot be displeased in response to creatures—even by horrendous atrocities—directly contradicting many biblical depictions of divine displeasure.[118]

Some might worry that if God is displeased by human evil, God's emotional state might be unstable and susceptible to mood swings. Yet given divine omniscience, God is aware of all events, and while any event in isolation might prompt divine pleasure or displeasure, God's overall state would rationally and evaluatively correspond to everything of which God is aware (see chap. 4).[119] While any mere creature would be utterly overwhelmed by awareness of all suffering, God in his infinite greatness is also cognizant of all past, present, and future goodness and capable of shouldering all the burdens of creatures without being overwhelmed.

Conversely, proponents of *strict* immutability and impassibility face the difficulty of explaining how Christ is fully divine and yet became incarnate and experienced change and suffering. As Jay Wesley Richards puts it, "No Christian theologian can tolerate definitions" of divine attributes "that contradict the claim that God became incarnate as the man Jesus, who mourned, suffered and died."[120] This has posed a significant problem in the Christian

115. Though he wishes to retain it, Daniel Castelo notes, "It could very well be the case that the language of divine impassibility has run its course" (Castelo, *Apathetic God*, 68). Robert Jenson goes further, stating that despite the "subtle qualifications and real insights involved in the tradition's sophisticated massaging of the notion of impassibility . . . in any sense of impassibility perceptible on the face of the word, it will not do as an attribute of the God of Scripture and dogma." Jenson, "Ipse Pater Non Est Impassibilis," 120.

116. Vanhoozer suggests, "Perhaps the Bible's depiction of divine suffering is less a matter of anthropopathic projection than it is a case of human suffering being theopathic (God-like)." Vanhoozer, *Remythologizing Theology*, 77–78.

117. Rogers, *Perfect Being Theology*, 51. See Mullins, "Why Can't the Impassible God Suffer?," 3–22.

118. Rogers, *Perfect Being Theology*, 51.

119. See the discussion of divine omnisubjectivity in chap. 4.

120. Richards, *Untamed God*, 41.

tradition. As R. T. Mullins notes, "Many of the early Christological heresies were motivated by the *prima facie* incompatibility of divine timelessness, immutability, impassibility, and the incarnation."[121] For example, as Gavrilyuk explains it, "The Arians argued that since the unbegotten God was impassible, he could not possibly be ontologically equal to the suffering Logos [Christ]."[122] Moreover, if Christ suffered only relative to his humanity and his divinity was untouched by any change or suffering, how can one avoid the conclusion that Christ's sacrifice was merely a human sacrifice?[123] If the atonement cost divinity nothing, in what sense does Christ's divinity contribute to the atonement?

These are not difficulties for covenantal theism, which maintains that, while remaining *fully* divine, Christ voluntarily condescended to become human (Phil. 2:6–8) and thereby made himself susceptible to things he was otherwise not susceptible to, such as hunger, thirst, fatigue (and others).[124] On this view, the divine nature is compatible with passibility and voluntary condescension such that what Christ did on behalf of humanity involved voluntary divine suffering with us and for us. As James Cone puts it, "The cross of Jesus reveals the extent of God's involvement in the suffering of the weak. He is not merely sympathetic with the social plan of the poor but becomes totally identified with them in their agony and pain. The pain of the oppressed is God's pain, for he takes their suffering as his own, thereby freeing them from its ultimate control of their lives."[125] Not only does covenantal theism straightforwardly affirm that God in Christ *voluntarily* offered himself as a sacrifice (John 10:17–18), suffering on our behalf, but this view also affirms that the Father and the Spirit voluntarily suffered because of the cross event (albeit in a very different manner than Christ)—specifically in giving the Son to die for us.[126]

Further, many argue, "If God is immutable in the traditional [strict] sense He cannot be the God of biblical revelation, a God who is a person and an agent, who loves His people, who responds to prayer."[127] In this regard, on the basis of his study of prayer in the NT, David Crump comments, "Despite

---

121. Mullins, *End of the Timeless God*, 158

122. Gavrilyuk, "God's Impassible Suffering," 142.

123. Jürgen Moltmann claims, "If God is incapable of suffering, then—if we are to be consistent—Christ's passion can only be viewed as a human tragedy." Moltmann, *Trinity and the Kingdom*, 22.

124. Adam Harwood argues that this involved "change among the persons of the Trinity." Harwood, "Did the Incarnation Introduce Change?," 45.

125. Cone, *God of the Oppressed*, 175. Indeed, Jesus voluntarily identified himself with the disinherited. See Thurman, *Jesus and the Disinherited*, 17–18.

126. Contrary to patripassianism, however, the Father did not suffer on the cross or take on human experience. On crucial distinctions between "God's suffering as human from his suffering as God," see Bauckham, "In Defence of *The Crucified God*," 112–13.

127. Rogers, *Perfect Being Theology*, 46. Rogers herself argues against this view.

certain Christian traditions disputing this claim, . . . we are quite correct in believing that God cares for us, that he makes plans concerning us, that he exercises personal decision and enters into true reciprocity with us in such a way that he allows himself to be affected by our words and decisions. Christian petition requires believing that the Father is honestly listening, is willing to be influenced, and is thus engaged in authentic two-way communication with the one who prays."[128] This, I believe, is what Scripture affirms. Throughout Scripture, God repeatedly hears and responds to prayer, being moved to compassionate action in response to human petitions (e.g., Judg. 2:18; 10:16; 2 Sam. 21:14; 24:25). The God of Scripture profoundly cares about *you*; what you do and what happens to you—all that happens in your life—matter deeply to God, in the real sense that it affects God's own life.

In the words of T. F. Torrance, "If God is merely impassible he has not made room for Himself in our agonied existence, and if he is merely immutable he has neither place nor time for frail evanescent creatures in his unchanging existence. But the God who has revealed himself in Jesus Christ as sharing our lot is the God who is really free to make himself poor, that we through his poverty might be made rich, the God invariant in love but not impassible, constant in faithfulness but not [strictly] immutable."[129]

This holds massive implications for how Christians should live. Oliver Davies writes, "We can only think about God in depth, and draw near to him in understanding where we re-enact within ourselves" the compassion of God directed toward others.[130] If the God we worship and to whom we pray voluntarily subjects himself to suffering *with us*, we also ought to stand with those suffering and in need. We ought to imitate God in tangibly caring for others; loving one another as God loves us (John 13:34–35); including others' best interests as part of our own, as Christ does for us, loving the church as his own body (Eph. 5:28–30); and drawing near to them with genuine empathy and presence and as much concrete assistance as is within our means to provide.

Conclusion

This chapter has made a case that the God of Scripture is self-existent (aseity) and needs nothing (self-sufficiency), changeless with respect to his essential nature and character (qualified immutability), but experiences relational changes, including changing emotions because he *freely* created the world and

128. Crump, *Knocking on Heaven's Door*, 285.
129. Torrance, *Divine and Contingent Order*, 7.
130. Davies, *Theology of Compassion*, 253.

voluntarily engages in back-and-forth covenantal relationship with creatures. As such, God is passible in a qualified sense, meaning God is *voluntarily* passible in relation to the world; God *freely* created and *freely* opened himself up to being affected by this world in a way that does not diminish or collapse the Creator-creature distinction. Such a view allows one to consistently affirm *both* the biblical testimony that God does not change with respect to his essential nature and character (Mal. 3:6) *and* the biblical testimony that God actually experiences (analogically) the kinds of relational "changes" Scripture regularly attributes to God, such as being pleased or angered by creatures, acting and interacting in covenant, and many others.

Three

The God of the Past, Present, and Future

Omnipresence and Eternity

They say Aslan is on the move—perhaps has already landed."[1] So says Mr. Beaver to the Pevensee children in the opening book of C. S. Lewis's the Chronicles of Narnia. The sound of Aslan's name fills the children with excitement, even though they do not yet know who Aslan is. Mr. Beaver later explains,

> He's the King. He's the Lord of the whole wood, but not often here, you understand. Never in my time or my father's time. But the word has reached us that he has come back. . . . He'll put all to rights, as it says in an old rhyme in these parts:
>
> > Wrong will be right, when Aslan comes in sight,
> > At the sound of his roar, sorrows will be no more,
> > When he bares his teeth, winter meets its death
> > And when he shakes his mane, we shall have spring again.[2]

The presence of the king is of paramount concern throughout Lewis's Chronicles. When Aslan is present, there is awe and wonder, joy and deliverance,

1. Lewis, *The Lion, the Witch, and the Wardrobe*, 64.
2. Lewis, *The Lion, the Witch, and the Wardrobe*, 74–75.

73

goodness and justice. When absent, Aslan is sorely missed, and his return—his presence and all that comes with it—is greatly longed for and anticipated. In the Chronicles of Narnia, as in so many other stories, the presence or absence of the true king makes all the difference.

Divine presence is likewise a major motif in Scripture. A major aspect of God's covenants with his people is his promise to dwell *with* them. The presence of God is associated with flourishing; divine "absence" is utterly disastrous. The pinnacle of divine presence comes via the incarnation and, with it, the promise of the eschatological return, when "the tabernacle of God is among men, and He will dwell among them, and they shall be His people, and God Himself will be among them, and He will wipe away every tear from their eyes; and there will no longer be any death; there will no longer be any mourning, or crying, or pain; the first things have passed away" (Rev. 21:3–4 NASB).

In theology, the issue of divine presence—spatial and temporal—is fraught with difficulties and loaded with implications. Christian theism affirms that God is omnipresent and eternal, but many questions arise regarding the nature of divine presence and eternity. Relative to spatial presence, Is God everywhere? Is God always with us? If so, what does that mean? Relative to temporal presence, Is God atemporal or temporal? Does God experience the passing of time? Does God have a future?

Omnipresence: God Is Present

Conceptions of Divine Omnipresence

Christian theists generally agree that God is present everywhere (omnipresent). In Anselm's words, "No place or time confines You [God] but You exist everywhere and always."[3] The nature of divine presence, however, is variously understood. Process theologians tend to hold that God is (in some sense) spatially present everywhere because the world is part of God's being—the world is "in God" (pan*en*theism).[4] Conversely, most Christian theists affirm that God is utterly distinct from creation; God is not essentially related to the world but *freely* created it. Further, most Christian theists deny that God is contained in or encompassed by any spatial location and deny that God is spatially extended—as if parts of God are in different places.[5] Some believe

3. Anselm, *Proslogion* 13, in *Major Works*, 94.
4. Charles Hartshorne writes, "In an undiluted sense [God] has all the world for body" (Hartshorne, *Man's Vision of God*, 200). For a different panentheist view, see McFague, *Body of God*.
5. See Moreland and Craig, *Philosophical Foundations*, 515.

God is "wholly present at every point in the universe."[6] Others deny that God is omnipresent in terms of being spatially located, maintaining instead that God is *derivatively* omnipresent[7]—that is, God is omnipresent "as a function of his knowledge and power . . . present everywhere in the sense that his perfect knowledge and power extend over all."[8]

Much of the discussion is driven by traditional commitments to divine incorporeality, the view that God has no physical body (*corpus*). Some hold that "God is essentially bodiless" such that "although he may sometimes have a body, he is not dependent on his body in any way."[9] Others (including strict classical theists) hold that divinity *cannot* occupy space or take bodily form. This is often described as the traditional view. According to Katherin Rogers, "Almost all Judeo-Christian philosophers of religion, past and present, have agreed that God is not spatial, and that nonetheless He is 'present' to all of space and it to Him."[10] However, drawing on Robert Pasnau's work, R. T. Mullins argues the opposite: "Traditionally, omnipresence holds that the entire being of God is wholly located in every point or region of space."[11] Just what the traditional view of omnipresence is, then, is disputed.[12]

Divine Presence in Scripture

There is an abundance of biblical material on divine presence, sometimes depicting God as (specially) present in particular locations yet also indicating

6. Moreland and Craig, *Philosophical Foundations*, 515. See Hud Hudson's arguments in favor of this view in "Omnipresence," 119–216.

7. I follow Ross Inman's distinction between derivative presence (presence "in virtue of standing in some particular relation or relations to a *distinct* entity") and fundamental presence (a non-derivative presence such that an entity is "located" at a "place in *its own right*"). Inman, "Omnipresence and the Location of the Immaterial," 169 (emphasis original).

8. T. Morris, *Our Idea of God*, 155. So Thomas Aquinas, *Summa Theologiae* I.8.3.

9. Swinburne, *Christian God*, 127.

10. Rogers, *Perfect Being Theology*, 59. Cf. the view of Joshua Hoffman and Gary S. Rosenkratz that "God is a nonphysical spirit, or soul" and such "a soul cannot literally be omnipresent" (Hoffman and Rosenkratz, *Divine Attributes*, 53). An exception to the near consensus in favor of some kind of incorporeality is found in Stephen H. Webb's argument for eternal divine matter and "heavenly flesh" in *Jesus Christ, Eternal God*.

11. Mullins, *End of the Timeless God*, 38. Mullins quotes Robert Pasnau's explanation: "Medieval Christian authors, despite being generally misread on this point, are in complete agreement that God is literally present, spatially, throughout the universe" (Pasnau, "On Existing All at Once," 19). Cf. Inman's case that Augustine and Anselm affirmed that God is "wholly located at . . . the [non-point sized] maximally inclusive place where the universe is entirely located" (Inman, "Omnipresence and the Location of the Immaterial," 187). See also Inman, "Divine Immensity and Omnipresence."

12. Bruce Ware argues that "God is nonspatial in himself (*in se*) apart from creation, and God is everywhere spatially present in relation to creation (*in re*)—and without conflict or contradiction" (Ware, "Modified Calvinist Doctrine of God," 87). Cf. Horton, *Christian Faith*, 256.

that God cannot be contained in any particular location and is—in some manner—present everywhere. To a survey of this material I now turn.

SPECIAL DIVINE PRESENCE

Many passages depict God as being *specially* present in a particular place. In Genesis 3:8, Adam and Eve "heard the sound of the LORD God walking in the garden at the time of the evening breeze." In Exodus 3, Moses encounters God at the burning bush and hears, "Remove your sandals from your feet, for the place on which you are standing is holy ground" (Exod. 3:4–5 NASB), suggesting that holiness and proximity to God are connected. This is one of many instances of theophany—a visible manifestation of God's presence. Some theophanies involve physical interactions. In Genesis 18, YHWH "appeared to Abraham by the oaks of Mamre" (18:1) in the form of a man, along with two "men" later identified as angels (19:1). YHWH is served food (18:8) and travels some distance with Abraham, and finally, when "He had finished speaking to Abraham the LORD departed" (18:33 NASB).[13] Later, in Genesis 32, Jacob wrestles with a "man" who turns out to be God (32:24–30; cf. Hosea 12:3–5).[14] Further, Exodus 24:10–11 reports that Moses and others "saw the God of Israel; and under His feet there appeared to be a pavement of sapphire" and "they saw God" (NASB; cf. Isa. 6:1–5).[15] Much later, in the unique and greatest theophany, "the Word [identified as God in John 1:1] became flesh, and dwelt among us, and we saw His glory" (John 1:14 NASB). He was thus called Immanuel, "God is with us" (Matt. 1:23). Further, God dwells in believers via the Holy Spirit (1 Cor. 3:16–17; 6:19; cf. John 16:7–8).

God's special presence *with* his people is of great import throughout Scripture. Indeed, as J. Ryan Lister unpacks it, the story line of Scripture is largely focused on the "restoration of God's presence" in terms of God's "relational

---

13. That YHWH is identified as one of the "three men" Abraham saw in Gen. 18 seems to be indicated by a combination of the following: (1) just before Abraham sees the three "men," Gen. 18:1 says that "the LORD appeared to Abraham by the oaks of Mamre"; (2) YHWH is depicted as speaking, including to Abraham, numerous times in the narrative (e.g., Gen. 18:13, 26–32); (3) Gen. 18:22 states that "the men [which seems to describe only two men given the language of Gen. 19:1] turned from there, and went toward Sodom, while Abraham remained standing before the LORD"; and (4) Gen. 19:1, which immediately follows a dialogue between Abraham and God, says, "The two angels came to Sodom in the evening," suggesting two of the "three men" were angels and the third was YHWH.

14. Cf. numerous appearances of the angel of the LORD, which many scholars identify as theophanies (see chap. 7).

15. Later, Isaiah has a vision of God, reporting, "I saw the Lord sitting on a throne, high and lofty; and the hem of his robe filled the temple" (Isa. 6:1; cf. Ezek. 1:15–28 and the heavenly throne scenes in Revelation).

nearness" that was "once lost in the fall."[16] Likewise, J. Scott Duvall and J. Daniel Hays make a compelling case that "God's relational presence" is "the most
comprehensive, pervasive, and unifying theme" of Scripture.[17] At the burning
bush, God promises Moses, "I will be with you" (Exod. 3:12 NASB). Yet after
the golden calf rebellion, whether God will continue to be specially present
"with" and "among" Israel is unsettled (33:3–5), the sanctuary God has commanded Moses to make "so that I may dwell among them" (25:8) is not yet
built, and the special covenant relationship itself appears to be in jeopardy.[18] So
Moses intercedes, pleading that God will graciously go with them and continue
treating Israel as his distinct covenant people. God graciously promises that his
special covenant relationship and presence will indeed continue *with* the people,
despite their rebellion (33:13–17). Indeed, God promises, "My presence [*pānîm*,
literally "face"] will go with you, and I will give you rest" (33:14).[19]

The back-and-forth dialogue climaxes with Moses requesting, "Show me
your glory, I pray" (Exod. 33:18). In response, God declares, "I will make all
my goodness pass before you, and will proclaim before you the name, 'The
Lord'" (33:19). However, God adds, "You cannot see my face [*pānîm*]; for
no one shall see me and live" (33:20). Instead, God instructs, "There is a
place by me where you shall stand on the rock; and while my glory passes by
I will put you in a cleft of the rock, and I will cover you with my hand until
I have passed by; then I will take away my hand, and you shall see my back;
but my face [*pānîm*] shall not be seen" (33:21–23).[20] Moses experiences the
special presence (*pānîm*) of God, but this is veiled divine presence. Yet Exodus
33:11 states earlier, "The Lord used to speak to Moses face to face [*pānîm
'el-pānîm*], as one speaks to a friend" (cf. Deut. 34:10) and, in Numbers 12:8,
God declares of Moses, "With him I speak mouth to mouth, . . . and he be-
holds the form of the Lord" (NASB).

While some have thought this implies a contradiction, Peter Craigie
notes, "The Hebrew idiom *face to face* . . . implies something like 'person to

16. J. Lister, *Presence of God*, 24.
17. Duvall and Hays, *God's Relational Presence*, 329.
18. On the motif of covenant jeopardy, see Walton, *Covenant*.
19. The word *pānîm* (plural of *pānê*) can literally mean "face" but often idiomatically refers
to presence and "carries strong connotations of relationship" (it can also refer to the entire
person, among other idiomatic usages) (Duvall and Hays, *God's Relational Presence*, 13). According to H. Simian-Yofre, in Exodus, *pānîm* "serves to express in some undefined sense the
personal presence of Yahweh" (Simian-Yofre, "פָּנִים," 11:595). Broadly, Simian-Yofre writes that
pānîm "describes relationships"; it refers to "real personal presence, relationship, and meeting
(or refusing to meet)" (Simian-Yofre, "פָּנִים," 11:606–7). Likewise, A. S. van der Woude stresses
that *pānîm* refers to "the personal presence of God." Van der Woude, "פָּנִים," 2:1004.
20. Nahum M. Sarna suggests that the term translated "back" here "means the traces of His
presence, the afterglow of His supernatural effulgence." Sarna, *Exodus*, 215.

person.'"[21] Notably, speaking with God "face to face" does not itself entail that one sees some "form" of God. While Deuteronomy 5:4 states that "the LORD spoke with you [the people of Israel] face to face at the mountain," Deuteronomy 4:15 reports that "you [the people] saw no form when the LORD spoke to you at Horeb out of the fire," though they were "shown" God's "glory and greatness" (5:24; cf. 4:12). In some instances, then, the presence of "the invisible God" (Col. 1:15) is described as somehow visible to humans (e.g., Exod. 24:9–11; 33:23; cf. Gen. 32:30; Num 12:8). Yet "no one has ever seen God" in his fullness (John 1:18); God is the one who "dwells in unapproachable light, whom no man has seen or can see" (1 Tim. 6:16 NASB; cf. Exod. 33:20). Exodus 34:5–6 describes the promised manifestation to Moses:

> The LORD descended in the cloud and stood with him there, and proclaimed the name, "The LORD." The LORD passed before him, and proclaimed,

> "The LORD, the LORD,
> a God merciful and gracious,
> slow to anger,
> and abounding in steadfast love and faithfulness."

Similarly, God tells Elijah, "Go out and stand on the mountain before the LORD, for the LORD is about to pass by." Then "there was a great wind, so strong that it was splitting mountains and breaking rocks in pieces before the LORD, but the LORD was not in the wind; and after the wind an earthquake, but the LORD was not in the earthquake; and after the earthquake a fire, but the LORD was not in the fire; and after the fire a sound of sheer silence" (1 Kings 19:11–12). Here, again, the text depicts some sense in which God "pass[es] by." While statements such as "the LORD was not in the wind" may seem to contradict omnipresence, James Arcadi suggests that "perhaps, this narrative and others in the Hebrew Scriptures train us to think of God's presence as a degreed attribute. God can be more in certain locales than others."[22] Indeed, Arcadi maintains, "The narratives of the Hebrew Scriptures commend us to think of theophanies as occurring in a degreed manner. There can be more or less theophanies—*strong theophanies* and *weak theophanies*"—that is, greater or lesser concentrations of divine presence (e.g., "a particular theophanic concentration of the divine presence, a strong theophany" in the burning bush

---

21. Craigie, *Book of Deuteronomy*, 148 (emphasis original). Duvall and Hays note that *pānîm* "frequently was used as a synecdoche to represent the entire person" (Duvall and Hays, *God's Relational Presence*, 13). Van der Woude adds that *pānîm ʾel-pānîm* "depicts the immediate and personal relationship between God and his chosen." Van der Woude, "פָּנִים," 2:1005.

22. Arcadi, *Incarnational Model of the Eucharist*, 95.

and "less of a concentration" of divine presence where Moses was standing, rendering it holy ground).[23]

Many other instances indicate God might be *specially* present in some locations. God promises his covenant people, "I will walk among you, and will be your God, and you shall be my people" (Lev. 26:12). Further, humans sometimes flee from or come into divine presence. Cain "went away from the presence of the LORD, and settled in the land of Nod, east of Eden" (Gen. 4:16; cf. 3:8). "Jonah set out to flee to Tarshish from the presence of the LORD" and got on a ship "to Tarshish, away from the presence of the LORD" (Jon. 1:3; cf. 1:10). According to Job 1:12, even the "Satan went out from the presence of the LORD" (cf. 2:7). Conversely, Psalm 95:2 exhorts, "Let us come into his [God's] presence with thanksgiving." Further, in 2 Chronicles 15:2, by the "Spirit of God" a prophet tells "Asa, and all Judah and Benjamin: the LORD is with you when you are with Him. And if you seek Him, He will let you find Him; but if you forsake Him, He will forsake you" (NASB; cf. Deut. 31:17–18; Acts 17:27). This suggests that God's special presence may in some sense be contingent on human response. Elsewhere, God himself declares, "I dwell in the high and holy place, / and also with those who are contrite and humble in spirit" (Isa. 57:15; cf. Rev. 3:20).

GOD CANNOT BE CONTAINED IN EARTHLY TEMPLES OR OTHERWISE

Scripture often indicates that God is sometimes specially present in chosen holy places (e.g., the sanctuary, the promised land), as if divine presence is sometimes localized or concentrated in holy places, and that such special presence is conditional and not uniform. God commands, "Make me a sanctuary, so that I may dwell among them" (Exod. 25:8; cf. 25:21–22) but warns that the people must "not defile their camp where I dwell in their midst" (Num. 5:3 NASB). Further, "the glory of the LORD filled" the wilderness tabernacle (Exod. 40:34, 35) and Solomon's temple (1 Kings 8:11; cf. 2 Chron. 5:14). Duvall and Hays comment, "The presence of God dwelling in the tabernacle and then in the temple was a reality and not a metaphor. The cloud surrounding his glory/presence as he entered the tabernacle was real and not figurative."[24] Further, they highlight the frequent OT instances of the expression *lipnê YHWH* ("before the face of the LORD" or "in the presence of the LORD") and contend that "while this expression is somewhat fluid, the majority of usages refer to the spatial presence of God, often in the tabernacle or in the temple."[25]

23. Arcadi, *Incarnational Model of the Eucharist*, 96–97.
24. Duvall and Hays, *God's Relational Presence*, 8.
25. Duvall and Hays, *God's Relational Presence*, 14.

Yet Ezekiel describes God's "glory" departing from the temple before the Babylonians destroyed it: "The cherubim lifted up their wings, with the wheels beside them; and the glory of the God of Israel was above them. And the glory of the LORD ascended from the middle of the city, and stopped on the mountain east of the city" (Ezek. 11:22–23; cf. Ezek. 9–10).[26] Much later, the presence of God comes to the second temple in Jesus, himself a "temple" of God's presence (John 2:19–21; cf. Matt. 12:6).[27] Later still, Paul writes, "You are a temple of God" and "the Spirit of God dwells in you" (1 Cor. 3:16 NASB; cf. 6:19). Scripture also speaks of "the greater and more perfect [heavenly] tabernacle, not made with human hands, that is to say, not of this creation," into which the risen Christ entered as high priest (Heb. 9:11 NASB).[28]

While depicting God's special presence in the sanctuary and otherwise, Scripture also attests that God cannot be contained in any spatial location. Solomon states, "Will God indeed dwell on the earth? Even heaven and the highest heaven cannot contain you, much less this house that I have built!" (1 Kings 8:27; cf. 2 Chron. 6:18). Similarly, God proclaims,

> Heaven is my throne
>   and the earth is my footstool;
> what is the house that you would build for me,
>   and what is my resting place? (Isa. 66:1; cf. Ps. 11:4)[29]

Before quoting this verse in Acts 7:49, Stephen adds, "The Most High does not dwell in houses made by human hands" (7:48 NASB; cf. 17:24).

26. Whether understood as a literal depiction or a vision figurative of divine presence, this passage describes God departing and stopping on the mountain east of the city, congruent with the motif of divine presence and (relative) absence in other passages. Christ later lamented over Jerusalem (Matt. 23:37–39), not long before he would depart, ascending from the Mount of Olives east of the city (Acts 1:9–12), and the temple would again be destroyed.

27. Duvall and Hays explain, "The restoration of God's presence is promised throughout the OT prophets and is fulfilled in the Gospels when Jesus, Immanuel (God with us), appears" (Duvall and Hays, *God's Relational Presence*, 1). Cf. Ezek. 43:1–12; Hag. 2:9.

28. David Moffit comments, "The author [of Hebrews] speaks in Heb. 9–10 about Jesus entering the tabernacle in heaven, the very tabernacle that Moses saw [cf. Exod. 25:8–9, 40; Heb. 8:5], and moving through its sancta into the place where God dwells. This concrete depiction of a heavenly structure where God dwells and where the angels serve as priests (Heb. 1) indicates the author's belief in a heavenly tabernacle upon which the earthly tabernacle/temple is modeled" (Moffit, *Atonement and the Logic of Resurrection*, 221n7). Cf. R. Davidson, *Typology in Scripture*, chap. 3. Moffit comments further that the "language in [Heb.] 9:11–12 encourages a spatial and temporal conception of Jesus entering and moving through a structure that actually exists in heaven," coinciding "with the author's claim that Jesus serves as a high priest in heaven." Moffit, *Atonement and the Logic of Resurrection*, 225.

29. It seems obvious that such imagery is figurative; otherwise it would refer to a gigantic body seated on heaven with legs and feet stretching to rest on earth.

Accordingly, Jesus replies to the Samaritan woman's question about whether God should be worshiped at Mount Gerizim or Jerusalem by saying, "An hour is coming when neither in this mountain nor in Jerusalem will you worship the Father. . . . God is spirit [*pneuma*], and those who worship Him must worship in spirit and truth" (John 4:21, 24 NASB). Since "God is spirit" (cf. Luke 24:39), God is not restricted to any location as physically embodied creatures are and thus may be present and worshiped in multiple locations.[30] God may dwell in particular locations (Exod. 29:45–46; Ps. 132:13–14), but God cannot be limited or restricted to any location; God can *specially* dwell in many locations simultaneously.[31]

GOD IS OMNIPRESENT

The psalmist proclaims,

> Where can I go from your spirit?
> Or where can I flee from your presence?
> If I ascend to heaven, you are there;
> if I make my bed in Sheol, you are there.
> If I take the wings of the morning
> and settle at the farthest limits of the sea,
> even there your hand shall lead me,
> and your right hand shall hold me fast. (Ps. 139:7–10)

---

30. J. P. Moreland and William Lane Craig comment that to say "God is spirit" (John 4:24) "is to say" that God is "a living, immaterial substance" (Moreland and Craig, *Philosophical Foundations*, 507). Many biblical commentators agree. See, e.g., L. Morris, *Gospel According to John*, 240. This understanding might be supported by Luke 24, wherein the risen Jesus assures his disciples that he is not a spirit, because "a spirit [*pneuma*] does not have flesh and bones," then eats "a piece of broiled fish . . . before them" (vv. 39, 42–43 NASB; cf. Isa. 31:3).

31. In this regard, Benjamin Sommer makes a case that at least some Israelites believed YHWH could "be present in more than one specific location on earth—as well as on a throne in heaven—at any given time" (Sommer, *Bodies of God*, 44). Sommer references Ps. 20:1–2, 6, in this regard. See also, e.g., Gen. 18, 32; Exod. 3–4, 23, 33; Judg. 6; Hosea 12:4–6, many of which refer to the theophanic *mal'ak YHWH* ("angel of the LORD"), discussed in chap. 7. Sommer maintains, however, that there are competing traditions in the Hebrew Bible, fluidity and nonfluidity, the former affirming that God can be physically present in multiple locations simultaneously (Sommer, *Bodies of God*, 38–57) and the latter denying this and seemingly resisting the view that God is present bodily (62–79). However, I do not believe the biblical passages Sommer sees as part of an antifluidity tradition actually exclude fluidity (relative to divine presence). Further, both passages that speak affirmatively of divine embodiment in a particular place and those resistant to claims that God is restricted to one particular location are compatible if God can manifest himself in physical form and locate his presence in particular places while remaining omnipresent (see the discussion later in this chapter). Sommer's larger fluidity thesis claims that ANE "gods" could also have many personalities. Here I am concerned only with Sommer's claims relative to presence, setting aside his view of fluidity relative to divine "selfhood."

Wherever the psalmist may go, God is there. As Leslie C. Allen puts it, "The psalmist, wherever he went, would find himself confronted with a God who was already there. As a human being he can be at only one place in the world at once, but he finds God everywhere."[32] Further, in Jeremiah, God says, "Am I a God near by, says the LORD, and not a God far off? Who can hide in secret places so that I cannot see them? says the LORD. Do I not fill heaven and earth?" (Jer. 23:23–24). This passage conveys that God is *both* near and far (immanent and transcendent) and somehow fills heaven and earth—indicating divine omnipresence without specifying the manner of such presence.[33]

Language of God "seeing" or "watching" everything also appears. Proverbs 15:3 states, "The eyes of the LORD are in every place, keeping watch on the evil and the good" (cf. Job 34:21; Ps. 139:1–3; Ezek. 8:12; Amos 9:2–4). The phrase "eyes of the LORD" cannot be taken as referencing physical anatomy without absurdity, since the "eyes" are said to be "in every place." This is figurative language using "eyes" to signal divine awareness *analogous to* physically seeing everything.[34] While texts depicting God as "all-seeing" indicate *at least* God's comprehensive awareness of all places, other texts indicate God's power extends to every location, "sustain[ing] all things" (Heb. 1:3). Together, such texts entail *at least* derivative omnipresence.

Offering comfort to those facing trials, Scripture often highlights the presence of God's power wherever one may go. Relative to Israel's entrance into Canaan, Moses proclaims, "Be strong and courageous, do not be afraid or tremble at them, for the LORD your God is the one who goes with you. He will not fail you or forsake you" (Deut. 31:6 NASB). Deuteronomy 31:8 continues, "The LORD is the one who goes ahead of you; He will be with you. He will not fail you or forsake you. Do not fear or be dismayed" (NASB). Here God's being "with" and going "before" involve God's power to sustain and deliver his people. Likewise, Joshua 1:9 proclaims, "Be strong and courageous! Do

32. L. Allen, *Psalms 101–150*, 328. Edward Wierenga adds, "This passage suggests, first, that God is really *present* at or *located* at various particular places. Second, it suggests that there is no place where God is not present; that is, that God is present *everywhere*" or "*omnipresent*" (Wierenga, "Omnipresence"). One might suppose that God merely goes wherever the psalmist goes, but (as Arcadi explains) "this does not fit the entirety of the poem. The psalmist is clearly in awe of God's immensity and ability to be anywhere," and the impact "is to likewise think that there is no place in the cosmos that one could go where God is not." Arcadi, *Incarnational Model of the Eucharist*, 87.

33. The term translated "fill" can refer to a material filling or a figurative filling (e.g., Ps. 119:64). See "מָלֵא," BDB 570.

34. Bruce K. Waltke comments that this "signifies [God's] presence in a situation and his evaluation of it." Waltke, *Book of Proverbs*, 614.

not tremble or be dismayed, for the LORD your God is with you wherever you go" (NASB). Elsewhere God promises his covenant people,

> When you pass through the waters, I will be with you;
> and through the rivers, they shall not overwhelm you;
> when you walk through fire you shall not be burned,
> and the flame shall not consume you. (Isa. 43:2; cf. Zech. 2:10–11)

Perhaps along similar lines, Jesus promises, "Where two or three are gathered in my name, I am there among them" (Matt. 18:20). Without indicating the manner of such presence, this text indicates the risen Christ can somehow be "there among" his followers even when they are scattered across the globe and while Christ is also somewhere else (see John 14:3). Similarly, in the Great Commission, Jesus promises, "Remember, I am with you always, to the end of the age" (Matt. 28:20; cf. Heb. 13:5), indicating that Christ can somehow be present with the disciples even as they disperse to spread the gospel to all nations.

A Constructive Model of Divine Omnipresence

The biblical data surveyed above seems to affirm both that God is present everywhere and that God may be specially present at some particular locations while not being contained in or encompassed by space. If this is correct, Scripture affirms that God is present everywhere (omnipresent), yet God is not present everywhere in the same sense.

A number of issues warrant consideration at this juncture. First, much hinges on what it means to be present, particularly the manner of divine presence. Just how is God present relative to a given spatial location? Second, if God is omnipresent, how can there be special divine presence? Special divine presence challenges the intuition that an omnipresent God would be uniformly present to all locations—that is, present everywhere in precisely the same fashion or to the same degree. Third is the issue of presence in particular locations without being contained in any particular locations. Fourth, and closely related, is the issue of whether God is incorporeal and, if so, whether God is incorporeal in a way that is incompatible with bodily presence.

Taking Stock of the Biblical Data

Relative to these issues, my aim in this section is to outline a minimal, constructive model of divine omnipresence that is biblically warranted and systematically coherent. Such a model must be able to account for the various streams of biblical data regarding divine presence without contradiction, including the following significant points I take to be biblically warranted in light of the preceding survey:

1. God specially manifests his presence to particular people in particular locations such that God is not uniformly present in all locations (Gen. 18:33; Exod. 3:4–5; 33:11–23; John 1:14).

2. God sometimes promises to be "with" particular people in some special fashion, often relative to covenant relationship (Exod. 33:17; Lev. 26:12; Deut. 31:6–8: Josh. 1:9; Isa. 43:2; Matt. 18:20; 28:20).

3. God may dwell with or in the midst of humans, especially in chosen holy places such as the sanctuary/temple (Exod. 25:8; Num. 5:3; 1 Kings 8:11; 1 Cor. 3:16).

4. God is spirit and cannot be contained in a particular location—even the highest heaven (1 Kings 8:27; Isa. 66:1; John 4:21–24; Acts 7:49).

5. The presence of God can—in some sense—"come" and "go," and creatures can also depart from God's presence or come into God's special presence, which itself may be contingent on the way humans relate to God (Gen. 4:16; 2 Chron. 15:2; Ezek. 11:22–23; Jon. 1:3).

6. Wherever one may go, God is there—one cannot escape from God's presence (Ps. 139:7–10; Prov. 15:3; Jer. 23:23–24).

7. God is both near and far—immanent and transcendent (Jer. 23:23; cf. Acts 17:27).

8. God is somehow present to all creation—that is, God "fills" heaven and earth (Jer. 23:24; cf. Prov. 15:3; Heb. 1:3).

9. God sometimes manifests his presence via physical form, including some kind of bodily form (Gen. 18:33; 32:24–30; Exod. 24:9–11; John 1:14), yet God is "invisible" (Col. 1:15; 1 Tim. 1:17) and no human can see God in his fullness (Exod. 33:20; John 1:18).

10. In Christ, the Word who is God *became* flesh (John 1:1, 14; cf. Phil. 2:6–8).

While other points are also relevant, any model committed to the standard of biblical warrant should be able to consistently account for these points or make a compelling case that such points are not actually biblically warranted. With this in mind, we return to the four issues outlined above, beginning with the manner of divine presence.

The Manner of Divine Presence

As far as I can see, the biblical data does not specify the precise manner of God's presence. God's omnipresence might be nonderivative—that is, God might be actually located at each particular location in the sense that God is *wholly* spatially located at *every* location (ubiquitous entension).[35] While some (e.g., Hud Hudson) have thought such a view might require that God is a material object, Ross Inman has argued that there are some ways of defining material objects such that God might be immaterial and yet omnipresent in the sense of actual spatial presence while avoiding the view that parts of God are spread throughout space.[36] On such an understanding, God can actually occupy spatial locations and nevertheless be *essentially* immaterial (as Jesus's assertion "God is spirit" is traditionally understood).

Alternatively, God's omnipresence might be *derivative* such that God is omnipresent in virtue of the fullness of his knowledge (omniscience) and/or power (omnipotence).[37] Scripture attests that God is aware of everything and

35. Roughly, entension means that an entity is wholly located at some extended place and all subplaces of that place (rather than *extended* over space in parts). See Hudson, "Omnipresence." Yet, Inman notes, "Being wholly located" at a place is compatible with multilocation; it does not entail "exclusivity of location" as "being entirely located" denotes. Inman, "Omnipresence and the Location of the Immaterial," 177.

36. Inman identifies these as (1) modal location, (2) modal pertension, and (3) dispositional pertension, claiming that each furnishes "the theist with an account of the material-immaterial divide that allows for immaterial objects to entend the non-point-sized places where they are located, and thus be spatially located in a strict and literal sense" (Inman, "Omnipresence and the Location of the Immaterial," 202). On the modal location understanding, an object is a material object if "it is part of the nature" of that object "to have a spatial location" (Inman, "Omnipresence and the Location of the Immaterial," 195). On this definition, as long as it is not part of God's nature to have a spatial location, God would not be defined as a material object. Alternatively, on the modal pertension understanding (which Inman claims is in "the general spirit" of some remarks of Augustine and Anselm), "to be 'material' is not to be essentially located in space per se, but to be essentially located in space *in a particular kind of way*, namely, by being partly located at distinct places via pertension" (pertension refers, roughly, to being spread out over a particular extended place) (Inman, "Omnipresence and the Location of the Immaterial," 197 [emphasis original]). On this definition, as long as God is not "partly located at distinct places via pertension," God is not a material object. Finally, one might revise modal pertension to a weaker account Inman calls dispositional pertension. On this understanding, an object is a material object if "it is part of the nature of" that object "to be disposed to be located in space via pertension" (Inman, "Omnipresence and the Location of the Immaterial," 200). On this definition, as long as God is not "disposed to be located in space via pertension," God is not a material object. Cf. Hudson, "Omnipresence," 210–11.

37. Conversely, Wolfhart Pannenberg wrote, "No power, however great, can be efficacious unless present to its object. Omnipresence is thus a condition of omnipotence." Pannenberg, *Systematic Theology*, 1:415.

that God's power-in-action extends to every location (see chaps. 4 and 5).[38] At least in these senses, God is omnipresent. Here, though, it is worth noting that Eleonore Stump argues that defining omnipresence in only these ways "misses something" relative to even "the minimal sense of *personal* presence."[39] This *minimal* sense, she maintains, requires "second-person experience"—that is, experience "in which one can say 'you' to another person."[40] Beyond this, *significant* personal presence requires closeness and shared attention wherein persons are consciously aware of and pay attention to one another, contrary to one being minimally present but absent relative to attention.[41] Such significant personal presence is lacking when two people sit in the same place, but one is not "present" in the sense that her attention is directed to, for example, her smartphone. Stump argues, "In order for God to be omnipresent," it must be "that God is always and everywhere *in a position to* share attention with any creature able and willing to share attention with God."[42] I will return to this in the following section.

As far as I can see, both (some kind of) derivative and nonderivative conceptions may be consistent with the biblical data on divine presence, at least insofar as a given nonderivative conception is compatible with special divine presence (see below).[43] In addition, some other conception might be correct. It is worth recalling here that there is disagreement over what the traditional view is. Further, it may be that understanding the precise manner of divine presence is beyond our ken. Indeed, given that humans face considerable difficulties

38. See Arcadi's proposal that accounts for divine omnipresence (and special presence) in terms of divine action, emphasizing what he considers a "presence-as-action motif" in Scripture that "accounts for the whole spectrum of types of divine presence: from weak theophany to strong theophany to omnipresence" (Arcadi, *Incarnational Model of the Eucharist*, 96). Cf. Gasser, "God's Omnipresence in the World," 43–62.

39. Stump, *Wandering in the Darkness*, 111, 112 (emphasis added).

40. Stump, *Wandering in the Darkness*, 52. That is, "it is necessary for a second-person experience" that one "interact consciously and directly with another person who is conscious and present to you as a person, in one way or another." Stump, *Wandering in the Darkness*, 77.

41. See Stump, *Wandering in the Darkness*, 116–18.

42. Stump, *Wandering in the Darkness*, 117 (emphasis added).

43. Arcadi maintains, "If God is all at every location [as ubiquitous entension supposes], he cannot be more at any location. Yet if this is the case, then it makes no sense for the faithful to utter anything like, 'God is there,' in any sense other than a truism" (Arcadi, *Incarnational Model of the Eucharist*, 94). Arcadi thus thinks the biblical "picture of God" does not fit with ubiquitous entension (Arcadi, *Incarnational Model of the Eucharist*, 95). Likewise, Georg Gasser argues that Hudson's account of ubiquitous entension faces difficulties accounting for "the biblical tradition and personal religious experiences" wherein "God acts differently at different places," noting numerous biblical instances (Gen. 18; Exod. 3; 1 Kings 8; Acts 2) that "seem to presuppose that God is manifesting Himself in a singular way at a particular place and that God is simultaneously not present in this specific way at another place." Gasser, "God's Omnipresence in the World," 59.

making sense of the phenomenon of light (e.g., wave-particle duality) and otherwise making sense of location (and claims of multilocation) in quantum physics, should we not expect to face difficulties understanding *divine* presence? Given my commitments to the humble posture of canonical theology, I affirm what I take to be the biblically warranted view *that* God is omnipresent without claiming to be able to explain precisely *how* God is omnipresent.

Divine Presence Is Not Uniform

Omnipresence, however, does not entail uniformity of presence (as sometimes assumed). As seen earlier, numerous biblical passages depict God as *specially* present in particular locations (e.g., the sanctuary), and Moses and others successfully petition for God's special presence. In this regard, Duvall and Hays demonstrate that the special "presence of God dwelling among his people is foundational to his covenant with them" and "the Triune God [of Scripture] desires to have a personal, encountering relationship with his people and enters into his creation in order to facilitate that relationship. Thus the Bible begins with God's presence relating to his people in the garden (Genesis) and ends with God's presence relating to his people in the garden (Revelation)."[44] In this regard, Lister distinguishes between "God's relational nearness and his being everywhere," noting that God's "particular presence" is "detailed in God's being in the midst of his people in Eden (e.g., Gen. 1:8, 10; cf. Rev. 21:22), in the tabernacle/temple (e.g., Exod. 25:8; 1 Kings 8:1–13), in the incarnation of Christ (e.g., Matt. 1:23; John 1:14; 2:21) and, ultimately, in the new heaven and the new earth (e.g., Isa. 66:22–23; Rev. 21:1–5, 22–27)."[45] Similarly highlighting "God's presence and absence in the covenantal drama," Michael Horton argues that "God is omnipresent in his essence, but the primary question in the covenantal drama is whether God is present for us, and if so, where, as well as whether he is present in judgment or in grace."[46] Accordingly, Horton distinguishes God's general *"ontological omnipresence"* from God's special *"covenantal-judicial presence"* in particular places, noting that "God's [special] dwelling in the midst of his people is a prominent motif from Genesis to Revelation."[47]

---

44. Duvall and Hays, *God's Relational Presence*, 1. Arcadi also affirms "divine special presence"—that is, "greater concentrations of God's presence" of the kind "the experience of the faithful indicates" (e.g., 1 Kings 19:9–13) (Arcadi, *Incarnational Model of the Eucharist*, 94). See also Feinberg, *No One Like Him*, 249–50.

45. J. Lister, *Presence of God*, 48, 49.

46. Horton, *Christian Faith*, 255. As Brunner puts it, "God is not present to all in the same way. . . . God may 'come near' and He may 'go away,' and we may 'come near' to, and 'move away' from Him." Brunner, *Christian Doctrine of God*, 258.

47. Horton, *Christian Faith*, 255 (emphasis original). Cf. Hermann Cremer's distinction between God's "general world-presence" and God's "saving presence," which is "his particular

This may complement Stump's account of omnipresence, which emphasizes the importance of personal presence, including shared attention. In this regard, she maintains that God's *significant* personal presence to a given human is contingent on that human's disposition toward God: "Because God is omnipresent, then, if Paula is able and willing to share attention with God, the presence omnipresent God has to her will be significant personal presence. If she is not able and willing, then God will have only minimal personal presence with respect to her" (cf. 2 Chron. 15:2; Acts 17:27).[48] As Jonathan Reibsamen puts it, "God cannot be unilaterally significantly present to those who are not willing to be present to God."[49]

Consistently holding that God is omnipresent, but not uniformly present, merely requires that in addition to God's *general* omnipresence, God may be *specially* present to particular locations in some way(s) he is not present to other locations. This may be so whether the manner of divine omnipresence is understood as derivative or nonderivative. For example, God might be derivatively omnipresent while also specially present in specific locations in some derivative fashion. Perhaps God is omnipresent in that God's power extends everywhere, sustaining all things (Heb. 1:3), while instances of special divine presence are special manifestations of divine power in creation (i.e., instances of special divine action) that do not involve God being *spatially* present.[50] In this way, general omnipresence and special divine presence *could* involve the same kinds of presence while being distinguished in terms of degree.

Alternatively, God's omnipresence might be *nonderivative*, and special divine presence might be *derivative*. God might be wholly spatially present at every spatial location (in some way) while exercising his power in special ways in some particular location(s). Conversely, God might be *derivatively* omnipresent, perhaps present in terms of his power sustaining all things, while God might be *nonderivatively* specially present in some particular location(s)—spatially localizing himself in one or more particular locations.[51]

---

work of redemption." He explains, "God's presence does not work the same everywhere, but it works everywhere. . . . Where God acts in electing love and thus establishes a particular connection between himself and humanity, there is saving presence." Cremer, *Christian Doctrine of Divine Attributes*, 64.

48. Stump, *Wandering in the Darkness*, 117. However, she adds, there may be "obstacles *internal* to a human person" that might interfere even when one is (in some sense) "willing" (emphasis original).

49. Reibsamen, "Divine Goodness," 140.

50. See, e.g., Gasser, "God's Omnipresence in the World," 59–60.

51. It is difficult to conceive of how this might be so, but perhaps God can make his presence entend in a discrete location or multiplicity of locations while being derivatively omnipresent. If divine ubiquitous entension is possible, and being wholly located at a place (entension) is consistent with multilocation (Inman, "Omnipresence and the Location of the Immaterial," 177),

These are some ways God's general omnipresence *might* be distinguished from special divine presence without apparent contradiction. Again, given that the Creator is vastly different from creation, we might lack the conceptual resources to understand the manner of divine presence. In this regard, as long as doing so involves no contradiction, I need not claim to know *how* God is present in order to affirm *that* God is present. Whatever we say about the manner of divine presence, and I think we should be careful not to claim too much, I believe Scripture consistently attests that God is (somehow) present to all creation (omnipresence) *and* that God is not uniformly present but may dwell with humans in some special manner (special divine presence).

God Cannot Be Contained

Whatever else we say, we must avoid the mistake of thinking God can be encompassed or contained in creation. Nor should we think that if God is specially present in some location(s), then God is bound or restricted to such location(s). This not only would run afoul of the Creator-creature distinction (if God created the universe, then God must transcend creation) but also would come into conflict with biblical affirmations that God transcends spatial limitations, such as "heaven and the highest heaven cannot contain" God (1 Kings 8:27 NASB). To account for the many passages that affirm God cannot be contained in any location, it seems best to affirm that God can (somehow) concentrate or localize his presence in a special way without being restricted to or contained in any spatial location.

Divine Incorporeality

This understanding provides a framework for thinking about divine incorporeality. Saying that God is *not restricted* to physical form or location

---

perhaps an omnipotent God could entend in discrete locations. If Inman is right that God can be present by entension without being an essentially material being, then this would not require essential corporeality. If special divine presence by entension is not reducible to a derivative kind of divine presence (it may be), then God could be derivatively omnipresent and may also be specially present in various locations derivatively *and* nonderivatively (e.g., the divine presence in Jesus might have been nonderivative, and God could also be specially present in some places derivatively as a matter of divine power). It *might* also be possible that God is omnipresent in some nonderivative manner and that God is also somehow specially present in some particular locations in a nonderivative manner, though I do not see how this might be the case. If God is present everywhere in the sense of ubiquitous entension—that is, as wholly present to every spatial location—it would be hard to see how God could be *specially* present in any given location in a nonderivative manner. If he is already wholly present, how could he be more present in some places unless special presence is a different kind of presence (i.e., derivative presence)?

is very different from saying that he is *incompatible* with physical form or location. God may be capable of (somehow) assuming physical and bodily form while neither being contained in or restricted by any spatial location nor being limited to physical form.

If God has taken physical form, then (on pain of contradiction) divinity cannot be incompatible with taking physical form. At least relative to the incarnation, there must be some sense in which divinity is compatible with genuinely being incarnated in physical form, some sense in which it is actually true that "the Word became flesh, and dwelt among us" (John 1:14 NASB) and that one who was "in the form of God . . . emptied himself, taking the form of a slave" (Phil. 2:6–7). While divinity transcends created matter, in the incarnation divinity *somehow* takes on material, bodily form—an addition without subtraction to Christ's divinity. In this regard, Katherine Sonderegger maintains that God "is not a *visible* God . . . not a local or explicit presence." But she immediately adds, "Of course God does have these modes as well! He can be and has been incarnate."[52] While *how* this is understood may vary, *that* God became incarnate in Christ is central to the Christian faith.[53]

It seems best to me to affirm that God is incorporeal in the sense that God is not *essentially* corporeal but is not incompatible with corporeality (in some sense). In other words, as the omnipotent Creator of all, "God is spirit" (John 4:24) and is not restricted to bodily form or physical characteristics, but he may "take" bodily form wherever he so wills (Col. 2:9)—while remaining omnipresent.[54] In this regard, Richard Swinburne argues, "God is essentially bodiless"; though God "may sometimes have a body, he is not dependent on his body in any way."[55] God might, then, be incorporeal (in this sense) and not be restricted to any spatial location or physical form but may also somehow take on physical form (in the incarnation and otherwise).[56] Although God may act in or upon particular locations without needing physical form to so act, God *might* have some preferred form(s) by which he consistently manifests himself to certain creatures. For example, the frequent biblical imagery of

52. Sonderegger, *Systematic Theology*, 526 (emphasis original).
53. In this regard, while he offers no dogmatic conclusion for theological conceptualization today in his sweeping historical study of divine corporeality, Christoph Markschies contends, "The God witnessed within the biblical Scripture cannot be reduced without substantial loss to a bodiless, absolutely transcendental being in the tradition of a biblical interpretation informed by Platonic philosophy and conventional since antiquity." Markschies, *God's Body*, 320.
54. Col. 2:9 seems to suggest that God is not essentially corporeal given that it emphasizes the incarnation as the fullness of deity in bodily form.
55. Swinburne, *Christian God*, 127.
56. Questions arise regarding how God might "take" physical form similar to those regarding the manner of divine presence.

God seated on a throne in the midst of the heavenly host *might* describe the way God chooses to visibly manifest his presence to the heavenly host, without being restricted thereby. While some anatomical imagery of God in the Bible is demonstrably idiomatic (see chap. 2), some "body language" relative to God (e.g., of Jacob wrestling with God) might be consistently interpreted as God's special divine presence wherein God chooses to manifest himself in visible and sometimes tangible physical and bodily form, without being restricted to any embodied state.

In this and other regards, considerable mystery remains. Yet Scripture attests that God is omnipresent *at least* in the sense that nothing escapes God's knowledge or power. As the omnipotent Creator, God transcends spatial limitations; creation cannot contain him. "God is spirit" (John 4:24), and according to Romans 1:20, the "divine nature" is "invisible." Yet the transcendent God can also be immanent and present in a special manner "with us" in particular locations, somehow localizing (and sometimes visibly manifesting) his presence without being restricted to or encompassed by any location or physical form. The God of Scripture is neither dependent on nor bound by creation but can act and interact in and with his creation. In this and other ways, God is both near and far (Jer. 23:23); God can be "with us" as immanent while remaining transcendent. This is closely related to the question of divine eternity, to which we now turn.

Eternity: God Has No Beginning or End

Conceptions of Divine Eternity

Christian theists agree that God is eternal—that is, God exists without beginning or end. However, Christians disagree over the nature of divine eternity, especially whether God is timeless or temporal (not to be confused with *temporary*). If God is timeless (or atemporal) in the strict sense, there can be no succession of moments—no passing of time—in God's life; "for God there is no before and after."[57] A strictly timeless God could not perform one action, then perform another. If God is timeless, what humans perceive as successive divine actions are merely the temporal effects of God's single, timeless act.[58] In strict classical theism, timelessness is closely associated with

57. Williams, "Introduction to Classical Theism," 96. In Paul Helm's words, "as timeless," God "cannot have temporal relations with any of his creation. He is time-less in the sense of being time-free." Helm, *Eternal God*, 39.
58. Dolezal, "Still Impassible," 147. As Rogers puts it, God "does all He does in one, perfect, eternal and immutable act." Rogers, *Perfect Being Theology*, 54.

incorporeality. As Rogers states, "God is neither spatial nor temporal. . . . Space and time are not categories which apply to God, but all spatial and temporal things are immediately known and caused by God."[59]

Many argue, conversely, that God is not timeless but temporal. God has a past and a future and *successively* acts and interacts within the flux of time. Nicholas Wolterstorff writes, "Scripture presents God as having a history, from which it is to be concluded that God is not timeless."[60] Further, Stephen T. Davis contends, "A timeless being cannot be the personal, caring, involved God we read about in the Bible. The God of the Bible is, above all, a God who cares deeply about what happens in history and who acts to bring about his will" and *temporally* "responds to what human beings do."[61]

Conversely, Paul Helm argues, "Only a God who is immutable in a particularly strong sense can (logically) perform all that Scripture claims that God performs, and a God can only be immutable in this strong sense if he exists timelessly."[62] While recognizing that divine timelessness is not taught by Scripture, timelessness advocates maintain that it is consistent with Scripture, required of perfect being theology, and "the classical view of God's relation to time."[63] Conversely, advocates of divine temporality maintain that temporality is consistent with perfect being, and some claim that the view that God is not timeless is "the view explicit or implicit in Old and New Testaments and in virtually all the writings of the Fathers of the first three centuries."[64]

Some have suggested that God might be both atemporal and temporal "in different senses."[65] However, most scholars in the discussion believe that God cannot be both atemporal and temporal, at least if atemporality is defined as the view that God *cannot* experience temporal succession (strict timelessness)

---

59. Rogers, *Perfect Being Theology*, 59.

60. Wolterstorff, *Inquiring about God*, 164. So also Padgett, "Response to Wolterstorff," 219.

61. Davis, *Logic and the Nature of God*, 14. Some notable advocates of divine temporality (at least with creation) include Craig, "Divine Eternity," 146; Mullins, *End of the Timeless God*; Swinburne, *Christian God*, 137; DeWeese, *God and the Nature of Time*; Zimmerman, "God inside Time and before Creation," 75–94.

62. Helm, *Eternal God*, 21–22.

63. Helm, "Divine Timeless Eternity," 28. So also Rogers, *Perfect Being Theology*, 54. Cf. Augustine, *Confessions* 11.11.13 (*NPNF* 1:167), 11.14.17 (*NPNF* 1:168); Boethius, *Consolation of Philosophy* 5.6 (LCL 74:423–25).

64. Swinburne, *Christian God*, 138.

65. So Ware, "Modified Calvinist Doctrine of God," 87. See also Horton, *Christian Faith*, 255–56; Frame, *Doctrine of God*, 549–59. Notably, according to Christophe Chalamet, Karl Barth claimed that God is "both timeless *and* temporal" in a way unique to God (Chalamet, "No Timelessness in God," 26). Cf. *CD* II/1, 608–40. Mullins, conversely, believes that Barth "explicitly reject[ed] the doctrine of divine timelessness" but inconsistently "affirm[ed] a doctrine of divine eternality that is indistinguishable from divine timelessness" (Mullins, *End of the Timeless God*, xvii). Cf. *CD* III/2, 438–39.

and temporality is defined as the directly contradictory view that God *can* experience temporal succession. So defined, God cannot be both atemporal (or timeless) and temporal.[66] While others may use these terms differently, in what follows I adopt these common definitions.[67] Accordingly, the question at hand is whether God is compatible with temporal succession.

Divine Eternity in Scripture

Some philosophers and theologians claim that the biblical data is underdetermined regarding God's relationship to time.[68] Before addressing this claim, let us first briefly survey some biblical data relevant to this issue.

GOD IS ETERNAL

The Bible repeatedly teaches that God is eternal. Isaiah 40:28 states, "The LORD is the everlasting God, / the Creator of the ends of the earth." Isaiah 57:15 adds that God "inhabits eternity" (NRSV) or "lives forever" (NASB; cf. Deut. 32:40).[69] Psalm 90:2 elaborates, "Before the mountains were brought forth, / or ever you had formed the earth and the world, / from everlasting to everlasting you are God." Psalm 102:27 adds, "You [God] are the same, / And Your years will not come to an end" (NASB; cf. Heb. 1:12). Likewise, the NT calls God "Him who lives forever and ever" (Rev. 4:9 NASB), "the eternal God" (Rom. 16:26), and "the King eternal, immortal, invisible, the only God" (1 Tim. 1:17 NASB; cf. Heb. 9:14).

GOD IS NOT TEMPORAL IN THE WAY THAT CREATURES ARE TEMPORAL

While there is little question that Scripture teaches God is eternal, there is dispute over what Scripture teaches about God's relation to time. Some texts highlight a vast difference between creatures' relation to time and God's relation to time. For instance, Psalm 90:4 proclaims, "For a thousand years in your [God's] sight / are like yesterday when it is past, / or like a watch in the night." Likewise, 2 Peter 3:8 states, "With the Lord one day is like a thousand years, and a thousand years are like one day" (cf. Job 10:4–5; 36:26). Some advocates of timelessness appeal to such texts as evidence

---

66. See Mullins, *End of the Timeless God*, xvi.

67. I have suggested elsewhere that, if consistent, views that claim to affirm divine temporality *and* atemporality amount to species of temporalism. See Peckham, *Doctrine of God*, 84–85.

68. So, e.g., Helm, "Divine Timeless Eternity," 31.

69. The Hebrew phrase is *šōkēn ʿad*, from a root that means "to dwell" and a root for "eternity" (literally "dwells eternally" or "forever"). Nothing in such language indicates timelessness.

that God is timeless. However, the conclusion that God relates to time very differently than creatures do, as these passages indicate, does not entail that God is atemporal but is consistent with the view that God is temporal in some analogical fashion. Richard Bauckham comments on 2 Peter 3:8, "The intended contrast between man's perception of time and God's is not a reference to God's eternity in the sense of atemporality"; the "point is rather that God's perspective on time is not limited by a human life span."[70] Moreover, the very next verse says that God "is not slow about His promise, as some count slowness, but is patient toward you, not wishing for any to perish but for all to come to repentance" (2 Pet. 3:9 NASB). "Patience" itself suggests temporality.[71]

Atemporalists sometimes also appeal to God's declaration to Moses in Exodus 3:14, "I AM WHO I AM." Yet this phrase—whether translated "I am who I am" or "I will be who I will be"—does not obviously indicate divine timelessness.[72] Further, Wolterstorff notes that Exodus's "representation of God as having a history" is "typical of Scripture's representation of God: God responds to what transpires in human affairs by performing a succession of actions, including actions of speaking."[73] Some atemporalists also appeal to the reference to God as he "who is and who was and who is to come" (Rev. 1:4; cf. 1:8; 4:8). Yet David Aune calls this a "temporal description of divinity," noting that "a similar threefold temporal description of divinity is widespread in Greco-Roman literature beginning with Homer."[74] As Mullins notes, this is "an odd proof-text for divine timelessness since it clearly speaks of God having a past [was] and a future [is to come]."[75]

While recognizing that Scripture does not teach divine timelessness and that the "interactive God [Scripture depicts] is more easily understood as temporal," Hugh McCann appeals to Exodus 3:14, John 8:58 (wherein Jesus says, "Before Abraham was, I am"), and Psalm 90:2 (which speaks of God as "from everlasting to everlasting").[76] He then comments, "It is not unreasonable to think passages like this aim at an atemporal conception."[77] However, while these texts in isolation *might* be read as consistent with the claim that God is timeless, none of these texts (or any others of which I am aware) provide

---

70. Bauckham, *Jude, 2 Peter*, 310.

71. R. T. Mullins comments, "A timeless God cannot be patient." Mullins, *End of the Timeless God*, 204.

72. See, e.g., Canale, *Criticism of Theological Reason*.

73. Wolterstorff, *Inquiring about God*, 158.

74. Aune, *Revelation 1–5*, 31.

75. Mullins, *End of the Timeless God*, 201.

76. McCann, "God beyond Time," 91.

77. McCann, "God beyond Time," 92.

biblical warrant for the claim that God is timeless.[78] While numerous passages indicate that God is not related to time in the way humans are, even advocates of divine timelessness agree that no texts explicitly portray God as atemporal or claim that God is atemporal.

Scripture Portrays God as Experiencing Temporal Succession

Numerous texts, conversely, portray God as enduring through time (i.e., in terms of temporal succession). Psalm 90:2 itself describes God as "from everlasting to everlasting" (cf. 103:17). As Mullins explains, "The from/to formula in this passage is a common formula in scripture used to denote a span of time," and "the Hebrew word *ʿōlām*—sometimes translated as eternity depending on context—is used twice here to refer to the span of God's life. It quite literally means from perpetual duration in the indefinite past to perpetual duration in the indefinite future. This is a deeply temporal portrayal of God."[79]

Likewise, Psalm 102 addresses God as "you whose years endure / throughout all generations." It continues,

> Long ago you laid the foundation of the earth,
> and the heavens are the work of your hands.
> They will perish, but you endure;
> they will all wear out like a garment.
> You change them like clothing, and they pass away;
> but you are the same, and your years have no end. (102:24–27; cf.
> Heb. 1:10–12)

Contrasting the transience of created things with the permanence of God, this passage portrays God as *enduring* through time and creating "long ago."

Scripture also frequently speaks of God as "before" creation. Jesus states, "Now, Father, glorify Me together with Yourself, with the glory which I had with You before the world [*kosmos*] was" (John 17:5 NASB). Likewise, Jesus says to the Father, "You loved Me before the foundation of the world [*kosmos*]"

---

78. Noting numerous texts that timelessness advocates appeal to (Exod. 3:14; Num. 23:19; Pss. 90; 139; Isa. 46; Mal. 3:6; James 1:17; Heb. 13:8; 2 Pet. 3; Rev. 1:4), Mullins comments, "None of these passages, however, give us the without succession clause. In fact, many of them directly, or indirectly, suggest that God does have succession in His life." Mullins, *End of the Timeless God*, 200.

79. Mullins, *End of the Timeless God*, 33.

(17:24 NASB).[80] Further, Colossians 1:17 teaches that the Son "is before all things," and Ephesians 1:4 adds that God "chose us in Christ before the foundation of the world" (cf. 1 Pet. 1:20; Rev. 13:8). Similarly, Jude 25 speaks of the "glory, majesty, power, and authority" that belong to God "before all time [aiōnos] and now and forever." One might read these texts as referring to a temporal "before," indicating "time" passing prior to the creation of this planet or the entire physical universe (a "time" before physical time), or one might interpret these texts as referring to a nontemporal "before," perhaps in reference to a timeless reality (nontemporally) "before" creation. Similar competing interpretations arise regarding phrases such as "before the ages" (pro + aiōn in 1 Cor. 2:7; cf. Eph. 3:9; Col. 1:26; and pro chronōn aiōniōn in 2 Tim. 1:9; Titus 1:2–3; cf. Rom. 16:25–26). While such phrases use temporal language, the question is what they teach, if anything, regarding God and time.[81]

Numerous other passages depict God as performing responsive and successive actions, otherwise acting temporally, and having a future. The God of Scripture successively makes and keeps covenants, temporally responds to creaturely actions, and performs mighty works—not least in the incarnation. Indeed, "when the fullness of the time came, God sent forth His Son, born of a woman," and now "God has sent forth the Spirit of His Son into our hearts" (Gal. 4:4, 6 NASB). Here and elsewhere God is described as acting in special ways at particular times and places. In this regard, Terence Fretheim maintains that Scripture "witnesses to a God who shares in our human history as past, present, and future, and in such a way that we may even speak of a history of God."[82]

Further, Zephaniah 3:16–17 describes a future time when God will dwell with and rejoice over his redeemed people:

> In that day it will be said to Jerusalem:
> . . . .
> "The LORD your God is in your midst,
> A victorious warrior.
> He will exult over you with joy,
> He will be quiet in His love,

80. Whether kosmos refers to the entire physical universe or some part of creation after the universe began, these verses portray trinitarian relations in temporal terms (Christ "had" glory "before the world").

81. In a seminal work, James Barr cautions against attempts to settle the question of temporality based on semantics, stating, "If such a thing as a Christian doctrine of time has to be developed, the work of discussing it and developing it must belong not to biblical but to philosophical theology" (Barr, Biblical Words for Time, 149). Yet, while word studies cannot settle the issue and the material that speaks explicitly of "time" might be underdetermined, other biblical teachings might illuminate the issue.

82. Fretheim, Suffering of God, 33.

He will rejoice over you with shouts of joy." (NASB; cf. Isa. 65:19; Jer. 32:41)

This text depicts God as having a future—complementing many other passages describing *future* reconciliation between God and his people—a future time evoked by Scripture's repeated motif of the eschatological "day of the Lord" when the covenantal God "will dwell among them, and they shall be His people, and God Himself will be among them, and He will wipe away every tear from their eyes; and there will no longer be any death; there will no longer be any mourning, or crying, or pain; the first things have passed away" (Rev. 21:3–4 NASB).

A Constructive Model of Divine Eternity

According to the brief survey above, Scripture teaches that God is eternal and that God does not relate to time in the way that humans do, and it depicts God as experiencing temporal succession. How might this data be theologically interpreted in a way that does justice to all the relevant biblical passages without injury to any of them? What do we have biblical warrant to claim relative to God and time?

Accommodative Language and Timeless Divine Action

Even advocates of timelessness agree that numerous passages depict God as experiencing temporal succession. For example, Rogers notes, "There certainly are scriptural passages which *prima facie* imply that God is temporal."[83] Likewise, McCann recognizes that there are "passages that portray God as temporal."[84] Helm adds, "Any reader of Scripture is forcefully struck by the language of time and change as applied to God."[85]

However, many advocates of divine timelessness argue that such passages should not be taken as indicating that God actually experiences temporal succession but as accommodative language wherein God represents himself as temporal. Helm explains, "If a timelessly eternal God is to communicate to embodied intelligent creatures who exist in space and time and to bring about his purposes through them, and particularly to gain certain kinds of responses from them, then he must do so by representing himself to them in

83. Rogers, *Perfect Being Theology*, 64. So also Helm, "Divine Timeless Eternity," 33.
84. McCann, "God beyond Time," 92.
85. Helm, "Divine Timeless Eternity," 42.

ways that are not literally true."[86] James Dolezal adds, "When God speaks in Scripture about undertaking new actions or acquiring new states of mind or affection he is simply accommodating his revelation to our creaturely way of thinking and speaking."[87] On this view, all passages that depict God as temporal, all depictions of successive divine action, should be reinterpreted according to an atemporal perspective, presupposing that "God's 'acts' in time are nothing but the unfolding temporal effects of the single, eternal, and unchanging action of his will."[88]

Yet as discussed before, all theological language accessible to humans is accommodative, and recognizing that language is accommodative does not inform us whether and to what extent it applies to God. Accommodative (and analogical) language conveys meaning, and as far as I can see, there is no biblical warrant for *negating* the biblical depictions of God as temporal or for the far-reaching claim that the many biblical portrayals of successive divine actions should be reinterpreted as temporal effects of a single timeless divine action. Such a sweeping maneuver would require that a vast array of biblical passages be read as conveying something rather different than, and sometimes directly at odds with, what the passages convey exegetically.

In this regard, McCann argues, "God is [also] presented as a spatial being: as having a head, hands and feet, as dwelling in cities and tabernacles, as moving from place to place. If it is fair to take this kind of talk as metaphorical, then surely passages that portray God as temporal can in principle be so taken as well."[89] However, as previously discussed, if Scripture is to be theologically normative, biblical "body language" of God also should not be negated without biblical warrant for doing so. Further, there is biblical warrant for the view that God is not *essentially* corporeal (see John 4:24) and abundant exegetical reasons for understanding *some* anatomical imagery used of God as demonstrably idiomatic (as seen in chap. 2). The fact that *some* instances that use body language of God are rightly interpreted as metaphorical, however, does not provide warrant for assuming that *all* instances that depict God as temporal should be taken as metaphorical.

The divine timelessness advocate may argue that to avoid predications that are unfit for the perfect being, one must sometimes negate what Scripture portrays or claims about God. Yet scholars disagree regarding which predications are fit for perfect being. How, then, does one know just what to negate? Some perfect being theologians argue God is timeless, and some argue God is

86. Helm, "Divine Timeless Eternity," 46.
87. Dolezal, "Still Impassible," 148.
88. Dolezal, "Still Impassible," 147.
89. McCann, "God beyond Time," 91–92.

temporal. So it is not obvious that a timeless God is greater than a temporal God. Further, if a particular view of what is compatible with perfect being is deemed a legitimate standard for deciding what biblical portrayals or claims to negate, then that particular view might thereby function as a theological norm over against Scripture itself. If one thinks, for example, that incarnation is unfit for perfect being (as some have supposed), then one might thereby negate biblical portrayals and claims regarding the incarnation itself. After all, "many of the early Christological heresies were motivated by the *prima facie* incompatibility of divine timelessness, immutability, impassibility, and the incarnation."[90]

To avoid this slippery slope, one might appeal to the *Christian* tradition as grounds to negate biblical depictions of God as temporal. This appeal hinges, however, on at least two points. First, it hinges on the claim that the Christian tradition is a definitively normative standard for deciding which biblical portrayals or claims to negate. Second, it hinges on whether there is a standard, consistent view of the Christian tradition (which tradition? whose interpretation?) by which such matters might be decided. Regarding the first point, it is difficult to see how employing the Christian tradition as a definitively *normative* standard for deciding which biblical depictions to *negate* could be compatible with allowing Scripture itself to function as the final norm that itself is not normed. Second, as noted earlier, while many Christian theists claim that divine timelessness is the standard view of the Christian tradition, some theists (e.g., Swinburne) claim that divine tempo- rality is "the view explicit or implicit in . . . virtually all the writings of the Fathers of the first three centuries."[91]

Even if divine timelessness is the standard traditional view, contemporary advocates typically agree that divine timelessness "entails" the "view [of eternal- ism] that the past and future are as real as the present, as opposed to presentism, the view that only the present actually exists."[92] If divine timelessness entails eternalism, however, then if presentism is true, divine timelessness must be false. In this regard, some scholars argue that "presentism is the classical Christian position" held by Augustine, Boethius, Anselm, Thomas Aquinas, and others.[93] If this is correct, then either the classical Christian position does not affirm

90. Mullins, *End of the Timeless God*, 158.
91. Swinburne, *Christian God*, 138.
92. Rogers, *Perfect Being Theology*, 59.
93. Mullins, *End of the Timeless God*, 75. Indeed, Mullins states, "It is not clear that anyone prior to the nineteenth century actually held the view that all times are literally present to God" (Mullins, *End of the Timeless God*, 84). For instance, Augustine writes, "Neither the future, nor that which is past, now is." Augustine, *Confessions* 11.20.26 (*NPNF* 1:170).

divine timelessness or the classical Christian position involves a contradiction (insofar as timeless eternity *and* presentism are incompatible).[94] If the latter, to be consistent, one must break with the tradition one way or another.[95] So why not break in the direction of biblical depictions of God as temporal?

A "Biblical" Model of God and Time?

While recognizing that Scripture often depicts God as temporal, Helm maintains that "the language of Scripture about God and time is not sufficiently precise so as to provide a definitive resolution of the issue one way or the other."[96] Thomas Morris adds, "The most natural reading of most biblical texts about God is one on which God is seen as a temporal being. He is talked about in temporal language and there is not any clear nonpoetic passage to the contrary."[97] Yet "there are no biblical passages which explicitly and undeniably settle the matter."[98]

It may be that the limited biblical data that explicitly addresses God's relation to time is underdetermined, as many scholars maintain. However, before addressing this further, it may be helpful to outline some significant points that I believe are biblically warranted in light of the earlier survey:

1. Scripture repeatedly affirms that God is eternal; God has no beginning and no end (Isa. 40:28; 57:15; Pss. 90:2; 102:27; Rom. 16:26).

2. There is a vast difference between creatures' relation to time and God's relation to time. God does not relate to time the way humans do (Pss. 90:4; 102:24–27; 2 Pet. 3:8).

3. Scripture represents God as having a history and performing successive actions, depicting God as an active and interactive covenantal God (see the introduction).

4. Numerous passages of Scripture depict God as enduring in terms of temporal succession, existing from everlasting to everlasting (Ps. 90:2). God is he "whose years endure throughout all generations" (102:24).

5. The Son had glory with the Father before the world existed, and the Father loved the Son before the foundation of the world (John 17:5, 24). Yet, when the fullness of time came, God sent his Son (Gal. 4:4) in the

94. Mullins, *End of the Timeless God*, 30. Mullins argues further that even if eternalism is true, God cannot be timeless.

95. In addition, Mullins argues that the incarnation is incompatible with divine timelessness (discussed below).

96. Helm, "Divine Timeless Eternity," 31.

97. T. Morris, *Our Idea of God*, 135.

98. T. Morris, *Our Idea of God*, 121.

incarnation to save the world, and in the future (eschaton), God will rejoice over his people (Zeph. 3:17).

Given this data, I believe a model committed to the standard of biblical warrant should be able to consistently affirm that God is eternal, God does not relate to time as mere creatures do, and Scripture at least *depicts* God as temporally enduring and acting successively throughout history—not least relative to the incarnation.

Nevertheless, numerous questions remain, and I readily affirm that Scripture does not articulate a developed philosophy of time.[99] Accordingly, my model makes no specific case regarding a thoroughgoing philosophy of time.[100] However, I believe it is important to affirm a minimal conception of God and time that is compatible with God actually doing the kinds of things that Scripture teaches that God does. Even if the biblical passages that specifically address God and time are underdetermined *by themselves*, other claims about God that hold implications for God's relationship to time may bear significantly on the matter.

To this point, the situation relative to biblical warrant is this. Scholars on both sides agree that no biblical data teaches that God is timeless. Conversely, scholars on both sides affirm that, in McCann's words, there are many biblical "passages that portray God as temporal."[101] Indeed, Helm recognizes that "any reader of Scripture is forcefully struck by the language of time and change as applied to God."[102] The claim that God is timeless, then, runs counter to the way many biblical passages portray God. Moreover, there appears to be no biblical warrant for negating the many biblical depictions of God as enduring through time and performing successive and temporally responsive actions. Given this situation, if other biblical data indirectly affirms divine temporality, absent a defeater at the level of systematic coherence or biblical warrant, such data coupled with the biblical data that portrays God as temporal would amount to a strong cumulative case (relative to biblical warrant) in favor of the view that God is (somehow) temporal.

Numerous lines of biblical data could be considered in this regard. Here, given space limitations, I mention only a few. First, divine temporality is consistent with the view of divine presence outlined earlier, including biblical passages that depict God as (sometimes) localizing his presence in particular

99. See Callender, *Oxford Handbook on the Philosophy of Time*.
100. For an excellent discussion from a temporalist perspective, see Mullins, *End of the Timeless God*.
101. McCann, "God beyond Time," 92.
102. Helm, "Divine Timeless Eternity," 42.

places at particular times. Further, the many biblical depictions of God undergoing changing emotions (see chap. 2) strongly point toward divine temporality. In this regard, Helm argues, "A timelessly eternal God is immutable and so impassible in a very strong sense; he *necessarily* cannot change for change takes time, or is in time, and a timelessly eternal God by definition is not in time, and so his actions cannot take time, nor can he experience" changing emotions.[103] I agree. It follows from this argument, conversely, that if God does experience changing emotions (or otherwise changes), then God cannot be timeless. If the God of Scripture undergoes change (as argued in chap. 2), then it follows that the God of Scripture is (somehow) temporal. As Wolterstorff states, "God the Redeemer is a God who changes. And any being that changes is a being among whose states there is temporal succession."[104]

To consider another line of inquiry all too briefly, some take the biblical teaching of the incarnation to be conclusive evidence of divine temporality. If God is (strictly) timeless, how could the Son be fully divine and yet become human and "enter into" time and space? Mullins makes an extensive and, in my view, convincing case that "divine timelessness is not compatible with the ecumenical model of the incarnation. One must pick either divine timelessness or the incarnation."[105] Likewise, in this respect, Richard Cross maintains that a coherent model of the incarnation may require "an abandonment of a strong form of classical theism"—specifically, "we need to abandon divine impassibility, immutability, and timelessness."[106] Wolterstorff also claims that divine timelessness is not "compatible with an orthodox understanding of what happens in the incarnation" and that "the doctrine of the incarnation implies that the history of Jesus is the history of God."[107] Conversely, Helm argues that since "there is no change or succession possible in the timeless

103. Helm, "Divine Timeless Eternity," 38–39 (emphasis original). Likewise, Dolezal states, "If temporal succession of life is denied to God, so then must be all those experiences, such as emotional change, that require time" (Dolezal, "Still Impassible," 131). Elsewhere Helm argues, "(1) God is timelessly eternal. (2) Whatever is timelessly eternal is unchangeable. (3) Whatever is unchangeable is impassible. (4) Therefore, God is impassible." Helm, "Impossibility of Divine Passibility," 119.

104. Wolterstorff, *Inquiring about God*, 134. John Feinberg adds, "A God who changes his relationship with a repentant sinner incorporates a sequence in his handling of that person, but that sequence necessitates time and so rules out atemporalism" (Feinberg, *No One Like Him*, 432). Moreland and Craig maintain, further, "In virtue of his real, causal relation to the temporal world, God must minimally undergo extrinsic change and therefore be temporal—at least since the moment of creation." Moreland and Craig, *Philosophical Foundations*, 527.

105. Mullins, *End of the Timeless God*, 194. See also Loke, *Kryptic Model of the Incarnation*.

106. Cross, "Incarnation," 471.

107. Wolterstorff, *Inquiring about God*, 178.

eternity of God's life," the "incarnation is the 'projection' of the eternal God."[108] This, however, excludes the view that the Son *became* human at some time, in contrast to what Scripture explicitly claims. At a particular time ("when the fullness of time came," Gal. 4:4 NASB), "the Word [the Son] became flesh, and dwelt among us" (John 1:14 NASB), which involved the Son lowering and humbling himself ("taking the form of a slave") but later being reexalted to his rightful throne (Phil. 2:6–11).

Apart from Helm's "projection" view, conceiving of the incarnation of a timeless God faces other considerable difficulties. In brief, (among other things) Mullins argues that "divine timelessness cannot meet the conditions for embodiment" that the doctrine of the incarnation requires.[109] Further, Mullins argues, the Christian doctrine of the incarnation requires that the Son is the same person as Jesus. Yet if the Son is the same person as Jesus, then the Son must entertain the same *de se* beliefs as Jesus, *de se* beliefs being defined as "a first-person belief that no one else can entertain," such as "I am suffering on the cross."[110] Put the other way around, "If God the Son cannot entertain the same *de se* beliefs as Jesus, God the Son is not the same person as Jesus."[111] However, "the *de se* beliefs of the human mind of Jesus" include "temporal beliefs that involve change, succession, variation of emotion, ignorance of the future, and an interruption of pure joy. These simply are not *de se* beliefs that any timeless, immutable, or impassible divine mind could entertain."[112]

Of course, there is much more that warrants discussion regarding this highly complex and contested issue. However, I believe there is enough here to at least give pause relative to the incarnation. Even if one thinks there is a way to consistently hold the incarnation with divine timelessness, the question of biblical warrant remains. I see no biblical warrant for the view that the Son is timelessly incarnate, but I do see abundant biblical testimony that the Son *became* incarnate at some point in time.[113]

In addition, the narratives of God's successive covenantal interactions with humanity suggest that God somehow relates temporally to creatures. As seen earlier, Scripture not only depicts God via temporal language but also portrays

108. Helm, "Divine Timeless Eternity," 54. For an argument that the incarnation and time-lessness can be consistently affirmed, see Blount, "On the Incarnation of a Timeless God," 236–48.

109. Mullins, *End of the Timeless God*, 192.

110. Mullins, *End of the Timeless God*, 193–94.

111. Mullins, *End of the Timeless God*, 193.

112. Mullins, *End of the Timeless God*, 194. On Christ's omniscience, see chap. 7, under the heading "Tenet 4."

113. On eternal generation, see chap. 7.

God as experiencing changing emotions, otherwise changing relationally, and acting in succession and in response to creaturely actions (often in the context of back-and-forth covenant relationship). As Morris writes, God "speaks to Abram, and then later he speaks to Moses. He sends his Son, becoming incarnate in the world, and later he pours out his Spirit. He creates and then he saves. This is sequence and succession. If it is succession *within* the life of God, God is a temporal being."[114]

Much more should be said about this and other lines of thought, but for the purposes of this brief chapter, suffice it to say that numerous lines of data provide biblical warrant for the conclusion that God *temporally* relates to the world. I do not mean to claim there is no other *possible* theological option, but I believe some kind of divine temporality best fits the biblical data exegetically and canonically. Absent defeaters, this much is sufficient to claim biblical warrant for the view that God is (somehow) temporal.

A Minimal Model of Analogical Temporality and Divine Eternity

As I understand it, then, Scripture affirms that God is eternal (without beginning or end) and that God is *analogically* temporal, meaning that God can temporally act and interact while not being related to (or restricted to) time in the way humans are.[115] In other words, *analogical* temporality affirms that God is temporal in the minimal sense of being capable of experiencing temporal succession while emphasizing that God experiences and relates to time very differently than mere creatures, without claiming to know just how God relates to time. Rather than attempting to offer a thoroughgoing philosophy of time, this minimal model of analogical temporality merely claims that God can act and interact *temporally* in the ways Scripture depicts, performing successive actions over time, *reacting* and *responding* to humans in back-and-forth covenant relationship, undergoing emotional and other relational changes, and otherwise relating temporally to creatures.

This model affirms that God existed "prior to" and apart from the world (cf. Col. 1:16–17), contra the view that God is essentially related to the world.[116] God freely created the universe and thereby brought it into existence and, with it, brought into existence what some call *created* time or *physical* time—that

---

114. T. Morris, *Our Idea of God*, 125–26.
115. See Canale, *Basic Elements of Christian Theology*, 71. Cf. Torrance, *Christian Doctrine of God*, 220, 241.
116. In this regard, Torrance states, "The creation of the world out of nothing is something *new even for God*. God was always Father, but he *became* Creator." Torrance, *Christian Doctrine of God*, 208 (emphasis original).

is, "time in any temporal world containing physical objects."[117] Perhaps God was timeless "before" he created the universe (and, with it, physical time) but became temporal at the very moment he brought the universe into being.[118] Alternatively, it may be that God created physical time, but God's (unmetricated) time prior to the creation of the world is a metaphysical time that "cannot be measured because it lacks an intrinsic metric."[119]

Which of these views is preferable is a matter of dispute among temporalists.[120] Because I aim to restrict the confident claims I make in this book to those for which I can show sufficient biblical warrant, I make no confident claim here regarding which view is preferable. Both *might* be consistent with the biblical material discussed in this chapter, and both affirm that "God's existence *with creation* is temporal," yet *physical* time is not intrinsic to God's being.[121]

According to the minimal model I affirm, time should not be thought of as a container, as if time encompasses God. Rather, time is minimally conceived in terms of succession in God's life, which (*at least* with creation) includes various instances of (temporally) responsive passion and compassion, pleasure and displeasure, delight and grief, and joy and sorrow. The God of Scripture has new experiences and does genuinely new things (Isa. 43:19). As T. F. Torrance puts it, "Far from being a static or inertial Deity like some 'unmoved mover,'" God "is absolutely free to do what he had never done before, and free to be other than he was eternally: to be Almighty Creator, and even to become incarnate as a creature within his creation, while nevertheless remaining eternally the God that he always was."[122]

Some Questions and Implications

A number of issues warrant further consideration, but space permits only brief consideration of a few select issues here. First, some atemporalists claim temporality would limit God. However, divine timelessness would itself limit

---

117. DeWeese, "Atemporal, Sempiternal, or Omnitemporal," 49. Cf. Torrance's distinction between "the uncreated Time of God and the created time of our world" (Torrance, *Christian Doctrine of God*, 220). See also MacDonald, *Metaphysics and the God of Israel*, 79–81.

118. William Lane Craig calls this omnitemporality, arguing that "before creation" God was "atemporal." Craig, "Timelessness and Omnitemporality," 132. So also Copan, *Loving Wisdom*, 76.

119. Mullins, *End of the Timeless God*, 35. See further Padgett, *God, Eternity, and the Nature of Time*, 122–36; Swinburne, *Christian God*, 72–95; Zimmerman, "God inside Time and before Creation," 75–94.

120. See, e.g., the dialogue between Craig and Padgett in Ganssle, *God and Time*.

121. Wolterstorff, "Response to Craig," 170 (emphasis original).

122. Torrance, *Christian God*, 208.

God. As Davis explains, "Not even a timelessly eternal God is free of all temporal limitations, for he is actually unable to experience 'before' or 'after.' . . . There is temporal limitation whichever view we take."[123] A timeless God could not act or interact temporally (as Scripture depicts).[124] A timeless God could not do or enjoy anything that requires the passing of time, including many kinds of things Scripture depicts God doing. A timeless God could not create or sustain a *temporal* world and could not engage in back-and-forth relationship with creatures.[125] And a timeless God could have no knowledge of the *present*, changing state of the temporal world, including things like Christ's sacrifice is *now* in the past (Heb. 10:12) and Christ's second coming is *now* in the future (cf. Zeph. 3:17).[126] Conversely, a temporal God could do all the things Scripture affirms that he does, without being restricted by time the way creatures are.[127]

While Scripture frequently depicts God temporally responding to creatures, a timeless God could not genuinely *re*spond to creatures—at least if to respond is to "do something later than, and on account of, another person's having done something."[128] Some atemporalists claim, however, that God can "respond" via timeless divine action, meaning God "eternally will[s] his own reactions in time to some human action."[129] However, suppose (as Rogers puts it) "the concept of a response requires that there be a certain sort of causal connection such that," for instance, a "prayer 'prompts' the response, and the response 'answers' the prayer."[130] If so, I do not see how divine responsiveness could be compatible with impassibility of the kind most atemporalists affirm,

123. Davis, *Logic and the Nature of God*, 24. Yet, Padgett emphasizes, God "is not limited or changed in any *fundamental* way by the passage of time." Padgett, "Eternity as Relative Timelessness," 108 (emphasis added).

124. Davis notes that we have "no acceptable conception of atemporal causation"—that is, "of what it is for a timeless cause to produce a temporal effect." Davis, *Logic and the Nature of God*, 13.

125. Craig argues that if God "is Creator of a temporal world" and thereby "creatively active in the temporal world," then God "is really related to the temporal world" and thus himself "temporal." Craig, "Timelessness and Omnitemporality," 141. So also Mullins, *End of the Timeless God*, 155.

126. See the discussion in Prior, "Formalities of Omniscience," 114–29; Kretzmann, "Omniscience and Immutability," 409–21; Wolterstorff, *Inquiring about God*, 134–45.

127. Craig argues there is no reason to think "timeless life" is "the most perfect mode of existence of a perfect person." Indeed, he contends that temporal succession enriches life (e.g., the passage of time required for music). Craig, "Timelessness and Omnitemporality," 136.

128. Wolterstorff, "Response to Critics," 232. So also R. Lister, *God Is Impassible and Impassioned*, 230. Cf. Pike, *God and Timelessness*, 128.

129. Helm, "Divine Timeless Eternity," 53–54; Rogers, *Perfect Being Theology*, 65–66; Stump, *God of the Bible*, 76.

130. Rogers, *Perfect Being Theology*, 66.

which entails that God cannot be affected by anything outside himself.[131] The same problem faces advocates of pure actuality, which denies that God can be causally influenced, holding that God relates to the world only in terms of a "relation of reason" such that the "relation of God to creatures can only be that of a cause to an effect."[132] As John Webster explains, there is a "non-reciprocity of the creator-creature relation, which is not real on the side of the creator."[133] In this regard, Rob Lister concludes, if God is "pure actuality," then "God is never, properly speaking, responsive."[134]

These puzzles aside, at best a timeless God could only "prespond."[135] Even if atemporalists could show how this suffices at the level of systematic coherence, the question of biblical warrant remains. Further, even if timeless divine action could be spoken of in terms of "*re*sponses" and "*re*actions" without equivocation, divine timelessness is simply incompatible with many of the kinds of reactions that Scripture depicts God having—including emotional changes in response to creaturely actions.

Conversely, if God is analogically temporal, God can act and respond in the temporal ways Scripture depicts; God can relationally change and temporally respond to humans in back-and-forth covenant relationship as Scripture portrays, compassionately hearing and responding to the prayers of humans such that petitionary prayer makes a difference to God himself.[136] As Swinburne puts it, "Only a God who acts and chooses and loves and forgives is the God whom we wish to worship, and the pursuit of these activities, since they involve change of state, means being in time."[137] In this regard, nothing signifies God's special loving concern for us and with us more than the incarnation. If Mullins and others are right that "divine timelessness is not compatible with the ecumenical model of the incarnation," then conceiving of God as analogically temporal has a massive advantage regarding consistency with the central doctrine of the Christian faith—the incarnation.[138] In this and other respects, God might be thought of as backward compatible. That is to say, God can condescend to be "God with us" and act and interact on the creaturely plane of time and space (as in the incarnation), but God is not

---

131. Rogers, *Perfect Being Theology*, 66.
132. Thomas Aquinas, *Truth* 4.5 (p. 189). He explains, "There are real relations in creatures, referring them to God. The opposite relations in God to creatures, however, are merely conceptual relations"; that is, the "relation is merely one of reason." Thomas Aquinas, *Truth* 4.5 (p. 191).
133. Webster, *God without Measure*, 1:93.
134. R. Lister, *God Is Impassible and Impassioned*, 157.
135. Creel, *Divine Impassibility*, 22–23.
136. On petitionary prayer, see chap. 6.
137. Swinburne, *Coherence of Theism*, 225.
138. Mullins, *End of the Timeless God*, 194.

dependent on or bound by creation nor reducible or restricted to time and space in the way mere creatures are.

Yet atemporalists also claim that a temporal God is deficient in that parts of God's life would continually slip "away into an unrecoverable past" with "only this tiny sliver of a 'now' presently accessible to him."[139] However, given divine omniscience and omnipotence, God would retain *perfectly vivid* recall of the past and, *if* God so wished, could simulate or project a perfectly vivid replica of the world as it was at any past moment.[140] Of course, a "projection" would not provide the same subjective experience as being actually present *now*, but a timeless God could not have the subjective experience of an actual time that is *now* in the first place. As such, it is difficult to see how anything of significance would be lost if God is analogically temporal.

On the other hand, if eternalism is true, all events in history (including all evil occurrences) are eternal such that evil is never eradicated, which runs counter to Scripture's assurances that the present evil state of affairs will pass away (e.g., Rev. 21:4). Davis cites this as one reason he rejects "the timelessness of either God or heaven. I hope events like the Holocaust recede further and further into the past rather than remain an aspect of an 'eternal present moment.'"[141] The presentist view that the past no longer exists seems to be in keeping with the momentous eschatological promise that God will finally

> wipe every tear from their eyes.
> Death will be no more;
> mourning and crying and pain will be no more,
> for the first things have passed away. (Rev. 21:4; cf. Zeph. 3:17)

In this and other ways, I believe the teaching that God is analogically temporal and omnipresent in a way congruent with special divine presence in particular times and places is exceedingly good news. Among other things, whereas one might wonder in what respect a timeless God could genuinely dwell "with us," analogical temporality affirms that God can genuinely be *with us* in some significance sense, including personal presence, and supports the hope that in the future the intimacy of divine presence that God intended in the beginning—ruptured by the entrance of sin—will be restored.

In the meantime, God calls his followers to set aside time and space for shared attention with God, to commune with him even now. This is

139. Williams, "Introduction to Classical Theism," 96.
140. Given divine omniscience, God's "experience of the past remains as vivid as ever." Craig, "Timelessness and Omnitemporality," 135.
141. Davis, "Free Will and Evil," 107. Cf. Mullins, "Four-Dimensionalism," 127–28.

particularly important in an age when people are more and more lonely, anxious, busy, and distracted, being bombarded by so much vying for their attention at all times. In an age when technology more often distances us from intimate relationships than draws us into them, the covenantal God of Scripture calls us to intimately commune with him and with others, which God himself modeled supremely in Christ and makes provision for now through the work of the Holy Spirit. Even as my nine-year-old son and I long to spend quality time together, the covenantal God of Scripture desires quality time with us, inviting us to come apart from our burdens and rest in and with him.[142] Christ invites, "Come to me, all you that are weary and carrying heavy burdens, and I will give you rest. Take my yoke upon you, and learn from me; for I am gentle and humble in heart, and you will find rest for your souls. For my yoke is easy, and my burden is light" (Matt. 11:28–30).[143] Many people today, with so many things distracting them from shared attention and communion with God and one another, are starving to rest in deep personal relationship and presence. The covenantal God of Scripture, however, seeks us and calls us and freely offers and draws each of us toward love relationship with him, which alone will fulfill what the human heart most longs for and will unite us together in Christ.

In many ways, the story of Scripture is itself the story of God's desire to be significantly and personally present *with us* in a covenantal union of love, the presence of intimate love relationship God originally intended, which was ruptured by sin and evil. This personal presence of divine love relationship is the best possible good for all creation, which the covenantal God of Scripture, in his unfathomably great love and compassion, wants to restore so much that (in Christ) God became human—to be "God with us" (Immanuel) in human flesh. This is interwoven with Scripture's emphasis on God's presence "with us" in space and time, which itself illuminates Scripture's emphasis on sacred places (e.g., the sanctuary and the promised land) and sacred times (e.g., Sabbath), and its consistent emphasis on a promised and assured future (including the promised eschatological "day of the Lord") wherein the covenant promises will be fulfilled—namely, God's covenant promise throughout Scripture that "I will be with you and be your God." In large part, Christ's priestly ministry itself, along with the associated work of the Holy Spirit,

142. Accordingly, my son's favorite day is the Sabbath we share as a family, connecting with God and putting aside work and other distractions to be personally *present* (shared attention) with one another.

143. This complements the significant Sabbath motif in Scripture, which also speaks to the rest and personal presence in intimate relationship that many people are starving for. See Swoboda, *Subversive Sabbath*. Cf. Tonstad, *Lost Meaning of the Seventh Day*.

is aimed at the kind of reconciliation ("at-one-ment") necessary for the full restoration of the personal and intimate presence of God *with* all creation.

In the eschaton it will be true in some special and largely unimaginable sense that "the tabernacle of God is among men, and He will dwell among them, and they shall be His people, and God Himself will be among them" (Rev. 21:3 NASB; cf. 1 Cor. 2:9). This is exceedingly good news, especially for all those who have been abandoned by wayward earthly parents or otherwise. Whether you have the companionship of an earthly father or mother, brother or sister, wife or husband, daughter or son, or no one at all, you have a Father in heaven who is not only in heaven but also with you in truth and desires to bring you into still greater intimate relationship with himself—that you and I might be where Christ is. As Christ himself said, "In my Father's house there are many dwelling places," and "I go to prepare a place for you" and "will come again and take you to myself, so that where I am, there you may be also" (John 14:2–3). In the meantime, the covenantal God of Scripture is not only far off but exceedingly near. As one children's tale I treasured as a child puts it, the king "is as far away as you could ever suppose and yet he's as close as the tip of your nose."[144]

Conclusion

This chapter has made a case that God is both omnipresent and yet may be specially present and that God is eternal and *analogically* temporal. The God of Scripture is present everywhere in some manner but not always present everywhere in the same sense. God is omnipresent *at least* in the sense that God's knowledge and power extend to all creation. Yet God can also localize his presence in particular places (special divine presence) and manifest his presence in physical form, while God is never encompassed by or restricted to any location or physical form. In this and other ways, God is both transcendent and immanent without contradiction. Relative to the matter of divine temporality, the God of Scripture is not timeless but *everlastingly* eternal— God has no beginning or end and (in some way unique to divinity) experiences succession of time and performs successive actions and reactions. God is *analogically* temporal—capable of experiencing succession and responding to humans in covenant relationship as Scripture portrays—but relates to time very differently than creatures do.

144. Wood and Irish, *Secrets of the Kingdom.*

Four

The God Who Knows Everything

Omniscience and Foreknowledge

I f you have ever played hide-and-seek with a young child, you have likely seen a child try to hide by covering their eyes or crouching behind a slim tree. I fondly recall how funny it was when my son as a toddler thought I could not see him merely because his eyes were covered or because his own view was obstructed by a tree. In analogous fashion, sometimes people relate to God as if God does not know everything that could be known about us— such as when people pray with the pretense that they might hide their flaws and shortcomings from God, while in reality nothing is hidden from God (Heb. 4:13). God's wisdom is all-encompassing. This holds massive implications relative to divine providence and the confidence Christians should have in God's plan and purpose for all.

Christians generally agree that God is omniscient, that God infallibly knows all that can be known. However, questions arise relative to God's knowledge of the future—the issue of divine foreknowledge—particularly relative to human free will. This chapter addresses ongoing debates over the nature and extent of God's knowledge, seeking to answer questions such as, Does God know absolutely everything? Does God know the future? If so, can humans have genuine free will?

Omniscience: God Knows Everything

Many biblical passages indicate God is all-knowing (omniscient). According to Scripture, God knows "the end from the beginning" (Isa. 46:10), God's "understanding is infinite" (Ps. 147:5 NASB; cf. Isa. 40:28), and God "knows everything" (1 John 3:20). If God knows *everything*, God cannot be wrong about anything. There is biblical warrant, then, for affirming that God has perfect, infallible knowledge of all things.

Yet Scripture also frequently depicts God asking questions and making statements that some take to mean that God lacks knowledge. After Adam and Eve eat the forbidden fruit, God asks Adam, "Where are you?" (Gen. 3:9). God later asks Eve, "What is this that you have done?" (3:13). After Cain murders his brother Abel, God asks, "Where is your brother Abel?" (4:9). In Genesis 32:27, while wrestling with Jacob, the "man" who turns out to be God asks Jacob, "What is your name?" From the burning bush, God asks Moses, "What is that in your hand?" (Exod. 4:2). At the Red Sea, with the Egyptians closing in on the fleeing Israelites, God asks Moses, "Why do you cry out to me?" (14:15). Later, God asks Elijah, "What are you doing here, Elijah?" (1 Kings 19:9) and asks Jonah, "Is it right for you to be angry?" (Jon. 4:9).

Do such passages portray God as lacking knowledge, as some suppose? If God knows everything, why would he ask questions? Notably, questions may be posed for many reasons other than to gain information. When I ask my students what the word "omniscience" means, I ask in order to teach. When I see cookie crumbs on my son's mouth and ask whether he got into the cookies, I already know the answer. In depositions and trials, lawyers often ask questions to which they already know the answers to get a person's testimony on record.

God's questions seem to function likewise. God's questioning of Adam and Eve is part of a judgment proceeding, evidenced by (among other things) God's judgment declarations in Genesis 3:14 and onward. God's question to Cain is also part of a judgment proceeding wherein God reveals that he already knows what Cain has done and declares judgment accordingly (4:10–12). Some biblical scholars identify these and many other instances of divine questioning as instances of covenant lawsuit proceedings.[1] In the context of judgment proceedings, the questions God asks do not indicate any lack of knowledge on God's part.[2] The questions serve a legal purpose consistent with the teaching of Hebrews 4:13 that "before him [God] no creature is hidden,

---

1. See R. Davidson, "Divine Covenant Lawsuit Motif," 45–84.
2. Thomas V. Morris contends, "When God asks a question, he seeks to teach, not to be taught." T. Morris, *Our Idea of God*, 85.

but all are naked and laid bare to the eyes of the one to whom we must render an account" (cf. Matt. 12:36–37; 2 Cor. 5:10).[3]

No biblical passages indicate or entail that God does not know the answer to any question he asks. In many instances, judgment proceedings and otherwise, the context indicates that God has some reason for questioning that does not involve obtaining information (e.g., Jon. 4:9). Even in instances where such reasons might not be apparent, however, absent any textual indication that God lacks knowledge and given the texts that teach that God knows everything (e.g., 1 John 3:20), we have considerable biblical warrant for interpreting such as instances of God asking questions for some purpose other than obtaining information.

Many other passages attest to God's comprehensive and intimate knowledge of humans. According to 1 Kings 8:39, God *alone* "know[s] what is in every human heart." Further, "the LORD searches every mind, and understands every plan and thought" (1 Chron. 28:9), and God "knows the secrets of the heart" (Ps. 44:21; cf. Jer. 20:12). Indeed, Psalm 139:1–5 states,

> O LORD, you have searched me and known me.
> You know when I sit down and when I rise up;
>   you discern my thoughts from far away.
> You search out my path and my lying down,
>   and are acquainted with all my ways.
> Even before a word is on my tongue,
>   O LORD, you know it completely.

Elsewhere God himself declares, "I know the things that come into your mind" (Ezek. 11:5). Likewise, Jesus teaches, "God knows your hearts" (Luke 16:15) and "your Father knows what you need before you ask him" (Matt. 6:8; cf. 9:4; Mark 2:8; Luke 5:22; Acts 15:8). This and other data of Scripture attest that God knows all things—God is omniscient.

Omniscience and Foreknowledge

Conceptions of Omniscience and Foreknowledge

While there is little controversy over whether God is omniscient, many disagree over the nature of divine omniscience, particularly concerning whether

---

3. Richard M. Davidson explains (regarding instances like Gen. 11; 18), "God comes to investigate, not because He needs to know, but so that it can be seen that He is fair and just in all His dealings." R. Davidson, "Divine Covenant Lawsuit Motif," 72.

God has exhaustive definite foreknowledge—that is, whether God knows the entirety of the future in precise detail. Most Christian theists maintain that omniscience includes exhaustive definite foreknowledge, which is widely considered to be the traditional view, "the overwhelming consensus of the Church's leading thinkers."[4] However, some (e.g., open theists and process theists) believe God is omniscient in that he knows all that can be known, but they maintain that future *free* decisions of creatures cannot be known.

In this regard, process theists, open theists, and (many) determinists agree that if creatures possess free will of the kind that is incompatible with causal determinism (*libertarian* free will), then God cannot have exhaustive definite foreknowledge.[5] However, determinists affirm that God possesses exhaustive definite foreknowledge and deny that creatures possess libertarian free will, while process and open theists affirm that creatures possess libertarian free will and deny that God possesses exhaustive definite foreknowledge. Yet many other Christian theists affirm both that God possesses exhaustive definite foreknowledge *and* that God grants libertarian free will to creatures.

The debate over whether God grants libertarian free will is addressed in chapter 5. This chapter focuses on the debate between those who affirm God has exhaustive definite foreknowledge (whether determinists or indeterminists) and those who deny it. Relative to the biblical data, one side appeals to passages that they claim teach that God has comprehensive knowledge of the future, while the other side appeals to passages that they claim teach that parts of the future remain unknown even to God. Given this situation, let us consider both cases relative to the standard of biblical warrant.

An "Openness Motif" in Scripture?

Many open theists claim that Scripture indicates that God does not know the future exhaustively. For instance, recognizing a foreknowledge "motif" in Scripture, Greg Boyd says he would affirm exhaustive definite foreknowledge if it were not for "other biblical material that depicts the future as partly open."[6] Specifically, Boyd argues that in Scripture "God asks questions about the future, speaks of the future in conditional terms, regrets the outcome of decisions he has made, changes his mind in response to changing situations, and so on."[7]

4. Hunt, "Simple-Foreknowledge View," 69. David Hunt points to Justin Martyr, Augustine, Boethius, Anselm, Thomas Aquinas, Martin Luther, John Calvin, Jacob Arminius, and John Wesley.

5. Theistic determinists believe that God exercises power in a way that determines all occurrences. Conversely, indeterminists believe that God does not causally determine history.

6. Boyd, "Open-Theism View," 15–16.

7. Boyd, "Open-Theism View," 23.

For example, Boyd claims that God tests Abraham because God "wants to know whether Abraham will choose to obey him or not."[8] He argues, "The verse clearly says that it was *because* Abraham did what he did that the Lord *now* knew he was a faithful covenant partner" (Gen. 22:12).[9] Boyd appeals, further, to passages wherein God's desires appear to be frustrated, including many texts depicting God's desire that all be saved and instances like Ezekiel 22:30, where God says, "I sought for anyone among them who would repair the wall and stand in the breach before me on behalf of the land, so that I would not destroy it; but I found no one." Boyd asks, "How can the Lord become frustrated trying to achieve things he is certain will never come to pass?"[10] Similarly, Boyd appeals to God's question regarding his vineyard in Isaiah 5:4, "Why, when I expected it to produce good grapes did it produce worthless ones?" (NASB). Boyd interprets this to mean that God "'expected' one thing to occur, only to discover something else occurred instead."[11]

Open theists also appeal to texts that depict God "repenting." These are often translated in terms of God changing his mind and having regrets, and open theists argue that such statements only make sense if God does not know the future. For example, Boyd appeals to Genesis 6:6: "The LORD was sorry that he had made humankind on the earth." Boyd comments, "If God truly wished he had never made humans—to the point of his wanting to destroy them and start over—shouldn't we conclude that the extent of their depravity *wasn't* a foregone conclusion at the time he created them?" Similarly, Boyd quotes 1 Samuel 15:11, where God says, "I regret that I made Saul king." Here Boyd asks, if God "was eternally certain that Saul would 'turn back' when he made him king, how can God regret making him king because he 'turned back'?"[12]

Do these passages (and others like them) provide evidence that God does not know the future free decisions of creatures? Some explain these texts by claiming that they are anthropomorphic such that God is merely portrayed in human terms as if God lacks knowledge of the future. In response, Boyd contends, "All God's revelatory language is 'accommodated' to our human condition" and sometimes includes "metaphors, symbols and anthropomorphisms," but such "nonliteral language," as revelatory, "communicates *something truthful about God.*" As such, "reinterpreting the passages that constitute the motif of future openness as 'metaphorical' does not *clarify*

8. Boyd, "Open-Theism View," 33. So also Pinnock, "Systematic Theology," 122.
9. Boyd, "Open-Theism View," 32.
10. Boyd, "Open-Theism View," 28.
11. Boyd, "Open-Theism View," 24.
12. Boyd, "Open-Theism View," 26.

these passages: it *undermines* them."[13] Boyd may be right that claiming such passages are anthropomorphic is insufficient to rebut the open theist's claims. However, one need not appeal to anthropomorphism (or accommodative language broadly) in this regard. Even on a literal reading, the passages themselves do not actually indicate that God lacks knowledge of the future. To see this, let us briefly revisit some representative texts, beginning with instances where God is said (in English translations) to repent, be sorry, regret, or change his mind (e.g., Gen. 6:6; 1 Sam. 15:11)—that is, instances where God is the subject of the Hebrew verb *nāḥam*.

First, the root *nāḥam* does not itself indicate or entail any *change of mind*. Rather, *nāḥam* (in the niphal stem) basically means to "suffer emotional pain," which may be "extended to describe the release of emotional tension" by God's relenting or "retracting a declared action" such as "punishment" or "blessing."[14] The verb *nāḥam* (in niphal) is often used to depict divine "sorrow" and God relenting of some declared or ongoing action, but it does not indicate any "suggestion of regret" for God's own actions.[15]

How, then, should one interpret phrases like "the LORD was sorry that he made humankind on the earth" (Gen. 6:6) and "I regret that I made Saul king" (1 Sam. 15:11)? Notably, neither these texts nor others indicate that God regretted his own actions as if he would do otherwise if he had them to do over again. Regarding Genesis 6:6, it is difficult to square the view that God "truly wished he had never made humans," as Boyd supposes, with the fact that God made provision to save humankind from destruction (not only in the flood narrative but also relative to the cross). It seems far more likely that God's sorrow and regret are directed at what humans became, though God would create humans just as he did if he had to do it over again. According to Kenneth A. Mathews, Genesis 6:6 displays the "emotional response of God" in "God's fervent passion" and his "wounded 'heart' filled with pain" and "emotional anguish."[16]

Regarding 1 Samuel 15, God had already warned Israel what would happen if they had a king and expressed he did not want them to have a king at that time (1 Sam. 8:6–22; cf. Deut. 17:14–20). Understandably, then, God would regret or be sorrowful that he made Saul king, not because God wished he had done otherwise or did not foreknow what would come of Saul's kingship but because he did not want to make Saul king in the first place and "regrets"

13. Boyd, "Open-Theist Response to Helm," 192 (emphasis original).
14. Parunak, "Semantic Survey of NḤM," 532.
15. Parunak, "Semantic Survey of NḤM," 513n1. See further Peckham, *Concept of Divine Love*, 266–68.
16. Mathews, *Genesis 1–11:26*, 341–42.

what has happened (in the sense of wishing it were different). With regard to both Genesis 6 and 1 Samuel 15, one can genuinely and consistently have "regret" with respect to something one has done even if one knew the results beforehand and would do that thing again. For example, I regret that we had to euthanize our beloved family cat, Cleo, some years ago, but given the pain she was in and the fact that we had no preferable alternatives, I would do the same thing again.

Boyd claims, however, that if God was "certain that he'd regret his decision to make [Saul] king—and then went ahead and made him king anyway—that would not only be unwise, it would be incoherent."[17] However, if there was no preferable alternative available to God at the time (given all God knows and God's benevolent purposes and commitments), this would neither be unwise nor incoherent. In this regard, students often ask me why God chose Saul to be king. I do not know why God chose Saul, but it is at least possible that Saul was the best available king that the people of Israel would accept as king at the time. That God took into account the people's preferences is evident in that he laments that Israel rejected him as king (see 1 Sam. 8:7; cf. 8:22).[18]

A similar line of thought applies to cases where God appears to be frustrated. Open theists such as Boyd suppose that if one is frustrated by something, one could not have certain prior knowledge thereof. However, this does not follow. Suppose a mother is about to appear in child custody court and she knows in advance exactly what false claims her ex-husband will make (suppose he told her what he was going to say). Does it follow that the mother would not be genuinely frustrated when her ex-husband actually states such false claims in custody court? Of course not. It does not follow that being frustrated about some occurrence entails that one lacked prior knowledge of that frustrating occurrence.

Regarding Boyd's appeal to God's stated desire that everyone be saved (e.g., 1 Tim. 2:4–6; cf. Titus 2:11; 2 Pet. 3:9), there is no incompatibility between God knowing someone would finally reject salvation and God sorrowing over their decision (more on this later). With respect to God saying, "I sought for anyone among them" to intercede, "but I found no one" (Ezek. 22:30), even on open theism God possesses comprehensive knowledge of the present such that God *must have* already known whether there was anyone willing and able to effectively intercede. The same goes for instances like the testing of Abraham and others, where God tests people "to know what is in their heart" (Deut. 8:2; cf. Gen. 22:12). The open theist account of such instances requires

17. Boyd, "Open-Theism View," 27.
18. Consider also David's long and circuitous path to the kingship many years after God anointed him.

that God does not already know what is in people's hearts. Yet if God knows everything about present reality, as open theists themselves affirm, then God must already know precisely what is in everyone's heart.[19]

Boyd attempts to rebut this objection by suggesting that, via testing, "God elicits a decision from the people he tests."[20] However, while it does seem that God tests in order to elicit a decision that makes known or *manifests* "what is in their heart," it does not follow from this that God himself does not already know "what is in their heart." Such a conclusion would flatly contradict the biblical teaching that God "know[s] what is in every human heart" (1 Kings 8:39; cf. Pss. 44:21; 139:1–5). Instead, just as God might ask questions for some reason other than obtaining information, God might test someone for some reason other than obtaining information for himself, perhaps to manifest what is in a person's heart to themselves or others (e.g., in the context of formal or informal judgment proceedings, as briefly discussed earlier).

What about instances like Isaiah 5:4, where God states, "Why, when I expected it to produce good grapes did it produce worthless ones?" (NASB). Here the meaning of the term translated "expected" (*qāwâ*) does not connote lack of knowledge but literally means "to wait." Even in English, the word "expect" may refer to an *expectation* or standard that one "expects" others to meet, regardless of whether one believes they actually will.[21] In this and numerous other cases, consideration of the original language clarifies what the text claims and does not claim.

Open theists also appeal to Jeremiah 3:7, translated as God saying, "*And I thought*, 'After she has done all this she will return to me'; but she did not return."[22] In this verse and others like it (e.g., 3:19), the verb translated "I thought" is *'āmar*, which typically means "to say." Accordingly, other translations render this as a command or expectation in the sense of a standard: "And I said, after she had done all these things, 'Return to Me'" (3:7 NKJV; cf. LXX). The Hebrew wording does not entail that God mistakenly "thought" they would return. Moreover, Boyd's interpretation would "implicate God in various *mistaken beliefs*," contradicting his own conception of divine omniscience.[23]

Similarly, Boyd argues, "Three times in Jeremiah the Lord expresses his surprise at Israel's behavior by saying his children were doing things 'which I did not command or decree, *nor did it enter my mind*' (Jer. 19:5; cf. 7:31;

---

19. As open theist William Hasker states, "God has complete, detailed, and utterly intimate knowledge of the entirety of the past and the present." Hasker, *God, Time, and Knowledge*, 192.

20. Boyd, "Open-Theism View," 33.

21. Hunt, "Simple-Foreknowledge Response [to Boyd]," 50.

22. Pinnock, *Most Moved Mover*, 47; Boyd, "Open-Theism View," 25.

23. Hunt, "Simple-Foreknowledge Response [to Boyd]," 51.

32:35)."[24] Yet the phrase translated "nor did it enter my mind" might refer to the previous clause, "which I did not command or decree." Rendered this way, God would be saying, "I did not command or decree" that you do such awful things, "nor did it enter my mind" *to command or decree* so. Such a reading is at least as plausible on a grammatical-syntactical level and has the advantage of being consistent with Scripture's teachings elsewhere. Further, even if one thinks the clause "nor did it enter my mind" refers to the evil actions of God's people, the phrase could be understood as analogous to saying that some horrendous evil is "unheard of." Boyd's interpretation, conversely, requires that God did not anticipate some possibilities, contradicting his own view that God "can never be caught off guard—for he anticipates all possibilities."[25]

While other instances might be considered, these are representative of the prominent texts and arguments open theists typically offer. However, neither these nor other biblical passages provide biblical warrant for the claim that God lacks exhaustive knowledge of the future.

Scripture Teaches That God Knows the Future Decisions of Humans

An abundance of biblical passages depict God as knowing the future, including the future free decisions of creatures. Indeed, narratives repeatedly portray God revealing the future in striking detail. In Genesis 37:5–11, God gives Joseph dreams foretelling that his brothers will someday bow to him (fulfilled in 42:6; 44:14). Later, God reveals to Joseph exactly what Pharaoh will decide regarding his cupbearer and baker (40:12–22). Still later, God reveals the interpretation of Pharaoh's dreams, foretelling seven years of plenty followed by seven years of famine (41:25–36).[26] God's prediction of the famine could be explained in terms of God foretelling what he himself will do (cf. 41:32), but unless God determines the decisions of humans, including *evil* decisions, the other two instances cannot be explained this way.[27] One predicts Pharaoh's decisions regarding his servants. The other involves a series of decisions by humans, including Joseph's brothers' *evil* decisions to sell him into slavery, the many decisions of people later encountering Joseph, Joseph's own decisions, and more (cf. Deut. 31:16–21).[28]

24. Boyd, "Open-Theism View," 24 (emphasis original). Cf. Pinnock, "Systematic Theology," 122.

25. Boyd, "Open-Theism View," 24. Cf. Rice, *Openness of God*, 49.

26. On these instances, Hunt comments, "We see God's foresight encompassing both the outcome of Pharaoh's most intimate thought processes *and* the long-term effects of large-scale climatic forces." Hunt, "Simple-Foreknowledge View," 68.

27. On whether the Joseph narrative should be interpreted deterministically, see chap. 5.

28. Likewise, Deut. 31:16–21 reports that God told Moses about the future rebellion of Israel in precise detail.

Elsewhere Scripture depicts prophecies about people, *by name*, long before their birth—the fulfillment of which would depend on many human decisions. According to 1 Kings 13:1–2, a prophecy mentioning King Josiah *by name* was given in the presence of Jeroboam, the king of Israel (ca. 931–910 BC), hundreds of years before Josiah (641/640–610/609 BC) was born, foretelling a specific action of Josiah's fulfilled roughly three hundred years later (see 2 Kings 23:19–20).[29] Elsewhere God foretells, "Cyrus, 'He is my shepherd, and he shall carry out all my purpose'" and Jerusalem "shall be rebuilt" (Isa. 44:28; cf. 45:1, 13).[30] If written by the prophet Isaiah (ca. 740–700 BC), as Scripture depicts, this prophecy calls the Persian ruler Cyrus by name and predicts his decree to rebuild Jerusalem (538 BC) long before Cyrus was born.[31] According to John Oswalt, this and other "Cyrus predictions" (Isa. 41:2, 25; 46:11) provide "evidence that God can and does tell the future" as part of God's argument "against the idols" centered on the fact "that they cannot declare the future."[32]

To explain these kinds of passages, some open theists claim that God sometimes *selectively determines* people to do what he predicted.[33] Appeals to selective determinism, however, run counter to the core conviction of open theism that God consistently grants humans libertarian free will and, William Lane Craig argues, amount to a "compatibilistic account of divine foreknowledge."[34] Even if selective determinism could suffice as an explanation of some smaller-scale cases, it faces significant difficulties relative to cogently explaining long-term prophecies like those in Daniel 2 and 7, which Scripture depicts as accurately predicting the rise and fall of specific successive empires over centuries (cf. God's foretelling of the centuries Israel would spend in slavery in Gen. 15:13–16). Additionally, a strong case can be made that, hundreds of years in advance, Daniel 9:24–27 predicts the precise timing of the beginning of Christ's ministry and of Christ's death.[35] If God

29. Some claim these texts were written much later, after the fact, but Scripture depicts this prophecy as given hundreds of years before Josiah was born (1 Kings 13:1–2).

30. Some also point to Isa. 45:1 as predicting the way Cyrus would defeat Babylon.

31. Some say this text was written later, after the fact, but the verse portrays a prediction of what Cyrus *would do in the future*, attributed to God himself.

32. Oswalt, *Book of Isaiah*, 196.

33. Boyd contends, "God determines whatever he sees fit and leaves as much of the future open as he sees fit" (Boyd, "Open-Theism View," 19). On 1 Kings 13:1–2 and Isa. 44–45, Boyd comments, "These decrees obviously established parameters around the parents' freedom to naming these individuals (cf. Lk 1:18–22, 59–64) and also restricted the scope of freedom these individuals could exercise regarding *particular foreordained* activities" (Boyd, "Open-Theism View," 19–20 [emphasis original]). As Jason Nicholls states, "God is able to keep his ultimate purposes on track through periodic instances of determinism"—that is, "*select determinism.*" Nicholls, "Openness and Inerrancy," 647 (emphasis original).

34. Craig, "Middle-Knowledge Response [to Boyd]," 58.

35. This is just one of many OT messianic prophecies, some of which the NT identifies as such.

gave these prophecies in the time of Daniel, as Scripture depicts, then the succession of the empires of Persia, Greece, Rome, and beyond is predicted in striking detail far in advance.[36] The fulfillment of such prophecies *depends on* countless human decisions—even a tiny difference can have massive long-term ramifications (consider the butterfly effect).[37] Explaining these via selective determinism would require that, over centuries, God *causally* determined countless human decisions—including many *evil* decisions, raising significant difficulties regarding the problem of evil.

The NT also contains many striking examples. For instance, Jesus tells his disciples, "You will all become deserters; for it is written, 'I will strike the shepherd, / and the sheep will be scattered'" (Mark 14:27, quoting Zech. 13:7). Here Jesus not only correctly foretells that these disciples will *all* desert him but also portrays this prediction as a fulfillment of a centuries-old prophecy. Likewise, despite Peter's protests (Mark 14:29), Jesus correctly and *precisely* foretells, "This very night, before the cock crows twice, you [Peter] will deny me three times" (14:30; cf. 14:13–15). Here some open theists appeal to the "settled character" hypothesis, claiming that "the Father knew and revealed to Jesus one solidified aspect of Peter's character that was predictable in the immediate future."[38] Yet Paul Kjoss Helseth points out that Peter's later repentance evinces that Peter's character was not "crystallized in the form of an irreversible character" when he denied Christ.[39] Moreover, William Lane Craig notes that even if "Jesus could infer that Peter would fail him, how could he infer that Peter's failure would come in the form of denials, rather than, say, flight or silence, and how could he infer *three* denials before the cock crowed *twice?*"[40] Moreover, Jesus predicted not only Peter's denial but also desertion by the other disciples.

The case of Judas's betrayal is also significant. John 6:64 records, "Jesus knew from the first who were the ones that did not believe, and who was the one that would betray him." Boyd interprets this to "mean that Jesus knew who would betray him *early on.*"[41] However, Jesus explains Judas's betrayal

---

36. Some date these prophecies of Dan. 2 and 7 to the Maccabean period (second century BC), claiming that the prophecies were fabricated after the fact. This contradicts Scripture's portrayal of the prophesies (among other significant difficulties), however, and fails to account for the predictions regarding Jesus in Dan. 9, since it is undisputed that Daniel was written long before Jesus was born.

37. A small change in one place can have massive effects elsewhere (e.g., the flapping of a butterfly's wing could set off a series of events that eventually produces a tornado far away).

38. Boyd, "Open-Theism View," 20.

39. Helseth, "Response to Boyd," 218.

40. Craig, "Middle-Knowledge Response [to Boyd]," 57 (emphasis original).

41. Boyd, "Open-Theism View," 21.

as a fulfillment of prophecy, saying, "It is to fulfill the scripture, 'The one who ate my bread has lifted his heel against me'" (John 13:18, quoting Ps. 41:9; cf. John 14:29).[42] Then Jesus explains, "I tell you this now, before it occurs, so that when it does occur, you may believe that I am he" (John 13:19). The phrase translated "I am he" is *egō eimi* (literally "I am"), which may echo YHWH's self-description in Exodus 3:14 as the great "I am" (*egō eimi* in LXX). It seems Christ's prediction is intended as evidence of divine foreknowledge. Christ succeeds where the "gods" YHWH mocks in Isaiah 41 failed: "they could not "tell . . . what is to come hereafter, / that [Israel] may know that [they] are gods" (v. 23; cf. 46:4, 9–10).

Such instances require that God somehow had precise foreknowledge of numerous *morally responsible* human decisions. Specifically, in Matthew 26, "we find Jesus predicting, in quick succession, that he will be betrayed on the feast of the Passover (v. 2) by a disciple (v. 21) 'who has dipped his hand into the bowl with me' (v. 23); that it is Judas in particular who will betray him (v. 25); that his other disciples will desert him (v. 31); and that Peter will deny him three times before morning (v. 34)—none of which looks like it could be foreknown with certainty in the absence of some supernatural insight into the future."[43] These instances might be explainable by determinism (selective or otherwise), but this explanation would require that God determined *evil* decisions—including the apostles' desertion, Peter's denial, and Judas's betrayal.[44]

Other passages teach that specific events related to the cross were foreknown and occurred according to God's detailed plan. Acts 2:23 states, "This man [Jesus], handed over to you according to the definite plan and foreknowledge [*prognōsis*] of God, you crucified and killed" (cf. 1 Pet. 1:20).[45] Here God's "plan and foreknowledge" refer not only to things God does but also to *evil* things people do, for which they are held morally responsible. Likewise, Acts 4:26 quotes a messianic prophecy:

> The kings of the earth took their stand,
> and the rulers have gathered together
> against the Lord and against his Messiah. (quoting Ps. 2:1–2)

42. Many other typological interpretations of OT prophecies (including many of Christ) depend on God foreknowing a vast array of details, including creaturely decisions.

43. Hunt, "Simple-Foreknowledge View," 68.

44. John Sanders suggests that perhaps "God removed the free will" of Judas and Peter to fulfill his predictions (Hall and Sanders, *Does God Have a Future?*, 30). Given that God holds Judas morally responsible for betraying Jesus, however, this hypothesis would require affirming the controversial claim that one can be causally determined to commit an evil act and yet be morally responsible for that evil act (compatibilism).

45. See also Jesus's many predictions about those who would kill him (Mark 8:31; 9:31; 10:32–34).

Acts then applies it to Herod, Pontius Pilate, and others who acted "against" Christ "to do whatever your hand and your plan had predestined [*proorizō*] to take place" (Acts 4:27–28; cf. Rom. 8:29–30). Boyd contends that "Scripture never suggests that these specific individuals were destined or foreknown to carry out these wicked deeds. It only teaches that these specific deeds were destined and foreknown to take place."[46] However, Acts 4 refers to Herod and Pontius Pilate by name, and Acts 2:23 explicitly states that Jesus was "handed over to you according to the definite plan and foreknowledge of God." Further, as noted earlier, Jesus quotes OT prophecies as predictions of Judas's betrayal and desertion by the Twelve.

In the above examples, God possesses detailed knowledge of humans' future decisions. However, the case for foreknowledge does not rest on these examples alone. Many other passages indicate that God possesses *exhaustive and definite* foreknowledge.

Scripture Teaches That God Knows the End from the Beginning

According to Isaiah 46:9–10, God declares,

> I am God, and there is no other;
> I am God, and there is no one like me,
> declaring the end from the beginning
> and from ancient times things not yet done. (cf. 48:3–5; Acts 15:18)

To declare "the end from the beginning," God must *know* "the end from the beginning," and the phrase "from ancient times" indicates that this knowledge is declared beforehand (i.e., foretold). Thus, God knows "the end from the beginning" beforehand. As J. Alec Motyer understands it, this passage refers to "the whole sweep of history, from its inception to the things still in process."[47]

While open theists argue that this passage (and others like it) only requires that God foretells *some* things, there are excellent reasons to interpret Isaiah 46:10 as referring to God foretelling the *entirety* of history.[48] Specifically, the

46. Boyd, "Open-Theism View," 22.
47. Motyer, *Isaiah*, 333.
48. John Sanders interprets Isa. 46:10 to mean "God is declaring the 'end' (exile and restoration) before it happens. But this does not entail exhaustive foreknowledge, only the ability of God to bring it about" (J. Sanders, *God Who Risks*, 130). Clark Pinnock likewise argues that Isaiah's prophecies "chiefly establish what God promises to do and do not prove limitless foreknowledge" (Pinnock, "Systematic Theology," 122). Boyd concurs, adding, "Neither this nor any other passage in Scripture says that God foreknows or declares *everything* that is going to occur." Boyd, "Open-Theism View," 17.

phrase "the end from the beginning" *may* be a merism—an expression that refers to a totality by mentioning contrasting parts (e.g., "*Young and old* are invited to church"). If so, it refers not only to "the end" and "the beginning" but also to *everything* in between, indicating God foreknows *everything*.[49] Notably, this passage (and the Cyrus prophecy in Isa. 44:28–45:1, 13) appears within a discourse referred to as the "trial of the gods" wherein God sets forth his knowledge of the future as evidence that he is God "and there is no other" (46:9).[50] As David Hunt puts it, Isaiah makes "God's ability to know what will happen before it happens . . . the chief mark by which the true God may be distinguished from false gods."[51] For example, in Isaiah 41:22–23, God says,

> Declare to us the things to come.
> Tell us what is to come hereafter,
>   that we may know that you are gods. (cf. 44:7–8, 21)[52]

Further, Psalm 139:16 indicates that God possesses exhaustive definite foreknowledge of the psalmist's entire life, stating,

> Your [God's] eyes beheld my unformed substance.
> In your book were written
>   all the days that were formed [*yāṣar*] for me,
>   when none of them as yet existed.

Noting that *yāṣar*, "'mold, devise,' is used of the divine purpose in the qal elsewhere," Leslie Allen translates this "In your book are all written down days that were planned [*yāṣar*] when none of them had yet occurred."[53] Allen comments, further, "Yahweh has foreknowledge of all the psalmist's

49. This passage does not specify *how* God knows the future; it teaches that God will bring about some things he predicts (Isa. 46:11; cf. 48:3–5), but that by itself does not entail determinism. To decide between determinism and indeterminism here and elsewhere, one must ask which reading is consistent with *all* the texts. See chap. 5.

50. See Hanson, *Isaiah 40–66*, 88.

51. Hunt, "Simple-Foreknowledge View," 68. Oswalt adds that here "predictive prophecy has been put forward as a proof of God's uniqueness" in contrast to the gods who could not predict the future (so also Isa. 41:21–29; 42:9; 43:8–13, 19–21; 44:6–10, 24–28). Oswalt, *Book of Isaiah*, 236.

52. Notably, merely predicting one's own actions would not by itself suffice as proof against the "gods," since even the demonic agencies behind the "gods" (Deut. 32:17; 1 Cor. 10:19–20; see chap. 6) could work some signs and wonders (see, e.g., 2 Thess. 2:9; cf. Exod. 7:10–12; Matt. 24:24; Rev. 19:20). Only extensive predictions could suffice for this purpose, but such predictions would involve many decisions of creatures.

53. L. Allen, *Psalms 101–150*, 317.

days."[54] Another robust claim of divine foreknowledge appears in Romans 8:29, "For those whom he foreknew [*proginōskō*, from *ginōskō*, "to know," and *pro*, "before"] he also predestined [*proorizō*, "decided beforehand"] to be conformed to the image of his Son, in order that he might be the firstborn within a large family." Likewise, 1 Peter 1:1–2 refers to those "chosen according to the foreknowledge [*prognōsis*] of God the Father." These two passages appear to depict God's foreknowledge of the salvation of individuals.[55]

In this regard, Ephesians 1:11 adds, "In Christ we have also obtained an inheritance, having been destined [*proorizō*] according to the purpose of him who accomplishes all things according to his counsel and will." According to this text, some "in Christ" have been "destined" beforehand (*proorizō*). Here not merely *some* things are accomplished according to God's will, but *all* things are said to be accomplished according to the "purpose" that God has "destined" beforehand. If so, God must (somehow) have knowledge of *all* things beforehand—that is, exhaustive definite foreknowledge (via determinism or otherwise). Notably, the term *proorizō* (often translated "destined" or "predestined)" basically means "to decide beforehand."[56] By itself, this term does not indicate determinism or indeterminism because one could decide something beforehand unilaterally *or* one could decide something beforehand in a way that takes into account the free decisions of others.

In my view, this passage and the others referenced above (*by themselves*) do not conclusively indicate determinism or indeterminism—an issue addressed in chapter 5. I do believe, however, that these passages indicate God knows the future exhaustively, whether he knows the future by causally determining history or some other way. As Katherin Rogers states, the "Bible expresses, clearly and often, the view that God knows the future."[57]

---

54. L. Allen, *Psalms 101–150*, 330. He goes on, "With respect to the apparent determinism of v 16, G. von Rad (*Wisdom in Israel*, 263, 282) commented that in the pre-apocalyptic concept the individual's freedom was scarcely affected."

55. Passages like these are sometimes understood in terms of corporate election, meaning the chosen *group* of believers is referred to without specific reference to the individuals who will finally make up that group. Yet, given that these passages directly link election to God's foreknowledge (*prognōsis*), I think it is more likely that these passages evince divine foreknowledge of who will *freely* respond.

56. L&N 359. Cf. BDAG 873. The term *proorizō* combines *pro* ("before") and *horizō* ("to decide or mark out boundaries or limits"). Accordingly, Louw and Nida render Rom. 8:30, "Those whom he decided upon ahead of time, these he called" (L&N 360). A. Chadwick Thornhill notes, "The term simply means to decide beforehand, and does not contain any inherently deterministic value within the term itself." Thornhill, *Chosen People*, 219.

57. Rogers, *Perfect Being Theology*, 64. Hunt adds, "The doctrine of divine foreknowledge appears firmly rooted in the plain meaning of scores of biblical texts." Hunt, "Simple-Foreknowledge View," 69.

A Constructive Model of Omniscience

In my view, the survey of biblical data above offers biblical warrant for the following claims:

1. God "knows everything" (1 John 3:20; cf. Ps. 147:5; Isa. 46:10; Heb. 4:13).
2. God possesses comprehensive and intimate knowledge of humans (1 Kings 8:39; 1 Chron. 28:9; Pss. 44:21; 139:1–5; Luke 16:15), including knowing "all the days" of the psalmist beforehand (Ps. 139:16).
3. Many biblical passages depict God as having detailed knowledge of the future decisions of humans (including evil decisions), sometimes portrayed as spanning centuries and thus including countless human decisions (Gen. 37:5–11; 40:12–22; 1 Kings 13:1–2; Isa. 44:28; Mark 14:27–30; John 13:18–19; cf. Gen. 15:13–16; Dan. 2, 7, 9).
4. Numerous passages teach that God possesses exhaustive definite foreknowledge—foretelling "the end from the beginning" (Isa. 46:10) and everything in between (Ps. 139:16; Isa. 41:21–23).
5. God saves "those whom he foreknew" (Rom. 8:29; cf. 1 Pet. 1:2) and "accomplishes all things according to his counsel and will" (Eph. 1:11).

Conversely, no biblical passages indicate that God lacks knowledge of the future. As Boyd himself states, the "Bible unequivocally celebrates God's foreknowledge and control of the future."[58] Further, Boyd himself writes that he would affirm God's exhaustive definite foreknowledge were it not for "other biblical material that depicts the future as partly open."[59] However, on closer inspection, the biblical material does not indicate, or even suggest, that God lacks knowledge of the future. I believe there is biblical warrant, then, to affirm that God is omniscient—God knows everything—and that God possesses exhaustive definite foreknowledge. However, questions remain relative to systematic coherence.

Is Affirming Exhaustive Foreknowledge Consistent with Free Will?

For reasons discussed in the next chapter, I believe there is biblical warrant for the view that God grants creatures libertarian free will and does so *consistently* (contra selective determinism). If Scripture indeed teaches that God possesses exhaustive foreknowledge and that God consistently grants persons libertarian free will, then an adequate model consistent with the

58. Boyd, "Open-Theism View," 14.
59. Boyd, "Open-Theism View," 16 (see also 14–15).

standard of biblical warrant will *consistently* affirm both conclusions. Yet is divine foreknowledge consistent with creaturely libertarian free will?

In my view, God's foreknowledge does not undermine the genuine free will of creatures. Creatures remain just as free to decide between options in a libertarian manner (including being free to will otherwise than God ideally desires) as they would be if God lacked foreknowledge. As Jacob Arminius once put it, "A thing does not come to pass because it has been foreknown or foretold; but it is foreknown and foretold because it is yet (*futura*) to come to pass."[60] Far earlier, Anselm argued, "No impossibility is involved in the coexistence of God's foreknowledge and our free choice."[61] Even John Calvin himself wrote, "I will freely admit that foreknowledge alone imposes no necessity upon creatures, yet not all assent to this."[62]

Yet people sometimes intuitively think there is some contradiction between God knowing the future decisions of humans and humans having libertarian free will. Specifically, some suppose that if God knew with certainty before I was born what I will do tomorrow, then I could not be free with respect to what I will do tomorrow. As Nelson Pike famously argued, if God foreknows with certainty that Jones will mow his lawn on Saturday, then Jones could not do otherwise than mow his lawn on Saturday.[63]

Alvin Plantinga and many other philosophers argue, however, that there is another option—namely, one could affirm that if Jones were to do otherwise than mow his lawn on Saturday, then God would not have believed that Jones would mow his lawn on Saturday.[64] In this regard, William Lane Craig cautions, it is crucial not to confuse "certainty with necessity."[65] That God knows with certainty that Jones will mow his lawn on Saturday does not render it necessary or causally determine that Jones will do so. Rather, Plantinga, Craig, and others argue that Jones has the power to refrain from mowing his lawn, and if Jones were to do so, then "God would have held a belief different from the belief he in fact holds."[66] The future, then, may be epistemically "settled" or closed from God's perspective while remaining causally open—what occurs genuinely depends (in part) on what creatures *freely* decide.[67]

60. Arminius, *Works of James Arminius*, 2:368 (Disputation 28.14).
61. Anselm, *De Concordia: The Compatibility of God's Foreknowledge, Predestination, and Grace with Human Freedom* 1.7, in *Works*, 449.
62. Calvin, *Institutes of the Christian Religion* 3.23.6 (Battles, 2:954).
63. See Pike, "Divine Omniscience and Voluntary Action," 27–46.
64. See A. Plantinga, *God, Freedom, and Evil*, 67–73.
65. Craig, "Middle-Knowledge View," 127.
66. Craig, *Only Wise God*, 70.
67. As Hunt puts it, "The future is *epistemically* settled in the divine mind: but it does *not* follow that the future is *causally* settled in any way that conflicts with human freedom." Hunt, "Simple-Foreknowledge Response [to Boyd]," 53 (emphasis original).

As Plantinga argues, "The claim that divine omniscience [including exhaustive foreknowledge] is incompatible with human freedom seems to be based upon confusion."[68] Particularly, some mistakenly confuse the necessity of consequence with the necessity of the thing consequent (the fallacy of necessity)—that is, some confuse the following two claims:

1. *Necessarily*, whatever God believes will occur.
2. Whatever God believes will *necessarily* occur.

Since God cannot be wrong, it is *necessarily* true that whatever God believes will occur, but it does not follow that whatever God believes will *necessarily* occur. What is necessary is not the event God foreknows itself but merely the fact that God will not be wrong about the future—it is necessary that what God foreknows is consistent with what will occur.[69]

To see the crucial difference between the two claims, consider the following example. It is *necessarily* true that if Henry is unmarried, Henry is a bachelor. However, it is *not* true that Henry is *necessarily* a bachelor. Henry could become married (and thus no longer be a bachelor).[70] Likewise, it is *necessarily* true that if God knows Jones will mow his lawn on Saturday, Jones will mow his lawn on Saturday. However, is not *necessarily* true that Jones will mow his lawn on Saturday because Jones could decide to refrain from mowing his lawn on Saturday. Just as a bachelor could become married, Jones could decide not to mow his lawn, and if Jones were to do so, it would simply be the case that God would have believed differently.[71] This does not amount to affirming that God's past belief could be changed but affirms instead that if Jones *were to decide* to refrain from mowing his lawn, God *would have* believed differently.[72]

68. A. Plantinga, *God, Freedom, and Evil*, 67.

69. As Craig explains, "What is impossible is the *conjunction* of God's belief" that *x* will happen and *x* *not* happening (Craig, "Middle-Knowledge Response [to Hunt]," 112). "From God's knowledge that I shall do *x*, it does not follow that I must do *x* but only that I shall do *x*. That is in no way incompatible with my doing *x* freely." Craig, "Middle-Knowledge," 127.

70. A. Plantinga, *God, Freedom, and Evil*, 66 (emphasis original).

71. Another way to see the modal fallacy involved in this issue is by considering the following fallacious argument:

1. *Necessarily*, if I know you are sitting in a chair, then you are sitting in a chair.
2. I know you are sitting in a chair.
3. Therefore, you are *necessarily* sitting in a chair.

Premise 3 is obviously false. My knowing you are sitting in a chair does not render it necessary that you are sitting. You could be standing instead. Similarly, God's knowing what you will decide does not render your decision necessary.

72. See A. Plantinga, *God, Freedom, and Evil*, 70–71. Some argue, however, that while there may be no logical necessity here, there is some kind of "accidental necessity" of the past,

Along these lines, William of Ockham (1287–1347) argued that divine knowledge of "all future contingents" does not render what God knows to itself be "necessary."[73] Instead, although God foreknows something, "it is still possible that it will never have been true. And in that case there is a capacity for its opposite."[74] Put simply, "just as it contingently will be, so God *contingently* knows that it will be."[75] Ockham believed that the claim that God knows "all future contingents" could "be proved by means of the authorities of the Bible and the Saints."[76] Yet he also frankly explained, "I do not know how to describe the way [in which God has foreknowledge]."[77]

I also do not claim to know just how God knows the future, but I agree with Uche Anizor that the "believer must allow" what "Scripture clearly affirms" to "set the agenda and dictate what is plausible and what is not."[78] It is widely recognized that as long as doing so involves no contradiction, there is no problem with maintaining *that* something is the case relative to God (especially if biblically warranted) without claiming to know *how* something is the case relative to God. Christian theists affirm *that* God is eternal, but no one knows precisely *how* it is that God is eternal. Christian theists affirm *that* God is omnipotent, but many questions remain regarding *how* it is that God is omnipotent. Likewise, as long as doing so involves no contradiction, one can cogently affirm *that* God possesses exhaustive definite foreknowledge without claiming to know just *how* God possesses such foreknowledge (cf. Ps. 139:6). In this regard, while Paul Helm and I disagree regarding the nature of divine foreknowledge, I agree with Helm that Christians should "hold" the biblical "witness as a set of fixed points,"

---

or "temporal necessity"; that is, they believe it is impossible that one's decision could be free such that were one to do A instead of B, God would have known that, and if one were to do B instead of A, God would have known that instead. The debate is ongoing, but I agree with those philosophers who maintain there is no definitive reason to believe this is impossible. Specifically, the Ockhamist "denies that propositions reporting God's past beliefs about the future need be accidentally necessary," while "Molinists deny the claim that accidental necessity is closed under entailment of contingent propositions." Edward Wierenga adds that the "central feature of Molinism seems independent of any of the premises of the argument" regarding the accidental necessity of the past (Wierenga, "Omniscience," 140). On the Ockhamist avenue, see A. Plantinga, "On Ockham's Way Out," 235–69. On the Molinist avenue, see Craig, "Middle-Knowledge," 129–32.

73. Ockham, *Predestination* 90.
74. Ockham, *Predestination* 90. See, e.g., A. Plantinga, "Ockham's Way Out." Cf. Anselm, *De Concordia* 1.7, in *Works*, 447–49.
75. Ockham, *Predestination* 91 (emphasis added). Likewise, Brunner claims, "God knows the future as something contingent." Brunner, *Christian Doctrine of God*, 268.
76. Ockham, *Predestination* 90.
77. Ockham, *Predestination* 90.
78. Anizor, *How to Read Theology*, 142.

recognizing that we might not be able to demonstrate how some parts of Scripture "cohere" but might "have to be content with showing that the ideas are not inconsistent."[79] Craig goes further, contending that even if one cannot show how foreknowledge and human freedom are compatible, if "Scripture teaches both," then one should "hold the biblical doctrines in tension rather than deny the Scripture's clear teaching that God does know the future."[80]

Models of Exhaustive Definite Foreknowledge

In my view, an Ockhamist-like defense of the compatibility of exhaustive definite foreknowledge and creaturely libertarian free will is sufficient. Beyond this, however, some existing models of how this *might* work warrant consideration. The approach of simple foreknowledge maintains that God somehow knows the future either directly as present to him or *as if it were* present to him. Advocates of this view often note that the conceptual problem is not that God knows with certainty what I will do but that he knows what I will do *beforehand*. If God's knowledge somehow transcends time as we know it, however, this conceptual problem disappears.

Accordingly, some advocates maintain that God is timelessly eternal such that all of history is "present" to God and God knows "the future" via direct apprehension. Some contend this resolves the "timing problem," while others claim the problem remains relative to "the past truth of God's eternal knowledge of propositions about our future."[81] Others argue that simple foreknowledge is a viable model even apart from affirming divine timelessness.[82] Yet it is not clear *just how* God possesses such foreknowledge.

Another approach maintains that God possesses middle knowledge, which includes knowledge of what anyone *would* freely decide (in the libertarian sense) in any particular situation, including situations that do not come to pass (*counterfactual* situations).[83] If God knows what anyone would freely choose to do in *every* possible situation, then God can take that knowledge into

---

79. Helm, "Augustinian-Calvinist View," 164.

80. Craig, "Middle-Knowledge," 126.

81. Wierenga, "Omniscience," 140. Likewise, Linda Zagzebski contends that divine timeless knowledge raises a "dilemma exactly parallel to" the purported necessity of the past. Zagzebski, *Dilemma of Freedom and Foreknowledge*, 61.

82. So Hunt, "Simple-Foreknowledge View."

83. The middle knowledge approach is usually called Molinism, named after Luis de Molina and, according to many scholars, held by Jacob Arminius as well. See Molina, *On Divine Foreknowledge*. Cf. MacGregor, *Luis de Molina*, 79–104. Regarding Arminius's view, see R. Muller, *God, Creation and Providence*, 155–66. See also Stanglin and McCall, *Jacob Arminius*, 64–69.

account in his own decision-making.[84] Then God could foreknow the entire future by "adding" his own decisions to his knowledge of what any creature would *freely* do in any given situation (alongside his perfect knowledge of all other factors). This is perfectly compatible with the libertarian free will of creatures because what creatures would *freely* do in any given situation is not itself determined by God.[85] It is not up to God whether creatures *freely* decide to do as God prefers in any given situation, and the timeline of history ("the world") that God brings about is limited to timelines consistent with the (good and bad) free decisions of creatures.

Questions arise, however, regarding God's usage of middle knowledge to providentially govern history, relative to the problem of evil and otherwise (see chap. 6). Further, critics question *how* God could possess middle knowledge: *How* could God know what creatures who do not yet exist and may never exist would do in any situation?[86] However, the question *how* does not defeat the view. As noted earlier, one may cogently affirm *that* something is the case without knowing precisely *how* it is the case. Much more should be said about this and other approaches.[87] The debate over various conceptions of divine

84. For more on middle knowledge, see Flint, *Divine Providence*, 11–71. Cf. Perszyk, *Molinism*.

85. While Boyd claims Molinism entails that the future is settled in some way that excludes creaturely libertarian freedom, Craig explains that Boyd mistakenly "equates God's *settling* something with God's *determining* or *controlling* it." Craig, "Middle-Knowledge Response [to Boyd]," 57 (emphasis original).

86. This objection is known as the grounding objection, which maintains that (absent determinism) there appears to be no ground or "truth-maker" of "'would' counterfactuals of creaturely freedom" (Boyd, "Open-Theist Response to Craig," 131). Cf. Davison, "Craig on the Grounding Objection to Middle Knowledge," 365–69; O'Connor, "Impossibility of Middle Knowledge," 2:45–67. Some Molinists suggest divine conceptualism in this regard. Alternatively, Craig and others respond that there is no good reason to think such counterfactuals need truth-makers (Craig, "Middle Knowledge," 2:81, 83). Alvin Plantinga comments, "It seems to me much clearer that some counterfactuals of freedom are at least possibly true than that the truth of propositions must, in general, be grounded" via a truth-maker (A. Plantinga, "Self-Profile," 374). Thomas Flint adds, "For every version of the grounding objection of which I am aware, some elaboration of the 'Are So!' or of the 'So What?' response can be made by a Molinist" (Flint, "Divine Providence," 281). Cf. Craig, "Ducking Friendly Fire," 161–66. Appealing to the principle of bivalence (i.e., any proposition is either true or false), Craig argues further, "If there are counterfactual truths, then an omniscient being must know them" (Craig, "Middle-Knowledge," 137). However, there is an ongoing debate over Boyd's claim that what "will" and "will not" occur in the future are contraries, not contradictories such that open theism does not deny the principle of bivalence. On this, see Hess, "Open Future Square of Opposition," 573–87; MacGregor, "Neo-Molinist Square Collapses," 195–206; Hess, "Has Molina Collapsed the Neo-Molinist Square?," 195–206.

87. For examples of alternative approaches to divine foreknowledge, see Jonathan Kvanvig's deliberative model, which he calls "philosophical arminianism" (Kvanvig, *Destiny and Deliberation*, 94–177), Linda Zagzebski's fourth spatial dimension approach (Zagzebski, *Dilemma*

foreknowledge is far more technical and nuanced than I can do justice to in this brief section. For our purposes, suffice it to say that both models meet their fair share of criticism, but competent advocates argue that there are no logical or ontological defeaters of their approach.

Other promising models may yet emerge, and perhaps humans are not currently in a position to know *how* God knows what he knows. For now, while stopping short of claiming to know that this is the way God knows the future, I personally find middle knowledge to be a plausible and helpful approach. Indeed, some biblical passages appear to support the claim that God has middle knowledge—that God knows what creatures *would* do in situations that never actually come about (counterfactual situations).[88]

To consider just one example, in Jeremiah 38:17–18, Jeremiah tells Zedekiah, "Thus says the LORD, the God of hosts, the God of Israel, If you will only surrender to the officials of the king of Babylon, then your life shall be spared, and this city shall not be burned with fire, and you and your house shall live. But if you do not surrender to the officials of the king of Babylon, then this city shall be handed over to the Chaldeans, and they shall burn it with fire, and you yourself shall not escape from their hand" (cf. 21:8–10; 38:2–3). In this case, God reveals to Zedekiah *precisely* what would happen to Zedekiah, his household, and the city *if he would* surrender and *if he would not*. Zedekiah chooses not to surrender, and precisely what God predicted occurs. In order for God to know with certainty just what would have occurred if Zedekiah had surrendered (e.g., his life and that of his household spared), however, God would have to know what the many humans involved *would* have done in that situation. This looks like one example of God possessing middle knowledge (see also 1 Sam. 23:8–13; Matt. 11:23; 1 Cor. 2:8).[89]

Further, something like middle knowledge might be at work in Romans 8:29–30, which states, "For those whom he foreknew he also predestined to be conformed to the image of his Son, in order that he might be the first-born within a large family. And those whom he predestined he also called;

---

of *Freedom and Foreknowledge*, 172–79), and T. Ryan Byerly's time-ordering account (Byerly, *Mechanics of Divine Foreknowledge and Providence*, 73–121).

88. Molina himself maintained, "It is clear from Sacred Scripture that the supreme God has certain cognition of some future contingents that depend on human free choice, but that neither have existed nor ever will exist in reality" (Molina, *On Divine Foreknowledge*, Disputation 49.9 [Freddoso, 116]). So also Craig, "Middle-Knowledge," 123, 140. For an interesting recent proposal regarding the mechanism by which God could know true counterfactuals of freedom (building on William Alston's direct acquaintaince model of divine knowledge), see Mooney, "How God Knows Counterfactuals of Freedom."

89. For a biblical case for middle knowledge, see Keathley, *Salvation and Sovereignty*, chap. 1. See also Laing, *Middle Knowledge*, chap. 9.

and those whom he called he also justified; and those whom he justified he also glorified." This passage might be read as meaning that God foreknew (*proginōskō*) what humans *would* freely do, *then* "predestined" (*proorizō*, "decided beforehand") what would actually occur by deciding what he would do in a way that took account of the free human decisions he foreknew—and then providentially executed this plan in history. Whether middle knowledge or some other position turns out to be true, I am convinced that exhaustive definite foreknowledge is affirmed by Scripture.

Some Questions and Implications

A number of questions and implications warrant further discussion, but space permits only brief consideration of a few relevant issues.[90] What follows focuses on the significance of omniscience relative to the intimacy with which God knows us and the confidence we can have in God's wisdom relative to the future.

Regarding the former, Linda Zagzebski maintains, "If God is omniscient, he must know every aspect of his creation, including the conscious states of his creatures" (cf. Ps. 139).[91] In other words, God must possess omnisubjectivity, which Zagzebski defines as "the property of consciously grasping with perfect accuracy and completeness the first-person perspective of every conscious being."[92] R. T. Mullins adds, "Omnisubjectivity is the perfect cognitive capacity to engage in maximal empathy."[93] Zagzebski explains that as omnisubjective, God not only must know "that Mary feels frustrated or sees the color of the paint" but also must somehow "know what it is like for" Mary to feel frustrated and/or see a particular color in a specific instance as well as "know what it is like for [all] conscious creatures to have their distinctive sensations and emotions, moods, and attitudes."[94]

If Zagzebski is right about this, then divine omniscience itself requires some kind of divine passibility that allows for maximal empathy, complementing the model outlined in chapter 2.[95] Yet to be consistent with other biblical claims about God, one must carefully qualify that God does not indiscriminately feel the feelings of all others (as appears to be the case in Charles Hartshorne's process theology) and perhaps otherwise qualify divine empathy to avoid

90. On questions regarding Christ's omniscience, see chap. 7, under the heading "Tenet 4."
91. Zagzebski, "Omnisubjectivity," 231.
92. Zagzebski, "Omnisubjectivity," 232.
93. Mullins, "Why Can't the Impassible God Suffer?," 10. Cf. Mullins, *God and Emotions*.
94. Zagzebski, "Omnisubjectivity," 232.
95. See Zagzebski, *Omnisubjectivity*, 45.

moral or other objections. God does not feel the feelings of the sadist, for instance. God knows what it is like for the sadist to have sadistic feelings, but God rejects empathizing with these and any other evil feelings.[96]

Here God's perfect knowledge of every conscious being's first-person perspective should be distinguished from knowledge *de se*—that is, knowledge "of oneself" that might be expressed in terms of the indexical "I." For example, "I" (John) feel hungry now because it is past lunchtime and "I" have not eaten yet. As omnisubjective, God would know not only that John feels hungry now but also precisely what it is like for John to feel hungry now—possessing "a conscious representation" of how John feels from John's perspective. Yet God would not affirm *of himself* "I (God) feel hungry now" or "I have not eaten yet." In Zagzebki's words, God has a "dual perspective," possessing a conscious representation of others' perspectives while retaining his own unique perspective as God.[97] God knows exactly what it feels like to be each person but without being limited to anyone else's single first-person perspective. God, then, takes into account the subjective viewpoints and feelings of all others in a way no one else could. As Zagzebski puts it relative to prayer and providence, "A being who has total empathetic identification with your subjective viewpoint has a much deeper grasp of what is good for you than one who does not." This has "radical consequences for the way God hears prayers," since "God would know your prayers the way you know them, when you first have the desire, then possibly struggle for the words, and perhaps use the wrong words" (cf. Rom. 8:26–27).[98]

Some claim, however, that if God has exhaustive definite foreknowledge, God could not experience genuinely responsive emotions like grief or joy. This mistakenly supposes that emotional experience requires the element of surprise. I have read the Gospel accounts of Christ's crucifixion countless times, but they still move me. Prior knowledge does not preclude emotional reaction.[99] Here it is helpful to distinguish between theoretical knowledge and experiential knowledge. While God's knowledge of the future is infallible, it is theoretical rather than experiential. Having theoretical knowledge of the

96. This follows from the fact that God rejects evil entirely and summarily. See chap. 6.

97. As Zagzebski explains, "When an omnisubjective being acquires a representation of Mary's conscious state of seeing red, he sees red as if he sees through Mary's eyes, but since he is aware of that state as a copy of Mary's state, there is no problem that he would be led to make judgments of the world from his own perspective based on conscious states that are copies of Mary's perspective. . . . He has a dual perspective." Zagzebski, "Omnisubjectivity," 242.

98. Zagzebski, "Omisubjectivity," 245.

99. One may have a loved one diagnosed with a terminal illness and thus know they will soon die but still feel grief when death occurs.

future is not the same as experiencing it as present.[100] Possessing knowledge of all facts (past, present, and future) is not the same as having all experiences as one's own *actual* experience.

Further, if God is omnisubjective (in a properly qualified way), God could vicariously enjoy (when appropriate) the surprise of his beloved humans, analogous to the way I might enjoy the surprise and delight of my son when he opens a Christmas present. Whereas a timeless God could not know what time it is "now," if God is analogically temporal (as argued in chap. 3), then God's knowledge of the present—of what is happening "now"—would change as the world changes. This is consistent with omniscience because God would have exhaustive and definite *theoretical* knowledge of all times (past, present, and future) while having experiential knowledge of the past and experiencing the present as present.

Conversely, if God lacks exhaustive definite foreknowledge and consistently grants libertarian free will such that creatures can will otherwise than God ideally desires, how could God *know* with certainty that he would accomplish his central purpose of love relationship with creatures or that evil would be defeated and not arise again in the eschaton, perhaps repeatedly?[101] If God does not know with certainty how things will turn out and refrains from determining creaturely wills, might God's plans and commands ultimately turn out to be unsuccessful (now or in the eschaton)? Might God's decisions end up allowing far more evil than God would have allowed had he known better? God might have made better decisions and given better commands if he had perfect foreknowledge of the ramifications of his decisions and commands rather than merely knowledge of *possible* ramifications. If God lacks

100. If so, God could make his decisions "prior to" creation (perhaps via middle knowledge) and also make those decisions in time (when situations arise), with the caveat that what God decides as he experiences the events always matches perfectly with what he decided beforehand via his perfect foreknowledge (without conflating the two). Even given open theism, wherein God perfectly anticipates all possibilities, God could theoretically make all his decisions beforehand by deciding what he would do in every *possible* situation. Yet, he would not foreknow which situations will actualize and thus could calculate only ranges of possible ramifications of decisions he might make.

101. Regarding the latter, open theists could maintain that redeemed humans achieve a stage of "perfected freedom," which Kevin Timpe defines as having formed a character by their own previous *free* decisions such that they cannot sin (Timpe, *Free Will in Philosophical Theology*, 83–101). Boyd affirms a similar view in *Satan and the Problem of Evil*, 190–91. However, this seems to require controversial views such as *postmortem* opportunity and moral growth (e.g., purgatory) (Cf. Boyd, *Satan and the Problem of Evil*, 381–85.) Regarding the former, Johannes Grössl and Leigh Vicens make a convincing case that if open theism is true and God grants humans libertarian freedom, God could not guarantee at creation "His central purpose in creating the world, that of creating a loving community between Himself and His creatures." Grössl and Vicens, "Closing the Door on Limited-Risk Open Theism," 485.

foreknowledge, might God have chosen not to create humans had he known what humans would do? If God lacks foreknowledge, did Christ really die for *you* and for *me*, specifically, or only for some people who *might* exist? Did God even know for sure you and I would be born?

Whereas these questions present significant problems for open theism, if God possesses exhaustive definite foreknowledge, we have grounds for confidence that God can know with certainty that evil will be eradicated once and for all—never to arise again—while perpetually granting creatures libertarian free will. We have grounds for confidence that God knows with certainty what is preferable in *every* situation such that God commands what is preferable in light of *all* factors. If God knows the future, God indeed foreknew *every* person and chose to die for *you* and *me* specifically; indeed, from all eternity, God elected (in an indeterministic sense) each one who would *freely* accept his love. If so, God truly chose to create *this* world, including each of us specifically, while knowing full well the unfathomable cost to himself, not merely hoping but being certain that "the sufferings of this present time are not worth comparing with the glory about to be revealed to us" (Rom. 8:18; cf. 2 Cor. 4:17).

Put simply, if God has exhaustive definite foreknowledge, one has no difficulty consistently affirming that:

1. God knows with certainty that sin and evil will never rise again.
2. God knows with certainty which course of action is preferable for all concerned relative to every situation.
3. God foreknew you and me and every other person, and Christ chose to die for you and me specifically.
4. God chose to create this world, despite knowing the enormous cost to himself, and can guarantee he made the right decision in doing so.

Sin and evil did not catch the God of Scripture by surprise. Rather, Scripture suggests that before the foundation of the world, there was a covenant within the Trinity (in at least the minimal sense of a jointly willed plan) regarding divine actions in the plan of salvation, including the distinct salvific roles of the trinitarian persons. This covenant of redemption *implicitly* appears in Scripture in numerous ways. For example, Scripture repeatedly teaches that the Father willed that the Son give himself for us—Christ "gave himself for our sins to set us free from the present evil age, according to the will of our God and Father" (Gal. 1:4; cf. John 5:30; 6:38–40; 17:4–12). Yet Scripture also teaches that the Son willed that he give *himself* for us—the Son lays down his life of his "own accord," consistent with the "command from" the "Father" (John 10:18; cf. Gal. 2:20; Eph. 5:2).

That this willing of the Father and the Son regarding the Son's sacrifice involves a *precreation* agreement or covenant is suggested by the fact that the Son's giving himself was itself central to the plan of salvation from *before* the foundation of the world (Acts 2:23; 1 Pet. 1:20; Rev. 13:8), which the NT repeatedly refers to as the "mystery" of the gospel and "God's wisdom, secret and hidden, which God decreed before the ages [*pro tōn aiōnōn*] for our glory" (1 Cor. 2:7; cf. Rom. 16:25–26; Col. 1:26) relative to "the hope of eternal life that God, who never lies, promised before the ages began [*pro chronōn aiōniōn*]" (Titus 1:2; cf. 2 Tim. 1:9). This mystery includes God's election "before the foundation of the world" according to "a plan for the fullness of time, to gather up all things in him, things in heaven and things on earth . . . according to the purpose [or plan] of him who accomplishes all things according to his counsel and will" (Eph. 1:4, 10–11; cf. Rom. 8:28–30; 2 Thess. 2:13; 2 Tim. 1:9; 1 Pet. 1:2). This is "the plan of the mystery hidden for ages [*apo tōn aiōnōn*] in God who created all things," the "eternal [*aiōnōn*] purpose that he has carried out in Christ Jesus our Lord" (Eph. 3:9, 11).[102]

In this regard, however, some claim that "the idea that God foresees future free decisions makes the problem of suffering particularly vexing because it gives God the perfect way to prevent it."[103] However, even without foreknowledge, an all-powerful God with perfect knowledge of the past and present could anticipate and prevent any instance of evil a millisecond before it would occur. If there is a morally sufficient reason why God does not prevent an evil event just before it would occur, such a morally sufficient reason would apply whether or not God possesses foreknowledge. Recognizing this, the open theist John Sanders writes, "It has become clear to me that presentism (openness) itself does not contribute much in the way of help in dealing with the question of evil," and "early statements of openness overstated its value."[104]

Why, some ask further, would God create those whom he foreknew would do evil? While the problem of evil will be discussed specifically in chapter 6, here it is worth noting that God not creating a person *because*

---

102. For numerous lines of biblical evidence supporting the covenant of redemption, see Fesko, *Trinity and the Covenant of Redemption*, 51–124, 132–41.

103. Rice, *Suffering and the Search for Meaning*, 91.

104. Hall and Sanders, *Does God Have a Future?*, 40. David Basinger adds, "A God with MK [middle knowledge] knew before creation what evil he would cause or allow while a God without MK knows now what evil he is causing or allowing." Basinger, *Case for Freewill Theism*, 92.

he foreknew they would do evil *might* (1) have been against God's character and/or moral commitments or (2) have led to worse results and/or have been less preferable in some other way. Here it is crucial to recognize that if God consistently grants creatures libertarian free will to impact the world (as I argue in subsequent chapters), then God cannot bring about just any world he wants. If God establishes and maintains a *consistent* order of cause and effect, as I believe consequential freedom and the flourishing of love require (more on this in subsequent chapters), then any creature's existence is itself bound up with countless antecedent factors (including all the decisions of any ancestors) and holds potentially enormous ramifications for future events—particularly given "the butterfly effect."[105] Thus, while one might think it would be simple for God to make it such that some evil person never existed, we do not know if that option was available to God without ramifications that were worse overall—relative to the entirety of history. Moreover, for all we know, God not creating a person—even the devil himself—*solely because* he foreknew that person would exercise freedom in opposition to God's ideal desires *might* compromise the kind of creaturely freedom to which God has committed himself for the good of the universe. Although some of God's decisions unavoidably affect who exists, it *might* be that God cannot exclude someone's existence for the *sole* purpose of denying their ability to depart from his ideal will without contravening his own commitments and/or perfect moral character of love (per impossibile).

One other possibility is that different worlds (meaning the entirety of all events in a given timeline) contain mutually exclusive values that are "incommensurable in the sense that there is no common measure, no fixed 'ratio' as it were, by which they can be measured against one another" to compare their overall value.[106] If so, perhaps God chose to actualize *this* world (i.e., this timeline of history) because of *this* world's unique, incommensurable values. Perhaps each world God could actualize without the devil in it would not include countless numbers of creatures of incommensurable value to God, including you. This scenario would indicate a profound aspect of divine election—an indeterministic conception of the riches of God's unfathomable love and grace in that, despite the immeasurable cost to himself, God "chose us in Christ before the foundation of the world" (Eph. 1:4). As I say elsewhere, "Perhaps similar to the way a mother chooses to endure the pain of childbirth for the joy of her child, God considered this world to be worth

---

105. Think of movies like *It's a Wonderful Life* and *Back to the Future*.
106. Hasker, *Triumph of God over Evil*, 79.

the cost in order to give us the joys of eternal life, which may comport with Paul's imagery of the 'birth pangs' of 'the whole creation' (Rom. 8:22)."[107]

We may not know exactly why God does what he does, but if God has foreknowledge, we can be confident that he makes his decisions with full knowledge of what is good and preferable, all things considered. On this topic, I sometimes ask my students whether they would prefer a physician who knows only that a treatment for an illness *might* resolve their malady and what side effects *might* occur or a physician who knows with certainty just what treatment will resolve the malady and what side effects will occur. Invariably, they choose the second physician—for good reason. I believe the God of Scripture is like the second physician and is thus repeatedly praised in Scripture as the all-wise one, who always knows, wants, and does what is best for all concerned.

The God of Scripture not only knows you and everything about you but also knows the end from the beginning and everything in between. This ensures that his decisions are not unwittingly reckless and potentially ill-fated but perfectly wise and good and that his promises can be trusted—he knows what is best and will certainly accomplish what he has declared (Isa. 46:9–10). Evil will one day be no more, and whoever trusts in him will live forever in perfect bliss—all injustices will be set right, for all creation and forevermore.

If God knows your heart, there is no sense pretending you can hide anything from him; God "understands every plan and thought" (1 Chron. 28:9) and "knows the secrets of the heart" (Ps. 44:21; cf. Jer. 20:12). The God of Scripture knows you better than you know yourself and perfectly empathizes *with* you. Why, then, should we pray and petition God if God "your Father knows what you need before you ask him" (Matt. 6:8), as Jesus explains? This question will be taken up in subsequent chapters after some other important factors have been addressed. For now, it is good news that God knows us perfectly because God knows what is best for us, and even though he knows everything about you and me—even that which may be unlovable—God loves us anyway. Indeed, God loves you and me more than we can imagine.

There is much more that we do not know (and perhaps cannot know) about God's infinite knowledge. Yet pondering the depths and majesty of God's perfect knowledge evokes praise and worship. As Paul writes,

O the depth of the riches and wisdom and knowledge of God! How unsearchable are his judgments and how inscrutable his ways!

"For who has known the mind of the Lord?
Or who has been his counselor?" (Rom. 11:33–34)

107. Peckham, *Theodicy of Love*, 143.

Conclusion

This chapter addressed the question of whether God knows everything, including the future, concluding that the God of Scripture is omniscient and outlining a case that God's omniscience includes exhaustive definite foreknowledge. Specifically, this chapter outlined a case that (1) Scripture teaches that God possesses exhaustive definite foreknowledge, (2) there is no apparent logical or ontological contradiction involved in affirming both that God has such foreknowledge and that he consistently grants libertarian free will to creatures, and (3) it is good news that God knows everything that can be known and has *certain* knowledge of all future occurrences. Chapter 5 turns to the issues of divine omnipotence and providence, including the debate over determinism.

Five

The Almighty Sovereign Who Creates, Sustains, and Covenants

Omnipotence and Providence

"God is sovereign," the youth pastor taught his middle-school group. "That means he controls everything that happens." One puzzled middle schooler replied, "So God was in control when my dog died? Why would God kill my dog?" The youth pastor replied, "That's a tough one. But sometimes God lets us go through hard times so that we're prepared for even more difficult things in the future. I remember how hard it was when my dog died. But going through that helped me deal with an even more difficult time later when my grandma died. Does that make sense?" The middle schooler thought for a bit, then replied, "So God killed my dog to prepare me for when he's going to kill my grandma?"[1]

The way we think about God's power and providence holds massive implications. Most Christian theists agree that God is all-powerful (omnipotent), meaning that God can do anything that is logically possible and consistent

---

1. Marc Cortez shared this on his *Everyday Theology* blog in June 2013, which is no longer accessible. Some of Cortez's original post is quoted here: https://nleaven.wordpress.com/2013/06/19/3-mistakes-we-make-when-talking-about-the-sovereignty-of-god.

with God's nature. However, Christian theists offer differing understandings of divine providence and sovereignty. As noted earlier, theistic determinists believe that God exercises power in a way that determines all occurrences. Conversely, indeterminists believe that God does not causally determine history.

This chapter focuses on the debates over divine omnipotence and providence, addressing questions such as, Can God do anything? Can he bring about any state of affairs? Is "omnipotence" a coherent idea? Does God always get what he wants? The implications for worship and prayer are far-reaching. If God controls *everything*, can prayer actually make a difference? If God lacks the power to have control over situations, does it make sense to pray to him to bring something about?

The Question of Omnipotence

Divine Power in Scripture

From beginning to end, Scripture emphasizes God's awe-inspiring power as the Creator. "In the beginning," Genesis 1:1 declares, "God created the heavens and the earth" (NASB). Indeed, "By the word of the LORD the heavens were made, / and all their host by the breath of his mouth" (Ps. 33:6). Additionally, "the worlds were prepared by the word of God" (Heb. 11:3). Creation itself manifests God's power: "Ever since the creation of the world his eternal power and divine nature, invisible though they are, have been understood and seen through the things he has made" (Rom. 1:20). Accordingly, in Revelation 4:11, God is praised as worthy of "glory and honor and power, for you created all things, and by your will they existed and were created."

The God of Scripture not only is the Creator of all but also "sustains all things by his powerful word" (Heb. 1:3).[2] Indeed, "all things have been created through him [the Son] and for him," and "in him all things hold together" (Col. 1:16–17; cf. John 1:3).[3] Throughout Scripture, God repeatedly acts in or on the world, performing special divine actions like parting waters, sending fire from heaven, shutting lions' mouths, preserving men unharmed in a fiery furnace, and even raising people from the dead. In the Gospels alone, among many other miracles, Jesus turns water into wine, heals withered hands, cures leprosy, gives sight to the blind, restores a severed ear, heals various other maladies and illnesses, casts out demons, walks on water, calms storms, multiplies food for crowds, raises the dead, and himself rises from the grave.

---

2. This verse refers to the Son. On the Son's divinity, see chap. 7.

3. F. F. Bruce interprets this as teaching that Christ "is the sustainer of the universe and the unifying principle of its life." Bruce, *Epistles to the Colossians*, 66.

Further, according to Scripture, God possesses maximal power. "Nothing is too hard for" the "great and mighty God whose name is the LORD of hosts, great in counsel and mighty in deed," who "showed signs and wonders in the land of Egypt, and to this day in Israel and among all humankind" (Jer. 32:17–20; cf. 32:27; Job 42:2; Ps. 147:5). Likewise, an angel tells Mary, "Nothing will be impossible with God" (Luke 1:37). And Jesus teaches, "For God all things are possible" (Matt. 19:26; Mark 10:27; cf. Mark 9:23; 14:36). Further, Ephesians 1:19 describes "the immeasurable greatness of his power for us who believe, according to the working of his great power."

Indeed, Scripture explicitly calls God all-powerful. God himself states in Revelation 1:8, "I am the Alpha and the Omega . . . who is and who was and who is to come, the Almighty" (*pantokratōr*, literally "all [*pan*] powerful [*krateō*]").[4] God is also repeatedly called "Almighty" (*pantokratōr*) elsewhere (2 Cor. 6:18; Rev. 16:14; 19:15; 21:22), often in the context of praise and worship, including thanking the

> Lord God Almighty,
>   who are and who were,
>   for you have taken your great power
>   and begun to reign. (Rev. 11:17; so also 4:8; 15:3; 16:7; 19:6–7)

While Scripture teaches that God is all-powerful, Scripture also explicitly states that there are some things God cannot do. God "cannot deny himself" (2 Tim. 2:13), and "God cannot be tempted by evil" (James 1:13). Accordingly, God "never lies" (Titus 1:2; cf. Num. 23:19), and God's promises are unchangeable, for "it is impossible that God would prove false" (Heb. 6:18; cf. Ps. 89:34). Other instances indicate God does not exercise all his power but operates within some restrictions. For example, while Jesus prays, "Father, for you all things are possible" (Mark 14:36), he also prays, "My Father, if it is possible, let this cup pass from me" (Matt. 26:39; cf. Mark 14:35). In some sense, then, *all things* are possible for God, and in another sense, some things might not be possible even for God. If (in some sense) "all things are possible" for God, then God must possess the power to do all things that are intrinsically possible. Anything that is not possible for God, then, could be due not to any lack of divine power but to some other factor (or factors). In the case of Christ's prayer in Gethsemane, while it was intrinsically possible for Christ to avoid the cross (cf. John 10:18), it was not possible insofar as God was to keep his commitment to save sinners while remaining perfectly just (cf. Rom. 3:25–26).

---

4. BDAG 755; L&N 138.

Along similar lines, Mark 6:5 reports that Jesus "could do no deed of power" in his hometown, "except that he laid his hands on a few sick people and cured them." Yet how could it be that he who "sustains *all things* by his powerful word" (Heb. 1:3) could be restricted from performing some miracles? Matthew 13:58 declares this was "because of their unbelief" (cf. Mark 6:6). However, unbelief could restrict the action of the all-powerful one *only* if God has somehow committed himself to acting (or refraining from acting) in a way that is tied to human faith. In this regard, Jesus himself explicitly ties what "can be done" to faith and prayer. In Mark 9:22, a man whose son is afflicted by an evil spirit pleads with Jesus, "If you are able to do anything, have pity on us and help us." Jesus replies, "If you are able!—All things can be done for the one who believes" (9:23; cf. Eph. 1:19).[5] Then the man cries out, "I believe; help my unbelief!" (Mark 9:24). When the disciples ask Jesus why they could not cast out this spirit, Jesus explains, "This kind can come out only through prayer" (9:29; cf. Matt. 17:20). Here, again, divine action could be restricted according to faith and prayer only if God commits himself to such restrictions.

If God's promises are unchangeable and "it is impossible that God would prove false" (Heb. 6:18), then (at least in some sense) God *cannot* do otherwise than he has promised. To the extent that God covenants or otherwise commits himself to do or refrain from doing something, God has thereby morally restricted his future action. If "God cannot deny himself" (2 Tim. 2:13) and "God cannot be tempted by evil" (James 1:13), it follows that divine action is restricted according to God's moral nature. While Scripture affirms that God is all-powerful (omnipotent), then, Scripture also indicates that God does not exercise all his power but operates (at least at *some* times) according to some restrictions—his commitments and moral nature. This raises further questions regarding divine providence. Before taking those up, however, we turn to questions about the coherence of divine omnipotence itself.

The Meaning of Divine Omnipotence

Some have claimed that if God is omnipotent, God should be able to do anything whatsoever.[6] However, many Christian theists have long understood omnipotence in a way that recognizes that even God cannot do things that would involve performing a contradiction. This is not because God lacks any

5. Interestingly, Paul's prayer in Eph. 1:19 refers to "the immeasurable greatness of his power *for us who believe*" (emphasis added).
6. Cf. Geach, "Omnipotence," 46–60. See also Peckham, *Theodicy of Love*, which this chapter draws on.

power but because bringing about two mutually exclusive states of affairs is impossible. As Thomas Aquinas puts it, "Power is said in reference to possible things" such that the "phrase, *God can do all things*, is rightly understood to mean that God can do all things that are possible."[7] Accordingly, "there does not fall under the scope of God's omnipotence anything that implies a contradiction."[8] As Richard Swinburne puts it, omnipotence entails only the "power to do what is possible."[9] This is consistent with the way Christ prays in Gethsemane, particularly the phrase "if it is possible, let this cup pass" (Matt. 26:39).

C. S. Lewis explains:

> Omnipotence means power to do all that is intrinsically possible, not to do the intrinsically impossible. You may attribute miracles to him, but not nonsense. This is no limit to his power. If you choose to say "God can give a creature free will and at the same time withhold free will from it," you have not succeeded in saying *anything* about God: meaningless combinations of words do not suddenly acquire meaning simply because we prefix to them the two other words "God can." . . . It is no more possible for God than for the weakest of his creatures to carry out both of two mutually exclusive alternatives; not because his power meets an obstacle, but because nonsense remains nonsense even when we talk it about God.[10]

Yet some raise so-called paradoxes of omnipotence, such as whether God can create a rock that he cannot lift. Whichever way one answers, there is something God cannot do. However, as George Mavrodes argues, this and other paradoxes of omnipotence fail "because they propose, as tests of God's power, putative tasks whose descriptions are self-contradictory. Such pseudo-tasks, not falling within the realm of possibility, are not objects of power at all. Hence the fact that they cannot be performed implies no limit on the power of God, and hence no defect in the doctrine of omnipotence."[11] As Thomas Morris states, the supposed dilemma here is "just an incoherent act-description."[12] J. P. Moreland and William Lane Craig add that if God is all-powerful, "'a stone too heavy for God to lift' describes as logically impossible a state of affairs as does 'a square triangle,' and thus it describes nothing at all."[13]

7. Thomas Aquinas, *Summa Theologiae* I.25.3.
8. Thomas Aquinas, *Summa Theologiae* I.25.4.
9. Swinburne, *Coherence of Theism*, 153.
10. Lewis, *Problem of Pain*, 18.
11. Mavrodes, "Some Puzzles Concerning Omnipotence," 223.
12. T. Morris, *Our Idea of God*, 74.
13. Moreland and Craig, *Philosophical Foundations*, 528.

Moreover, as seen earlier, Scripture itself teaches that there are some things God cannot do. God "cannot deny himself" (2 Tim. 2:13). God, then, cannot act in a way that is incompatible with his own essential nature. Further, if God "cannot be tempted by evil" (James 1:13) and never lies or breaks his promises (Titus 1:2; Heb. 6:17–18), it follows that God only does good and always acts consistently with his promises and commitments.[14] As Katherin Rogers puts it, "God cannot break His promises, because that would be wicked."[15] This does not count against divine omnipotence, however, because (Morris explains) "any action from which God is debarred by having made a promise is not, in virtue of its inaccessibility to him, thereby indicative of a lack of *power.*"[16] Although God does not lack any power, the way God might use his power is limited to that which is compatible with whatever God covenants and/or promises.

God's action, then, might be *morally* limited in a way consistent with his omnipotence. To say God is omnipotent, then, is to say God possesses the power to do anything that does not involve a contradiction, relative to his own perfectly consistent essential nature (cf. 2 Tim. 2:13) and any commitments God has made.[17] The almighty God of Scripture is a covenantal God who never

14. A chorus of voices in the Christian tradition maintain that, by nature, God *cannot* do evil. Some Christians maintain, however, that God *could* do evil but never *would.* Some maintain that love requires libertarian freedom relative to moral decisions, and if so, God must possess freedom to do evil. However, one might affirm that God *cannot* do evil and yet possesses morally significant libertarian freedom by adopting a sourcehood conception of libertarian freedom wherein (roughly put) one has libertarian freedom if one is the ultimate source of one's decisions. Even if God cannot do evil, God would nevertheless be the ultimate source of his free decisions because God is essentially good *of himself* (*a se*)—nothing external to God caused God's essential goodness. Whereas it seems that *creatures* must possess the ability to do evil in order to possess morally significant libertarian freedom (because they are not the ultimate source of their own nature), this would not be the case for the Creator. On this debate, see Timpe, *Free Will in Philosophical Theology,* 103–18; Loke, "Divine Omnipotence and Moral Perfection," 525–38; Yandell, "Divine Necessity and Divine Goodness," 313–34; Manis, "Could God Do Something Evil?," 209–23; Reichenbach, *Evil and a Good God,* 139–53. This discussion is inextricably linked to numerous other issues, such as the Euthyphro dilemma, divine command theory, and theories of moral praiseworthiness. On these, see the excellent work of Baggett and Walls, *Good God.*

15. Rogers, *Perfect Being Theology,* 99–100.

16. T. Morris, *Our Idea of God,* 75 (emphasis original). Regarding the "stone paradox," Morris suggests God could "just create an ordinary stone and promise never to move it, thereby rendering it true that he subsequently cannot lift it."

17. This has long been understood by theists and atheist philosophers alike. As atheist philosopher William Rowe put it, "God can do anything that is an absolute possibility *and not inconsistent with any of his attributes.* Since doing evil is inconsistent with being perfectly good, and since being perfectly good is a basic attribute of God, the fact that God cannot do evil will not conflict with the fact that he is omnipotent" (Rowe, *Philosophy of Religion,* 8 [emphasis original]). Anthony Kenny adds that omnipotence is "the possession of all logically possible

denies himself and always keeps his commitments. In this regard, Scott Hahn demonstrates that in biblical covenants God "bound himself by divine oath to bless his people and all nations."[18] Likewise, Michael Horton writes that God "has bound himself to us . . . by a free decision to enter into covenant with us," and "God is not free to act contrary to such covenantal guarantees."[19]

Notably, then, *if* God has decreed or covenanted that nature will operate according to some consistent "laws" of nature, then God himself is not free to act in any way that contravenes those "laws" of nature.[20] Further, *if* God grants creatures a kind of free will that is incompatible with God determining what those creatures do (libertarian free will), then God's exercise of power would be *self*-limited to that which is compatible with creaturely free will. Accordingly, if any particular good is contingent on the free decisions of creatures (in the libertarian sense), whether God can bring that particular good about would depend on the free decisions of creatures.[21] For example, putting aside for now whether one thinks this is the case, suppose that reciprocal love relationship is a good that requires both parties to exercise a kind of free will that cannot be determined by another. If so, even if I possessed the power to control the will of my wife, I could not make her love me. No matter how much power I possess, I could not—by myself—make it the case that my wife and I enjoy reciprocal love relationship. If love requires this kind of free will, even the omnipotent God could not unilaterally bring about reciprocal love relationship with creatures (or among creatures). This involves no deficit of divine power; no amount of power could bring about a good that is contingent on whether someone else cooperates *without being determined to do so.*[22]

Models of Omnipotence and Providence

Process theologians maintain, however, that creation is necessarily free such that even God cannot causally determine history. On this view, God has the

---

powers which it is logically possible for a being with the attributes of God to possess." Kenny, *God of the Philosophers*, 98.

18. Hahn, *Kinship by Covenant*, 334.

19. Horton, *Lord and Servant*, 33. In this regard, Karl Barth writes, "Loyally binding Himself to this work [of "creation, reconciliation and redemption"] He does not cease to be omnipotent in Himself as well as in this work" (*CD* II/1, 527). Emil Brunner adds, "God wills the independence of the creature" and thus "limits Himself" and "enters into the life of His creatures." Brunner, *Christian Doctrine of God*, 269.

20. See chap. 6.

21. If so, God can do "anything logically possible *that does not require creaturely cooperation.*" Rice, *Suffering and the Search for Meaning*, 52 (emphasis original).

22. As Brian Leftow explains, "It is not due to lack of power in anyone that nothing but its agent can cause an incompatibilistically free action." Leftow, "Omnipotence," 191.

"greatest conceivable power" but is not omnipotent in the traditional sense.[23] God *cannot* prevent the evil in the world because God's power is limited to persuasion.[24] Indeed, process theologian David Ray Griffin contends that if "God could intervene to prevent any specific instance of evil" but does not, then God is culpable for that evil.[25] However, I believe this view is inconsistent with biblical depictions of divine power and thus fails relative to the standard of biblical warrant. Scripture repeatedly depicts God exercising his power in astonishing ways to prevent evil (e.g., Christ cures leprosy, gives sight to the blind, restores a severed ear, calms storms, multiplies food for crowds, and raises the dead). If God actually worked such evil-preventing miracles in the past, as Scripture teaches, it cannot be true that God (by nature) *lacks the power* to prevent such kinds of evil in our world today.

In contrast, most Christians affirm that God is omnipotent in the sense that he possesses the power to determine that all creation does as he wills. Many Christian theists believe God *could* causally determine history but instead freely grants creatures *libertarian* free will (within limits), which is incompatible with causal determinism.[26] In contrast to process and similar views, I call this *sovereignty* indeterminism. On the other hand, theistic determinism maintains that everything happens as God determines it should happen; either God causally determines all of history in a direct fashion or God determines some occurrences directly and determines prior factors that causally determine all other occurrences.[27] Paul Helm takes the latter view, claiming that "nothing happens that God is unwilling should happen."[28]

23. Hartshorne, *Divine Relativity*, 138.

24. Individuals "can only be influenced, they cannot be sheerly coerced" (Hartshorne, *Man's Vision of God*, xvi). David Basinger, however, raises questions about this account of divine power. See Basinger, *Divine Power in Process Theism*.

25. D. Griffin, "Creation out of Nothing," 117. Griffin maintains that most "problems of Christian theology" stem from "the traditional doctrine of divine omnipotence" (D. Griffin, "Critique of the Free Will Defense," 96). Thomas Jay Oord adopts a very similar view (essential kenosis). Oord, *Uncontrolling Love of God*, 141, 148, 181.

26. The most prominent conceptions of libertarian free will are leeway and sourcehood conceptions. Leeway approaches require the ability to do otherwise. Sourcehood approaches, instead, maintain that libertarian free will requires that an agent is the ultimate source of what she chooses to do (not causally determined by external factors); an agent might act freely even in some instances where she does not possess the ability to do otherwise (e.g., if the agent has formed a character that renders some action impossible). My proposal is congruent with either approach. See further Timpe, "Leeway vs. Sourcehood Conceptions of Free Will," 213–24; Timpe, *Free Will*.

27. As Kevin Timpe defines it, "Causal determinism is the thesis that the course of the future is entirely determined by the conjunction of the non-relational past and the laws of nature." Timpe, *Free Will in Philosophical Theology*, 8.

28. Helm, "Augustinian-Calvinist View," 178.

Indeed, Helm believes that "the existence of an omniscient, timelessly eternal God is logically inconsistent with the libertarian freedom in any of his creatures."[29] Like many others, Helm affirms compatibilism, the view that determinism is *compatible* with free will, defined by Cowan and Spiegel as "the ability to act according to one's desires and intentions."[30] According to this compatibilist definition of free will, one is free to do what one "wants to do," but what one wants to do (one's desires and intentions) is itself causally determined by prior factors, which are themselves causally determined according to God's will.[31]

Relative to the Christian tradition, many scholars maintain that indeterminism was the most prevalent view in the early patristic tradition and beyond, including being held by Anselm (1033/34–1109).[32] Indeed, Swinburne claims, "All Christian theologians of the first four centuries believed in human free will in the libertarian sense, as did all subsequent Eastern Orthodox theologians, and most Western Catholic theologians from Duns Scotus (in the fourteenth century) onwards."[33] Many scholars trace determinism in the Christian tradition to Augustine (354–430). However, scholars hold conflicting views in this regard, including whether Augustine changed his view from indeterminism to determinism.[34] Eleonore Stump comments, "Historians of philosophy read Augustine on free will so variously that it is sometimes difficult to believe they are reading the same texts."[35] Likewise, some claim Thomas Aquinas was a

29. Helm, *Eternal God*, 144.

30. Cowan and Spiegel, *Love of Wisdom*, 237.

31. I use "compatibilism" to refer to broad compatibilism, the view that determinism is compatible with free will *and* moral responsibility. Narrow compatibilism (aka semicompatibilism) maintains that determinism is compatible with moral responsibility, whether or not it is compatible with "free will." On various understandings of compatibilism, see Kane, *Oxford Handbook of Free Will*, 153–242.

32. Rogers, *Perfect Being Theology*, 101. Cf. Anselm, *De Concordia* 1.7, 3.1, 3.5, in *Works*, 447–49, 452–53, 457–58.

33. Swinburne, *Providence and the Problem of Evil*, 35. This is consistent with the findings of Kenneth Wilson, who offers a sweeping survey of Christian (and relevant pre-Christian) thought leading up to Augustine, concluding that among early Christian thinkers there was a "rare theological unanimity over hundreds of years" in favor of what he calls "traditional free choice" (Wilson, *Augustine's Conversion*, 94). Paul Gavrilyuk notes further, "The common core of patristic theodicy" held that God was not culpable for creatures' "free evil choice" because "God did not causally determine these choices." Gavrilyuk, "Overview of Patristic Theodicies," 6, 4.

34. According to one prominent theory, early in his writing career, Augustine adopted something like what is now called libertarian free will (see *On Free Choice of the Will*) but later adopted a deterministic perspective akin to compatibilism. For an extensive case that this hypothesis is correct, see Wilson, *Augustine's Conversion*.

35. Stump, "Augustine on Free Will," 124. For instance, David Hunt maintains that Augustine was not a determinist, and Paul Helm holds the opposite view (Hunt, "Simple-Foreknowledge

determinist, while others interpret him as affirming creaturely libertarian free will.[36] Indeed, theists on both sides of the debate claim the same prominent thinkers as proponents of their views. Thinkers on both sides also claim biblical support for their views, raising the question, Does Scripture indicate whether human free will is compatibilist or libertarian?

Divine Providence and Creaturely Freedom in Scripture

One might initially think this question can be settled by appeal to numerous biblical passages that emphasize human choice. For example, in Deuteronomy 30:19, God says, "I have set before you life and death, blessings and curses. Choose life so that you and your descendants may live" (cf. Deut. 11:26–28; 2 Chron. 15:2; Jer. 18:7–10). Further, Joshua proclaims, "Choose this day whom you will serve," the gods of Canaan or YHWH (Josh. 24:15; cf. 1 Kings 18:21). In the NT, Paul exhorts, "If you confess with your lips that Jesus is Lord and believe in your heart that God raised him from the dead, you will be saved" (Rom. 10:9; cf. John 3:16–18; 8:31–32; Acts 16:31; Heb. 3:8–12; Rev. 3:20).

One might read these (and many similar) texts as evidence of the view that humans have libertarian free will. However, compatibilists argue that these and similar texts are consistent with compatibilist free will—humans can choose what they want, as such texts indicate, but what humans want is itself causally determined according to God's decree. Further, compatibilists appeal to texts like Genesis 50:20, where Joseph tells his brothers who had sold him into slavery, "Even though you intended to do harm to me, God intended it for good, in order to preserve a numerous people, as he is doing today" (cf. Phil. 2:12–13). This text (and others like it), they claim, indicates that human free will is compatible with determinism. Conversely, advocates of libertarian free will contend that biblical texts like this affirm divine providence without indicating causal determinism.

Given that both sides appeal to Scripture, is the biblical data sufficient to indicate which view is correct? On one hand, there is abundant textual support for divine sovereignty, which determinists argue supports their position. On the other hand, numerous biblical passages depict humans as doing

---

Response [to Helm]," 196; Helm, "Augustinian-Calvinist View," 162n3). For his part, Jesse Couenhoven concludes, "Augustine the bishop was one of the first theological compatibilists." Couenhoven, "Augusine of Hippo," 247.

36. For the view that Thomas Aquinas was a determinist, see Garrigou-Lagrange, *God, His Existence and Nature*, 2:538–39; Helm, "Augustinian-Calvinist View," 163. For the opposite view, see Stump, *God of the Bible*, 44n40, 23–24n14.

otherwise than God desires, indicating that creatures possess libertarian free will, minimally defined as the ability to will otherwise than God actually desires. This apparent impasse requires a closer look at some prominent biblical data relevant to this debate.

God Is Sovereign

Scripture teaches that God is sovereign. God, the Creator and sustainer of all, rules over all—"everything apart from God, the entire world, owes its existence and continuation to the omnipotence of God."[37] Nothing falls outside God's providence. Not even one sparrow "will fall to the ground apart from your Father" (Matt. 10:29). God not only declares "the end from the beginning" but also assures,

> "My purpose shall stand,
>   and I will fulfill my intention,"
> calling a bird of prey from the east,
>   the man for my purpose from a far country.
> I have spoken, and I will bring it to pass;
>   I have planned, and I will do it. (Isa. 46:10–11)

Likewise,

> The LORD of hosts has sworn:
> As I have designed,
>   so shall it be;
> and as I have planned,
>   so shall it come to pass:
> . . . .
> For the LORD of hosts has planned,
>   and who will annul it?
> His hand is stretched out,
>   and who will turn it back? (Isa. 14:24, 27; cf. Dan. 4:35)

Indeed, God "does whatever he pleases" (Ps. 115:3; cf. 135:6; Job 42:2).

Accordingly, Ephesians 1:11 proclaims that God "accomplishes *all things* according to his counsel and will." This (like many other passages about God's will and purpose) focuses on God's plan of salvation. Specifically, God "chose us in Christ before the foundation of the world" and "destined us for adoption as his children through Jesus Christ, according to the good pleasure of his

37. Cremer, *Christian Doctrine of Divine Attributes*, 56.

will" (1:4–5). Further, it is God's "plan for the fullness of time, to gather up all things in him [Christ], things in heaven and things on earth. In Christ we have also obtained an inheritance, having been destined [*proorizō*] according to the purpose of him who accomplishes all things according to his counsel and will" (1:10–11).[38] Likewise, Acts 13:48 declares regarding some Gentiles who heard the gospel, "As many as had been destined [*tassō*, "appointed"] for eternal life became believers."[39] Earlier, Peter explains, Jesus was "handed over to you according to the definite plan and foreknowledge of God" (2:23).

Regarding God's providential plan of salvation, Romans 8:28–30 elaborates: "We know that all things work together for good for those who love God, who are called according to his purpose. For those whom he foreknew he also predestined to be conformed to the image of his Son, in order that he might be the firstborn within a large family. And those whom he predestined he also called; and those whom he called he also justified; and those whom he justified he also glorified." Determinists read this (and similar texts) as evidence that God unconditionally and irresistibly elects some to salvation. Others contend that God "predestines" those to salvation whom he foreknows will freely accept God's call.[40]

These verses immediately precede the discourse in Romans 9–11, which determinists often highlight.[41] Some interpret the phrase "I have loved Jacob, but I have hated Esau" (9:13) to mean that God unconditionally elected Jacob for salvation and unconditionally damned Esau. However, while the preceding verses (9:11–12) describe what Rebekah was told "before they had been born," the phrase "I have loved Jacob, but I have hated Esau" was *not* declared before Jacob and Esau were born; it quotes a post-exilic statement from Malachi 1:2–3 about God's dealings with Israel and Edom. In context, it highlights God's continued, *undeserved* covenantal love for the elect people of Israel ("Jacob").[42] Although both Israel and Edom ("Esau") were descendants of

38. As noted earlier, *proorizō* means "decide beforehand" (see L&N 359–60; BDAG 873) and can refer to something decided unilaterally or in a way that takes account of others' free decisions. See the further discussion of Eph. 1:11 below.

39. One could be appointed (*tassō*) deterministically or in a way contingent on one's free decisions. John Polhill sees here "the same balance between human volition and divine providence that is found throughout Acts." While "the Gentiles took an active role in believing," this "was in response to God's Spirit moving in them, convicting them, appointing them for life." Polhill, *Acts*, 308.

40. Augustine himself commented, "The purpose [of God] relates to God's foreknowledge and predestination. God only predestined those whom he knew would believe and follow the call." Augustine, *Augustine on Romans* 55 (ACCS 6:235).

41. For further discussion of Rom. 9–11, see Peckham, *Concept of Divine Love*, 391–96.

42. God's choice of Jacob as son of the covenant promise was entirely unmerited, as Paul highlights by emphasizing that Jacob was chosen "before" he "had been born or had done

Abraham (cf. Rom. 9:6–13) and neither deserved God's favor, God preserved the nation of Israel, while the nation of Edom ceased to exist.[43] This passage emphasizes God's election of and faithfulness to Israel according to his covenant promises (for the sake of *all* nations), without any "injustice on God's part" (Rom. 9:14), but it does not indicate unconditional election to salvation. Earlier Paul explains, "Not all Israelites truly belong to Israel, and not all of Abraham's children are his true descendants," for "it is not the children of the flesh who are the children of God, but the children of the promise are counted as descendants" (9:6–8; cf. 4:11; Gal. 4:28). Paul illustrates this by highlighting that both Isaac and Jacob had older brothers (Ishmael and Esau) who were not elect "children of the promise" (Rom. 9:9–14), thus teaching that Israel did not merit election and that merely being Abraham's descendant does not entail being elect (9:6).[44] Even as God had the right to elect Israel, God has the right to cut off those who persist in unbelief and include in the elect others who believe in Christ (cf. 3:22; 4:11, 24; 10:9–13; Matt. 22:1–14). Accordingly, some Gentiles were "grafted in," while some "branches" of Israel "were broken off because of their unbelief" (Rom. 11:19–20), highlighting "the kindness and the severity of God: severity toward those who have fallen, but God's kindness toward you, *provided you continue in his kindness*; otherwise you also will be cut off. And even those of Israel, *if they do not persist in unbelief*, will be grafted in, for God has the power to graft them in again" (11:22–23; cf. 9:31–32; 10:9, 21). Among other things, this indicates significant conditionality relative to election.[45] As Robert Mounce understands the discourse of Romans 9 and beyond, Paul

anything good or bad"—thus, "not by works but by his [God's] call" (Rom. 9:11–12). On this passage, contrary to the view that "freedom of the will" was "taken away," Augustine comments, "God did this by foreknowledge, by which he knows what even the unborn will be like in the future." Yet God chooses not according to works, "but by foreknowledge he chose faith. He chose the one whom he knew in advance would believe in him." Augustine, *Augustine on Romans* 60 (ACCS 6:250).

43. James D. G. Dunn comments, "Paul's aim is to prick the bubble of Israel's presumptuousness as the elect, not to affirm Esau's rejection" (Dunn, *Romans 9–16*, 545). Further, Scripture teaches that God "does not reject arbitrarily," but "Edom brought judgment upon themselves" (Mason, *Books of Haggai, Zechariah, and Malachi*, 141). See, e.g., Lam. 4:22; Ezek. 25:12–13; 35:15; 36:5; Joel 3:19; Amos 1:9, 11; Obad. 10–14. As Elizabeth Achtemeier puts it, God responds to Israel questioning his love in Mal. 1 by highlighting that "Edom has not gone unpunished for his violation of his brotherly covenant with Israel." Achtemeier, *Nahum–Malachi*, 176.

44. See Thornhill, *Chosen People*, 234–37.

45. Joseph Fitzmyer comments, "God's election, though gratuitous, is conditioned by Christians' responsible fulfillment of obligations to him" (Fitzmyer, *Romans*, 616). Dunn likewise states, "Paul underlines the point that perseverance is a Christian responsibility rather than an unconditional promise" (Dunn, *Romans 9–16*, 665). Douglas J. Moo adds, "Ultimate salvation is dependent on continuing faith." Moo, *Epistle to the Romans*, 707.

was not "teaching double predestination" but explaining that God had not failed "to maintain his covenant relationship with Israel. He had not broken his promise to the descendants of Abraham."[46]

Some argue, however, that Romans 9:15–16 indicates determinism:

For he says to Moses,

"I will have mercy on whom I have mercy,
and I will have compassion on whom I have compassion."

So it depends not on human will or exertion, but on God who shows mercy.[47]

However, this quotes God's words in the aftermath of the golden calf rebellion (Exod. 33:19), which were not about electing some to salvation and rejecting others but highlighting God's freely bestowed mercy; in the narrative, people were given a choice to come to God's side or not (32:26).[48] As Joseph Fitzmyer notes, Paul quotes Exodus 33:19 "in order to underscore Yahweh's freedom of merciful activity; he does not act arbitrarily, as Israel itself knows."[49] In Romans 9, the quotation continues the theme of Israel's *unmerited* election, highlighting the fact that Israel has no right to complain about God's grace to the Gentiles because Israel repeatedly received profoundly *undeserved* mercy and only thereby continued as God's covenant people after they rebelled and forfeited any right to covenant relationship. As Nijay K. Gupta puts it, "God's going with this people, his self-revelation as the God of mercy and compassion, is the fulfillment of a promise *in spite of Israel's failure*."[50]

46. Mounce, *Romans*, 199. While adopting a Calvinist approach, Moo notes there is a "strong case" for a "corporate and salvation-historical interpretation." Moo, *Epistle to the Romans*, 585.

47. Augustine, however, comments, "Paul does not take away the freedom of the will but says that our will is not sufficient unless God helps us" (Augustine, *Augustine on Romans* 62 [ACCS 6:256]). Jerome adds, "Free will is preserved as far as our willing and running is concerned," and "everything depends on the [mercy and] power of God as far as the fulfillment of our willing and running is concerned." Jerome, *Against the Pelagians* 1.5.19 (ACCS 6:256).

48. Many scholars argue that Exod. 33:19 echoes and adds to Exod. 3:14, rendering it something like, "I will proclaim before you the name LORD, and the grace that I grant and the compassion that I show" (JPS). On this, G. S. Ogden concludes, "The point being made is that God's mercy and goodness are freely given to all the people" (Ogden, "Idem Per Idem," 117). Many other scholars agree that this phrase signifies an emphasis on God's mercy, not discrimination between objects of divine mercy. See Stuart, *Exodus*, 708; Janzen, *Exodus*, 248; Freedman, "Name of the God of Moses," 154; Brueggemann, "Book of Exodus," 940; Sarna, *Exodus*, 214; Childs, *Book of Exodus*, 76, 596; Fretheim, *Exodus*, 305.

49. Fitzmyer, *Romans*, 567. Likewise, William S. Campbell comments, "These words are intended not as proof that the divine election is arbitrary, but as proof to the contrary" (W. Campbell, "Freedom and Faithfulness of God," 30). So also Lenski, *Interpretation of St. Paul's Epistle to the Romans*, 608–9. Cf. Staudinger, "ἔλεος," 1:431; Esser, "ἔλεος," 2:597.

50. Gupta, "What 'Mercies of God'?," 87 (emphasis original).

The claim that God has the right to bestow mercy on whomever he chooses is perfectly consistent with indeterminism. In this regard, Paul goes on to reference God's hardening of Pharaoh's heart shortly before the golden calf rebellion, commenting, "So then he has mercy on whomever he chooses, and he hardens the heart of whomever he chooses" (Rom. 9:18). Notably, Exodus states both that Pharaoh hardened his heart (e.g., Exod. 8:15, 32) *and* that God hardened Pharaoh's heart (e.g., 9:12). While consistent with determinism, this is also consistent with the indeterminist view that Pharaoh *freely* chose to stubbornly harden his heart against God *and* that God acted to bring about this outcome without determining Pharaoh's will (more on this later).[51] As many recognize, Exodus says Pharaoh hardened his own heart (8:15, 32) before it says God hardened his heart (9:12), and Leon Morris comments, "Neither here nor anywhere else is God said to harden anyone who had not first hardened himself."[52] Augustine himself comments that it should not "be thought that Pharaoh did not obey because he could not, on the ground that his heart had already been hardened. On the contrary, Pharaoh had deserved his hardness of heart by his earlier unbelief."[53] However, some determinists argue that the next verse indicates God's will cannot be resisted: "You will say to me then, 'Why then does he still find fault? For who can resist his will?'" (Rom. 9:19). Yet these statements are not positive claims Paul makes but questions Paul anticipates others asking, to which Paul responds.[54] Instead of teaching that God's will is irresistible, Paul himself later teaches that "whoever resists authority resists what God has appointed, and those who resist will incur judgment" (13:2; cf. Luke 7:31; Acts 7:51).

In Romans 9, Paul goes on to reference OT imagery of the potter and the clay, asking, "Does not the potter have a right over the clay, to make from the same lump one vessel [*skeuos*] for honorable use and another for common use? What if God, although willing to demonstrate His wrath and to make

51. God may "harden" someone's heart without causally determining their will, perhaps akin to how I could "harden" my nine-year-old son's heart by bringing about some circumstances without controlling his will.

52. L. Morris, *Epistle to the Romans*, 361. Morris goes on, "God's hardening follows on what Pharaoh himself did. . . . God does not harden people who do not go astray first (cf. Jas. 1:13)." As Craig Keener understands it, God does not make "an honorable man . . . become stubborn," but God "judge[s] a wicked leader" (Keener, *Romans*, 119). Fitzmyer thinks this is a "protological way of expressing divine reaction to persistent human obstinacy against him." Fitzmyer, *Romans*, 568.

53. Augustine, *Augustine on Romans* 62 (ACCS 6:257).

54. Ambrosiaster comments, "Here Paul assumes the role of an objector who makes these assumptions" (Ambrosiaster, *Commentary on Paul's Epistles* [ACCS 6:258]). Likewise, Augustine comments, "Paul plays devil's advocate by asking a rhetorical question." Augustine, *Augustine on Romans* 62 (ACCS 6:259).

His power known, endured with much patience vessels of wrath prepared for destruction?" (vv. 21–22 NASB; cf. Isa. 45:9).[55] These verses again highlight God's sovereignty over creatures but do not entail determinism.[56] Not only does Paul highlight God's "patience" with such vessels (cf. Rom. 2:4; 1 Tim. 1:16), but elsewhere he also teaches that whether one is a "vessel for honor" is contingent on how one responds to God, saying, "If anyone cleanses himself . . . he will be a vessel [*skeuos*] for honor" (2 Tim. 2:21 NASB; cf. 1 Thess. 4:3–4).[57] This complements the potter and clay imagery in Jeremiah 18:1–10, which highlights that how God relates to nations is contingent on their own decisions. Specifically, God declares, "If that nation against which I have spoken turns from its evil, I will relent [*nāḥam*, niphal] concerning the calamity I planned to bring on it" (18:8 NASB; cf. 18:9–10).[58]

While the passages considered above teach that God is sovereign and that God's providence is all-encompassing, I do not believe any passages indicate or entail that history is causally determined by God. Such passages may be consistent with determinism, but they are also consistent with the view that God indeterministically foreknows the future *free* decisions of creatures and factors those free decisions into his (consequent) will or purpose. The indeterminist might consistently affirm, then, that God "accomplishes all things according to his counsel and will" (Eph. 1:11) alongside the understanding that God's "counsel and will" already include the *free* decisions of creatures, which God foreknew and factored into his decisions. Likewise, the indeterminist can consistently affirm that God chooses and "predestines" some to salvation, with the understanding that God chooses and "predestines" those to salvation whom he foreknows will *freely* accept God's call. On this view, God "does whatever he pleases" (Ps. 115:3), but part of what pleases God is to grant creatures libertarian free will.

As far as I can see, then, all these (and other) passages that emphasize divine sovereignty are consistent with indeterminism and thus do not by themselves indicate whether determinism or indeterminism is true. Other passages, however, indicate that creatures sometimes reject God's will (e.g., Luke 7:30) and choose otherwise than God desires.

---

55. Keener comments, "God makes vessels for honor, which is his interest, but endures those that are objects of his wrath for the sake of the others (9:22–23)." Keener, *Romans*, 120.

56. God choosing someone for "special" use does not entail determinism any more than my choosing to hire someone as a graduate assistant would entail determinism.

57. Philip Towner comments, this "metaphor opens into a general invitation to respond. . . . 'Anyone' can become an 'instrument for noble purposes,'" but this requires "'cleansing,'" which, as the object of the action ('themselves') shows, is an individual decision (cf. 2 Cor. 13:5)." Towner, *Letters to Timothy and Titus*, 541.

58. See Peckham, "Passible Potter and the Contingent Clay."

Creatures Sometimes Rebel and Will Otherwise than God Commands and Desires

According to Scripture, creatures sometimes rebel, refuse to listen, and reject God's will—willing otherwise than God prefers. God gives creatures choices, saying to Israel, "I have set before you life and death, blessings and curses. Choose life so that you and your descendants may live" (Deut. 30:19; cf. Lev. 26). Sadly, the people repeatedly break God's law, break the covenant, and reject and forsake God. As 2 Chronicles 36:16 puts it, "They kept mocking the messengers of God, despising his words, and scoffing at his prophets" (cf. Amos 2:4–5). Of such repeated rebellion, God laments,

> But my people did not listen to my voice;
>   Israel would not submit to me.
> So I gave them over to their stubborn hearts,
>   to follow their own counsels.
> O that my people would listen to me,
>   that Israel would walk in my ways!
> Then I would quickly subdue their enemies,
>   and turn my hand against their foes. (Ps. 81:11–14; cf. 78:22)

God's words indicate that the people did otherwise than God wanted and thereby affected God's own action—a common theme throughout Scripture.

Elsewhere God states, "I reared children and brought them up, / but they have rebelled against me" (Isa. 1:2). Later, God calls his people

> rebellious children, . . .
> who carry out a plan, but not mine;
> who make an alliance, but against my will,
>   adding sin to sin. (30:1)

Further, they are "rebellious people" who "refuse to listen / To the instruction of the LORD" (30:9 NASB; cf. 30:10–11). God declares judgment against them "because [they] reject this word" (30:12). He offered to save them if they would repent, but they "were not willing" and "said, 'No'" (30:15–16 NASB). Nevertheless, God tells them, "The LORD waits to be gracious to you," and "he will surely be gracious to you at the sound of your cry; when he hears it, he will answer you" (30:18–19). Later, Isaiah 63:10 states, "They rebelled / and grieved his holy spirit." Thereafter, God declares,

> I held out my hands all day long
>   to a rebellious people,

who walk in a way that is not good
    following their own devices;
a people who provoke me
    to my face continually. (65:2–3)

Notably, Paul quotes God's words from this very passage in the discourse of Romans 9–11: "All day long I have held out my hands to a disobedient and contrary people" (10:21). A few verses later in Isaiah, God proclaims,

When I called, you did not answer,
    when I spoke, you did not listen,
but you did what was evil in my sight,
    and chose [*bāḥar*] what I did not delight [*ḥāpēṣ*] in. (65:12)

God repeats this in nearly identical words in Isaiah 66:4, saying, "I will choose" (*bāḥar*) their treatment,

because, when I called, no one answered,
    when I spoke, they did not listen;
but they did what was evil in my sight,
    and chose [*bāḥar*] what did not please [*ḥāpēṣ*] me.

The Hebrew verb *ḥāpēṣ* signifies willing, desiring, or delighting or taking pleasure in.[59] In these instances, the people refused to listen to God and chose directly contrary to what God desired.

Elsewhere God decries his people's "wickedness in forsaking me" (Jer. 1:16). While God "planted" his people "as a choice vine, a completely faithful seed," God declares to them, "You turned yourself before Me / Into the degenerate shoots of a foreign vine" (2:21 NASB). God further declares judgment "because they have not given heed to my words" and "rejected" his law (6:19). Later, God states, "You have rejected me," and "I am weary of relenting [*nāḥam*]" (15:6).[60] Yet God nevertheless promises that if they repent, he will relent (*nāḥam*) (18:7–10). Here and elsewhere God repeatedly sets choice before the people, warning, "If you will not listen to me" and "the prophets

59. The Hebrew term *ḥāpēṣ* and the Greek terms *thelō* and *boulomai* might signify willing or desiring (among other connotations), depending on the context. Since one tends to *will* what one desires and "pleases," the concepts of willing and desiring are closely linked. See Talley, "חָפֵץ," 2:232; Müller, "βούλομαι, θέλω," 3:1015–18.
60. Here the people's actions "weary" God in the sense of displeasure or trying his patience but not in the sense of fatigue. Isaiah 40:28 teaches that God does not "faint or grow weary" as creatures do.

whom I send to you urgently," then "I will make this city a curse for all the nations of the earth" (26:4–6).

Over and over again, God instructs the people to "not devise evil in your hearts against one another," but like Pharaoh, "they refused to pay attention and turned a stubborn shoulder and stopped their ears from hearing. They made their hearts like flint so that they could not hear the law and the words" God sent; "He called and they would not listen" (Zech. 7:10–13 NASB). The fact that people may harden *or* not harden their hearts is further indicated in this exhortation: "Today, if you hear his voice, do not harden your hearts as in the rebellion, as on the day of testing in the wilderness" (Heb. 3:7–8, quoting Ps. 95:7–8).

Christ's words in the NT further indicate that people sometimes will otherwise than God desires. Jesus repeatedly speaks of blessings for those who do God's "will" (*thelēma*) (e.g., Matt. 7:21), indicating that some do not, and teaches his disciples to pray, "Your will be done, on earth as it is in heaven" (6:10), suggesting that sometimes God's will is not done. On this, I. Howard Marshall comments that if "we freely yield ourselves to God," then "he is able to accomplish his will through us and our prayers. In a very real sense, therefore, the accomplishment of God's will in the world does depend on our prayers."[61] Jesus's lament over Jerusalem further echoes OT instances of God's unfulfilled desires: "Jerusalem, Jerusalem, the city that kills the prophets and stones those who are sent to it! How often have I desired [*thelō*] to gather your children together as a hen gathers her brood under her wings, and you were not willing [*thelō*]!" (23:37; cf. Isa. 30:15–16).

Likewise, Jesus tells a parable in which some were "invited [or "called," *kaleō*] to the wedding feast," but "they were unwilling [*thelō*] to come" (Matt. 22:3 NASB).[62] So others were invited and accepted the call instead (22:9–10). Explaining this, Jesus concludes, "Many are called, but few are chosen" (22:14).[63] As Craig Blomberg notes, this is not an "irresistible calling" but an

61. Marshall, *Epistles of John*, 245.

62. The *kaleō* word group refers to a call or invitation that is contingent on acceptance (Matt. 22:14; Heb. 11:8), consistent with corresponding OT language (*qārā'*) (2 Sam. 15:11; 1 Kings 1:41, 49). The word group does not itself indicate whether a call/invitation has been (or will be) accepted, but the context may (e.g., Rom. 8:28–29). While some contend that the term *klētos* ("called") refers to "effectual" calling that "cannot be frustrated" and "not merely an invitation" (Schreiner, *Epistle to the Romans*, 450–51), in my survey of all instances throughout Scripture, I found no instance of an irresistible call but many instances indicating that the call may be accepted or rejected (e.g., Matt. 22:1–14). See Peckham, *Concept of Divine Love*, 378–87.

63. As Donald Hagner explains, "πολλοί ["many"] is probably to be taken as a universalizing Semitism, which can be translated 'everyone'" (Hagner, *Matthew 14–28*, 632). So also Meyer, "Many [= All] Are Called," 89–97. Moo also recognizes this as "a 'general' call." Moo, *Epistle to the Romans*, 530.

invitation. "Those responding properly may be said to have been chosen," but they "must freely respond to the Spirit's work. . . . Election does not violate free will nor occur irrespective of" one's decisions.[64] Gottlob Schrenk adds, "The whole point of the parable is that one does not have to decline [the invitation] or to appear in an unsuitable garment."[65] Further, Luke 7:30 explicitly states that some people rejected God's will, saying, "By refusing to be baptized by him [John], the Pharisees and the lawyers rejected God's purpose [boulē] for themselves."[66] Later, Stephen proclaims, "You men who are stiff-necked and uncircumcised in heart and ears are always resisting the Holy Spirit; you are doing just as your fathers did" (Acts 7:51 NASB; cf. Rom. 13:2).

Elsewhere God proclaims, "Why will you die, O house of Israel? I have no pleasure [ḥāpēṣ] in the death of anyone. . . . Turn, then, and live" (Ezek. 18:31–32; cf. 33:11).[67] Here and elsewhere God proclaims that he does not desire that *anyone* die and exhorts the people to turn and live. Numerous other texts indicate that God desires to save all. For instance, Paul writes that God "desires [thelō] everyone to be saved and to come to the knowledge of the truth," noting that Jesus "gave himself a ransom for all" (1 Tim. 2:4, 6; cf. 4:10; Titus 2:11).[68] Some argue the term translated "everyone" or "all" refers to all kinds of people rather than everyone.[69] However, as even determinists such as Thomas Schreiner and John Piper note, such an interpretation seems unlikely and does not suffice to explain texts like 2 Peter 3:9, which states, "The Lord is not slow about his promise, as some think of slowness, but is patient with you, not wanting anyone to perish, but all to come to repentance" (cf. Ezek. 18:32; 33:11). This text, Schreiner comments, "refers to God's desire that everyone without exception be saved."[70] Going further, Peter H. Davids

---

64. Blomberg, *Matthew*, 329. J. Eckert adds, "A predestinarian misunderstanding of the belief in election is thus rejected. . . . The elect are those who have followed the invitation into the kingdom of God through Jesus Christ" (Eckert, "ἐκλεκτός," 4:417). Cf. 2 Esdras 8:3, 41. Likewise, Robert H. Stein comments, the "'chosen ones' designates those who have responded to God in repentance and faith," not "the elect by some kind of predestination" (Stein, *Luke*, 446). L. Coenen, however, thinks this is attributed "to the divine choice alone," but this view conflicts with Matt. 22. Coenen, "καλέω," 1:540.

65. Schrenk, "εκλεγομαι, εκλογη, εκλεκτος," 4:186. Similarly, France, *Gospel of Matthew*, 827; Nolland, *Gospel of Matthew*, 892.

66. H. J. Ritz notes, "The βουλή [will/purpose] of God can be hindered." Ritz, "Βουλή," 1:224.

67. Daniel I. Block comments, "Without repentance God cannot forgive." Block, *Book of Ezekiel*, 589.

68. Anton Vögtle contends that 1 Tim. 2:4 excludes determinism. Vögtle, *Der Judasbrief*, 231–32. Cf. Müller, "θέλω," 3:1020.

69. See, e.g., the survey in Moo, *2 Peter and Jude*, 188.

70. Schreiner, *1, 2 Peter, Jude*, 382. Likewise regarding Ezek. 18:32—God does not want *anyone* to die. So also Piper, "Are There Two Wills in God?," 108.

says that God wants "'everyone'/'all' to come to repentance. . . . God's will may not be done, but it will not be for lack of trying on his part."[71] Yet if some will not be saved, as Scripture appears to teach (John 3:18; Heb. 10:36; 1 John 2:17; Rev. 9:20–21; 16:9–11), it follows that God's desire that "everyone without exception be saved" is unfulfilled.[72]

A Constructive Model of Divine Power and Providence

On one hand, numerous passages teach that God is sovereign and "accomplishes all things according to his counsel and will" (Eph. 1:11). On the other hand, numerous passages teach that creatures sometimes reject God's will, refuse to listen, rebel against and reject God, and will otherwise than God desires (Ps. 81:11–14; Luke 7:30).[73] How are we to understand these two sets of texts? What reading consistently affirms both sets without injury to either of them?

In my view, the preceding material indicates biblical warrant for the following points:

1. God is all-powerful (e.g., Rev. 1:8), yet God cannot do some things—God "cannot deny himself" (2 Tim. 2:13) or "be tempted by evil" (James 1:13).
2. God "does whatever he pleases [*ḥāpēṣ*]" (Ps. 115:3), yet creatures sometimes do that which does not please God; God's people "chose [*bāḥar*] what I did not delight [*ḥāpēṣ*] in" (Isa. 65:12).
3. God declares, "My purpose ['*ēṣâ*] shall stand, / and I will fulfill my intention. . . . / I have planned, and I will do it" (Isa. 46:10–11). Yet God also refers to his people as "rebellious children, . . . / who carry out a plan, but not mine; / who make an alliance, but against my will, / adding sin to sin" (30:1; cf. Hosea 8:4).
4. God declares, "I have spoken, and I will bring it to pass" (Isa. 46:11), yet sometimes God's people despised God's words (2 Chron. 36:16) and "did not listen to [God's] voice," "would not submit to" God (Ps. 81:11), and "refuse[d] to listen / To the instruction of the LORD" (Isa. 30:9 NASB; cf. 65:12; Jer. 6:19).

71. Davids, *Letters of 2 Peter and Jude*, 281. Further, Eric Fuchs and Pierre Reymond understand 2 Pet. 3:9 as evidence against determinism. Fuchs and Reymond, *La deuxième Épitre de Saint Pierre*, 115–16.

72. For a compelling biblical case that some will not be saved, see Marshall, "New Testament Does Not Teach," 55–76.

73. See further Peckham, *Concept of Divine Love*, 205–8, 236–41, 372–78, 577–82.

5. God's providence is all-encompassing. God "accomplishes *all things* according to his counsel [*boulē*] and will" (Eph. 1:11), yet some creatures "rejected God's purpose [*boulē*] for themselves" (Luke 7:30; cf. Isa. 30:15; Matt. 23:37) and resisted the Holy Spirit (Acts 7:51).

6. Those whom God foreknew, he predestined, and those he predestined, he called, justified, and glorified (Rom. 8:29–30). Yet sometimes God called his chosen people, but they did not answer (Isa. 65:12; 66:4; cf. Ps. 81:13); God "called and they would not listen" (Zech. 7:13 NASB). God desired to save them, but they "were not willing" (Isa. 30:15 NASB; Matt. 23:37); some who were invited (*kaleō*, "called") to God's wedding feast refused the invitation, whereupon others were invited and chosen instead (Matt. 22:1–14; cf. Rom. 11:20–23).

7. God declares, "I will be gracious to whom I will be gracious, and will show mercy on whom I will show mercy" (Exod. 33:19, also quoted in Rom. 9:15). Yet God also declares, "The LORD waits to be gracious to you" and "will surely be gracious to you at the sound of your cry; when he hears it, he will answer you" (Isa. 30:18–19).

8. Whereas God hardened Pharaoh's heart (Exod. 9:12), Pharaoh is earlier said to have hardened his own heart (8:15, 32); God's people "made their hearts like flint" (Zech. 7:12 NASB); and the Holy Spirit exhorts, "Today, if you hear his voice, do not harden your hearts as in the rebellion, as on the day of testing in the wilderness" (Heb. 3:7–8; cf. Ps. 95:7–8).

9. God is the potter and can do with the clay what he wills (Rom. 9:21), declaring, "Like the clay in the potter's hand, so are you in My hand, O house of Israel" (Jer. 18:6 NASB), yet he also declares, "If that nation against which I have spoken turns from its evil, I will relent" (18:8 NASB; cf. 18:9–10).

10. Paul speaks of "vessels [*skeuos*] of wrath prepared for destruction," yet he also says that God "endured [such vessels] with much patience" (Rom. 9:22 NASB) and elsewhere teaches that "if anyone cleanses himself . . . he will be a vessel [*skeuos*] for honor" (2 Tim. 2:21 NASB). Further, God "is patient . . . not wanting any to perish, but all to come to repentance" (2 Pet. 3:9; cf. Rom. 10:21), and God has "no pleasure [*ḥāpēṣ*] in the death of anyone" but calls people to "turn, then, and live" (Ezek. 18:32; cf. 33:11; 1 Tim. 2:4).

These and many other biblical instances affirm God's sovereignty and comprehensive providence *and* affirm that humans sometimes rebel against God and reject God's will.

God's Two "Wills"?

How can it be that God accomplishes *all* things according to his will if creatures sometimes reject God's will? If Scripture is consistent, both sets of texts must be true in what they affirm. Yet how can they be true together without contradiction? To address this, many theologians posit two kinds of divine "wills," but there is disagreement regarding how to understand God's "wills."

Many determinists posit a distinction between God's hidden will and God's revealed will. God's hidden will is what God *actually* prefers. Accordingly, God determines history such that God's hidden will always comes to pass, including all instances of evil. Conversely, God's revealed will refers to what God reveals as his will, including his commandments. When God's revealed will does not come to pass, such as when creatures violate God's commandments, it is because God determined that something else occur instead (his hidden will).[74]

Many indeterminists, in contrast, emphasize the distinction between God's antecedent will and God's consequent will. God's antecedent will is what God wills logically prior to taking account of any creaturely decisions and is thus what God actually prefers—what would occur if everyone did as God wants. God's consequent will is what God wills after taking into account creaturely decisions—including all the bad decisions that depart from what God prefers. As Eleonore Stump explains, "God's antecedent will is what God would have willed if everything in the world had been up to him alone," and "God's consequent will is what God actually does will, given what God's creatures will."[75]

Determinists and indeterminists agree that some things God wills do not come to pass, but they disagree about the reason why. Many indeterminists maintain that some things God (antecedently) wills do not occur because creatures will otherwise than God prefers. God's consequent will always comes to pass not because God determines history but because God's consequent

---

74. Some determinists maintain that God "positively governs all acts that are not evil" and "governs all other acts, evil acts, by permitting them" (Helm, "Augustinian-Calvinist View," 178). However, William Lane Craig argues that if determinism is true, "divine permission" does not make sense and God "is still implicated in evil" (Craig, "Middle-Knowledge Response [to Helm]," 205). So also Rogers, *Perfect Being Theology*, 101. Hunt adds that if "universal causal determinism is true," as Helm maintains, then God is "the ultimate cause of *all* our actions (and not just of our good actions)." This is to say that if (as Helm believes) God "created the initial state of the universe and the causal rules by which one state is succeeded by another state," unless God "created *something* with the power to make an undetermined contribution to reality [contrary to determinism], God is the sufficient cause of absolutely everything—including our sins." Hunt, "Simple-Foreknowledge Response [to Helm]," 198 (emphasis original).

75. Stump, *Wandering in the Darkness*, 385.

will takes into account the *free* decisions of all creatures (via foreknowledge), including many things contrary to what God prefers (i.e., occurrences of evil). God laments evil because God genuinely prefers (or wishes) that such instances of evil had not occurred. Determinists, conversely, maintain that some things God says he wills (God's revealed will) do not come to pass because God does not actually prefer those things and determines otherwise. God's hidden will always comes to pass because God determines history. As such, when God laments creaturely decisions and instances of evil (see the texts surveyed earlier), God does not actually wish it had been otherwise; whatever occurs is what God actually preferred and thus deterministically decreed (his hidden will).

Which account fares better relative to the standards of systematic coherence and biblical warrant? Indeterminists have no difficulty explaining why some things God wills do not come to pass. Some things God prefers do not occur because God grants creatures libertarian free will and creatures sometimes will otherwise than God prefers. Accordingly, the indeterminist can affirm that many things God wills and actually prefers (God's antecedent will) do not come to pass while also consistently affirming that God's consequent will always comes to pass but includes many things (e.g., evil) that God does not prefer because it includes the free decisions of creatures.

The determinist, however, faces difficulties regarding coherently accounting for the view that God wills some things that do not come to pass. If God causally determines history such that what God actually prefers (hidden will) always occurs, how could there be any instances of God genuinely willing things that do not come to pass? If, as Paul Helm claims, "nothing happens that God is unwilling should happen," then how could it be that God is "not wanting any to perish" (2 Pet. 3:9) but some finally do perish?[76]

Many determinists argue that God may genuinely desire one outcome (in his revealed will) but may desire another outcome more (in his hidden will) and that the second outcome may be incompatible with the first outcome such that God cannot determine that both occur. God, then, may have unfulfilled desires in the sense that he desires one outcome but determines that another (more desirable) outcome takes place instead. For example, Piper claims that "God wills not to save all, even though he is willing to save all, because there is something else that he wills more, which would be lost if he exerted his sovereign power to save all."[77] For Piper and many other determinists, the

---

76. Helm, "Augustinian-Calvinist View," 177.
77. Piper, "Are There Two Wills in God?," 123. Helm maintains, similarly, "God ordains evil because it is logically necessary for his goal of the greater good" (Helm, "God, Compatibilism, and the Authorship of Sin," 122). Cf. Calvin, *Commentaries on the Catholic Epistles*, 419–20.

outcome God desires more is "the manifestation of the full range of God's glory in wrath and mercy (Rom. 9:22–23) and the humbling of man so that he enjoys giving all credit to God for his salvation (1 Cor. 1:29)."[78] However, for this line of thought to work, there must be some incompatibility between two or more outcomes that God desires *and* whether the two outcomes are incompatible must not be contingent on God's will.

Yet it is difficult to see how two things God values could be incompatible *if determinism is true*. If everything is the way it is due to either God's will or God's nature, as determinists typically suppose, then two things God values might be incompatible in one of two ways. They might be incompatible in a way that is subject to God's will, or they might be incompatible in a way that is not subject to God's will because it is intrinsic to reality according to God's essential nature. If the incompatibility of two divinely desired values were subject to God's will, however, then God could effectively will that the two values be compatible instead. If, on the other hand, the incompatibility of the two things God values is intrinsic to reality (and thus to God's essential nature), then for God to desire that the two values be compatible would mean that God desires something that is contrary to his own essential nature, per impossibile (cf. 2 Tim. 2:13). Accordingly, if determinism is true, it seems impossible that God could desire or will two values that are incompatible with each other. Yet if this is so, unless God claims to will something that he does not truly will, God's revealed will and hidden will would always correspond. For any outcome that God could desire or will *without self-contradiction*, God could causally determine or effectively will it to be the case.

To see how this is so, consider the claim of some determinists that God desires "the manifestation of the full range" of his "glory in wrath and mercy" more than he desires that none perish or that there be no (or less) evil in the world.[79] This claim is problematic because if God causally determines *all* events (which would include all mental events), then God could *immediately* make every mind humbly and joyfully recognize "the full range" of God's glory, without any sin or evil whatsoever.[80] Further, Jerry Walls notes that if God "must display justice by punishing evil in order fully to manifest his

78. Piper, "Are There Two Wills in God?," 124. Some call this the divine glory defense. See Johnson, "Calvinism and the Problem of Evil," 43–48.

79. See Piper, "Are There Two Wills in God?," 124.

80. John Calvin himself maintains that God causally determines humans' mental actions, saying, the "internal affections of men are not less ruled by the hand of God than their external actions are *preceded* by his *eternal decree*," and, as such, "God performs not by the hands of men the things which He has decreed, without *first working* in their hearts the *very will* which *precedes* the acts they are to perform." Calvin, "Defence of the Secret Providence of God," in *Calvin's Calvinism*, 2:23 (emphasis original).

glory," then "God needs evil or depends on it fully to manifest his glory. This consequence undermines not only God's goodness, but his sovereignty as well."[81] Conversely, if wrath is not essential to God's nature but is the proper response of goodness and love against evil (as argued in chap. 2), then there is no need or benefit to manifesting wrath in the absence of evil. Where there is no evil, there is no wrath.[82]

Even if we set aside these objections, however, the determinist Piper himself affirms, "There is nothing beyond God's own will and nature which stops him from saving people," and yet "there are people who are not objects of God's electing love."[83] However, if it is a matter subject to "God's own will" that some must be damned for his glory, then God could simply will that this be otherwise. Alternatively, if it is a matter of God's essential nature that some must be damned for his glory, then for God to will or desire that no one be lost would be to will or desire something that contradicts his own essential nature and glory, which would be absurd.[84]

Given determinism, then, if God has unfulfilled desires, it seems that God either has desires that conflict with his own nature, amounting to self-contradiction, or wills against his own will, amounting to another kind of self-contradiction. If so, a deterministic God would not have any unfulfilled desires; everything God wills would come to pass.[85] Determinism, then, stands in considerable tension with the many biblical depictions of God having un-fulfilled desires. To coherently claim God has unfulfilled desires, as Scripture portrays, one must posit some operative factor beyond God's own nature and will.[86] However, by definition, any such factor would be a (theistically)

81. Walls, "One Hell of a Problem," 94.

82. Some might claim that where there is no sin, there could be no mercy, but I believe the semantic range of biblical terms for mercy (see Peckham, *Concept of Divine Love*) includes positive aspects of love (compassion and lovingkindness) that would occur even without sin or evil. See my critique of *felix culpa* approaches in chap. 6.

83. Piper, "How Does a Sovereign God Love?," 10.

84. Similar problems face Paul Kjoss Helseth's suggestion that God "ordained" the "particular evils" in this world (at least in part) because they "cultivate in" believers "the Christian virtues of perseverance, proven character, and hope" (Helseth, "God Causes All Things," 44). If God caus-ally determines humans' mental actions, however, he could causally determine that each person immediately possess all Christian virtues, unless such virtues themselves require indeterminism.

85. See Peckham, *Theodicy of Love*, 35–39.

86. Yet, Piper maintains, "There is nothing beyond God's own will and nature which stops him from saving people" (Piper, "How Does a Sovereign God Love?," 10). In this regard, Walls highlights the fact that if compatibilism is true, God could causally determine that every indi-vidual "*freely* accept his love and be saved" (Walls, "One Hell of a Problem," 90). See further Jordan Wessling's argument that "God loves every human person with what" he calls "*supreme love*: a love that values and seeks an individual's supreme or highest good" such that God seeks to save all. Wessling, *Love Divine* (forthcoming).

indeterministic factor, such as creatures willing otherwise than God prefers. The indeterminist, on the other hand, has biblical warrant to affirm that creatures possess libertarian free will. Specifically, if Scripture teaches that creatures sometimes will otherwise than God actually prefers, as I have argued, it follows that at least some creatures at some times have libertarian free will, minimally defined as the ability to will otherwise than God prefers.[87]

If this is so, while the determinist can adequately account for the texts that affirm God's comprehensive providence and sovereignty, the determinist seems to lack an adequate account of the many passages wherein creatures will otherwise than God wills. The sovereignty indeterminist (who affirms exhaustive definite foreknowledge), on the other hand, can consistently account for both the passages that teach that God is sovereign and "accomplishes all things according to his counsel and will" (Eph. 1:11) and the passages that teach that creatures sometimes will otherwise than God prefers (Ps. 81:11–14; Luke 7:30). The sovereignty indeterminist can consistently affirm both, without twisting the content of either, by distinguishing between God's antecedent and consequent wills, which I call God's ideal will and God's remedial will.

A Constructive Model of God's Providence of Sovereign Love

God's ideal will refers to what God actually prefers from some time onward—that is, God's ideal will is what would occur, from some point onward, if all creatures did what God actually prefers (i.e., ideally desires). God's remedial will is God's will that has already taken into account every other factor, including the *free* decisions of creatures that sometimes depart from what God actually prefers. Accordingly, God's remedial will includes not only what God himself causes in history but also what all creatures *freely* cause. If God foreknows the free decisions of creatures (perhaps via middle knowledge), including all instances wherein creatures *freely* will otherwise than God actually prefers (i.e., against God's ideal will), God can take into account all the *free* decisions of creatures, plan his own actions accordingly to bring about the most preferable outcome available given the free decisions of creatures (i.e., God's remedial will), then providentially execute his plan in history via divine action (Rom. 8:29–30; Isa. 46:9–11). I believe this understanding consistently accounts for all the biblical passages descriptive of God's sovereign and comprehensive providence as well as all the passages descriptive of creatures rejecting God's will and willing otherwise than God (ideally) desires.

87. See further Peckham, *Theodicy of Love*, 40–41.

Specifically, this model of providence coherently affirms that God grants creatures libertarian freedom and also "destined" or planned all things according to his "purpose" and "accomplishes all things according to his counsel and will" (Eph. 1:11). This model simply understands God's "purpose" and "will" in this passage as God's *remedial* purpose and will—inclusive of the free decisions of creatures, including the bad ones that depart from God's ideal will. Accordingly, one can affirm a strong conception of divine providence, affirming that God indeed accomplishes *all* things according to his (remedial) will (1:11) while also affirming libertarian free will and thus accounting for the many passages wherein God's will is unfulfilled (e.g., Luke 7:30). God does "whatever he pleases" (Ps. 115:3), but what pleases God takes account of the free decisions of creatures.[88]

Here it is crucial to distinguish between instances wherein God causes some outcome directly, apart from any free contribution by others (strong actualization), and instances wherein God brings about some outcome in a way that depends on the free actions of others (weak actualization).[89] Given this distinction, God cannot *strongly* actualize any outcome that depends on creatures' *free* decisions, and whether or not God can weakly actualize some desired outcome depends on what creatures *freely* decide. Given God's exhaustive foreknowledge, however, God may weakly actualize some desired outcome by directly causing some things that, combined with the contributions of free creatures, God knows will bring about that outcome.

Given this understanding, passages that speak of both God and creatures bringing about some outcome may be understood as instances of weak actualization.[90] For example, with this understanding, one can consistently and straightforwardly affirm that Pharaoh *freely* hardened his own heart (Exod. 8:15, 32) while affirming that God also hardened Pharaoh's heart (without determining Pharaoh's will) by doing some things that, combined with Pharaoh's *free* decisions, resulted in Pharaoh's heart being hardened (e.g., bringing

---

88. Since the Creator sustains all things, there can be no *competition* between divine and creaturely causation. However, insofar as God grants creatures freedom to do otherwise than he ideally wills, creatures can act contrary to what God prefers.

89. Alvin Plantinga explains, "In the strong sense, God can actualize only what he can cause [by himself] to be actual," but weak actualization refers to what God actualizes in a way that depends on the free decisions of others. A. Plantinga, *Nature of Necessity*, 173.

90. Scripture depicts many divine judgments as instances in which, in response to people's decisions to reject God and serve the "gods" of the nations (Judg. 10:6–16; cf. Deut. 29:24–26), God reluctantly withdraws his protection and "gives" them over to their enemies (e.g., Judg. 2:13–14; Ezra 5:12; Neh. 9:30; Ps. 106:41–42; Jer. 38:18; cf. Ps. 81:12). Accordingly, God laments the excessive devastation Babylon inflicted and judges Babylon and her gods for it (Jer. 51:24–25, 44; cf. 25:12–14; 50–51; Zech. 1:15).

Pharaoh to points of decision via the plagues). On this understanding, God takes into account what creatures freely will but also acts in a way that greatly affects history, bringing about the most preferable outcome that is available without infringing on the free will of creatures.

This also provides a consistent interpretation of the case of Joseph, particularly Joseph's explanation to his brothers about their selling him into slavery: "Even though you intended to do harm to me, God intended it for good, in order to preserve a numerous people, as he is doing today" (Gen. 50:20). Given the above understanding of weak actualization and the distinction between God's ideal will and his remedial will, one can consistently affirm that Joseph's brothers sold him into slavery of their own libertarian free will, against what God actually preferred (God's ideal will) since it was evil, while also affirming that God weakly actualized this outcome according to his remedial will, for the good purpose of preserving many people (50:20). Notably, the very fact that "God intended" this for the purpose of saving many people points toward indeterminism because if God was causally determining everything to occur just as he preferred, he could have preserved the people from famine in many other ways (e.g., providing manna from heaven). Here and in many other cases, God takes what appears to be a circuitous route to his purpose, which suggests God works around numerous unseen factors and impediments (see chap. 6).[91]

Although God possesses the power to determine all events, God also grants creatures libertarian free will. God does so, I believe, because God is love, and as I have argued elsewhere, genuine love relationship requires *consequential freedom*—that is, libertarian freedom to bring about in the external world what one internally wills (to some limited extent).[92] If so, the flourishing of love relationship involving creatures requires that creatures possess freedom to act within some noncapricious limits in a context in which relatively predictable effects follow from causal actions. As Michael Murray puts it, "Free and effective choice" requires some "nomic regularity"—that is, a "natural order" that "operate[s] by regular and well-ordered laws of nature," within which creatures may "form intentions" and have "reason to believe . . . certain bodily movements" will likely actualize those intentions.[93] If this is correct, love is not only the fulfillment of the law (Rom. 13:10), but the law is also

91. Even in the cases of Balaam and Jonah, the context indicates God was not causally determining their wills. God was displeased by Balaam's attempts to curse Israel after God told him not to (e.g., Num. 22:12, 22), and Balaam later gave Balak a successful plan to corrupt Israel (31:16; cf. Rev. 2:14), which makes little sense if God determined Balaam's will all along. Likewise, if God determined Jonah's will, he could have made Jonah go directly to Nineveh.

92. See Peckham, *Theodicy of Love*, 41–45.

93. Murray, *Nature Red in Tooth and Claw*, 7, 139–40.

integral to the flourishing of love. In my view, there is good reason to believe that God has ordered the world to operate according to some consistent "laws" of nature, which he himself covenants not to contravene because such order is conducive to the maximal flourishing of love.[94]

Notably, insofar as God commits to consistently granting creatures consequential freedom and upholding the nomic regularity he has established for the good of all, God's own freedom is thereby limited. Even as God does not break his promises, God does not break his own laws (Pss. 89:34; 111:7–8; 119:160). Because God invariably keeps his promises, God's actions are (morally) limited by whatever promises and covenants he makes without in any way limiting God's sheer power. Because some creatures exercise their consequential freedom to do otherwise than God prefers, many things occur that God does not ideally desire. Yet God's remedial will takes all this into account such that God's (remedial) purpose will finally come about and all creation will enjoy the endless, uninterrupted, blissful flourishing of love (Rev. 21:3–4).

This model of God's providence of sovereign love offers a consistent account of God's unfulfilled desires that are prominent throughout Scripture alongside a robust account of God's sovereignty and exhaustive foreknowledge, affirming both that God actually prefers that no evil ever occur and that God's purpose ultimately triumphs. Love triumphs over evil.[95] God does not always get what he wants (his ideal will), but God will certainly accomplish his all-encompassing purpose (his remedial will).

Some Questions and Implications

A number of implications warrant further discussion, but space permits only brief consideration of a few relevant issues.[96] First, the doctrine of divine omnipotence is crucial to affirming that God has the ability to respond to our prayers and bring about what he has promised and covenanted (cf. 2 Cor. 6:18), including the full restoration of the universe to perfect goodness and harmony. As Thomas Morris puts it, "Unless he is sufficiently powerful, we cannot be confident that he will succeed" in keeping his promises.[97] If God is all-powerful, however, God has the power to heal the brokenhearted, set the

94. See the discussion in chap. 6.
95. Cf. Bruce R. Reichenbach's treatment on the interrelationship of love, creaturely freedom, and divine sovereignty. Reichenbach, *Divine Providence.*
96. Another issue that warrants further discussion, but cannot be addressed in any detail here, is the nature of divine action. For a case that "special divine action in the world—causing a miracle" is compatible with science, see A. Plantinga, *Where the Conflict Really Lies,* 91–125. See further Abraham, *Divine Agency and Divine Action.*
97. T. Morris, *Our Idea of God,* 65–66.

captives free, make the lame to walk again, cause the blind to see, feed the hungry, restore justice, and raise the dead to eternal life. The one who alone has the power to create, sustain, redeem, and restore the universe is the God of Scripture who is worthy of all worship and praise (Rev. 4:11).

Yet given that the covenantal God of Scripture always keeps his promises, insofar as God commits himself to granting consequential freedom, the way creatures exercise that freedom is not up to God. While remaining omnipotent, God morally limits his actions to whatever parameters he has covenanted or committed to (Ps. 89:34) for the sake of love. As John Wesley once put it:

> [God] cannot counteract himself, or oppose his own work. Were it not for this, he would destroy all sin, with its attendant pain, in a moment. He would abolish wickedness out of his whole creation, and suffer no trace of it to remain. But in so doing he would counteract himself; he would altogether overturn his own work. . . . If, therefore, God were thus to exert his power, there would certainly be no more vice; but it is equally certain, neither could there be any virtue in the world. Were human liberty taken away, men would be as incapable of virtue as stones. Therefore (with reverence be it spoken) the Almighty himself cannot do this thing. He cannot thus contradict himself or undo what he has done.[98]

One might ask whether such a view undermines divine sovereignty. I believe it does not. Even as a ruler may remain sovereign while granting some power and jurisdiction to a vice-regent, God remains sovereign even as he grants creatures consequential freedom. As A. W. Tozer put it:

> God sovereignly decreed that man should be free to exercise moral choice, and man from the beginning has fulfilled that decree by making his choice between good and evil. When he chooses to do evil, he does not thereby countervail the sovereign will of God but fulfills it, inasmuch as the eternal decree decided not which choice the man should make but that he should be free to make it. If in His absolute freedom God has willed to give man limited freedom, who is there to stay His hand or say, "What doest thou?" Man's will is free because God is sovereign. A God less than sovereign could not bestow moral freedom upon His creatures. He would be afraid to do so. . . . Certain things have been decreed by the free determination of God, and one of these is the law of choice and consequences.[99]

One might further protest that God should not grant *so much* consequential freedom, precisely because it can be so misused. However, as discussed

---

98. Wesley, "On Divine Providence," in *Works of John Wesley*, 6:339–40.
99. Tozer, *Knowledge of the Holy*, 111–12.

in the next chapter, God might have morally sufficient reason(s) to grant consequential freedom just as he has—love itself may depend on it. For now, it is important to note that insofar as God grants us consequential freedom to impact history, we are (in a limited and circumscribed sense) coauthors of history. While I believe God has good reasons that morally restrict him from intervening in some cases (see chap. 6), many evils are within our power to prevent or mitigate, if we are willing. It is within the power of many humans to feed many other humans; indeed, there is enough food produced on this planet to feed everyone. Further, many humans possess the means to significantly reduce, and perhaps eventually eliminate, the poverty of others.

It is within our power to reject racism and sexism and stand against systemic injustice in our societies—working individually and collectively to bring about a state of affairs that is closer to justice and doing so as a way of keeping the great commandment that we are to love our neighbor as ourselves. Scripture itself is replete with calls to establish justice (e.g., among many others, Mic. 6:8; Zech. 7:9–10). A major theme of the prophets is the lack of justice in society, and Jesus himself laments and rebukes the neglect of "justice and mercy and faithfulness," "the weightier provisions of the law" (Matt. 23:23 NASB). In the end, we will be judged relative to how we treated the poor, imprisoned, and oppressed (see Matt. 25). Here the words of 1 John 4:20–21 ring loud and clear: "Those who say, 'I love God,' and hate their brothers or sisters, are liars; for those who do not love a brother or sister whom they have seen, cannot love God whom they have not seen. The commandment we have from him is this: those who love God must love their brothers and sisters also."

Further, God calls humans to be stewards—even in some sense co*rulers*—of this planet (Gen. 1:28), as he commissioned Adam and Eve to "cultivate" and "keep" the garden of Eden (2:15 NASB). Humans are to be caretakers rather than dominators, valuing fellow creatures as God's creation and taking care of creation as best we can.[100] As such, we might encourage practices that take better care of creation—individually doing what we can and encouraging systemic changes that are better for the environment. We might foster a way of life that treasures slowing down and resting—even as Genesis 2 depicts God himself resting from his work on the seventh day—resting from both work and mass consumerism that drive a considerable amount of the depletion of natural resources and contribute to environmental harm. We might pay closer attention to our diet, fostering ethical eating and moving toward diets that are more earth-friendly and (as my colleague and friend Rahel Wells puts it) cruelty free. As Scripture repeatedly emphasizes, God cares for animals, and

100. See, in this regard, Moo and Moo, *Creation Care.*

a "righteous man has regard for the life of his animal" (Prov. 12:10 NASB; cf. Ps. 36:6; Jon. 4:11).[101]

In these and other respects, if God actually prefers those things that Scripture consistently depicts God as preferring (love, goodness, justice, care for creation), then there are many states of affairs that God does not prefer that might be within our power to at least mitigate if not prevent altogether. If so, what we do and fail to do matters a great deal. After all, according to Psalm 115:16, "The heavens are the LORD's heavens, / but the earth he has given to human beings."

If God's ideal will is often unfulfilled, it will not do to think and act as if everything in the world takes place as God prefers. If it makes sense to pray that God's will be done on earth as it is in heaven (Matt. 6:10), it follows that God's will might not be done on earth. Moreover, it makes little sense to pray for God's will to be done on earth (as crucial as that is) while doing little or nothing to bring about what God has revealed to be his will on earth—like those who pass by the beaten man on the side of the road in Christ's parable of the good Samaritan (cf. Isa 1:15–17). We should not only heed Christ's instructions relative to prayer in the Sermon on the Mount but also heed the rest of the sermon (and Christ's wider counsel) on how we ought to treat others and thereby love and serve the Lord by loving and serving others (Matt. 25).

This understanding of divine providence highlights the importance of our moral agency in the world as Christ followers (consistent with Scripture's emphasis on how we are to live and treat others and the mandate to be caretakers of God's good creation) while also upholding a robust model of the providence of sovereign love that gives us confidence that the many problems that are beyond our ability to resolve will one day be resolved by the omnipotent Creator himself. In the meantime, I am convicted that we should do what we can within our sphere of influence to bring about good in this world and stand against evil and injustice of all kinds.

Conclusion

This chapter addressed the issues of divine power and the exercise of divine power, concluding that God is omnipotent, meaning God has the power to do anything that is logically possible and consistent with his essential nature. God possesses the power to determine all events but has chosen not to exercise his power to causally determine history, instead consistently granting libertarian free will to creatures (within consistent limits). On this view, God is

---

101. See Schafer, "'You, YHWH, Save Humans and Animals.'"

the all-powerful, sovereign ruler who grants genuine power to creatures and himself acts in accordance with his covenant promises. Tragically, because some creatures exercise their free will to do otherwise than God ideally desires, God's ideal desires are often unfulfilled. Yet because God has exhaustive definite foreknowledge, God takes into account all the free decisions of creatures, including the bad ones (which are not up to God), and remedially wills the most preferable outcome given such decisions. In this way, God sovereignly governs all of creation such that God's *remedial* will always comes to pass, but much of what occurs in creation is *not* what God actually prefers. Accordingly, God calls his followers to be agents of change for good in this world and identifies those who truly love and belong to him as those who love others not only in word but also in deed.

Six

The Goodness of God and the Problem of Evil

Faithfulness and Omnibenevolence

I vividly remember the day my then eighteen-month-old son Joel required a blood draw to determine whether he needed a potentially lifesaving medical procedure. The nurse asked my wife and me to hold Joel's little arms and legs while she drew his blood. I will never forget the way Joel looked at me as I held him down and the nurse stuck him with a needle. He was too young to talk, but his tear-filled eyes said it all: "Why are you doing this to me, Daddy? Why are you holding me here and letting her hurt me? It hurts! Why aren't you helping me?!"

There was nothing I could have said to Joel at the time to make him understand why it appeared that I was hurting him—or was at least complicit in inflicting pain on him. If he could have known and understood what I knew, then he would have recognized that I had no better alternative. I did not want to hold him down. I did not want him to be stuck with a needle. I did not want him to be hurt—I never want him to be hurt. When he broke his arm a few years later in a playground accident, I wished my arm had been broken instead of his. When I held him down as the nurse drew his blood, I was doing everything I could for his best good. Thankfully, Joel was fine, but I will never forget that look in his little tear-filled eyes.

Faced with the suffering of this world, we might similarly wonder why God does not prevent evil and end suffering. We might even think God should be doing x, y, or z. Yet even as Joel could not understand why I held him down, we may not be in a position to understand why God acts as he does. Perhaps there is far more going on than we can see.

This chapter takes up the issue of God's goodness, particularly in light of the problem of evil, addressing questions such as, Is God entirely good and loving? If so, why is there *so much* evil in this world?[1]

The Goodness of the Covenantal God of Scripture

The covenantal God of Scripture is good—entirely good. The God of Scripture is the God of goodness, truth, and beauty.[2] Scripture teaches that God is entirely faithful, righteous, holy, and loving. God's "work is perfect, / and all his ways are just.[3] / A faithful God, without deceit, / just and upright is he" (Deut. 32:4). "God is a righteous judge" (Ps. 7:11) and "has established his throne for judgment. / He judges the world with righteousness; / he judges the peoples with equity" (9:7–8; cf. 67:4; 96:10). "Good and upright is the LORD" (25:8; cf. Isa. 26:7), so "taste and see that the LORD is good" (Ps. 34:8). God "is upright; / he is my rock, and there is no unrighteousness in him" (92:15; cf. 129:4). God "is righteous; he does no wrong" (Zeph. 3:5). God is omnibenevolent—he always does what is preferable for all concerned. Indeed, "the LORD is good to all, / and his compassion is over all that he has made"; he "is just in all his ways, / and kind in all his doings" (Ps. 145:9, 17). "No evil dwells with" God (5:4 NASB). "God is light and in him there is no darkness at all" (1 John 1:5). As such, "God cannot be tempted by evil" (James 1:13; cf. 1:17; Hab. 1:13). God's "righteousness endures forever" (2 Cor. 9:9), and in the end, his "righteous judgment will be revealed" (Rom. 2:5; cf. 3:25–26). Finally, the redeemed will sing,

> Great and amazing are your deeds,
>   Lord God the Almighty!
> Just and true are your ways,
>   King of the nations!
> Lord, who will not fear
>   and glorify your name?

---

1. This chapter draws from and revises sections of Peckham, *Theodicy of Love*.
2. See J. Davidson, *Toward a Theology of Beauty*.
3. Indeed, a case can be made that the entire biblical canon functions as a covenant witness document, documenting God's love and faithfulness. See Peckham, *Canonical Theology*, 21–28.

For you alone are holy.
All nations will come
and worship before you,
for your judgments have been revealed. (Rev. 15:3–4)

Further, they proclaim,

Hallelujah!
Salvation and glory and power to our God,
for his judgments are true and just. (19:1–2; cf. Pss. 89:5;
119:137–38)

Scripture repeatedly highlights the close link between God's goodness, righteousness, faithfulness, and steadfast love. Psalm 33:4–5 declares,

The word of the LORD is upright,
and all his work is done in faithfulness.
He loves righteousness and justice;
the earth is full of the steadfast love of the LORD. (cf. 37:28)

Further, Psalm 36:5–6 states,

Your steadfast love, O LORD, extends to the heavens,
your faithfulness to the clouds.
Your righteousness is like the mighty mountains,
your judgments are like the great deep.

Again, Psalm 89:14 proclaims, "Righteousness and justice are the foundation of your throne; / steadfast love and faithfulness go before you" (cf. 85:10; Isa. 16:5; Mic. 6:8). Indeed, God himself declares, "I act with steadfast love, justice, and righteousness in the earth, for in these things I delight" (Jer. 9:24; cf. Hosea 2:19).[4] Accordingly,

The steadfast love of the LORD is from everlasting to everlasting
on those who fear him,
and his righteousness to children's children. (Ps. 103:17; cf. 101:1;
119:149)

---

4. Divine *ḥesed* ("steadfast love," "lovingkindness") is frequently associated with justice, especially *ṣədāqâ* ("righteousness") (1 Kings 3:6; Pss. 36:10; 40:10; 85:10; 103:17; Prov. 21:21; Hosea 10:12) and *mišpāṭ* ("justice/judgment") (Pss. 101:1; 119:149; Hosea 12:6; Mic. 6:8; Zech. 7:9). The three terms appear together numerous times (e.g., Pss. 33:5; 89:14; Isa. 16:5; Jer. 9:24; Hosea 2:19).

God is "the faithful God, who keeps His covenant and His lovingkindness to a thousandth generation with those who love Him and keep His commandments" (Deut. 7:9 NASB). Indeed, God's "steadfast love is established forever"; his "faithfulness [*'ĕmûnâ*] is as firm as the heavens" (Ps. 89:2). Again,

> The LORD is good;
>   his steadfast love endures forever,
>   and his faithfulness [*'ĕmûnâ*] to all generations. (Ps. 100:5; cf. 57:10; 89:1, 24, 33)

Even amid lament,

> The steadfast love of the LORD never ceases,
>   his mercies never come to an end;
> they are new every morning;
>   great is your faithfulness. (Lam. 3:22–23)

The God of Scripture is the covenantal God, "abounding in steadfast love [*ḥesed*] and faithfulness [*'ĕmet*]" (Exod. 34:6). As Nahum Sarna explains, this "combination of terms [*ḥesed* and *'ĕmet*] expresses God's absolute and eternal dependability in dispensing His benefactions."[5]

While God's steadfast love far exceeds all reasonable expectations—including covenant responsibilities—it does not override or contravene justice but brings justice and mercy together (cf. Ps. 85:10). In the aftermath of the golden calf rebellion, God demonstrates that he is

> merciful and gracious,
> slow to anger,
> and abounding in steadfast love and faithfulness,
> keeping steadfast love for the thousandth generation,
> forgiving iniquity and transgression and sin,
> yet by no means clearing the guilty. (Exod. 34:6–7)

This text and others emphasize that God will not turn a blind eye to injustice. Yet while the consequences of parents' iniquity extends to the third and

---

5. Sarna, *Exodus*, 216. Scripture repeatedly links God's steadfast love (*ḥesed*) and faithfulness (*'ĕmet*) or truth (e.g., Gen. 24:27; Exod. 34:6; Pss. 40:10–11; 57:3; 61:7; 85:10; 86:15; 89:14; 138:2; Mic. 7:20). *Ḥesed* is also frequently linked with *'āman*, the verb "to be faithful" (e.g., Deut. 7:9; cf. Ps. 89:1–2), and *'ĕmûnâ*, the noun "faithfulness" (e.g., Pss. 36:5; 89:2; 92:2; 98:3; 100:5). See Jepsen, "אמן," 1:314.

fourth generations of those who hate God, God keeps "steadfast love to the thousandth generation" (20:6; 34:7; Deut. 5:10; 7:9; Jer. 32:18).[6] God forgives abundantly but does not thereby forsake justice. God can forgive without injustice because, in Christ, God provided "a sacrifice of atonement" and "did this to show his righteousness . . . to prove at the present time that he himself is righteous" even as he "justifies the one who has faith in Jesus" (Rom. 3:25–26; cf. 1 John 1:9). God's demonstration of his righteousness is also the supreme demonstration of love: "God proves his love for us in that while we still were sinners Christ died for us" (Rom. 5:8).

Importantly, in this regard, Scott Hahn makes a case for understanding divine justice and mercy "as aspects of covenant fidelity." He explains, "In the context of covenant, the justice of God does not consist merely in enforcing obedience to the law, but also in fidelity to his own sworn covenant commitments. Thus, it is a matter of *justice* for God to keep his covenant obligations," which include his promise of "showing mercy to the seed of Abraham, and through that seed to the whole human family. Therefore, through the covenant relationship God establishes between himself and his people, he has devised a just way to dispense his mercy and a merciful way to dispense justice."[7]

From beginning to end, in the midst of triumphs and trials, Scripture affirms that "God is faithful" (1 Cor. 1:9; 10:13; cf. 2 Cor. 1:18). In all things, God's "way is perfect; / the promise of the LORD proves true; / he is a shield for all who take refuge in him" (Ps. 18:30). Further, "the Lord is faithful; he will strengthen you and guard you from the evil one" (2 Thess. 3:3). Again, "he who has promised is faithful" (Heb. 10:23; cf. 1 Thess. 5:24; Heb. 11:11); even "if we are faithless, he remains faithful—for he cannot deny himself" (2 Tim. 2:13). Accordingly, Revelation 3:14 identifies Christ as "the Amen, the faithful and true witness" (cf. John 14:6; Heb. 2:14; Rev. 1:5; 19:11).

God's faithfulness is inextricably linked to his holiness. God alone is entirely "faithful, the Holy One of Israel" (Isa. 49:7; cf. Rev. 3:7). God's holiness not only relates to God's faithfulness and absolute moral purity but also

---

6. John I. Durham proposes that the phrase "steadfast love for the thousandth generation" might "better be read 'innumerable descendancy'" (Durham, *Exodus*, 287). Rather than direct divine judgment (cf. Deut. 24:16; 2 Kings 14:6; Ezek. 18:20), the iniquity to the third and fourth generations might be understood as "natural" consequences of the web of history; a parent's life has significant impact, for good or ill, on lives of descendants. Significant generational affects would stem from children and grandchildren lacking the proper Torah instruction that "was essential to their life and well-being" (Craigie, *Book of Deuteronomy*, 154). Cf. Sarna, *Exodus*, 110.

7. Hahn, *Kinship by Covenant*, 336.

reveals God as the one who is essentially "set apart" from creation[8]—that is, God's holiness emphasizes the Creator-creature distinction, closely linked to God's moral purity and the importance of God's relational presence, recalling that (absent mediation) evil cannot be in the presence of the perfectly holy God.[9] As Psalm 5:4 puts it, "No evil dwells with" God (NASB; cf. Isa. 59:2; Hab. 1:13). Created things may be holy in proximity to God (cf. the "holy ground" in Exod. 3:5 and the sanctuary and its compartments as "holy" [hagios] places, e.g., Heb. 9:12). Wherever God dwells is holy by virtue of God's special presence.[10] Even sinful creatures may be sanctified ("made holy," hagiazō) by relationship with God through the atoning work of Christ (Heb. 10:10) and mediation of the Holy Spirit (2 Thess. 2:13; 1 Pet. 1:2). But God "alone" is "holy" in and of himself (Rev. 15:4), the source of goodness, love, and holiness in relation to whom creatures may be holy, as God commands (Lev. 11:44; Matt. 5:48; 1 Pet. 1:15–16) and wills (1 Thess. 4:3; Heb. 10:10).[11] As uniquely holy, God alone is worthy of worship. The seraphim before God's throne thus sing, "Holy, holy, holy is the LORD of hosts; / the whole earth is full of his glory" (Isa. 6:3). And they sing,

> Holy, holy, holy,
> the Lord God the Almighty,
>   who was and is and is to come. (Rev. 4:8)

God's glory is itself linked with God's holiness and his name and character of perfect goodness. When Moses asked God, "Show me your glory," God replied, "I will make all my goodness pass before you, and will proclaim before you the name," YHWH (Exod. 33:18–19; cf. 34:6–7; Rom. 3:23–26). Thus, to God's "name" we are to "give glory, for the sake of [his] steadfast love and [his] faithfulness" (Ps. 115:1; cf. 96:1–4). Because God's reputation affects the way people view him, potentially impeding love and worship, God repeatedly

8. Scripture uses the Hebrew term qādôš ("holy") of God to signify that God is "separate, apart, and so sacred, holy" ("קָדֹשׁ," BDB 872). The root (often via the noun qōdeš) also refers to created objects that may be set apart or consecrated (and thus sacred or holy) in connection to God.

9. Thomas E. McComiskey explains, "The biblical viewpoint would refer the holiness of God not only to the mystery of his power, but also to his character as totally good and entirely without evil. Holy objects" are "dedicated to what is good and kept from what is evil." McComiskey, "קָדֹשׁ," 2:787.

10. As James Arcadi understands it, holy objects "become holy due to the concentration of divine presence at a location of divine action." Arcadi, Incarnational Model of the Eucharist, 98.

11. Notably, if holiness involves proximity to God, but proximity to God in terms of personal presence can be impeded by sin and evil (cf. Ps. 5:4; Isa. 59:2), how we relate to God and live have massive implications.

shows great concern for his name throughout Scripture.[12] For this, and much more, God is to be praised: "O give thanks to the LORD, for he is good; / for his steadfast love endures forever" (Ps. 106:1; cf. 2 Chron. 5:13; Ps. 136). "To the King of the ages, immortal, invisible, the only God, be honor and glory forever and ever" (1 Tim. 1:17).

The Problem of Evil in Scripture

The dissonance between God's goodness and the horrendous evil in this world is not merely a recent philosophical problem; the problem appears prominently in Scripture itself. For instance, Habakkuk 1:13 states, "Your eyes [God] are too pure to behold evil, and you cannot look on wrongdoing" but then immediately asks, "Why do you look on the treacherous, and are silent when the wicked swallow those more righteous than they?" Isaiah adds,

> Justice is far from us,
>   and righteousness does not reach us;
> we wait for light, and lo! there is darkness;
>   and for brightness, but we walk in gloom. . . .
> We wait for justice, but there is none. (59:9, 11; cf. Ps. 53:1–3; Hab. 1:4)

Likewise, Ecclesiastes repeatedly laments the injustice and "grievous evil" in this world (5:13 NASB; cf. 3:16; 6:1; 7:15; 8:14; 10:5), suggesting it would be "better" to have "never existed" and "never seen the evil activity that is done under the sun" (4:3 NASB). Job suffered so much that he "cursed the day of his birth" (Job 3:1) and questioned God's justice (9:24; cf. 16:9, 11). He further laments,

> I cry to you and you do not answer me; . . .
> You have turned cruel to me;
>   with the might of your hand you persecute me. . . .
> But when I looked for good, evil came;
>   and when I waited for light, darkness came. (30:20–21, 26)

Over and over, the problem of evil is raised in Scripture. "Where is the God of justice?" (Mal. 2:17). "Why, O LORD, do you stand far off? Why do you hide yourself in times of trouble?" (Ps. 10:1). Lord, "How long shall the wicked exult?" (94:3; cf. 77:7–10; 94:4–7). "Why does the way of the guilty

---

12. See, among many other examples, Ps. 109:21; Isa. 48:9, 11; Ezek. 18:25; 20:9, 14, 22, 44; cf. Gen. 18:24–25; Exod. 32:12–13; Num. 14:15–16; Deut. 9:28; Josh. 7:7–9. See also Rom. 3:26; 5:8.

prosper? Why do all who are treacherous thrive?" (Jer. 12:1; cf. Job 12:6; 21:7). "Why has the LORD our God done all these things to us?" (Jer. 5:19). "Why is the land ruined and laid waste?" (9:12). "Why have these things come upon me?" (13:22; cf. 16:10). Even Jesus asks, "My God, my God, why have you forsaken me?" (Mark 15:34; cf. Ps. 22; Matt. 27:46).

Why does evil seem to reign in this world? How could God be entirely good, loving, and righteous given the enormity of evil and injustice in this world? If God is omniscient, God is aware of all the evil in this world. If God is omnipotent, God has the power to prevent all evil. If God is omnibenevolent, God would desire to prevent every evil.[13] How, then, can there be evil in this world, and so much of it? These last questions relate to the logical and evidential problems of evil. The logical problem claims that the premise "there is evil in the world" is logically inconsistent with the premises that God is omnipotent, God is omniscient, and God is omnibenevolent.[14] The evidential problem claims that the kind and amount of evil in this world are such that it is *improbable* that an omnipotent, omniscient, and omnibenevolent God exists.[15]

These philosophical problems are distinct from the religious or existential problem of evil, which relates to how people deal with experiences of suffering and evil. This chapter focuses on the philosophical problems, concerned primarily with how one might reconcile the goodness and love of God with the fact that there is so much evil in the world, without justifying, explaining away, or trivializing evil itself. Rather than attempting a full-blown solution to the philosophical problems, the remainder of this chapter offers a brief discussion of some approaches to the problem of evil, focusing finally on some avenues that might be helpful, including a cosmic conflict theodicy of love, premised on the view that God is a covenantal God of love.

---

13. Moral evil may be defined as (but not reduced to) what is opposed to God's (ideal) desires (cf. Ps. 5:4) and thus opposed to God's love. This does not mean that if God desired some evil *x*, *x* would cease to be evil but presupposes that God desires only that which is congruent with his perfect character. See Baggett and Walls, *Good God*. At first glance, however, some texts may appear to attribute moral evil to God (e.g., Isa. 45:7). Such passages employ the term *rāʿaʿ*, which broadly refers to that which is undesirable from someone's point of view (whether or not it is unjust or morally wrong) and thus often refers to calamities and disasters. When predicated of God, *rāʿaʿ* refers to judgments (i.e., calamities) God righteously brings against moral evil (Ps. 44:2; Isa. 45:7; Jer. 25:29; 31:28; Mic. 4:6; Zech. 8:14). As David W. Baker explains, the primary OT root translated "evil" (*rāʿaʿ*) is "a uniting into one word of what in English is expressed by two words, physical (bad) and moral (evil)." Baker, "רָעַע," 3:1155.

14. See Mackie, "Evil and Omnipotence," 201–2. Cf. Hume, *Dialogues Concerning Natural Religion*, 134.

15. On the evidential problem of evil, see Rowe, *God and the Problem of Evil*, 121–233.

Some Common Approaches to the Problem of Evil

Denying the Premises, Modifying the Premises, or Felix Culpa

One way to resolve the conceptual problem is to deny some premise of the logical problem of evil. Given that there is evil in the world, one might deny that God is omnipotent, omniscient, or omnibenevolent.[16] Denying omnibenevolence is not a live option for me, however, because denying God's goodness contradicts Scripture and undermines the core of Christian faith. Denying omniscience is not a live option for the same reasons. Yet some argue that God lacks exhaustive definite foreknowledge such that God cannot be blamed for not preventing or warning us about evils he did not foreknow.[17] However, not only do I believe that Scripture affirms that God possesses exhaustive definite foreknowledge; I do not believe that denying this provides any conceptual advantage regarding the problem of evil. As discussed earlier, even if God possessed only exhaustive knowledge of the past and the present, God would thereby possess sufficient knowledge to anticipate any evil just before it would occur and could thus exercise his power to prevent it. If God has good reasons for not doing so, such reasons would apply whether or not God possesses exhaustive definite foreknowledge.

However, if one denies God is omnipotent, at least in the traditional sense, then evil might be explained by claiming that God does not possess the power to prevent the evils that occur in this world.[18] Yet not only does this deny the traditional notions of divine omnipotence and sovereignty, but it also can provide no assurance that evil will finally be defeated in the end.[19] Moreover, as discussed in chapter 5, Scripture is filled with miracle accounts. If God actually worked such miracles in the past, as Scripture claims, it cannot be true that God cannot (by nature) work the kinds of miracles that would prevent evils that occur in this world. If God actually provided manna from heaven (Exod. 16:35), sent his angel to shut the mouths of lions (Dan. 6:22; cf. 3:24–28), calmed storms (Mark 4:39–41), healed various kinds of illnesses

16. See Roth, "Theodicy of Protest," 1–20.

17. As Richard Rice explains, "Open theodicy" maintains that since future "free decisions" are "not there to be known," God is not only "not responsible for these decisions" but also "cannot be blamed for not knowing them, not preventing them or not warning us about them." Rice, *Suffering and the Search for Meaning*, 104.

18. David Ray Griffin contends, "We must fully surrender" the "traditional doctrine of divine omnipotence" in order to maintain that God "is unambiguously loving" (D. Griffin, "Critique of the Free Will Defense," 96). See also Oord, *Uncontrolling Love of God*, 141, 148, 181.

19. Griffin states that whether "God will be effectual in bringing about this new form of civilization will depend on whether we respond to this call." D. Griffin, "Critique of a Theodicy of Protest," 28.

(Luke 4:40), and raised people from the dead (e.g., 1 Kings 17:17–24), then God must possess the power to do things that would assuage starvation, cure illnesses, and even reverse death.

One might claim, instead, that it is actually fortunate there is evil in this world—a view called *felix culpa* (literally "happy fault").[20] Those who affirm *felix culpa*, of various kinds, claim evil is somehow *necessary* for some greater good(s).[21] Many advocates of *felix culpa* even claim that "each evil or possible evil removed takes away one more actual good."[22] Each evil, then, is actually an instrumental good.[23] Preventing any evil would actually reduce the goodness of the world, and any "evil" deed actually ends up increasing the goodness of the world.[24] Yet Paul directly rejects that we should "do evil so that good may come" (Rom. 3:8; cf. 6:1–2).

A *felix culpa* advocate might instead claim that the world would be better off without some evil, but it is better that evil has occurred because at least some evil is necessary for greater good(s). Many biblical passages indicate that God frequently brings good out of evil occurrences.[25] As Richard Rice puts it, "While in themselves [evils] have no benefit, God can respond even to life's greatest losses in ways that bless and benefit us."[26] However, I do not see any evidence that evil itself is *necessary* for good, and I believe that the many

20. As Thomas Aquinas put it, "God allows evils to happen in order to bring a greater good therefrom," and thus "we say: 'O happy fault, that merited such and so great a Redeemer'" (Thomas Aquinas, *Summa Theologiae* III.1.3). Cf. Ambrose, *De Institutione Virginis* 17, 104; Augustine, *Enchiridion* 27 (*NPNF* 3:246).

21. Consider Gottfried Leibniz's claim that this world must be the best possible world because "God cannot fail to produce the best" (Leibniz, *Theodicy*, 264). Yet many have argued there may not be a *best* possible world. See Adams, "Must God Create the Best?," 24.

22. Swinburne, "Some Major Strands of Theodicy," 258. Richard Swinburne's "higher-order goods defense" claims that some higher-order goods (e.g., sympathy, courage) can only be performed "in the face of evils" (Swinburne, "Some Major Strands of Theodicy," 250). Other prominent *felix culpa* approaches include John Hick's soul-making theodicy and the divine glory defense favored by some determinists. Hick's soul-making theodicy claims that genuine morality and love can result only from a free process of development, requiring an evil environment with suffering and significant (epistemic) distance from God. See Hick, *Evil and the God of Love*. Divine glory defenses claim evil is necessary for the manifestation of God's glory via wrath against evil. For more discussion of such approaches, see Peckham, *Theodicy of Love*, chap. 6.

23. Hick "reluctantly" admits his view involves "some kind of instrumental view of evil." Hick, *Evil and the God of Love*, 239.

24. If so, Kevin Diller notes, "We can no longer condemn evil and injustice as wholly antithetical to what is good" (Diller, "Are Sin and Evil Necessary?," 402). Karl Barth adds, if "sin is understood positively" such that it "counterbalances grace and is indispensable to it, it is not real sin." *CD* III/3, 333.

25. Some biblical passages indicate suffering might assist in building character and reliance on God (e.g., Rom. 5:3–4; 1 Pet. 4:12–14; cf. 2 Cor. 12:8–10). However, such passages presuppose a fallen world wherein humans are sinful, need reconciliation, and face the devil's attacks.

26. Rice, *Suffering and the Search for Meaning*, 152.

biblical commands to "hate what is evil" (Rom. 12:9; cf. Ps. 97:10; Prov. 8:13; Amos 5:15) and the affirmations that God himself hates evil (Ps. 5:4–5; Prov. 6:16–19; Isa. 61:8) amount to the conclusion that God actually prefers that evil had never occurred.[27] I could be wrong about this, and *felix culpa* approaches warrant further discussion, but given this and other serious concerns I have regarding the view that evil is necessary for good, I will turn to focusing on approaches I believe are more promising relative to the standards of biblical warrant and systematic coherence.

Skeptical Theism

The approach of skeptical theism argues that, given our limited cognitive abilities and perspective, we should not expect to be in a position to know what God's reasons relative to evil are.[28] The skeptical theist, then, is "skeptical" about human capacity to be aware of and understand God's reasons relative to the evil in this world. As Alvin Plantinga puts it, just because one "can't see what God's reason might be," it "doesn't follow that probably God doesn't have a reason."[29] Indeed, Stephen Wykstra explains that just as one might not be able to see some "tiny flies" ("noseeums") that are present but so small that you "no see 'um," one might not be in a position to see God's reasons with respect to evil.[30]

Something like skeptical theism appears in Scripture. At the end of the book of Job, God asks a series of questions that highlight how limited human understanding is regarding God's ways:

> Who is this that darkens counsel by words without knowledge? (38:2)

> Where were you when I laid the foundation of the earth?
>   Tell me, if you have understanding. (38:4)

> Have the gates of death been revealed to you,
>   or have you seen the gates of deep darkness?
> Have you comprehended the expanse of the earth?
>   Declare, if you know all this. (38:17–18; cf. 38:33; 40:2, 8)

27. It seems to me that the value of virtuous responses to evil is grounded in love's value and, presumably, that in a world without evil, there would be comparable or better virtuous actions that more deeply manifest love. See Peckham, *Theodicy of Love*, 24.

28. On skeptical theism, see McBrayer and Howard-Snyder, *Blackwell Companion to the Problem of Evil*, 377–506.

29. A. Plantinga, *Warranted Christian Belief*, 497.

30. Wykstra, "Rowe's Noseeum Arguments from Evil," 126.

Whatever else one might say about evil, we should recognize how little we know (cf. Job 42:3). In this regard, Paul writes, "O the depth of the riches and wisdom and knowledge of God! How unsearchable are his judgments and how inscrutable his ways!" (Rom. 11:33; cf. Isa. 55:8–9). God alone, as omniscient and perfectly good, possesses the perspective necessary to judge comprehensively and righteously. While I believe that skeptical theism is a viable avenue with respect to the problem of evil, however, I also think that Scripture reveals more regarding the problem of evil.

The Free Will Defense

The free will defense maintains that evil is the result of the misuse of creaturely free will such that "God is not to be blamed for the existence of moral evil. We are."[31] The free will defense has a long history in the Christian tradition. As Paul Gavrilyuk puts it, "Relatively early among patristic theologians, a broad agreement emerged that the free will of some rational creatures accounted for the actualization of evil. The Creator could not be held responsible for the free evil choices that rational creatures made, since God did not causally determine these choices."[32] Rather, the "misuse of angelic and human free will is the cause of evil."[33]

More recently, Alvin Plantinga set forth a widely lauded articulation of the free will defense.[34] Indeed, the atheist philosopher William Rowe wrote, "The logical problem of evil has been severely diminished, if not entirely resolved" as a "result of Plantinga's work."[35] Plantinga posits that a world with "significantly free" creatures might be "more valuable, all else being equal, than a world containing no free creatures."[36] Yet "to create creatures capable of moral good," God "must create creatures capable of moral evil; and He can't give these creatures the freedom to perform evil and at the same time prevent them from doing so."[37] Indeed, if God grants free will to Maurice "with respect to" a particular "action, then whether or not he actually performs the action is up to Maurice—not God."[38] Tragically, some free creatures "went wrong

---

31. Davis, "Free Will and Evil," 75.
32. Gavrilyuk, "Overview of Patristic Theodicies," 4. See, e.g., Augustine, *On Free Choice of the Will*.
33. Gavrilyuk, "Overview of Patristic Theodicies," 6.
34. Plantinga's defense describes only what "God's reason [for evil] might possibly be." A. Plantinga, *God, Freedom, and Evil*, 28.
35. Rowe, "Introduction to Part II," 76.
36. A. Plantinga, *God, Freedom, and Evil*, 30.
37. A. Plantinga, *God, Freedom, and Evil*, 30.
38. A. Plantinga, *God, Freedom, and Evil*, 44.

in the exercise of their freedom," and "this is the source of moral evil," but it "counts neither against God's omnipotence nor against His goodness; for He could have forestalled the occurrence of moral evil only by removing the possibility of moral good."[39]

In my view, the free will defense succeeds regarding the logical problem of evil. Further, with Stephen Davis, I believe the free will defense "grows out of the witness of the Christian scriptures," particularly in light of the many instances of Scripture wherein creatures will otherwise than God prefers (see chap. 5), alongside Scripture's portrayal of God as the covenantal God—the promise-making and promise-keeping God who always keeps the commitments he makes.[40] I believe that, while valuable in other ways, the greatest value of free will is that it makes love possible. As C. S. Lewis puts it, "Free will, though it makes evil possible, is also the only thing that makes possible any love or goodness or joy worth having. A world of automata—of creatures that worked like machines—would hardly be worth creating. The happiness which God designs for His higher creatures is the happiness of being freely, voluntarily united to Him and to each other. . . . And for that they must be free."[41]

Elsewhere I have argued that love is of supreme outweighing value and that love relationship requires libertarian free will (minimally defined as freedom to will otherwise than God desires).[42] If to will otherwise than God actually prefers is itself evil, as I believe it is, then love relationship itself requires the *possibility* of evil. Yet love does *not* require the actuality of evil. Creatures might have *freely* chosen to do only good. As Davis explains, "It was not necessary that evil exist," but the "possibility of freely doing evil is the inevitable companion of the possibility of freely doing good."[43]

As helpful as it is, however, the free will defense faces some challenging questions. First, if God possesses exhaustive definite foreknowledge, couldn't God have chosen to create only those beings whom he knew would *freely* do only what is good? Here it is crucial to recognize that if creatures are *free* to

39. A. Plantinga, *God, Freedom, and Evil*, 30. So also Leftow, "Omnipotence," 191.

40. Davis, "Free Will and Evil," 89.

41. Lewis, *Mere Christianity*, 48.

42. See Peckham, *Theodicy of Love*, 41–46, 150–52. As Eleonore Stump writes regarding the "mutual love" God desires with humans, "what is mutual cannot be produced unilaterally" (Stump, *Wandering in the Darkness*, 138). Vincent Brümmer adds, "Love is by definition free." Brümmer, *Model of Love*, 175.

43. Davis, "Free Will and Evil," 75. Likewise, the determinist Millard Erickson claims, "Genuine humanity requires the ability to have and do some things contrary to God's intention." Accordingly, "the possibility of evil was a necessary accompaniment of God's good plan to make people human." Erickson, *Christian Theology*, 395.

will otherwise than God prefers, a world (i.e., the entire history of a universe) in which every creature always *freely* chooses to do only good might not be actualizable by God because it depends on what decisions creatures freely make.[44] Further, even if God could "actualize a world including moral good but no moral evil," perhaps such a world would include only a few people or otherwise be less than preferable.[45] Moreover, while God's decisions have ramifications regarding who ends up existing, *perhaps* it would be inconsistent with God's own character and/or morally justified commitments (e.g., to free will) to exclude persons from existing for the *sole purpose* of denying their ability to do otherwise than he ideally desires. Further, as discussed in chapter 4, it may be that various actualizable worlds are of incommensurable value and that God chose to actualize the unique, incommensurable value of this world.

Second, why does God not simply remove the consequences of evil decisions? I have argued elsewhere that the maximal flourishing of love relationship requires that creatures possess *consequential* freedom—that is, freedom to actually impact the world within some consistent parameters or limits. Consequential freedom requires the freedom to act in a context where causal actions bring about relatively predictable effects. This requires some "nomic regularity," a "natural order" that "operate[s] by regular and well-ordered laws of nature," accounting for the consistent relationship of causes and effects in the world.[46] As noted earlier, if God has decreed or covenanted that nature will operate according to some consistent laws of nature (cf. Jer. 33:20–26; 31:35–37), which are themselves conducive to the maximal flourishing of creation, then God himself is not free to act in any way that contravenes those laws of nature (more on this later).

Yet what about evil that it seems God could prevent without undermining anyone's consequential freedom, such as "natural" disasters or evil that could be prevented by advance warning (as in the case of an angel warning Joseph about Herod in Matt. 2:13)? For example, God could prevent a plane crash caused by mechanical difficulties by alerting an appropriate party of the need for repair. In addition, the free will defense faces the problem of (seemingly) selective miracles.[47] Scripture repeatedly portrays God as working miracles to prevent or mitigate some evil (e.g., multiplying food, calming storms, healing all kinds of illnesses). If God acted in history in the ways Scripture claims,

44. Plantinga suggests that perhaps "every creaturely essence suffers from transworld depravity," which means "it was not within God's power to actualize any world in which that person is significantly free but does no wrong." A. Plantinga, *Nature of Necessity*, 189, 186.
45. A. Plantinga, *Nature of Necessity*, 190.
46. Murray, *Nature Red in Tooth and Claw*, 7.
47. See Oord, *Uncontrolling Love of God*, 192.

such special divine actions must not contravene the kind and extent of free will that God is committed to consistently upholding. Free will by itself, then, does not seem adequate to explain why God (at least sometimes) does not intervene in similar instances today. Here I believe there is more to the story, a cosmic conflict.[48]

A Cosmic Conflict Theodicy of Love

The Cosmic Conflict Motif

Scripture repeatedly depicts an ongoing conflict between God's kingdom and the devil and his angels (see, e.g., Matt. 13:24–30, 37–39; Rev. 12:7–10; cf. Matt. 12:24; 25:41), who are fallen celestial creatures who rebelled against God's government (cf. 2 Pet. 2:4; Col. 1:16–17).[49] The Gospels alone are filled with conflict between Jesus and the demonic realm.[50] Jesus repeatedly "by the Spirit of God . . . cast out demons," declaring, "The kingdom of God has come" against the devil's kingdom (Matt. 12:28; cf. Mark 3:23–24; Luke 11:18–20).[51] Indeed, Brian Han Gregg writes, "The conflict between God and Satan is clearly a central feature of Jesus' teaching and ministry."[52] In this regard, 1 John 3:8 teaches that "the Son of God was revealed for this purpose, to destroy the works of the devil" (cf. Gal. 1:4). Further, Christ became human "so that through death he might destroy the one who has the power of death, that is, the devil" (Heb. 2:14; cf. John 12:31–32; Rev. 12:9–11).

Accordingly, at the outset of Christ's ministry, the Spirit drives him "into the wilderness to be tempted by the devil" (Matt. 4:1). In addition to tempting Jesus to turn stones into bread (4:3) and throw himself off the "pinnacle of the temple" as a test of faith (4:5–6), the devil shows Jesus "all the kingdoms of the world and their splendor; and he said to him, 'All these I will give you, if you will fall down and worship me'" (4:8–9). Here the devil seeks to usurp

48. Plantinga himself suggests that so-called natural evils *might* result from the rebellion of "Satan and his cohorts." A. Plantinga, *Nature of Necessity*, 192.

49. Space permits only a brief survey of selected biblical evidence for the cosmic conflict motif. For much more, see Peckham, *Theodicy of Love*, chaps. 3–5. See also Arnold, *Powers of Darkness*; Page, *Powers of Evil*; Noll, *Angels of Light*; Boyd, *God at War*; Heiser, *Unseen Realm*; Cole, *Against the Darkness*.

50. See, e.g., Matt. 4:1–10; 8:28–33; 9:33; 10:1, 8; 17:18; Mark 1:13; 3:15, 22–23; 5:13–15; 7:25–30; 9:17–30; Luke 4:33–36; 8:2, 27–33; 9:38–42; 10:18–19; 11:14; 13:16; John 8:44; cf. Acts 5:3; 26:18; Heb. 2:14; 1 John 3:8.

51. David George Reese comments that God's "kingdom was confronting more than a loose confederation of hostile forces. It faced an opposing kingdom of evil spirits." Reese, "Demons," 2:141.

52. Gregg, *What Does the Bible Say about Suffering?*, 66.

worship due to God alone (cf. Rev. 13:4) and claims jurisdiction over all the world's kingdoms (cf. Luke 4:6). Regarding this episode, Joel B. Green comments, "We discover that the world of humanity is actually ruled by the devil."[53] Here and elsewhere, Scripture portrays an ongoing clash between God's kingdom of light and the demonic kingdom of darkness (Acts 26:18; Rom. 8:38; 13:12; 2 Cor. 10:3–5; Eph. 1:19–21; 6:11–12; Col. 2:15; 1 Tim. 4:1; 1 Pet. 3:22).[54] This, however, is no conflict between equals. Not even close. The devil and his minions are mere creatures (Col. 1:16) who rebelled against God of their own accord, and their domain is both limited and temporary (Matt. 25:41; Rev. 12:12; 20:10), ruling out eternal cosmic dualism.[55] Yet the demonic realm has significant power in the world. Accordingly, Paul exhorts, "Put on the whole armor of God, so that you may be able to stand against the wiles of the devil. For our struggle is not against enemies of blood and flesh, but against the rulers, against the authorities, against the cosmic powers of this present darkness, against the spiritual forces of evil in the heavenly places" (Eph. 6:11–12).[56] As Kevin Vanhoozer states, "The world is now under the

53. Green, *Gospel of Luke*, 194. François Bovon adds that the devil is "saying that God has given him the political authority over the kingdoms of this world" (Bovon, *Luke 1:1–9:50*, 143). Erickson likewise comments, "Satan is actually the ruler of this domain," though a usurper. Erickson, *Christian Theology*, 588.

54. See especially Arnold, *Powers of Darkness*.

55. The constituents of the "domain of darkness" are creatures, as are all things other than God, "things visible and invisible, whether thrones or dominions or rulers or powers" (Col. 1:16). Further, according to 2 Pet. 2:4, at least some evil spirits are fallen "angels" who "sinned." Likewise, Jude 6 refers to "angels who did not keep their own position, but left their proper dwelling." There are various theories about the nature of these angels' sin. For our purposes, it suffices to note they fell by somehow overreaching their "position." As Sydney Page notes, other texts "allude to fallen angels," such as Paul's statement that humans will "judge angels" (1 Cor. 6:3). Further, the "dragon and his angels" (Rev. 12:7) warring against God presupposes "a number of fallen angels," perhaps also referenced via the "stars" swept from heaven by the dragon (12:4) as is "widely held" (Page, *Powers of Evil*, 258). These and other passages have led many to conclude that Satan and his demons are fallen angels. Christians have traditionally interpreted Isa. 14:12–15 and Ezek. 28:12–19 as depicting Satan's fall from perfection. See, e.g., Origen, *De Principiis* 1.5.4; John Cassian, *Conference* 8.8.2; Cyril of Jerusalem, *Catechetical Lectures* 2.4; Jerome, *Homilies on the Psalms* 14; Tertullian, *Against Marcion* 2.10; Ambrose of Milan, *On Paradise* 2.9; Augustine, *City of God* 11.15 (ACCS 13:94–96). While this interpretation has become controversial since the rise of modernistic biblical criticism, I believe the weight of the canonical evidence supports the traditional interpretation (though the cosmic conflict perspective does not hinge on this interpretation). On this, see Peckham, *Theodicy of Love*, 65–66. See also Cole, *Against the Darkness*, 90–92; Boyd, *God at War*, 157–62; L. Cooper, *Ezekiel*, 268. Cf. Heiser, *Unseen Realm*, 75–91.

56. Some have interpreted biblical references to Satan, demons, principalities, and powers as referring to human systems of power or world systems with inner spirituality. See Wink, *Walter Wink*. However, I believe the biblical data points decidedly toward understanding these powers as personal agents that also have systematic impact. See Clinton Arnold's convincing case

dominion of the powers of darkness," and as such, "the world resists and rejects God's authoritative rule."[57]

Just as the devil sought to usurp worship in the temptation, throughout biblical history, demons sought to usurp worship through idol worship. Paul explains that the Gentiles "sacrifice to demons and not to God" (1 Cor. 10:20; cf. 2 Cor. 6:14–15; Rev. 9:20).[58] Behind the idols were demons who passed themselves off as "gods" (cf. 1 Cor. 8:4–6; Acts 17:18), and Satan himself is referred to as "the god of this world" who "has blinded the minds of the unbelievers" (2 Cor. 4:4). This echoes the more subtle depiction of the cosmic conflict in the OT, where "the gods of the nations" central to OT narratives are actually demons in disguise.[59] As Deuteronomy 32:16–17 reveals, the people made God "jealous with strange gods. . . . / They sacrificed to demons, not God, / to deities they had never known" (cf. Lev. 17:7; Deut. 32:8; Pss. 82; 106:37).[60]

Satan is repeatedly depicted as "the ruler of the demons" (Matt. 9:34; 12:24–29), who, along with "his angels," battles God's kingdom (Rev. 12:7–9; cf. Matt. 25:41; Rev. 12:3–12). "The dominion of Satan" is directly opposed to God's

---

for the reality, personhood, and systemic impact of evil celestial agencies in Arnold, *Powers of Darkness*, 194–205. Cf. Page, *Powers of Evil*, 240; Noll, *Angels of Light*, 119.

57. Vanhoozer, *Faith Speaking Understanding*, 100.

58. Reese explains that this refers to "pagan gods," the "spiritual reality behind the apparent nothingness of idols" (Reese, "Demons," 2:140, 142). Gordon Fee adds that Israel "had rejected God their Rock for beings who were no gods, indeed who were demons" (Deut. 32:17) (Fee, *First Epistle to the Corinthians*, 472). So Arnold, *Powers of Darkness*, 95; Noll, *Angels of Light*, 81.

59. John Goldingay comments that behind the idols were "so-called deities [that] do indeed exist, but they do not count as God, and they are subject to God's judgment." Yet, these "supernatural centers of power" can "deliberately oppose Yhwh's purpose" (Goldingay, *Old Testament Theology*, 2:43). Notably, God "executed judgment on" Egypt's "gods" (Num. 33:4; cf. Exod. 12:12; 18:10–11). Many other instances refer to the "gods" of the nations (Exod. 12:12; 15:11; 23:32; Deut. 4:19–20; 6:14; 32:8, 17; Josh. 24:15; Judg. 6:10; 10:6; 11:24; 1 Sam. 5:7; 6:5; 1 Kings 11:5, 33; 18:24; 20:23, 28; 2 Kings 17:29–31; 18:33–35; 19:12–13; 1 Chron. 5:25; 2 Chron. 25:14–15, 20; 28:23; 32:13–17; Isa. 36:18–20; 37:12; Jer. 5:19, 30–31; 46:25; 50:2; 51:44; Zeph. 2:11). Scripture is clear, however, that YHWH is utterly superior (1 Chron. 16:25–26; 2 Chron. 2:5–6): "There is none like" YHWH "among the gods" (Ps. 86:8; cf. 2 Chron. 6:14; Pss. 77:13; 95:3; 96:4–5; 97:9; 135:5). See further Block, *Gods of the Nations*.

60. Many scholars believe that Deut. 32:8 teaches that celestial beings ("gods") were allotted territory to rule on earth: "When the Most High apportioned the nations, when he divided humankind, he fixed the boundaries of the peoples according to the number of the gods" (cf. Gen. 11; Deut. 4:19–20; 29:26). The MT reads "sons of Israel," but most scholars agree that the most likely original corresponds to the DSS—"sons of God"—which corresponds to the LXX rendering, "angels of God." So, among many others, Tigay, *Deuteronomy*, 302; Craigie, *Book of Deuteronomy*, 377; Christensen, *Deuteronomy 21:10–34:12*, 791; Miller, *Deuteronomy*, 228; Thompson, *Deuteronomy*, 326; Clements, "Deuteronomy," 2:529. For support of the reading "sons of God," see Heiser, "Deuteronomy 32:8," 52–74. Cf. Jubilees 15:31. This view is also represented among early church fathers. See, e.g., Theodoret of Cyrus, *Commentary on Daniel* 10.13; Jerome, *Commentary on Daniel* 10.13; John Cassian, *Conference* 8.13.2 (ACCS 13:276–78).

kingdom of light (Acts 26:18 NASB; cf. Col. 1:13–14), and Christ himself repeatedly refers to Satan as "the ruler of this world" (John 12:31; 14:30; 16:11; cf.
Luke 4:5–6; 2 Cor. 4:4; Eph. 2:2). Indeed, according to 1 John 5:19, "the whole
world lies under the power of the evil one." Scripture also identifies Satan as the
accuser and slanderer (e.g., Rev. 12:10; 13:6; cf. Job 1–2; Zech. 3:1–2; Jude 9)
and the deceiver and tempter of the world from the beginning (Matt. 4:3; Rev.
12:9; cf. John 8:44; Acts 5:3; 2 Cor. 11:3; 1 John 3:8; Rev. 2:10).[61] He is "the great
dragon," "the serpent of old who is called the devil and Satan, who deceives the
whole world," and "the accuser of our brethren . . . who accuses them before
our God day and night" (Rev. 12:9–10 NASB; cf. Gen. 3:1–5; Rev. 20:2).

Some question the plausibility of cosmic conflict approaches in a post-
Enlightenment and secular age. However, Alvin Plantinga notes, "Plausibility,
of course, is in the ear of the hearer, and even in our enlightened times there are
plenty of people who think both that there are non-human free creatures and
that they are responsible for some of the evil that the world contains."[62] Indeed, most people throughout history have believed in supernatural agencies.[63]
Moreover, not only does the cosmic conflict motif enjoy abundant biblical
warrant, but the reality of a cosmic conflict has also been affirmed by the vast
majority of Christians throughout the ages and was part of "the common core
of patristic theodicy."[64] As Jeffrey Burton Russell puts it, "The devil has always
been a central Christian doctrine, an integral element in Christian tradition."[65]

Calling for what she calls "biblical realism," Esther Acolatse points out the
"internal inconsistency in a position that acknowledges one kind of unseen

61. The term for devil (*diabolos*) itself basically means "slanderer." See Bietenhard, "Satan,
Beelzebul, Devil, Exorcism," 3:468.
62. A. Plantinga, "Self-Profile," 42. For a philosophical defense of the existence of Satan
and his cohorts, see Guthrie, *Gods of This World*.
63. See Greg Boyd's survey of the "nearly universal intuition of cosmic conflict" across cul-
tures (Boyd, *God at War*, 18). See also Reese, "Demons," 2:140; Ferdinando, *Triumph of Christ*,
376. In this regard, Kabiro wa Gatumu notes, "Some scholars regard the Western church as
having failed" to "give sufficient or serious attention to the topic of supernatural powers" due
to "anti-supernaturalistic prejudice." Gatumu, *Pauline Concept of Supernatural Powers*, 52, 51.
64. Gavrilyuk, "Overview of Patristic Theodicies," 6. Irenaeus (referring to the rule of faith)
speaks of "the angels who transgressed and became apostates" (Irenaeus, *Against Heresies* 1.10.1
[*ANF* 1:330]). Likewise, Tertullian notes a baptismal formula wherein "we solemnly profess
that we disown the devil, and his pomp, and his angels" (Tertullian, *De Corona* 3 [*ANF* 3:94]).
A similar statement appears in many ancient baptismal formulas. See Gilmore and Caspari,
"Renunciation of the Devil in the Baptismal Rite," 488–89. Stephen Noll adds, "Confession
of 'things visible and invisible' [in the Nicene Creed, apparently drawing on Col. 1:16] seems
indeed to be the dogmatic position of the historic catholic faith." Noll, "Angels, Doctrine of," 47.
65. Russell, *Satan*, 226. See also Boyd, *Satan and the Problem of Evil*, 39; Tonstad, "Theodicy and the Theme of Cosmic Conflict," 169–202; Burns, *Christian Understandings of Evil*,
27–39, 45–58.

realm, that of God, and not another, that of spirits. We cannot label one aspect as myth without relegating all aspects to myth."[66] Further, Garrett DeWeese contends that rejecting the reality of "spiritual beings" entails that one "dismiss totally the worldview of both the Old and the New Testaments, and indeed of Jesus himself."[67] In this regard, C. S. Lewis explained,

> One of the things that surprised me when I first read the New Testament seri-
> ously was that it talked so much about a Dark Power in the universe—a mighty
> evil spirit who was held to be the Power behind death and disease, and sin. . . .
> Christianity thinks this Dark Power was created by God, and was good when
> he was created, and went wrong. . . . This universe is at war. . . . It is a civil
> war, a rebellion, and . . . we are living in a part of the universe occupied by the
> rebel. Enemy-occupied territory—that is what this world is.[68]

The Nature of the Conflict

The basic *nature* of this conflict is reflected in Christ's parable of the wheat and the tares. A landowner sows good seeds in his field, but weeds spring up among the wheat, prompting his servants to ask, "Master, did you not sow good seed in your field? Where, then, did these weeds come from?" (Matt. 13:27). The landowner replies, "An enemy has done this" (13:28). The servants ask in reply, "Then do you want us to go and gather them?" But the landowner replies, "No; for in gathering the weeds you would uproot the wheat along with them. Let both of them grow together until the harvest" (13:28–30). Jesus later identifies himself as the landowner and "the enemy who sowed" the tares as "the devil" (13:37–39).

This parable portrays evil as the work of the devil in "the cosmic struggle between God and Satan."[69] Whereas God could immediately uproot evil (the weeds), doing so prematurely would result in significant collateral damage to the good (uprooting the wheat). To defeat evil while minimizing collateral damage, evil must be allowed to persist for a time. For some good reason, Satan is temporarily allowed to work evil in this world. On this parable, N. T. Wright comments, "God's sovereign rule over the world isn't quite such a straightforward thing as people sometimes imagine."[70]

---

66. Acolatse, *Powers, Principalities, and the Spirit*, 204.
67. DeWeese, "Natural Evil," 63. Cf. Page, *Powers of Evil*, 180.
68. Lewis, *Mere Christianity*, 45.
69. Davies and Allison, *Matthew 8–18*, 431. Grant R. Osborne adds, "This is the age of the cosmic conflict." Osborne, *Matthew*, 536.
70. Wright, *Matthew for Everyone*, 168.

Yet how could there be any conflict between the omnipotent God and mere creatures? Satan and his minions could only be in conflict with God if the nature of the conflict is not one of sheer power but a different kind of conflict. Scripture depicts this conflict as a cosmic courtroom drama over God's character, caused by the devil's slanderous allegations against God's goodness, justice, and government, made before the heavenly council (more on this below). As such, the cosmic conflict is primarily an epistemic conflict, which cannot be won by the exercise of sheer power but requires an extended demonstration of God's character.

The epistemic nature of the conflict is revealed from the beginning of Scripture to the end. In Genesis 3, the serpent sets forth the first of many slanderous allegations against God recorded in Scripture. The serpent first massively distorts God's command, asking Eve, "Did God say, 'You shall not eat from any tree in the garden'?" (3:1). Eve replies that there is only one tree they are not to eat from, lest they die (vv. 2–3). Then the serpent directly contradicts God, claiming, "You will not die; for God knows that when you eat of it your eyes will be opened, and you will be like God, knowing good and evil" (vv. 4–5). The serpent thus alleges that God is a liar who does not really intend what is best for Eve but is withholding some good (knowledge) from Eve to keep her from being like God. According to Victor P. Hamilton, this is "a direct frontal attack" against God's character via a "mixture here of misquotation, denial, and slander fed to the woman by the snake."[71] The serpent's allegation presents Eve with the choice of whom she will believe—an epistemic choice within an epistemic conflict.[72]

Scripture elsewhere identifies this "ancient serpent" as the devil himself, "the deceiver of the whole world," "the accuser of our comrades . . . who accuses them day and night before our God" (Rev. 12:9–10), and "the god of this world" who "has blinded the minds of the unbelievers" (2 Cor. 4:4; cf. Acts 26:18).[73] According to Jesus himself, the devil "is a liar and the father of lies" (John 8:44).[74] As G. K. Beale describes it, "After the Fall, the serpent

71. Hamilton, *Book of Genesis*, 189. Kenneth Mathews adds that the "motivation for God's command is impugned by the serpent" and that "the adversary argues the same case in Job" (Mathews, *Genesis 1–11:26*, 236). Similarly, Sarna, *Genesis*, 25; Page, *Powers of Evil*, 13, 17–18.

72. Donald E. Gowan notes that the very "setting of a limit shows that" Eve "does indeed have a choice and thus establishes" her "freedom" (Gowan, *From Eden to Babel*, 42). Cf. Westermann, *Genesis 1–11*, 222; Sarna, *Genesis*, 21.

73. Tremper Longman III explains that the "serpent, as later Scripture (Rev. 12:9) makes clear, was not an ordinary animal, but rather an incarnation of the evil one, Satan himself." Longman, *Daniel*, 256.

74. Gerald L. Borchert contends that Jesus's "reference [in John 8:44] is obviously to the garden of Eden text where the deceit of the serpent/devil led to the 'death' of Adam and Eve (Gen. 3:1–4; cf. Wis 2:24; Rom. 5:12)." Borchert, *John 1–11*, 305.

and his agents do on a worldwide scale what he began in the garden," putting forth "claims" that "slander the character of God."[75]

This epistemic conflict, with slanderous allegations, is also front and center in Job 1–2. Therein (the) Satan appears before a host of "heavenly beings" (*bənê hā'ĕlōhîm*, literally "sons of God"; 1:6; 2:1), which biblical scholars identify as the heavenly council or court that "discusses and makes decisions about earthly events," one of many such scenes in Scripture.[76] As John E. Hartley explains, "Several passages in the OT" appear "to assume that God governs the world through a council of the heavenly host" while also upholding "monotheistic belief."[77] John Goldingay adds, "This heavenly cabinet discusses and makes decisions about earthly events more broadly (see, e.g., 1 Kings 22:19–22; Ps. 82; Isa. 6; Dan. 7:9–14), and its members are then involved in the implementing of these decisions."[78] As part of an apparently ongoing dispute, God declares Job "blameless and upright" (Job 1:8), but (the) Satan alleges that Job fears God only because God blesses him and has "put a fence around him" (1:10), claiming that Job would curse God if calamity befell him (1:11). This amounts to an allegation not only against Job but also against God because it directly contradicts God's judgment that Job is blameless, upright, and God-fearing (1:8; cf. 2:3; Rev. 12:10).[79] This, Lindsay Wilson comments, "is a questioning not just of Job's motives but also of God's rule. The accuser is saying to God that Job does not deserve all his blessings, and thus God is not ruling the world with justice."[80] Victor P. Hamilton adds that this is "patently slanderous."[81]

Before this heavenly court, (the) Satan argues that the "fence around" Job prevents him from proving his case that God's judgment of Job is false. In the

75. Beale, *Revelation*, 656.

76. Goldingay, *Old Testament Theology*, 2:45.

77. Hartley, *Book of Job*, 71. See, e.g., 1 Kings 22:19–23; 2 Chron. 18:18–22; Job 1:6–12; 2:1–7; Pss. 29:1–2; 82; 89:5–8; Isa. 6:1–13; Dan. 7:9–14; Zech. 3:1–7; cf. Isa. 24:21–23; Jer. 23:18, 22; Ezek. 1–3; Dan. 4:13, 17; Amos 3:7–8. This heavenly council or court is often referred to as the divine council or divine assembly. See Mullen, "Divine Assembly," 2:214; Heiser, "Divine Council."

78. Goldingay, *Old Testament Theology*, 2:45.

79. The identity of (the) Satan in Job and other OT passages (1 Chron. 21:1; Zech. 3:1–2) is disputed. Some claim "the satan" is a title referring to a benign court prosecutor, not the Satan of the NT. However, I have argued elsewhere that the satan's speech and actions indicate that he is antagonistic to God and match the modus operandi of the devil of the NT—"the accuser" (Rev. 12:10; cf. Jude 9) and "the father of lies" (John 8:44). See Peckham, *Theodicy of Love*, 76–82. As Hartley puts it, (the) Satan "acts as a troublemaker, a disturber of the kingdom," displaying a "contemptuous attitude," which "deviates from" the "explanation" that he is a benign "prosecuting attorney of the heavenly council." Hartley, *Book of Job*, 71, 71n8.

80. L. Wilson, *Job*, 34. Frances Andersen adds, "God's character and Job's are both slighted" (Andersen, *Job*, 89). Cf. Alden, *Job*, 55.

81. Hamilton, "Satan," 5:985.

midst of what Richard Davidson identifies as a "cosmic covenant lawsuit," God responds by agreeing to allow (the) Satan to test his allegations, within limits, twice publicly agreeing to modify the limits on (the) Satan's power.[82] Yet while (the) Satan brings numerous horrible afflictions against Job and his household, Job does not curse God (Job 1:20–22; 2:9–10), falsifying (the) Satan's allegations. Although some blame God for allowing (the) Satan to harm Job, Frances Andersen argues that God has "good reason" for handling (the) Satan's allegations before the heavenly council as he does, "namely to disprove the Satan's slander" of God's character.[83] Wilson adds, "If God is treating Job as righteous when he is not, then God is not acting fairly. Much is at stake."[84]

Here, again, it is crucial to recognize that (the) Satan had brought charges against God's judgment and protection of Job—before the heavenly court. This is not a private dialogue but part of open court proceedings. In his response, God takes into account the way this case is viewed by members of the heavenly council and others. If (the) Satan is not allowed to make his case, his allegations against Job and God would remain open in the heavenly court, casting significant doubt on the justice and transparency of God's character and government, with widespread ramifications for creatures everywhere. In this regard, Hartley notes, "The main function of this assembly here is to provide an open forum in which Yahweh permits the testing of Job. That is, the plan to test Job was not hatched in a secret meeting between Yahweh and the *satan*. Rather it was decided openly before the heavenly assembly. In this setting Yahweh's motivation, based on his complete confidence in Job, was fully known and thus it was above question."[85]

Not only does the case of Job depict the conflict as an epistemic conflict— a cosmic courtroom dispute over allegations against God's moral character and government—but this case also sheds light on what I call the rules of engagement in this cosmic conflict, to which I now turn.[86]

The Rules of Engagement

For there to be a conflict between God and a mere creature like the devil, there must be some consistent parameters—or rules of engagement—within which the adversary is allowed to make his case against God. In the case of

82. Indeed, "several studies contend that the entire book of Job may be regarded as a cosmic covenant lawsuit." R. Davidson, "Divine Covenant Lawsuit Motif," 79.

83. Andersen, *Job*, 95.

84. L. Wilson, *Job*, 32.

85. Hartley, *Book of Job*, 72. Cf. L. Wilson, *Job*, 34.

86. Even if one discounts Job, however, there is enough biblical data elsewhere to support the cosmic conflict approach I outline below.

Job, (the) Satan's reference to the "fence around" Job indicates some specific preexisting boundaries or limits within which (the) Satan could work. Toward answering (the) Satan's slanderous allegations, before the heavenly council God (twice) agrees to a modification of the parameters. If God always keeps his promises and commitments (see Titus 1:2; Heb. 6:18), insofar as God agrees to extend the limits on (the) Satan's power, God (morally) cannot prevent (the) Satan from exercising his power within those parameters.

Yet one may ask, Why would God agree to any such rules of engagement in the first place? Insofar as God grants and respects epistemic freedom (see Gen. 3:1–5), exercising divine power could do nothing to counter the enemy's slanderous allegations. A king cannot prove that he is just by the use of force. A president cannot clear his name of corruption in the minds of citizens by a display of executive power. It may be that due to the demonic allegations against God's character, God could not immediately bring it about that everyone *freely* recognize his perfect love and goodness. A conflict over allegations against one's character cannot be settled by sheer power but requires some fair and open demonstration to prove the allegations true or false (1 Cor. 4:9; cf. Matt. 13:29; 1 Cor. 6:2–3). Yet as noted earlier, a creature cannot make a case against the omnipotent God unless that creature is permitted to operate within some consistent parameters, some rules of engagement that God covenants not to contravene or override.[87]

If such rules are not unilaterally determined by God but the product of heavenly court proceedings that take into account other minds and petitions from the enemy, the rules may be far from ideal. These, then, may be thought of as "covenantal" rules of engagement in the minimal sense of covenant as a nonunilateral agreement that is jointly recognized and binding—in this case limiting the enemy's power while morally limiting God according to his commitments.[88] As such, there may be many instances wherein God would otherwise decide to prevent evil events but doing so would be against the rules of engagement, which God did not unilaterally set and which God (morally) cannot contravene or unilaterally modify.

Many biblical passages provide evidence of such rules of engagement. For example, in Daniel 10, an angel sent by God in response to Daniel's prayer is delayed for three weeks because, he explains, "the prince of the kingdom of Persia opposed me twenty-one days," until Michael the prince

---

87. Cf. what Michael Bergmann and Daniel Howard-Snyder call "omnipotence-constraining connections," which might exist "between" outweighing "goods and the permission of" evil. Bergmann and Howard-Snyder, "Reply to Rowe," 138.

88. While I do not claim these are "covenantal" in the formal sense, there are biblical examples of asymmetrical covenants involving less than friendly parties (Ezek. 17:12–14; cf. Job 41:4).

"came to help" (10:13; cf. 10:20–11:1). Most biblical scholars believe this prince of Persia is a celestial ruler, in keeping with the common OT motif of celestial rulers behind earthly rulers, which the NT often refers to in terms of principalities and powers.[89] For example, Tremper Longman III sees this as "a clear case of spiritual conflict," commenting, "Though the divine realm heard and began responding immediately to Daniel's prayers three weeks earlier, there was a delay because of a conflict, an obstacle in the form of the 'prince of the Persian kingdom' (v. 13)."[90] Notably, the angel tells Daniel, "I must return to fight against the prince of Persia, and when I am through with him, the prince of Greece will come," but "there is no one with me who contends against these princes except Michael, your prince" (10:20–21).

How could this be? For there to be such a conflict in which God's angel is delayed for three weeks and must "contend" with "princes," God must not be exercising all his power; the enemy must be allotted some power and jurisdiction to operate within some specified parameters (rules of engagement) known to both parties, the details of which are beyond our ken.

This motif of celestial rulers behind earthly rulers also appears in Revelation 12–13, which identifies the devil as "the great dragon," "the deceiver of the whole world" (12:9), the worship-usurping celestial ruler behind earthly rulers who oppose God's rule and oppress God's people throughout the ages (cf. the worship-usurping idols/"gods" in the OT). Indeed, "the dragon gave" a beast from the sea "his power and his throne and great authority" (13:2; cf. 13:5; 17:13–14), and "the whole earth followed the beast" and "worshiped the dragon, for he had given his authority to the beast, and they worshiped the beast" (13:3–4).

Then the sea beast "was allowed to exercise authority for forty-two months" and "to utter blasphemies against God, blaspheming his name and his dwelling," and "was allowed to make war on the saints and to conquer them. It was given authority over every tribe and people and language and nation" (Rev. 13:5–7; cf. 17:13–14). According to G. K. Beale, among others, the composite beast from the sea signifies the successive oppressive regimes of Babylon, Persia, Greece, Rome, and beyond (13:1–2, echoing Dan. 7:4–8) such that the "dragon in Revelation 12 was seen as the ultimate force behind the

---

89. Many church fathers also held this view of demonic rulers behind earthly rulers and applied it to Dan. 10. See, e.g., Origen, *De Principiis* 3.3.2; Theodoret of Cyrus, *Commentary on Daniel* 10.13; Jerome, *Commentary on Daniel* 10.13, 10.20; John Cassian, *Conference* 8.13.2 (ACCS 13:276–78, 280).

90. Longman, *Daniel*, 249.

earthly kingdoms of the world."[91] If this is right, Satan has been the celestial ruler behind various oppressive earthly rulers throughout history.

Many other passages also provide evidence of rules of engagement that govern the cosmic conflict. Here are a few NT examples:

Jesus repeatedly refers to Satan as "the ruler of this world" (John 12:31; 14:30; 16:11; cf. 2 Cor. 4:4), indicating that the devil has some ruling authority in this world, which Christ came to destroy (Heb. 2:14; 1 John 3:8; cf. Eph. 6:11–12; Rev. 12:9–11).

Scripture repeatedly refers to the kingdom or domain of darkness (e.g., Acts 26:18; Col. 1:13) and states, "The whole world lies under the power of the evil one" (1 John 5:19; cf. Matt. 12:24).

The temptation of Christ by the devil is evidently prearranged according to some parameters—the Spirit drives Christ into the wilderness to fast and be tempted for forty days (Matt. 4:1–2; Luke 4:1–2). Only after "the devil left him" then "suddenly angels came and waited on him" (Matt. 4:11). And after "the devil had finished every test, he departed from him until an opportune time" (Luke 4:13; cf. 22:53).[92]

In one temptation, the devil tells Jesus, "All the kingdoms of the world," all "their glory and all this authority . . . has been given over to me, and I give it to anyone I please. If you, then, will worship me, it will all be yours" (Luke 4:5–7; cf. John 19:11).

When demons encounter Christ in Matthew 8:29, they shout, "What have you to do with us, Son of God? Have you come here to torment us before the time?" This suggests some parameters known to both parties.

In Christ's hometown, Christ's miraculous power is restricted "because of their unbelief" (Matt. 13:58). Jesus "could do no deed of power there, except that he laid his hands on a few sick people and cured them" (Mark 6:5).

Regarding an unclean spirit the disciples fail to cast out, Jesus explains, "This kind can come out only through prayer" (Mark 9:29). This episode indicates that there are rules regarding demonic agency, which may be impacted by prayer and faith (cf. Matt. 17:20).

91. Beale, *Revelation*, 683.
92. Notably, there would be nothing wrong with Christ turning stones to bread, unless there were some rules prohibiting such action.

At the Last Supper, Jesus tells Peter, "Satan has demanded to sift all of you like wheat, but I have prayed for you" (Luke 22:31–32; cf. 1 Pet. 5:8; Jude 9).[93]

In 1 Thessalonians 2:18, Paul explains, "We wanted to come to you— certainly I, Paul, wanted to again and again—but Satan blocked our way" (cf. Rev. 2:10).

According to Revelation 12:12, "The devil has come down to" earth "with great wrath, because he knows that his time is short!" Here Scripture makes clear that Satan's domain is temporary and limited (cf. the specified time of "forty-two months" in Rev. 13:5).

These and other biblical passages provide strong evidence of a cosmic conflict governed by rules of engagement, with demonic agents possessing some temporary jurisdiction to work within specified limits, which God has committed to in the context of heavenly court proceedings.

A Cosmic Conflict Theodicy of Love in Outline

Without claiming to answer why God acts or refrains from acting as he does in specific cases, this understanding of the cosmic conflict provides a framework for understanding why God sometimes does not prevent evil while affirming divine omniscience, omnipotence, and sovereignty. As seen throughout this book, the God of Scripture is a covenantal God who always keeps his promises. If God has agreed to "covenantal" rules of engagement, which are far from ideal due to the involvement of other minds, there may be many evil occurrences that God desires to prevent, but God is *morally* prohibited from doing so by the rules of engagement. Some evil thus falls within the temporary domain of the kingdom of darkness (e.g., Rev. 13:1–8). While God loves justice and hates evil (Isa. 61:8), and thus desires to prevent all evil, doing so in some instances would be against the rules, which God has covenanted not to violate. Further, since these rules appear to be dynamically related to things like faith and prayer (and the confluence of many other unseen factors), it might be morally permissible for God to intervene to prevent evil in one situation but not morally permissible for God to do so in another situation that seems nearly identical to us.

Given our limited human perspective, we are not privy to all the various factors at work in any particular scenario. In any given situation, the options

---

93. The verb *exaiteō* ("demand") "includes the idea that the one making the request has a right to do so." Here "both God and Satan seem compelled to operate within certain constraints." Gregg, *What Does the Bible Say about Suffering?*, 64.

morally available to God may be far from ideal. While some avenues might not be morally available to God due to the rules of engagement, others might contravene the kind of free will God grants creatures for the sake of love, and still others might result in worse evil overall. Whereas God does everything he (morally) can to prevent and eliminate evil, in some cases preventing a particular evil might (1) contravene the kind of creaturely free will that is necessary for love, (2) violate the rules of engagement to which God has committed himself, and/or (3) result in greater evil or less flourishing of love.

Further, just as God unwaveringly keeps his covenants with creatures and acts in ways congruent with his moral law, I believe God always acts in ways consistent with the so-called laws of nature—the regularities of the natural world—*at least* some of which God ordained in the beginning as the requisite context for creaturely flourishing.[94] This does not prohibit God from working miracles, however, because God might work miracles that are in accord with such laws, analogous to the way I might, without breaking any such laws, prevent a glass in midair from falling to the ground by catching it in my hand.

While miracles, then, are not prohibited by such "laws of nature," it may be that, for the good of all concerned, God has committed himself to consistently uphold some laws or regularities of nature (nomic regularity) such that God may only work miracles consistent with such regularities. In this regard, Alvin Plantinga notes that while "intelligent free action would not be possible in a world without regularity and predictability, . . . *such* action would be possible in a world in which God often intervened, provided he did so in a regular and predictable way."[95] Notably, God uses the language of covenants and ordinances (or statutes) to speak of the natural order, referring to "my covenant with the day and my covenant with the night" such that they "come at their appointed time" (Jer. 33:20–26; 31:35–37). Further, God proclaims that he "established [his] covenant with day and night and the ordinances of heaven and earth" (33:25; cf. Gen. 8:22). In some sense, then, Scripture speaks of the natural order as a "covenantal" order governed by "ordinances" or laws.

This relates to the problem of so-called natural evils—typically defined as evils that are not direct results of the free decisions of creatures. On this cosmic conflict framework, evil in nature may be understood as a by-product of the entrance of moral evil into this world (Rom. 8:20–22). The world as it

94. Joshua Rasmussen highlights that God operates "along lines of pre-established order—rules of engagement with other sentient beings. The purpose of the rules is to maintain orderly arenas" (Rasmussen, "Great Story Theodicy," 239). As part of his great story theodicy, he suggests that within the story there are "consistent rules that cannot be broken at the characters' whims" (227).

95. A. Plantinga, *Where the Conflict Really Lies*, 102–3.

is now, including the natural world, is not as God intended it (Gen. 3:14–19); due to creaturely rebellion, this world is in a fallen state awaiting restoration. What we think of as "laws of nature" *might* include both (1) those "laws" God primordially ordained as requisite to the maximal flourishing of creatures, unchangeable given God's commitment to creaturely flourishing, and perhaps (2) additional rules and/or forces introduced after evil originated, part of the "covenantal" rules of engagement, which thus cannot be contravened by God without breaking his promises.[96] Given the commitments God has made for the good of all concerned, then, many evils in nature might not be preventable by God (morally).

Again, one might think that God should not have committed to any such rules of engagement in the first place. Yet given our limited perspective and knowledge, we are in no position to judge what God *should have* done (cf. Job 42:3). God possesses perfect righteousness, wisdom, and knowledge, including precise knowledge of all factors and outcomes from the end to the beginning. The infinitely wise and loving God alone is in a position to know just what love requires and just what parameters and demonstrations will defeat the enemy's slanderous allegations once and for all and bring about the maximal flourishing of love.

Attention to the unfolding of the covenantal plan of redemption provides more than sufficient evidence for us to be confident that God works to bring about what is good for all concerned in the end. The God of Scripture always does what is good and preferable given the avenues available to him (Deut. 32:4; 1 Sam. 3:18; Ps. 145:17; Dan. 4:37; Hab. 1:13; Rom. 3:25–26; Rev. 15:3; cf. Gen. 18:25). In Christ, God has provided the ultimate demonstration of his righteousness and love at the cross (Rom. 3:25–26; 5:8), thereby defeating the allegations of the enemy in the heavenly council and preparing the way for the final eradication of the devil's temporary domain.[97] As Kevin Vanhoozer puts it, the "cross is the climax of the courtroom drama where God judges

96. As Rice puts it, perhaps demonic "interference with the processes of nature has transformed the world from the perfect home God intends it to be into an ominous and threatening environment, marked by pain, disease and death" (Rice, *Suffering and the Search for Meaning*, 78). This does not require the view that demons directly cause natural disasters or the like but that "natural causes" might have been affected by the demonic rebellion, negatively affecting how nature operates today. Many scholars have suggested something like this, including A. Plantinga, "Supralapsarianism or 'O Felix Culpa,'" 15–17; DeWeese, "Natural Evil"; Ortlund, "On the Fall of Angels," 114–36; Lloyd, "Fallenness of Nature," 262–79; Boyd, *Satan and the Problem of Evil*, 242–318; Page, *Powers of Evil*, 268; von Balthasar, *Theo-Drama*, 4:197–99. Cf. Pannenberg, *Systematic Theology*, 2:274; Torrance, *Divine and Contingent Order*, 123; Creegan, *Animal Suffering and the Problem of Evil*, 143–51.

97. For much more on how the work of Christ defeats Satan's allegations and prepares for the final eradication of Satan's domain, see Peckham, *Theodicy of Love*, chap. 5.

the covenantal unfaithfulness of humankind and displays his own covenant faithfulness, his love and his justice. . . . Jesus' death on the cross is the victory of God not merely over Israel's covenant rebellion but over the cosmic powers of sin, Satan, and death."[98]

Here it is crucial to recall that one primary aspect of Christ's mission was "to destroy the works of the devil" (1 John 3:8; cf. Gal. 1:4) and ultimately "destroy the one who has the power of death, that is, the devil" (Heb. 2:14). This involved defeating the enemy's slanderous allegations against God and his government. In large part, Christ's mission was to reveal God's kingdom of truth, love, and justice. In direct contrast to the "liar and the father of lies" (John 8:44), "that ancient serpent, who is called the Devil and Satan, the deceiver of the whole world" (Rev. 12:9), Jesus was "born" and "came into the world, to testify to the truth" (John 18:37), and Christ's followers are also enlisted to *testify* as witnesses (cf. 15:26).[99] In this regard, Revelation 12:10–12 proclaims, "Now have come the salvation and the power and the kingdom of our God and the authority of his Messiah, for the accuser of our comrades has been thrown down, who accuses them day and night before our God. But they have conquered him by the blood of the Lamb and by the word of their testimony. . . . But woe to the earth and the sea, for the devil has come down to you with great wrath, because he knows that his time is short!" Satan has been defeated at the cross, and one day soon, he and his kingdom will be destroyed.[100] As Beale explains, the "legal defeat of Satan [via the cross] is part of the essence of the inaugurated kingdom that has 'now come about,'" even though the "actual execution of the devil and his hordes comes at the consummation of history."[101]

In the meantime, while we often do not understand why things occur as they do, the God of the cross can be trusted; he knows what is best (omniscience) and wants only what is best for all concerned (omnibenevolence). God has done and continues to do everything that can be done for this world without undermining love relationship (cf. Isa. 5:1–4; Matt. 21:33–40), including the Son subjecting himself to the cross (Phil. 2:8). And he will finally eradicate evil, without compromising love. Because the infinitely loving God of the cross

---

98. Vanhoozer, *Drama of Doctrine*, 52, 55.

99. Richard Bauckham comments that in Revelation the "world is a kind of courtroom in which the issue of who is the true God is being decided. In this judicial contest Jesus and his followers bear witness to the truth." Bauckham, *Theology of the Book of Revelation*, 73.

100. On Rev. 12:10–11, Beale explains, "Christ was wrongfully accused and executed by Satan's earthly pawns. But his resurrection vindicated him in the law court of heaven and enabled him to take away the devil's right and power as heavenly prosecutor (cf. 1:18)." Beale, *Revelation*, 664.

101. Beale, *Revelation*, 661.

knows the end from the beginning, we can be assured that "the sufferings of this present time are not worth comparing with the glory about to be revealed to us" (Rom. 8:18; cf. 8:28; 2 Cor. 4:17). While creatures suffer greatly due to evil, the voluntarily suffering God of the cross suffers most of all—not only at the cross but also whenever creatures suffer—conclusively demonstrating his utter righteousness and love. God alone is impacted by the sum total of all evil. Yet despite knowing the unfathomable cost to himself, God chose to create and suffer *with* this world. If there had been any preferable way to ensure the unending bliss and flourishing of the universe, God would have chosen it. While many questions remain about why things occur as they do, the God of the cross can be trusted. The Lamb who was slain is worthy of all praise (Rev. 5:12), and one day God himself will "dwell among" us and "wipe away every tear," and "there will no longer be any death; there will no longer be any mourning, or crying, or pain; the first things have passed away. . . . These words are faithful and true" (21:3–5 NASB).

Some Questions and Implications

Numerous questions remain and warrant further discussion, but space permits only brief consideration of a few relevant issues. First, it is crucial to emphasize that often the last thing people need when facing acute suffering is a philosophical or theological explanation. The best thing one can do in such situations is to draw near the suffering one and offer tangible compassion and comfort. Yet there is a time and place for consideration of how to reconcile God's goodness with the kind and amount of evil in this world.

One question many people ask is, Why doesn't God miraculously intervene to prevent states of affairs that he does not prefer? Why, for example, doesn't God miraculously provide food for many who are starving? A simple appeal to the "laws of nature" does not seem to suffice because there are numerous instances in Scripture where God miraculously provides food (e.g., God provides manna for Israel in the wilderness, and Jesus multiplies food for hungry crowds). If God actually did such things in the past, as Scripture claims, then working a miracle to provide food cannot be an intrinsic violation of the kind of nomic regularity and consequential freedom that God commits to uphold for the flourishing of love. Why, then, might God do such miracles some times but not other times?

The theodicy of love outlined in this chapter addresses this problem of (seemingly) selective miracles by suggesting that God may be *temporarily* restricted (morally) from preventing some specific evils because doing so would violate the rules of engagement in the cosmic conflict. Because the rules of engagement are dynamically related to a broad matrix of factors such as faith and prayer (and the confluence of many other unseen factors), divine intervention may be within the rules in one situation but against the rules in another situation that seems nearly identical from our limited perspective. While God may be temporarily restricted (morally) from preventing some evil, however, the God of Scripture desires to eliminate all evil, possesses the sheer power to do so, and will finally eradicate *all* evil without compromising his perfect goodness and love (Rev. 21:3–4).

This relates closely to questions like, Why does God sometimes appear to be hidden? Why does God sometimes appear to answer prayers but other times appears not to do so? In brief, this theodicy of love suggests that when God appears to be hidden and/or does not respond to prayers in the way we might have hoped, doing so might have impinged on creaturely freedom, been against the rules of engagement, or resulted in greater evil or less flourishing of love.

Yet additional questions arise relative to petitionary prayer, regarding which Peter Baelz states, "It is no exaggeration to say that intercession provides a test-case for theological understanding."[102] For one, does it make sense to offer petitionary prayer aimed at influencing God to bring about some good(s) that God otherwise would not have brought about, as many Christians do?[103] The problem this question raises is sometimes referred to as the problem of petitionary prayer. Specifically, if God is all-knowing (omniscient), entirely good (omnibenevolent), and all-powerful (omnipotent), it seems that God would know all preferable goods he could bring about, would prefer to bring about such goods, and would be capable of doing so. How, then, could it make sense to offer petitionary prayer with the aim of influencing God to bring about some good?

A number of biblical passages seem to indicate that divine activity is somehow linked to "belief" and "prayer" (see Matt. 17:20; Mark 9:23–29; 11:22–24; cf. 2 Chron. 7:14). For instance, when the disciples ask Jesus why they could not cast out a demon, Jesus replies, "This kind can come out only through prayer" (Mark 9:28–29). This text (and others) indicates that at least some impediments to divine action are dynamically related to factors such as faith and prayer. If so, prayer may grant God jurisdiction to intervene in ways that otherwise would not be (morally) available—that is, the rules of engagement might (morally) restrict God from preventing some evils or bringing about some goods unless God is petitioned by an appropriate party to prevent such

---

102. Baelz, *Prayer and Providence*, 14.
103. As Scott A. Davison puts it, "One of the primary purposes of petitionary prayer, according to those who practice it, is to influence God's action in the world." Davison, *Petitionary Prayer*, 7.

evils or bring such goods about. Petitionary prayer, then, might make a significant difference in the world by opening up avenues for God to bring about goods he already wanted to bring about but was (morally) restricted from bringing about in the absence of petitionary prayer.[104]

Although prayer may open up avenues for God within the rules of engagement that were not otherwise available (morally), however, there are many other unseen factors such that prayer and faith do not open *every* avenue. When prayers are not answered as we hoped, we should not assume we did not pray hard enough or did not have enough faith or otherwise did something wrong (see Matt. 26:39; Luke 22:32). Some prayers might not be answered as we desire or expect because we might be praying for the wrong outcome (see Rom. 8:26; 1 John 5:14–15) and/or with the wrong motives (see James 4:2–3). But as noted earlier, it may be that some things we pray to God to do would contravene God's commitment to consequential freedom and/or to the rules of engagement in the cosmic conflict. Many outcomes are not strictly up to God, and the God of Scripture is frequently portrayed as wishing things were different (e.g., Ps. 81:11–14) and lamenting the evil in this world (e.g., Isa. 66:4). Notably, Christ's prayer in Gethsemane itself indicates that some avenues might not be available to God: "My Father, *if it is possible*, let this cup pass from me; yet not what I want but what you want" (Matt. 26:39 [emphasis added]; cf. 6:10).

One day God will finally eradicate evil, never to arise again (Rev. 21:4). In the meantime, we should stand against evil. Many evils are within our power to prevent or mitigate, if we are willing to act. Those of us who believe there is an ongoing cosmic conflict should do what we can to bring about what God has expressed as his will in this world—among other things, "to do justice, and to love kindness, and to walk humbly with your God" (Mic. 6:8). Toward this end, we should act according to the understanding that, as C. S. Lewis puts it, "There is no neutral ground in the universe. Every square inch, every split second is claimed by God, and counterclaimed by Satan."[105] Yet evil cannot be defeated by evil; only love can defeat evil. "By this everyone will know that you are my disciples, if you have love for one another" (John 13:35).

Conclusion

This chapter addressed the question of whether God is entirely good and loving, particularly given the kind and amount of evil in the world. Without

104. See Peckham, "Influence Aim Problem of Petitionary Prayer."
105. Lewis, "Christianity and Culture," 33.

attempting to answer all questions relative to the problem of evil, this chapter briefly discussed some avenues relative to the problem of evil, finally outlining a cosmic conflict theodicy of love that is based on a close canonical reading of Scripture.

In brief, this theodicy of love maintains that God consistently grants creatures consequential freedom because such freedom is necessary for love relationship and that there is evil in the world because creatures have tragically misused this freedom. Moreover, this world is embroiled in a cosmic conflict wherein the devil and his minions, creatures who rebelled against God and fell from perfection of their own free will, oppose God's moral government of love. As Jesus put it, "An enemy has done this" (Matt. 13:28). Although neither the devil nor any other creature could oppose the omnipotent God at the level of sheer power, this cosmic conflict is primarily an epistemic conflict, caused by the devil's slanderous allegations against God's character and government. Left undefeated, such allegations would disrupt the flourishing of love in the universe. For the good of all creatures in the universe, then, such allegations must be answered. However, such allegations cannot be defeated by sheer power but require a cosmic demonstration, within which the devil and his cohorts are afforded the opportunity to make their case within some consistent parameters—some rules of engagement agreed upon via proceedings in the heavenly court.

Because God is a covenantal God who always keeps his promises, the rules of engagement God agrees to thereby (morally) limit God's action relative to evil. In this age, then, there are some evils that God *temporarily* cannot (morally) prevent because doing so would undermine free will, contravene the rules of engagement, or result in greater evil. This provides a framework for understanding why the entirely good and loving God sometimes does not prevent horrendous evil while upholding divine omnipotence and omniscience and a robust conception of God's providence. God has done everything that could be done for this world without undermining love relationship, and God will finally eradicate evil without undermining love. In the meantime, while creatures suffer greatly due to evil, the voluntarily suffering God of the cross suffers most of all, providing the conclusive demonstration of God's utter love and justice. As Scripture assures us, "The Lord is faithful; he will strengthen you and guard you from the evil one" (2 Thess. 3:3).

Seven

Trinity of Love

A Canonical Exploration of Divine Triunity

The hobbits knew him simply as Strider, a mere ranger. Little did the hobbits know that this man, who seemed ordinary, was the rightful heir to the throne. Only as *The Lord of the Rings* unfolds do they (and the reader) learn this man is Aragorn, son of Arathorn—the one who would finally be the high king.

In very different fashion, Scripture unfolds the revelation of Christ, the Son of the Father, and the revelation of the Holy Spirit, sent by the Father and the Son. To fulfill God's covenant promises, Christ humbles himself and shrouds his glory behind flesh. To those who encounter him, it is not immediately apparent who Jesus of Nazareth really is—the covenant heir as son of David and divine Son of God, himself the true King deserving of ultimate glory, honor, and allegiance, which belong to God alone. Accordingly, his followers come to recognize and worship him as "Lord" and "God" (John 20:28). If Christ is not God, addressing him as God is blasphemy. If Christ is not God, worshiping him is idolatry. If Christ is not God, Christianity is a false religion.

Because Christ came in the manner he did, many have doubted his divine identity and the doctrine of the Trinity, asking questions like, How can God be three and one? Further, numerous issues regarding the Trinity doctrine are disputed even among trinitarians. Before briefly addressing some prominent issues upon which trinitarians sometimes disagree, this chapter focuses on what I call the core Trinity doctrine, for which there is extensive biblical warrant and regarding which there is deep and wide consensus among Christians. I define the core Trinity doctrine as follows: there is one and only one God, and God is three distinct (fully) divine persons. While a single chapter cannot do justice to the majestic doctrine of the Trinity, this chapter aims to offer a brief, constructive proposal for (1) affirming the core doctrine of the Trinity as biblically warranted and systematically consistent and (2) understanding the triune God as the Trinity of love, alongside a brief discussion of divine simplicity.

The Core Trinity Doctrine

Unpacking the Core Trinity Doctrine

The core Trinity doctrine might be parsed into the following four tenets:

1. There is one and only one God.
2. There is a Trinity of Father, Son, and Spirit.
3. The three persons of the Trinity are distinct from one another.[1] The Father is not the Son or the Spirit, the Son is not the Spirit or the Father, the Spirit is not the Father or the Son.
4. The three persons of the Trinity are fully divine and thus coequal and coeternal.[2] The Father is God, the Son is God, and the Holy Spirit is God.[3]

Put more simply, the core Trinity doctrine affirms (1) God's oneness, (2) God's triunity, (3) the distinctness of the three persons of the Trinity, and (4) the full divinity of the three persons of the Trinity.[4] Together, these amount to the affirmation of the core Trinity doctrine: there is one and only one God, and God is three distinct (fully) divine persons. If the four tenets above are biblically warranted, then the core Trinity doctrine is biblically warranted.

1. In other words, the trinitarian persons are not numerically identical (i.e., not the same *in every respect*).

2. In Nicene terms, there are three hypostases yet one ousia (*homoousios*). As John Calvin puts it, "Say that in the one essence of God there is a trinity of persons; you will say in one word what Scripture states." Calvin, *Institutes of the Christian Religion* 1.13.15 (Battles, 1:128).

3. The Athanasian Creed states, "The Father is God: the Son is God: and the Holy Spirit is God. And yet they are not three Gods: but one God." Schaff, *Creeds of Christendom*, 2:67.

4. Though I do not believe one could be *partially* divine (if divinity requires possessing the essential attributes of God), I use the phrase "fully" divine to differentiate this tenet from claims of *partial* divinity.

These four tenets also exclude numerous views most Christians have rejected as heresies, including tritheism, modalism, and subordinationism. Tritheism (excluded by tenets 1 and 2) maintains that there are three gods, overemphasizing God's threeness to the exclusion of God's oneness. Modalism (excluded by tenet 3) is the view that God is only one person manifested in three modes in salvation history, overemphasizing God's oneness to the exclusion of God's distinct threeness. Subordinationism (excluded by tenet 4) claims that the Son and/or the Spirit are by nature subordinate to the Father. Subordinationism takes many forms, including claims that Christ and/or the Holy Spirit are less than fully divine (e.g., claims of "partial divinity") and/or came into existence. One form, Arianism, claims that the Son is not eternal but was created by the Father such that "there was a time when he [the Son] was not."[5]

In contrast, the core Trinity doctrine affirms that the Father, Son, and Spirit are eternal and coequal. There can be no gradation of divinity; one cannot be *partially* divine. As Scripture consistently teaches, "There is no one like" YHWH and "no God besides" YHWH (1 Chron. 17:20), who alone is worthy of worship (e.g., Deut. 10:20; Luke 4:8). If being divine refers to being the supreme being who alone is worthy of worship (God), then one cannot be more or less divine. Likewise, if being divine is to possess the essential divine attributes, which are unique to the supreme being, then one cannot be partially divine any more than one can be a little bit pregnant. As Thomas McCall explains, "The Father does not have A+ divinity, while the Son has A divinity and the Spirit is relegated to A− divinity. There is only one divinity (on pain of polytheism), and either you have it or you don't."[6]

Is the Core Trinity Doctrine Biblically Warranted?

Whether the Trinity doctrine is biblically warranted is a question of considerable importance to Christian doctrine. As McCall explains, "Christians have been Trinitarians because they have been convinced that the revelation of God in Jesus Christ demands it." He goes on, "So far as I can see, the only reason for Christians to believe in the doctrine of the Trinity at all is on the basis of God's revelation in Jesus Christ as seen in Scripture."[7] Likewise, Fred Sanders states, "The church has always confessed the doctrine of the Trinity as something to be believed on the grounds of revelation alone as recorded

5. See Schaff, *Creeds of Christendom*, 1:29.
6. McCall, "Trinity Doctrine," 51.
7. McCall, *Which Trinity?*, 231.

in Scripture alone. The church should continue to do so. The doctrine of the triune God must be known to be biblical and shown to be biblical."[8] I agree.

However, some claim the Trinity doctrine is not biblical, which immediately raises the question of which conception of the Trinity one has in mind. Some who claim this, including many trinitarians, mean that the word "Trinity" is not in the Bible or that the doctrine of the Trinity *as it is explicitly stated in the Nicene Creed* is not explicitly found in the Bible. Because the Nicene Trinity doctrine requires a number of philosophical claims that go beyond any explicit claims in Scripture, it is difficult to make the claim that the Nicene doctrine is *taught* by the Bible. Yet, relative to the standard of biblical warrant, the issue is not whether the word "Trinity" or a particular metaphysical articulation of the doctrine (e.g., the Nicene articulation) is explicitly found in Scripture but whether the concept is taught by Scripture. The issue, relative to the standard of biblical warrant, is not whether the word "Trinity" or a particular metaphysical articulation of the doctrine is explicitly found in Scripture but whether the concept is taught by Scripture. In this regard, Sanders rightly emphasizes, "In our own time, it has become crucial for Trinitarian theology to demonstrate as directly as possible that it is biblical."[9]

For clarity, in what follows, I distinguish between the core Trinity doctrine and other prominent issues regarding the relationship among the persons of the Trinity (e.g., questions regarding the precise nature of triunity and eternal relations), focusing in the next few sections on showing that there is biblical warrant for the core Trinity doctrine.

Tenet 1: There Is One and Only One God

Scripture repeatedly teaches that there is one and only one God. Deuteronomy 4 states, "The LORD is God; there is no other besides him," and "the LORD is God in heaven above and on the earth beneath; there is no other" (vv. 35, 39; cf. Exod. 8:10; Deut. 32:39). Deuteronomy 6:4 adds, "The LORD is our God, the LORD is one ['eḥād]!" (NASB; cf. Zech. 14:9).[10] Further, 2 Samuel 7:22 attests, "There is no one like you [God], and there is no God besides you" (cf. 22:32; 1 Chron. 17:20). Elsewhere YHWH himself states,

> I am the LORD, and there is no other;
> besides me there is no god. (Isa. 45:5)

8. F. Sanders, *Triune God*, 155.
9. F. Sanders, *Triune God*, 162.
10. Notably, the term *'eḥād* does not require strict numerical oneness but may be used of oneness in unity (see Gen. 2:24).

> I am God, and there is no other;
> I am God, and there is no one like me. (46:9; cf. 1 Kings 8:60;
> 2 Kings 19:15, 19; Neh. 9:6; Pss. 18:31; 83:18; 86:10; Isa. 37:20;
> 44:6; 45:14, 18, 21; Joel 2:27)

God alone is the great "I AM" (Exod. 3:14; cf. Isa. 43:10; John 8:58). He states,

> I am the first and I am the last;
> besides me there is no god.
> Who is like me? (Isa. 44:6–7; cf. 44:8)

God alone is the Creator, declaring in Isaiah 44:24,

> I am the LORD, who made all things,
> who alone stretched out the heavens,
> who by myself spread out the earth. (cf. 2 Kings 19:15; Neh. 9:6;
> Isa. 37:16)

Further, God states,

> I am the LORD [YHWH], that is my name;
> my glory I give to no other,
> nor my praise to idols. (Isa. 42:8; cf. John 5:44)

God alone is worthy of worship; "you shall worship no other god" (Exod. 34:14; cf. Deut. 5:7–9). As Jesus himself states, "It is written, 'Worship the Lord your God, and serve only him'" (Matt. 4:10; cf. Deut. 10:20; Luke 4:8; Rev. 19:10).

Jesus also affirms, "The Lord our God, the Lord is one" (Mark 12:29, quoting Deut. 6:4; cf. Mark 12:32). Elsewhere Jesus speaks of "the one who alone is God" (John 5:44; cf. 17:3; Eph. 4:4–6). Indeed, 1 Corinthians 8:4 declares, "There is no God but one" (cf. 8:6; Gal. 3:20; 1 Tim. 2:5), and 1 Timothy 1:17 speaks of "the only God." James 2:19 adds, "You believe that God is one; you do well" (cf. Rom. 3:30; 16:27).

Again, if God is "one" (Deut. 6:4) and "there is no one like" God and "no God besides" God (2 Sam. 7:22; 1 Chron. 17:20; cf. Deut. 4:35, 39; Isa. 46:9), there can be no partial or quasi-God—no partial divinity.[11] If "there is no one like God," there cannot be someone who is not God but possesses

---

11. One complicating factor is that Scripture sometimes uses the OT and NT terms *ʾĕlōhîm* and *theos* (often translated "God") to refer to supernatural creatures like angels; the context indicates whether the terms refer to the one God.

attributes unique to God alone. No one other than God could be "the reflection of God's glory and the exact imprint of God's very being," as Hebrews 1:3 declares of Christ.

The above passages teach that there is only one God and posit numerous things that are true of God alone (e.g., being the Creator and worthy of worship). This brings us to the second claim.

Tenet 2: There Is a Trinity of Father, Son, and Holy Spirit

Scripture not only repeatedly affirms divine oneness but also repeatedly refers to the Trinity of Father, Son, and Holy Spirit, at least in the minimal sense of *trinitas* referring to a triad or trio. When the Son is baptized, "the Spirit of God" descends "like a dove," and the Father speaks via "a voice from heaven," proclaiming, "This is my Son, the Beloved, with whom I am well pleased" (Matt. 3:16–17). Christ's discourse in John 14–16 also includes numerous explanations of the interrelationship of the Father, the Son, and the Holy Spirit.

While the NT directly reveals the trio of Father, Son, and Spirit, the OT also indicates plurality in God.[12] The context of numerous references to "the angel of the Lord" suggests that this particular "angel" (*mal'āk*, which simply means "messenger") is no creature but a manifestation of YHWH.[13] As James Kugel puts it, as many scholars have long recognized, this "angel" of the Lord "is not some lesser order of divine being; it is God Himself, but God unrecognized, God intruding into ordinary reality," indeed, "God Himself in human form."[14] This angel of the Lord appears to Hagar and is identified with YHWH when Hagar "named the Lord [YHWH] who spoke to her, 'You are El-roi'; for she said, 'Have I really seen God and remained alive after seeing him?'" (Gen. 16:13; cf. 21:17; 22:11–12; 31:11–13; 48:16). Later, Jacob wrestles with a "man" who turns out to be God (32:24–30), so Jacob says, "I have seen God face to face, and yet my life is preserved" (32:30; cf. 32:28). Hosea 12:3–5 explains that Jacob "strove with God. He strove with the angel and prevailed" and "he spoke with him. The Lord the God of hosts." The "angel of the Lord" also appears to Moses in the burning bush (Exod. 3:2), and yet "God called to him out of the bush" and told him, "The place on which you are standing is holy ground" and "I am the God of your father,

---

12. In some instances, God uses plural pronouns, referring to "us" and "our" (e.g., Gen. 1:26; 3:22; 11:7; cf. Isa. 6:3), but the meaning of these instances is disputed.

13. The word *mal'āk* may refer to a human messenger, an angelic creature, or even a divine messenger. See *HALOT* 2:585–86.

14. Kugel, *God of Old*, 34.

the God of Abraham, the God of Isaac, and the God of Jacob" (3:2–6; cf. Josh. 24:15). Then "Moses hid his face, for he was afraid to look at God" (Exod. 3:6). Later, God tells Moses that he will "send an angel" before Israel, commanding them, "Listen to his voice," for "my name is in him" (23:20–21; cf. 14:19). The "angel of the LORD" also appears to Gideon (Judg. 6:11–23) and later to Manoah and his wife. When "Manoah realized that it was the angel of the LORD," he stated, "We shall surely die, for we have seen God" (13:21–22; cf. 13:13–20; Zech. 3:1–5).

Many scholars interpret such instances of the "angel of the LORD" as manifestations of the preincarnate Son. Such an interpretation would complement Isaiah 63, which refers to the "angel of the LORD" who appeared in Exodus as "the angel of His presence" (v. 9 NASB). According to J. Alec Motyer (and many others), this angel is "an Old Testament anticipation of Jesus."[15] Further, some see an apparent reference to the Trinity in Isaiah 63, which references "the lovingkindness of the LORD," then goes on,

> He became their Savior.
> In all their affliction He was afflicted,
> And the angel of His presence saved them;
> In His love and in His mercy He redeemed them,
> And he lifted them and carried them all the days of old.
> But they rebelled
> And grieved His Holy Spirit. . . .
> Where is He who put his Holy Spirit in the midst of them? (vv. 7–11
>   NASB; cf. Gen. 1:2; Eph. 4:30)

According to John Oswalt, "Most commentators recognize that the understanding of the Holy Spirit here and in v. 11 is close to the fully developed NT concept of the third person of the Trinity. Here he is clearly a person who is capable of being hurt by human behavior, and in v. 11 he is the empowering and enabling presence in the human spirit."[16]

As the covenant revelation of God is unfolded in the carrying out of the covenant of redemption, the NT contains more explicit references to the

---

15. Motyer, *Prophecy of Isaiah*, 387. John N. Oswalt notes, "The angel is the Lord himself as visibly present (see Exod. 20:21–23; 33:2, 14–15; Num. 20:16; Josh. 5:13–15; Judg. 13:6, 21–22). Delitzsch makes a good case for this being an expression of the second person of the Trinity" (Oswalt, *Book of Isaiah*, 607). J. Ridderbos adds that this cannot refer to "one of the created angels, for it could not be said of any of them that He redeemed Israel from all their affliction. So the reference is to the Angel of the LORD who is Himself God and is also distinguished from God." Ridderbos, *Isaiah*, 557.

16. Oswalt, *Book of Isaiah*, 607.

Trinity, including many so-called trinitarian formulas. According to Roderick K. Durst, there are "seventy-five triadic order passages" in the NT in which all three persons of the Trinity are mentioned within a range of one to five verses.[17] Indeed, Durst states, "The quantity of divine triadic instances is so profound and in such a diversity of orders that it constitutes a qualitative *matrix* of Trinitarian consciousness. Trinity is how the New Testament authors inadvertently thought and viewed reality."[18]

For example, while Deuteronomy 6:13 commands one to "swear" by YHWH's "name alone," Jesus commands the disciples to baptize "in the name of the Father and of the Son and of the Holy Spirit" (Matt. 28:19; cf. Exod. 23:20–21). Here the word "name" is singular, which Leon Morris explains "points to the fact that they [Father, Son, and Spirit] are in some sense one"; he concludes, "That God is a Trinity is a scriptural idea."[19] Likewise, Craig Blomberg comments, "The singular 'name' followed by the threefold reference to 'Father, Son, and Holy Spirit' suggests both unity and plurality in the Godhead. Here is the clearest Trinitarian 'formula' anywhere in the Gospels."[20]

A similar juxtaposition of oneness and threeness *in unity* appears in 1 Corinthians 12:4–6: "Now there are varieties of gifts, but the same Spirit; and there are varieties of services, but the same Lord; and there are varieties of activities, but it is the same God who activates all of them in everyone."[21] In 2 Corinthians 13:13, Paul likewise writes, "The grace of the Lord Jesus Christ, the love of God, and the communion of the Holy Spirit be with all of you." In Ephesians 4:4–6, Paul even more explicitly juxtaposes God's oneness alongside a threefold reference: "There is one body and one Spirit, just as you were called to the one hope of your calling, one Lord, one faith, one baptism, one God and Father of all, who is above all and through all and in all" (cf. Heb. 9:13–14).

Some critics of the Trinity doctrine, however, point to the phrase "one God and Father of all" (Eph. 4:6), Christ's reference to the Father as "the only [*monos*] true God" (John 17:3), and Paul's words "there is one God, the

---

17. Durst, *Reordering the Trinity*, 68.

18. Durst, *Reordering the Trinity*, 66 (emphasis original). Michael Horton adds, "The confession 'one God in three persons' arises naturally out of the triadic formulas in the New Testament." Horton, *Christian Faith*, 274–75.

19. L. Morris, *Gospel According to Matthew*, 748. "That the early followers of Jesus thought of God as triune seems clear from the passages that speak of the three together (e.g., Rom. 8:11; 1 Cor. 12:4–6; 2 Cor. 13:14; Gal. 4:6; Eph. 4:4–6; 2 Thess. 2:13, etc.)." L. Morris, *Gospel According to Matthew*, 748.

20. Blomberg, *Matthew*, 432.

21. Gordon Fee sees "clear Trinitarian implications in this set of sentences." Fee, *First Epistle to the Corinthians*, 588.

Father" (1 Cor. 8:6), arguing that such phrases indicate that *only* the Father is God. However, 1 Corinthians 8:6 also states that there is "one Lord, Jesus Christ, through whom are all things and through whom we exist" (cf. Eph. 4:5). If phrases like "there is one God, the Father" exclude the Spirit and the Son from being "God," then phrases like there is "one Lord, Jesus Christ" exclude the Father from being "Lord." However, this cannot be, since many texts speak of the Father as "Lord." For instance, Jesus says, "I thank you, Father, Lord of heaven and earth" (Matt. 11:25; cf. Rev. 11:15). Likewise, as shall be surveyed below, other texts also refer to the Son and the Spirit as "God" (e.g., John 1:1–3; Acts 5:3–4). Just as it would be inconsistent to take references to Christ as the "one Lord" as excluding the Father from being "Lord," it would be inconsistent to take references to the Father as the "one God" as excluding the divinity of the Son and the Spirit. To be consistent, such phrases should be understood as claims of monotheism—over against false gods (cf. 1 Cor. 8:5).[22]

In this regard, if the one God of Scripture is Father, Son, *and* Spirit, then referring to the Father as the "only God" does not exclude the Son and the Spirit—who are one with the Father—from being "God." And speaking of the Son as the "one Lord" does not exclude the Father from being "Lord," since the Father and the Son are ontologically united as "one" (John 10:30; 14:9). The conclusion that the Father, Son, and Spirit are *somehow* ontologically united as one God—the triune God—follows from tenets 1–4 of the core Trinity doctrine. We turn now to tenets 3 and 4, which affirm that the Father, Son, and Spirit are distinct persons and (fully) divine.

Tenet 3: The Three Persons of the Trinity Are Distinct from One Another

Scripture affirms that the Father, Son, and Holy Spirit are three distinct persons. There is little dispute over the personhood of the Father and the Son. Some have disputed, however, whether the Holy Spirit is a person. Here it is crucial to note that in the Trinity doctrine, "person" does not refer to a physically individuated person like a mere human but to a subject with self-consciousness, reason, and will. Further, persons possess attributes that only a person can possess. Accordingly, if Scripture teaches that the Holy Spirit possesses attributes that only persons can possess, then Scripture teaches that the Holy Spirit is a person.

22. Fee comments regarding 1 Cor. 8:6, "The formulae 'one God' and 'one Lord' stand in specific contrast to the 'many gods' and 'many lords' of the pagans" (1 Cor. 8:5). Fee, *First Epistle to the Corinthians*, 374.

In my view, many instances in Scripture attribute to the Holy Spirit characteristics that only persons can possess. For example, the Holy Spirit

shares the "name" with the Father and the Son (Matt. 28:19; cf. Exod. 23:21);

teaches (Luke 12:12; cf. John 14:26);

testifies or bears witness (John 15:26; cf. Rom. 8:16);

guides (John 16:13; Acts 8:29);

can be lied to and tested (Acts 5:3–4, 9);

speaks (Acts 8:29; cf. 10:19–20; 28:25; 1 Tim. 4:1; Heb. 3:7);

calls to ministry and sends out (Acts 13:2–4);

forbids or allows (Acts 16:6–7);

intercedes (Rom. 8:26–27; cf. 15:16; Titus 3:5);

possesses a "mind" or "mindset" (Rom. 8:27);

reveals, searches, and knows the thoughts of God (1 Cor. 2:10–11);

gives gifts to whom he wills—indicating he has a will (1 Cor. 12:11); and

can be "grieved" (Eph. 4:30; cf. Isa. 63:10; Heb. 10:29).

A mere force or power cannot be grieved, cannot intercede or bear witness, and has no will. Only a person can give gifts to whomever that person wills (1 Cor. 12:11), and only a person can be grieved.

Some concede that Scripture teaches that the Holy Spirit possesses attributes only a person can possess but deny that the Holy Spirit is a person *distinct* from the Father and/or the Son—that is, some argue that the Holy Spirit is just the Spirit of the Father and/or the Son such that references to the Spirit are actually references to the person of the Father and/or the Son (depending on the context).

However, Scripture portrays the Father, the Son, and the Holy Spirit as *distinct* persons. Beyond instances like the appearance of Father, Son, and Spirit as distinct at Christ's baptism (Matt. 3:16–17), numerous passages portray the Father and the Son as having relations and conversations in which one is an "I" and the other is a "you," indicating *distinct* persons. For example, Christ (the Son) prays to the Father in Gethsemane, "My Father, if it is possible, let this cup pass from Me; yet not as I will, but as You will" (26:39 NASB). To take another example, Jesus declares that he and the Father shared a personal love relationship before the foundation of the world (John 17:24; cf. 3:35; 5:20). These and other instances of I-Thou relations explicitly distinguish the persons of the Father and the Son.

Numerous texts also distinguish the person of the Holy Spirit from the Father and the Son. For instance, Jesus refers to the Holy Spirit as "another Advocate," distinct from himself (John 14:16), who will remind people of Jesus's teaching and "teach" the apostles more (14:26; cf. Luke 12:12). Indeed, Jesus explains, "The Advocate, the Holy Spirit, whom the Father will send in my name, will teach you everything, and remind you of all that I have said to you" (John 14:26).[23] Here and elsewhere the Spirit is not the Son or the Father but is *sent by* the Son from the Father. As Jesus explains, "When the Advocate [the Holy Spirit] comes, whom I will send to you from the Father, the Spirit of truth who comes from the Father, he will testify on my behalf" (15:26; cf. 16:7–8, 13).[24] The Holy Spirit, then, is not identical to the Son. The Holy Spirit is "another" sent to *testify about* Christ—a testimony that would not be valid if Christ testified about himself, since Christ himself said, "If I testify about myself, my testimony is not true. There is another who testifies on my behalf, and I know that his testimony to me is true" (5:31–32). Conversely, "everyone who speaks a word against the Son of Man [Jesus] will be forgiven; but whoever blasphemes against the Holy Spirit will not be forgiven" (Luke 12:10; cf. Matt. 12:32).

These and other passages indicate that the Father is not the Son or the Spirit, the Son is not the Spirit or the Father, and the Spirit is not the Father or the Son. This is consistent with Scripture speaking of the Holy Spirit as the Spirit *of* God (e.g., 1 Cor. 2:11; Eph. 4:30) or as the Spirit *of* Jesus (e.g., Acts 16:7). Even as the Father belongs to the Son and the Son belongs to the Father because the Father is the Father *of the* Son and the Son is the Son *of the* Father, the Spirit belongs to the Father and the Son because the Spirit is the Spirit of the Father and the Spirit of the Son. If the core Trinity doctrine is true, then the Father, the Son, and the Spirit are ontologically united as one and belong to one another while also being distinct persons.

Tenet 4: The Three Persons of the Trinity Are Fully Divine and Thus Coequal and Coeternal

While the divinity of the Father is typically not disputed, some dispute the divinity of the Son and/or the Spirit. Here it is crucial to recall that Scripture rules out the possibility that one could be *partially* divine; there is only one God and "there is no one like" him (1 Chron. 17:20).

23. Noting the "Trinitarian implications of v 26," George Beasley-Murray observes, "His role as representative of Jesus and his task of recalling and interpreting the revelation brought by Jesus make very clear the [distinct] personal nature of the Spirit." Beasley-Murray, *John*, 261.

24. W. F. Albright and C. S. Mann comment that throughout John the Holy Spirit is "clearly represented as being neither Father nor Son." Albright and Mann, *Matthew*, 362.

Scripture contains more information about the Son than about the Holy Spirit—a product of the progressive and unfolding revelation of the covenant of redemption. The Holy Spirit is most explicitly revealed only as the time came for the Spirit to be sent to follow Christ's earthly ministry, toward the end of what is recorded in Scripture—an example of progressive revelation unfolding as elements of the covenant of redemption come to fruition. What is written about the Holy Spirit, however, indicates that the Holy Spirit is (fully) divine. For instance, in Acts 5:3–4, Peter asks Ananias, "Why has Satan filled your heart to lie to the Holy Spirit?" Then in parallel, Peter tells Ananias, "You did not lie to us but to God!" (cf. 1 Cor. 3:16). As Ben Witherington III comments, "The Spirit here is treated as a person, one who can be lied to, not merely a power," and "the Spirit is equated with God, as a comparison of vv. 3 and 4 shows."[25] As such, Ananias "is guilty of lying not merely to human beings but to God in the person of the Spirit."[26]

In addition, the Holy Spirit shares with the Father and the Son the "name" (singular) in which Christ's followers are to baptize (Matt. 28:19). Moreover, Scripture teaches that the Holy Spirit possesses uniquely divine attributes—attributes only God possesses—such as eternality ("the eternal Spirit," Heb. 9:14), omniscience (the Spirit knows and "searches all things, even the depths of God," 1 Cor. 2:10 NASB), and omnipresence (the Spirit is present wherever Christ's followers would separately go; see John 14:16; cf. 1 Cor. 3:16–17; 6:19). Further, "God is love" (1 John 4:8, 16), and "God's love has been poured into our hearts through the Holy Spirit" (Rom. 5:5; cf. 15:30; Gal. 5:22). Likewise, while God alone is holy in and of himself, one of the tasks of the Spirit is to "sanctify" or make holy (e.g., Rom. 15:16; 1 Pet. 1:2).

The NT also attributes to the Holy Spirit sayings that the OT attributes to God. For example, just before quoting words attributed to "the voice of the Lord" from Isaiah 6, Paul states, "The Holy Spirit was right in saying to your ancestors through the prophet Isaiah . . ." (Acts 28:25). Likewise, Hebrews 3 attributes what God says in Psalm 95:7–9 to the Holy Spirit:

Therefore, as the Holy Spirit says,

"Today, if you hear his voice,
do not harden your hearts as in the rebellion,
as on the day of testing in the wilderness,

25. Witherington, *Acts of the Apostles*, 216n80.
26. Witherington, *Acts of the Apostles*, 216. Further, 1 Cor. 3:16 refers to believers as "God's temple," while 1 Cor. 6:19 refers to believers as "a temple of the Holy Spirit."

where your ancestors put me to the test,
though they had seen my works for forty years." (Heb. 3:7–10)

God's words such as "put *me* to the test" and "had seen *my* works" (cf. Exod. 16:7) can be attributed to the Holy Spirit without blasphemy only if the Holy Spirit is God. The consistent witness of Scripture, then, is that the Holy Spirit is indeed (fully) divine.

Regarding the divinity of the Son, John 1:1–3 teaches, "In the beginning was the Word, and the Word was with God, and the Word was God. He was in the beginning with God. All things came into being through Him, and apart from Him nothing came into being that has come into being" (NASB; cf. Rom. 9:5; 2 Thess. 1:12; Titus 2:13; Heb. 1:8–9; 2 Pet. 1:1).[27] John 1 later identifies the Word with the Son and in doing so both identifies the Son as God ("the Word was God") and distinguishes the Son from another who is also called God ("the Word was with God") (v. 1).[28] It further teaches that the Son did not come into being, since "apart from Him nothing came into being that has come into being" (v. 3 NASB; cf. Isa. 9:6; Col. 1:16–17; Rev. 22:13). Rather, the Word was "with God . . . in the beginning" and is thus eternally preexistent.

Christ's divinity is also explicitly proclaimed in John 20:28, where Thomas addresses Jesus, "My Lord and my God!"[29] Further, though Scripture teaches only God is to be worshiped (Exod. 34:14; cf. Matt. 4:10; Luke 4:8; Rev. 19:10), Jesus accepts worship on numerous occasions (John 9:38; cf. Matt. 2:11; 14:33; 28:9, 17; Luke 24:52; Rev. 5:8–14).[30] And in Hebrews 1:6, the Father himself even commands, "Let all God's angels worship him" (cf. Deut. 32:43 LXX; Ps. 97:7). Further, although God declares, "My glory I give to no other" (Isa. 42:8), Jesus refers to "My glory which You [Father] have given Me" (John 17:24 NASB; cf. 17:5; Heb. 1:3) and declares,

27. Leon Morris comments, "All that may be said about God may fitly be said about the Word." L. Morris, *Gospel According to John*, 68.

28. Such wording avoids both modalism and tritheism without technical language. The lack of the article does not indicate that the Word is a lesser "god," but "if John had included the article," he "would have been so identifying the Word with God" that "it would be nonsense to say . . . that the Word was *with* God." Carson, *Gospel According to John*, 117 (emphasis original).

29. It is not merely that the Son is referred to as *theos* that affirms his (full) divinity but the way he is so referred to (as agent of creation in John 1:1–3 and "Lord" in John 20:28), alongside Scripture attributing properties to the Son that belong to God alone (e.g., being worthy of worship).

30. Some argue there are no biblical instances of worshiping the Spirit (the closest thing is we "worship in the Spirit," Phil. 3:3). However, this is an argument from silence (absence of evidence is not evidence of absence).

"All will honor the Son even as they honor the Father" (John 5:23 NASB). Jesus further calls "God his own Father, thereby making himself equal to God" (5:18; cf. Matt. 14:33) and claims, "The Father and I are one" (John 10:30) and "Whoever has seen me has seen the Father" (14:9). Jesus speaks of "his angels" (Matt. 13:41) and of "my kingdom," which "is not from this world" (John 18:36), and he claims "authority" to "forgive sins" (Mark 2:10)—authority belonging to God alone (2:7; Luke 5:20–21).

Perhaps most striking, Jesus proclaims, "Before Abraham was, I am" (John 8:58), which scholars typically understand as a reference to YHWH's statement to Moses from the burning bush, "I AM WHO I AM" (Exod. 3:14) and thus a claim to be the great "I AM."[31] Likewise, while in Revelation 1:8 God says, "I am the Alpha and the Omega" (cf. Isa. 44:6), Christ later declares, "I am the Alpha and the Omega, the first and the last, the beginning and the end" (Rev. 22:13). Yet Paul Copan notes, "There can't be two Alphas and Omegas."[32] According to G. K. Beale, "These titles, which are used in the OT of God, are combined and applied to Christ to highlight his deity."[33] Accordingly, Christ rightly shares the throne with the Father such that the throne is called "the throne of God and of the Lamb" (22:3). "He will reign

31. Regarding John 8:58, Leon Morris comments, "'I am' must here have the fullest significance it can bear. It is in the style of deity (see on vv. 24 and 28), 'a reference to his eternal being' (Haenchen)" (L. Morris, *Gospel According to John*, 419).

Christ's statement "I tell you now, before it occurs, so that when it does occur, you may believe that I am he [*egō eimi*]" (John 13:19) echoes the "I AM" statement of Exod. 3:14 (*egō eimi* in the LXX) and thus seems to refer to *divine* foreknowledge. Further, while 1 Kings 8:39 teaches that "only" God "know[s] what is in every human heart," Jesus "knew all people" and "knew what was in everyone" (John 2:24–25; cf. Matt. 9:4; Rev. 2:23). And Jesus's disciples proclaim, "Now we know that you know all things" (John 16:30), and Peter says to the resurrected Christ, "Lord, you know everything" (John 21:17). Yet, if Christ is divine, how could he say, "About that day or hour no one knows, neither the angels in heaven, nor the Son, but only the Father" (Mark 13:32)? There are more nuances to this issue than I can address here, but one traditional avenue maintains that statements indicating that Christ lacked knowledge (e.g., Mark 13:32) apply only to his human nature. Another way (compatible with the former, depending on how both are construed) is the suggestion that during his earthly ministry, Christ possessed all knowledge (qua divinity) but did not access his divine knowledge of many things (perhaps doing so would contravene his covenantal role as the second Adam, limited by human nature). In human experience at least, one can possess knowledge (e.g., vivid childhood memories) that one is not currently thinking about or otherwise accessing. In this regard, Andrew Loke contends, "There is no good reason, biblically or philosophically, to think that it is essential to God that the divine knowledge be contained in the conscious awareness of the divine mind such that He cannot freely choose to let part of that knowledge reside in a preconscious part of His mind if He so desires." Loke, "On the Coherence of the Incarnation," 54.

32. Copan, *Loving Wisdom*, 58.

33. Beale, *Revelation*, 1138.

over the house of Jacob forever, and of his kingdom there will be no end" (Luke 1:33; cf. Dan. 2:44; 7:14; Isa. 9:7; Heb. 1:8; Rev. 11:15).

Moreover, Colossians 2:9 explicitly asserts the *full* divinity of Christ, saying, "In him the whole fullness of deity dwells bodily" (cf. Phil. 2:6).[34] Before this, Christ is declared

> the image of the invisible God, the firstborn of all creation. For by Him all things were created, both in the heavens and on earth, visible and invisible, whether thrones or dominions or rulers or authorities—all things have been created through Him and for Him. He is before all things, and in Him all things hold together. He is also head of the body, the church; and He is the beginning, the firstborn from the dead, so that He Himself will come to have first place in everything. For it was the Father's good pleasure for all the fullness to dwell in Him, and through Him to reconcile all things to Himself, having made peace through the blood of His cross; through Him, I say, whether things on earth or things in heaven. (Col. 1:15–20 NASB)[35]

The language of "firstborn" here cannot consistently be interpreted as meaning Christ had a beginning to his existence, because that would contradict the teaching that "apart from Him [Christ] nothing came into being that has come into being" (John 1:3 NASB). If nothing has come into being apart from Christ, then Christ himself did not come into being. Further, Colossians 1:16–17 itself teaches that "he is before all things" (cf. Isa. 9:6; Mic. 5:2; Rev. 22:13).[36]

In Colossians 1 and elsewhere, such "firstborn" language appears to be covenantal language referring to Christ's status as the promised Messiah, the "son of David" (Matt. 21:9) who would fulfill the Davidic covenant and other covenant promises as the true king who would usher in God's everlasting kingdom (cf. Dan. 2). This takes birthright language used of David as

---

34. F. F. Bruce comments that in Christ "(truly man as he was) the plenitude of deity was embodied." Bruce, *Epistles to the Colossians*, 100.

35. Regarding Paul's understanding of divine Christology, David Capes makes a compelling case that Paul often "consciously quotes and alludes to scriptural texts referring to YHWH, the unspeakable [covenant] name of God, and applies these to Jesus" (Capes, *Divine Christ*, xiv). For example, Capes argues that Paul quotes from Isa. 45, "the most stridently monotheistic passage in the Hebrew Bible," and applies this YHWH text to the "Lord" (*kyrios*) Jesus (in both Phil. 2:10–11 and Rom. 14:11; cf. Isa. 45:23) (Capes, *Divine Christ*, 120). He details this and other features in Paul's writings that "point unambiguously to a divine Christ in the mind and devotion of Paul" (Capes, *Divine Christ*, 186). Cf. Wright, *Paul and the Faithfulness of God*, 701.

36. James D. G. Dunn comments, "That 'firstborn' must denote primacy over creation, and not just within creation, is indicated by the conjunction linking the two verses: he is 'firstborn of all creation because in him were created all things (τὰ πάντα).'" Dunn, *Epistle to the Colossians*, 90.

God's covenant son (e.g., God declares of David, "I also shall make him My firstborn," Ps. 89:27 NASB; cf. 2:6–7) and applies it to Jesus, the unique Son and fulfillment of the covenant promises.

Similar language of Christ's covenantal role in the plan of redemption appears in Hebrews 1. Drawing on Psalm 2:7 and 2 Samuel 7:14, Hebrews 1:5–6 asks,

> To which of the angels did God ever say,
>
> > "You are my Son;
> > today I have begotten you"?
>
> Or again,
>
> > "I will be his Father,
> > and he will be my Son"?
>
> And again, when he brings the firstborn into the world [*oikoumenē*], he says,
>
> > "Let all God's angels worship him."

More will be said about references to Christ as "begotten" and "firstborn" later in this chapter. Here it is important to note that interpreting such references in Hebrews 1:5–6 as referring to Christ coming into being not only would contradict other passages that teach that Christ is eternal and did not come into being (e.g., John 1:1–3; Col. 1:16–17; Rev. 22:13; cf. Isa. 9:6; Mic. 5:2) but also would contradict Hebrews 1 itself. First, at the time described in Hebrews 1:5–6, the angels already exist, since "when he brings the firstborn into the world," the Father says, "Let all God's angels worship him." However, Colossians 1:16–17 explicitly teaches that the Son existed before the angels were created; indeed, "he himself is before all things" (1:17; cf. John 1:1–3). Moreover, only God is to be worshiped. Thus, God's command of the angels to worship the Son evidences that the Son himself must be God.

Consideration of the passages Hebrews 1:5–6 quotes from further indicates that such references are to the eternally preexistent Son coming into the economy (*oikoumenē*) in the context of taking on a prophesied role in the covenantal plan of redemption. Specifically, the phrase "You are my son; today I have begotten you" is quoted from Psalm 2:7, which "is widely understood as a royal [installation] psalm" that is "associated with a coronation."[37] Further, the phrase "I will be his Father, and he will be my Son" draws from 2 Samuel 7:14 and is originally said of David. Taken together, the references to Psalm

---

37. Ellingsworth, *Epistle to the Hebrews*, 111–12.

2 and 2 Samuel 7 manifest Jesus as the promised king, the fulfillment of the Davidic covenant as the Messiah—the ultimate claimant of the covenant "birthright," as it were. Hebrews 1:5–6 appears, then, to be imagery of the enthronement and/or installation of the Son in a covenantal role according to the promised plan of redemption (cf. Rom. 1:2–4).

This fits with Hebrews 1:8–9, which quotes Psalm 45:6–7 as a reference to the Father addressing the Son:

> But of the Son He [the Father] says,
>
> "Your throne, O God [the Son], is forever and ever,
> And the righteous scepter is the scepter of His kingdom.
> "You have loved righteousness and hated lawlessness;
> Therefore God [the Son], Your God [the Father], has anointed You
> With the oil of gladness above Your companions." (Heb. 1:8–9 NASB;
> cf. Ps. 110:1)

According to these verses, "God" (the Son) is anointed by "God" (the Father).[38] Further, Hebrews 1:10–12 quotes the words of Psalm 102:24–27, which there refer to God as Creator who ever remains the same, as being spoken by the Father "of the Son."

This complements the beginning of Hebrews 1, which teaches that God "made the world" through the Son and that the Son "is the radiance of His [God's] glory and the exact representation of His [God's] nature, and upholds all things by the word of His power" (vv. 2–3 NASB). Yet Scripture consistently teaches that "there is no one like" God (1 Chron. 17:20) and that God does not give his glory to another (Isa. 42:8). Only one who is God could be "the radiance of [God's] glory and the exact representation of His nature" (Heb. 1:3 NASB).[39] Only the omnipotent God could uphold "all things by the word of His power" (1:3 NASB). Only God could rightly be worshiped (1:6). Only God could rightly be described as the one who "in the beginning . . . founded the earth" such that "the heavens are the work of your hands" (1:10; cf. Neh. 9:6). Only the eternal and immutable God could rightly be described as ever "the same" (Heb. 1:11–12)—indeed, "the same yesterday and today and forever" (13:8). If there is no other like God, yet the Son possesses

---

38. Paul Ellingsworth sees this "double ὁ θεός" as "continu[ing] the 'dialogue of divine persons' found implicitly in earlier quotations." Ellingsworth, *Epistle to the Hebrews*, 124.

39. Ellingsworth writes, "In the present verse, χαρακτὴρ τῆς ὑποστάσεως αὐτοῦ ["exact representation of His nature"] reinforces ἀπαύγασμα τῆς δόξης ["radiance of His glory"] in describing the essential unity and exact resemblance between God and his Son." Ellingsworth, *Epistle to the Hebrews*, 99.

uniquely divine attributes and is like God—indeed, "the exact representation of His nature" and the "radiance" of God's "glory" (which God does not share)—then the Son is God.[40]

The data surveyed in this and the previous three sections provides strong evidence that Scripture affirms the four tenets of the core Trinity doctrine: there is one and only one God, and God is three distinct (fully) divine persons. With this in place, we now turn to consider the coherence of the core Trinity doctrine.

Is the Core Trinity Doctrine Coherent?

Among other things, the core Trinity doctrine claims that God is both one and three. Yet how can this be affirmed consistently? Affirming that God is both one and three involves a contradiction only if one claims that God is one and three *in precisely the same way*. Affirming that God is one in some respect and three in another respect, as the core Trinity doctrine affirms, involves no contradiction. A three-leaf clover is one and three in different respects, without any contradiction; it is only one clover, but it has three leaves. In a *very different* way, the Trinity is one and three in different respects, without any contradiction; the Trinity is one God but three persons. God is certainly not one and three in a way that is like a three-leaf clover. I do not intend this example as an *analogy* of the Trinity (all analogies of the Trinity are inadequate) but merely as a demonstration that something can be simultaneously both one and three in different respects, without any contradiction.

However, one might think it is inconsistent to specifically claim that there is one *God* but three *persons* who may be called God. Some worry that to say the Father is God, the Son is God, and the Holy Spirit is God amounts to the conclusion that there are three "Gods." By such language, however, trinitarians mean that the Father is divine, the Son is divine, and the Holy Spirit is divine (i.e., possess the essential attributes of deity). This involves the crucial distinction between the "is" of identity and the "is" of predication. The phrase "Strider is Aragorn" is an example of the "is" of identity because Tolkien's fictional character introduced first as Strider is the same character whose given name is Aragorn. The phrase "Aragorn is king," however, is an example of the "is" of predication. It is (eventually) true of Aragorn that

40. Put simply, there appears to be biblical warrant to affirm that Christ possesses uniquely divine attributes such as immutability (Heb. 1:11–12; 13:8), eternity (John 1:1–3; Col. 1:16–17; Rev. 22:13), omnipresence (Matt. 18:20; 28:20), omnipotence (Heb. 1:3), omniscience (John 16:30; 21:17; cf. 13:19), and sharing God's glory, nature, and status as the one who alone is worthy of worship as the Creator of all (cf. Rev. 14:7).

Aragorn is king (the predication "king" is true about Aragorn), but being "king" is not identical to being Aragorn.

When trinitarians say that the Father is God, the Son is God, and the Spirit is God, they mean this in the sense of the "is" of predication. It is true of the Father that the Father is divine, true of the Son that the Son is divine, and true of the Spirit that the Spirit is divine. However, it is *not* true that the Father is God in the sense of the "is" of identity or that the Son or the Spirit is God in the sense of the "is" of identity.[41] The Father is God, but not by himself; the Father is God in essential unity with the Son and the Spirit (and vice versa). What is meant by the term "Father" or "Son" or "Spirit" is *not* identical with everything the word "God" means.[42] Each of the three persons is God (in the sense of the "is" of predication), but there are not three "Gods." A true example of the "is" of identity relative to the Trinity would be the following: God is the Father, Son, *and* Spirit.

One might further think that the claim that God is three distinct *persons* involves a contradiction. One might believe that more than one person must amount to more than one separate being (and, hence, more than one God). This confusion arises if one thinks the trinitarian persons are "persons" in the same way mere humans are "persons." If so, the trinitarian persons would be limited in the same way that creaturely persons are—physically and otherwise. Yet God is not limited as creatures are, physically or otherwise (see chap. 3).[43] Rather, according to the Trinity doctrine, the Being of God is shared by and inclusive of the three trinitarian persons such that the three persons are (somehow) ontologically one. As long as the trinitarian "persons are related in such a way that there is only one God, and not three Gods," the Trinity doctrine is consistent with monotheism.[44] While it may be difficult to understand just how this is so, to be consistent, the core Trinity doctrine need only affirm that God somehow transcends creaturely limitations such that the Father, the Son, and the Holy Spirit are ontologically united as one God (more on this later).

Comprehending precisely how the trinitarian persons are ontologically one may be beyond the limits of human understanding. However, just as I do not need to know *how* God is eternal or omnipotent in order to consistently affirm *that* God is eternal and omnipotent, I do not need to know *how* the

41. See Copan, *Loving Wisdom*, 58–59.

42. As Murray J. Harris puts it, "While Jesus is God, it is not true that God is Jesus. There are others of whom the predicate 'God' may be rightfully used. The person we call Jesus does not exhaust the category of Deity." M. Harris, *Jesus as God*, 297.

43. Notably, some creatures have multiple heads (e.g., two- or three-headed snakes and conjoined human twins). While multiheaded creatures are not analogous to the Trinity, they evince that it is not impossible for one "being" to have two or more minds.

44. Mullins, "Hasker on the Divine Processions," 183.

Father, the Son, and the Spirit are ontologically one in order to consistently affirm *that* God is one God in three persons. The Creator God transcends creaturely and physical limitations. Accordingly, it should not be surprising that God's Being transcends the limitations and categories of creaturely being and creaturely conceptions of being (indeed, we have difficulty enough making sense of the wave-particle duality of light). While there is mystery here, as far as I can see there is no actual contradiction in affirming that there is one and only one God and that God is three distinct (fully) divine persons.

The Trinity of Love: Toward Understanding the Triune Relations

With the basic parameters of the core Trinity doctrine in place, the remainder of this chapter turns to a very brief consideration of some issues regarding the relations between trinitarian persons. The overarching question of what follows is, How are the trinitarian persons distinguished and related as one *in se*—that is, apart from God's relation to the world? Trinitarians hold varying positions regarding the eternal relations of the Father, the Son, and the Spirit, including regarding (1) the sonship of the Son and the proceeding of the Spirit, (2) the distinctness and ontological unity of Father, Son, and Holy Spirit, and (3) the way the trinitarian persons are "persons."

The core Trinity doctrine is compatible with various positions regarding these disputed issues. In my view, on these disputed and complex issues, it is wise to tread lightly and not make dogmatic claims beyond what one has biblical warrant to affirm with confidence. Accordingly, without claiming to fully comprehend the eternal relations of the trinitarian persons, I make a *tentative* case for understanding the Trinity as the Trinity of love. Again, however, one could affirm the core Trinity doctrine while disagreeing with my views regarding the issues discussed below.

The Economic Trinity, the Immanent Trinity, and Submission

Within the economy of biblical revelation, at least relative to Christ's earthly ministry, the Son is sent by the Father (John 5:36–37; 6:44, 57; 8:16, 18; 10:36; 12:49; 1 John 4:14) and voluntarily submits to the Father (John 10:18; cf. 14:28), lovingly obeying (14:31) and doing only what the Father wills (5:19, 30; 6:38; 8:28). Likewise, the NT depicts the Spirit in what some describe as a subordinate role—being sent by the Father and the Son (14:26; 15:26; 16:13)—but which might be best understood as voluntary submission.

How one theologically interprets this data depends a great deal on how one navigates the relationship between what theologians call the economic

Trinity and the immanent Trinity. The economic Trinity refers to the Trinity as the Trinity appears in relation to the world—that is, in the economy. The immanent Trinity refers to the Trinity as the Trinity is apart from the world (*in se*)—that is, in intratrinitarian relationship. The question is, To what extent does the Trinity as revealed in relation to the world (the economic Trinity) correspond to the inner life of God (the immanent Trinity)? Some trinitarians emphasize the "vast distinction between God's actions in the world [the economic Trinity] and God's eternal being [the immanent Trinity]."[45] Other trinitarians emphasize continuity between the two, employing various understandings of Rahner's Rule, the "proposition that the economic Trinity *is* the immanent Trinity and vice versa."[46]

Is the economic Trinity the immanent Trinity and vice versa? In one sense (at least), the answer must be yes; there are not two "trinities" but only one Trinity. However, the question goes deeper, asking whether the economic Trinity *as portrayed in Scripture* corresponds to God as he is in himself (*in se*) and, if so, to what extent. Here some theologians are deeply concerned about what Fred Sanders calls "an economizing of God and a deflationary historicizing of triunity."[47] In my view, there are (at least) two opposite dangers here. One is to conceptually separate the economic Trinity and the immanent Trinity such that the immanent Trinity is conceived of in a way that does not account for the biblical revelation regarding trinitarian relations in the economy. The other danger is to conflate the economic Trinity and the immanent Trinity such that one thinks that everything affirmed of a person of the Trinity in the economy of biblical revelation applies to that person eternally and essentially.

Conflating the two may lead to mistakenly thinking that, since Jesus experienced thirst, the Son is eternally thirsty, or otherwise erroneously reading every part of Jesus's life back into the Son's eternal life. Conversely, the economic Trinity and the immanent Trinity might be too sharply distinguished, leading one to conclude that the divine Christ could not have actually dwelled among humans, acted, suffered, or otherwise been temporally affected as Jesus was. By way of what some call "partitive exegesis," which attributes some things to the divine nature alone and some to the human nature alone, suffering (for example) might be attributed to Christ's humanity alone, with only predications compatible with strict timelessness, immutability, and impassibility corresponding to Christ's divinity. Yet as discussed earlier in this book, if

45. F. Sanders, *Triune God*, 144.
46. Rahner, *Theological Investigations*, 114 (emphasis original).
47. F. Sanders, *Triune God*, 150. Further, John Webster worries that "attention to God's outer acts" may be "thought to license talk of God as some sort of magnified historical agent acting on the same plane as other such agents." Webster, *God without Measure*, 8.

the divine Christ could not suffer, it is difficult to escape the conclusion that Christ's sacrifice was merely a human sacrifice.

In this and other regards, while it is crucial to recognize that many things are true of Christ's humanity that are not true of Christ's divinity and vice versa, I worry that using an extrabiblical standard to determine what corresponds to divinity and what does not might conflict with and sometimes overrule the revelation of God in Jesus Christ that Scripture records, perhaps (conceptually) reducing the incarnate Christ to a mere projection of God. As Paul Helm puts it, because "there is no change or succession possible in the timeless eternity of God's life," the "incarnation is the 'projection' of the eternal God."[48] In my view, however, the incarnation is not merely a projection of God, and the economic Trinity is not merely a projection of the immanent Trinity. I believe Scripture teaches that the Son actually *became* human without becoming any less divine and that the Holy Spirit actually came to *specially* dwell with humans in creation (the economy) without being reduced to or contained by creation. T. F. Torrance comments, in this regard, "Jesus Christ is not a mere symbol, some functional representation of God detached from God, but God in his own Being and Act come among us, exhibiting and expressing in our human form the very Word which he is eternally in himself."[49]

As I see it, if Scripture is trustworthy as the final norm of theological interpretation, then whatever Scripture actually affirms to be true of the Trinity in the economy (the economic Trinity) must be *compatible with* the way God is apart from the world (the immanent Trinity), without conflating the two. For instance, if the Bible teaches that "the Word was God" (John 1:1) and that the Word *actually* "became flesh" (1:14), then whatever is true of God *in se* must be *compatible with* the divine Word becoming flesh (in the economy). However, saying the two are compatible does not mean they are the same *in every way*. If the Word *became* flesh, then the Word was not always flesh. If the Word *actually* lowered himself from a previously exalted state (Phil. 2), being sent "when the fullness of time had come" (Gal. 4:4), then there was a time before the Son so condescended.[50] If so, the Son was not always just as he becomes in the incarnation, yet the Son's becoming human at some time is compatible with the Son's divine nature.[51]

---

48. Helm, "Divine Timeless Eternity," 54.
49. Torrance, *Christian Doctrine of God*, 95.
50. It seems that partitive exegesis cannot be employed to avoid this conclusion because (by their very description) such actions must correspond to the Word without flesh (the *logos asarkos*).
51. This is consistent with the view of divine temporality set forth in chap. 3.

As a result, the Son's declaration "The Father is greater than I" (John 14:28) describes something true of the Son at some time but need not be descriptive of something *eternally* true of the Son. While some trinitarians have recently argued that the Son's submission to the Father is an eternal *functional* submission and thus eternally true of God *in se*, I do not believe the Son's submission in the economy should be extrapolated to the eternal relations between the Father and the Son.[52] Instead, I believe this and other biblical data are best interpreted as referring to the Son voluntarily and temporarily lowering himself to fulfill his crucial covenantal role in the plan of redemption (the outworking of the covenant of redemption made among the trinitarian persons). If so, the Son's submission is a temporary functional subordination.

If it is correct to interpret Philippians 2:6 as teaching the Son possessed "equality with God" but did not hold on to it and instead lowered himself, then the Son could not be *eternally* subordinate to the Father.[53] Numerous biblical passages exhibit the pattern of Christ lowering himself according to the covenantal plan of salvation and then being reexalted to his throne—"the throne of God and of the Lamb" (Rev. 22:3). However, no biblical data indicates that the Son was already lower than the Father before he lowered himself. Rather, the Son shared glory with the Father "before the world was" (John 17:5 NASB; cf. 17:24), and at the appointed time (Gal. 4:4), the Son lowered and humbled himself (Phil. 2:5–8). But eventually the Son is re-elevated and exalted to his rightful throne (2:9–11; cf. Matt. 28:18; 1 Cor. 15:24–28; Eph. 1:20–23; Heb. 1:3–4).[54] Ultimately, Christ declares, "All will honor the Son *even as* they honor the Father" (John 5:23 NASB).

According to John 10:17–18, Christ's condescension was a voluntary lowering in the context of mutual (covenantal) love relationship: "For this reason the Father loves me, because I lay down my life in order to take it up again. No one takes it from me, but I lay it down of my own accord. I have power to lay it down, and I have power to take it up again" (cf. Gal. 2:20; Eph. 5:2). In the economy, not only does the Son lovingly obey the Father

52. This view that the Son and the Spirit are eternally subordinate is often referred to as eternal relations of authority and submission (ERAS) or eternal functional subordination (EFS). The difference between this and subordinationism is the claim that the subordination of the Son and the Spirit is merely functional. However, many critics have argued that this nevertheless amounts to subordinationism. For an introduction to the debate, see Jowers and House, *New Evangelical Subordinationism?*

53. Fee interprets this as teaching that "prior to his 'having taken the "form" of a slave' he was already 'in the "form" of God,'" which "presupposes prior existence as God." Fee, *Paul's Letter to the Philippians*, 203.

54. This re-elevation takes place in stages, corresponding to stages in the cosmic conflict (Satan is defeated at the cross but not yet destroyed). See Peckham, *Theodicy of Love*, chap. 5.

(and come to serve humanity rather than be served), but the Father also delegates to the Son in the context of love relationship, effectively "binding Himself to the results of Christ's salvific mission"[55] (see 2 Cor. 5:19; 1 John 4:14). Indeed, Jesus states, "The Father loves the Son and has given all things into His hand" (John 3:35 NASB; cf. 5:22–23; 13:3; 16:15). The Father thereby "submits" to the Son relative to whatever he has "given . . . into His [the Son's] hand."

In the economy of redemption, the Son also operates in submission to the Holy Spirit, being incarnated via the Spirit (Matt. 1:18–20; Luke 1:35), filled and anointed by the Spirit (Luke 4:1, 18; cf. Matt. 3:16; 12:28), and driven into the wilderness by the Spirit (Mark 1:12; cf. Matt. 4:1; Luke 4:1).[56] Later, however, the Spirit is sent both by the Father and the Son (e.g., John 14:26; 15:26; 16:7), apparently operating in a *functionally* submissive role (John 16:13–15) relative to both the Father and the Son (missional submission). Relative to "the relationship between the Spirit and Christ," Graham Cole sees "a story of successive subordinations. In the state of humiliation the Messiah is directed by the Spirit. In the state of glory, the vindicated Messiah directs the Spirit."[57] If this is right, the persons of the Trinity take on different roles and (functionally) submit to one another at various times according to the plan of salvation. If so, such *particular* submissions among the trinitarian persons are not eternal but temporary. If these "submissions" are indeed functional, if they are for the sake of achieving specific "missions," then such submissions would not be eternal but would continue only as long as needed to fulfill their missional function.[58] In this regard, McCall has argued that if the Son is eternally subordinate (in the sense of hierarchical ordering), then the Son cannot be of the same "essence" as the Father—amounting to subordinationism. While I cannot get into the details of the arguments here, I tend to agree with McCall (and many others) about this. At the same time, if Nozumu Miyahira is right that trinitarian love is "humble" and "seeks to

55. Canale, "Doctrine of God," 128.

56. Graham Cole comments, "There is a subordination of the Son to the Spirit as the Son carries out his messianic vocation" (Cole, *He Who Gives Life*, 171). So also Gulley, *Systematic Theology: God as Trinity*, 147–48.

57. Cole, *He Who Gives Life*, 207. See also Tinkham, "Neo-subordinationism," 269–73.

58. Drawing on the Gospel of John, Nozumu Miyahira makes a case that in "mutual co-subordination the three are equal." Such "subordination does not contain any pejorative implication in the triune God, because it is based on the love which is closely connected with the mutual and voluntary act," and thus "the subordination of the triune God is tantamount to the service of one to the other," involving "mutual loving, knowing, entrusting and glorifying." And "the more any one member carries out the entrusted work, the more they glorify each other." Miyahira, *Towards a Theology of the Concord of God*, 188–89.

subordinate itself to others," then there would appear to be a broader and different sense in which the trinitarian persons "subordinate" themselves to one another in love without thereby being inferior to one another relative to nature, status, position, or function.[59]

Here it is important to recognize that sonship does not entail subordination in the sense of inferior nature, status, position, or function. Even among mere humans, a son might not be subordinate to his father. A son might become his father's boss at work or his caretaker when his father is elderly. Mere human sons must begin life subordinate to their parents because, while young, they lack awareness of dangers and otherwise need to be under their parents' authority for their own protection. Yet Christ is not a "son" of the Father in the way mere humans are sons of their fathers. Among many other differences, Christ's life did not begin (John 1:1–3; Col. 1:16–17; Rev. 22:13), the Son is not younger than the Father, and the preincarnate Word had no need (of protection or anything else). Further, while King David is frequently called "son of Jesse" (his human father), as king he was not subordinate to his human father. Jesus is frequently called "son of David," but he was not subordinate to David. Jesus highlights just the opposite when he asks how David could refer to the "son of David" as "Lord" (Matt. 22:41–46; cf. Ps. 110:1). Moreover, at least in John 5:18, Christ's claim of Sonship is taken as indicating *equality* with the Father, and only if the Son is equal with the Father could it be appropriate that "all may honor the Son just as they honor the Father" (5:22–23; cf. 2 Sam. 7:14; Ps. 2:6–7; Heb. 1:2–14).

To support the view that the Son continues to be subjected to the Father even in the eschaton, however, some appeal to 1 Corinthians 15:28: "When all things are subjected to him, then the Son himself will also be subjected to the one who put all things in subjection under him, so that God may be all in all" (cf. Eph. 1:23).[60] However, I believe this text is best interpreted as referring to the end of the Son's functional covenantal role (and rule) as the mediatorial second Adam—the function of which was to defeat sin and the devil and to reclaim the rulership the first Adam forfeited—and the full resumption of the glory Christ shared with the Father before the world began (John

---

59. Miyahira, *Towards a Theology of the Concord of God*, 189. See McCall, *Which Trinity?*, 175–88. See also Erickson, *Who's Tampering with the Trinity?* Though holding a different view of trinitarian relations, Kevin Giles also argues that if Christ's "subordination is eternal, it is not a role or functional subordination" but "an ontological status that cannot be otherwise," a "hierarchical ordering in the eternal or immanent Trinity" that amounts to "subordinationism." Giles, "Trinity without Tiers," 283–84, 285.

60. Notably, Scripture affirms both that "God may be all in all" (1 Cor. 15:28) and that Christ "fills all in all" (Eph. 1:23).

17:5).[61] Otherwise, as John Calvin comments, this text would be "at variance with what we read in various passages of Scripture respecting the eternity of Christ's kingdom," such as Daniel 7:14, 27; Luke 1:33; and 2 Peter 1:11.[62] To be consistent with other biblical passages, the statements that Christ "must reign until he has put all his enemies under his feet" and thereafter "hands over the kingdom to God the Father" (1 Cor. 15:24–25) cannot mean the Son actually ceases to rule.[63] Indeed, "of the Son," the Father himself declares, "Your throne, O God, is forever and ever" (Heb. 1:8; cf. Isa. 9:7; Rev. 11:15).[64] It seems, then, that the Son reigns *as the second Adam* until he fulfills his covenantal (messianic, son of David and of Adam) function of vanquishing the principalities and powers in the cosmic conflict, but then he resumes his place on his throne—"the throne of God and of the Lamb" (Rev. 22:3)—and "he will reign forever and ever" (11:15; cf. Isa. 9:6–7).

Eternal Relations of Origin?

Yet there remains the question of whether the Son is eternally the Son of the Father (eternal Sonship) or whether the Son became the Son in the incarnation (incarnational Sonship) or some other view (e.g., the eternal Word took on a Sonship role prior to the incarnation, perhaps as mediator between Creator and creatures).[65] Some affirm eternal Sonship because they believe some biblical language of Christ's Sonship refers to Christ prior to the incarnation. However, while references to the "Son" prior to the incarnation could refer to Christ taking on a Sonship role prior to the incarnation, such references could instead be proleptic, foreshadowing the Sonship role Christ

61. See Gulley, *Systematic Theology: God as Trinity*, 152–55.

62. Calvin, *Commentary on the Epistles of Paul*, 2:31. Calvin concludes, "Nor will [Christ] in this way resign the kingdom, but will transfer it in a manner from his humanity to his glorious divinity" (2:32–33).

63. Notably, if the Father having "given all things into His [the Son's] hand" is rightly understood as the Father delegating to the Son relative to (among other things) defeating the devil's allegations according to the plan of redemption (a judicial transfer of jurisdiction within the cosmic conflict), then this "hand[ing] over the kingdom to God the Father" (1 Cor. 15:24) by the Son could be understood as just the reversal of such temporary juridical transfer, "after he has destroyed every ruler and every authority and power" and "put all enemies under his feet" (1 Cor. 15:24–25)—that is, once the cosmic conflict is ended with no longer any need for such allotted jurisdiction.

64. Just as Jesus can consistently affirm that the "Father judges no one but has given all judgment to the Son" (John 5:22) and also that "it is not I alone who judge, but I and the Father who sent me" (8:16; cf. 1 Pet. 1:17), it can be true that the Son ceases to rule in one respect (as the second Adam) but continues to rule in another (as the divine Word).

65. Such a view would fit, but not require, the view of some theologians that the incarnation would have occurred even if there was no sin from which humanity required redemption. See van Driel, *Incarnation Anyway*.

covenanted within the Trinity to carry out, analogous to the way I might say I met my wife in high school but do not thereby mean she was my wife then. Even as Scripture calling Jesus "son of David" does not require that Jesus was eternally David's son, Scripture calling Christ the "Son of God" does not by itself *require* eternal Sonship.

Yet a prominent view in the Christian tradition is that the Son is eternally generated (or "begotten") by the Father and that the Holy Spirit eternally proceeds from the Father (and, in the West, also from the Son).[66] This view of eternal relations of origin is not without its critics, however. Many argue this view lacks biblical support, and some even claim the view leads to subordinationism.[67] Supporters of eternal relations of origin, however, vigorously deny this.[68] In addition to its roots in the Nicene Creed (at least as most interpret it), supporters of eternal generation often appeal to biblical data regarding Christ's Sonship, particularly references to the Son as *monogenēs* (often translated "only begotten") and *prōtotokos* ("firstborn").

As seen earlier, interpreting these terms as indicating that Christ came into existence would be inconsistent with biblical passages that teach Christ had no beginning (e.g., John 1:1–3; Col. 1:17; Rev. 22:13; cf. Isa. 9:6; Mic. 5:2) and with the immediate context of many instances of these terms (e.g., Col. 1:15–20; Heb. 1:5–6). Accordingly, many advocates of eternal generation interpret references to the Son as *monogenēs* to mean the Son is generated by the Father, but eternally. This traditional view interprets *monogenēs* as partially derived from the verb *gennaō*, which often refers to literal birth. However, most recent NT scholars believe that *monogenēs* does not derive from *gennaō* but from another root such that it refers to being of a kind. As Leon Morris puts it, *monogenēs* "means no more than 'only,' 'unique.'"[69]

---

66. As Stephen Holmes describes the patristic view, Father, Son, and Spirit "are distinguished by eternal relations of origin—begetting and proceeding—and not otherwise" (Holmes, *Quest for the Trinity*, 146). See also Anatolios, *Retrieving Nicaea*; Ayres, *Nicaea and Its Legacy*.

67. For example, Millard Erickson argues, "The concept of eternal generation does not have biblical warrant and does not make sense philosophically. As such, we should eliminate it from theological discussions of the Trinity" (Erickson, *Who's Tampering with the Trinity?*, 251). See also Feinberg, *No One Like Him*, 489–92; Mullins, "Divine Temporality," 281–83. J. P. Moreland and William Lane Craig contend further, "Although creedally affirmed, the doctrine of the generation of the Son (and the procession of the Spirit) is a relic of Logos Christology which finds virtually no warrant in the biblical text and introduces a subordinationism into the Godhead which anyone who affirms the full deity of Christ ought to find very troubling." Moreland and Craig, *Philosophical Foundations*, 594.

68. For a defense of eternal generation relative to Scripture and philosophy, see F. Sanders and Swain, *Retrieving Eternal Generation*, 29–146. See also F. Sanders, *Triune God*.

69. L. Morris, *Gospel According to John*, 93. Harris similarly concludes, "It may be safely said that [in the NT] μονογενής is concerned with familial relations, not manner of birth. Neither the

Even if *monogenēs* is derived from *gennaō*, however, it might be understood as a reference to the incarnation, according to the angel's pronouncement to Mary, "The Holy Spirit will come upon you, and the power of the Most High will overshadow you; and *for that reason* the holy Child shall be called the Son of God" (Luke 1:35 NASB; cf. Gal. 4:4). According to this text, the incarnation is the "reason" Jesus is "called the Son of God." Moreover, *gennaō* itself does not always refer to literal birth or progeny. In the very chapter where the most famous instance of *monogenēs* appears (John 3:16), Jesus uses *gennaō* of humans being "born of the Spirit" (3:3–8). Along similar lines, 1 John 4:7 declares, "Everyone who loves is born [*gennaō*] of God." Later, Paul calls Onesimus one "whom I have begotten [*gennaō*] in my imprisonment" (Philem. 10 NASB; cf. 2 Tim. 1:2). The term *monogenēs*, then, might be derived from *gennaō* but employed as a metaphor of special status (e.g., covenantal "birthright"), as language of Christ as *prōtotokos* ("firstborn") may be understood (see tenet 4).[70]

The term *monogenēs* itself is sometimes used as a term of endearment—indicating one's uniquely beloved. Hebrews 11:17 refers to Isaac as Abraham's *monogenēs*, drawing on Genesis 22:2, which refers to Isaac as Abraham's *yāḥîd* ("only or unique one," often translated "only son") and son whom he loved. Yet Isaac was not Abraham's *only* son (remember Ishmael). Isaac was Abraham's uniquely beloved son (22:2), *the elect son of the covenant promise.* Interestingly, the Septuagint translates *yāḥîd* as *agapētos* ("beloved") in Genesis 22:2 rather than *monogenēs*. Both *monogenēs* and *agapētos* are sometimes used to translate *yāḥîd* in the Septuagint, and therein *agapētos* also translates the very similar-looking Hebrew term *yādîd* ("beloved"). Indeed, some believe the "originally distinct meanings of *yāḥîd* and *yādîd* became conflated" in the Septuagint.[71] Accordingly, R. L. Roberts argues that *yāḥîd* and *monogenēs* are "used as hyperboles of affection" such that *monogenēs huios* in John 3:16 and elsewhere may be rendered "uniquely" or "only beloved Son."[72]

Curiously, however, while the Synoptic Gospels repeatedly refer to Jesus as the "beloved" (*agapētos*) Son (Matt. 3:17; 17:5; Mark 1:11; 9:7; Luke 3:22; cf. Matt. 12:18; Mark 12:6; Luke 20:13), the Gospel of John never uses *agapētos*.[73]

---

virgin birth of Jesus nor the 'eternal generation' of the Son is in John's mind when he uses the adjective μονογενής." M. Harris, *Jesus as God*, 86–87.

70. It might, then, refer to a shift in Christ's role in the plan of redemption, as *gennaō* seems to be used in Heb. 1:5 ("today I have begotten [*gennaō*] you," the context of which excludes the possibility that this refers to a time when the Son came into existence).

71. M. Barth, *Ephesians 1–3*, 82.

72. Roberts, "Rendering 'Only Begotten,'" 15.

73. Of the Johannine writings, only 1 and 3 John use *agapētos*, always of believers, "children" of God.

This all may relate to why only Johannine writings use *monogenēs* of Christ, and only of Christ (John 1:14, 18; 3:16, 18; 1 John 4:9). While other NT writings refer to believers as "sons" (*huios*) of God, Johanine writings refer to believers as "children" (*teknon*) of God but never "sons" (*huios*) of God, reserving the term "Son" (*huios*) of God for Jesus alone. Reserving such language uniquely for Christ may just be John's way of identifying Jesus as the Father's uniquely beloved Son; others may be "children" (*teknon*) and "beloved" (*agapētos*), but Jesus is uniquely the Father's *huios* and *monogenēs*—his "only beloved Son" (*monogenēs huios*). Given that Isaac, the uniquely beloved son of his father and the uniquely elect son of the covenant promise, was a type of Christ, it is only fitting that John identifies Christ the antitype as the Father's "only beloved Son" (*monogenēs huios*) and that Scripture identifies Christ as the uniquely elect and beloved Son of the covenant promise, par excellence (Matt. 12:18; cf. Luke 9:35).

While debate continues over how *monogenēs* should be interpreted, and I do not intend to offer a dogmatic conclusion here, I see no biblical warrant for confidently interpreting *monogenēs* or other language of Sonship as evidence for eternal generation.[74] Likewise, I see no biblical warrant for the eternal procession of the Spirit. NT language of the Holy Spirit being sent and the one "who proceeds from the Father" (e.g., John 15:26) seems to refer to the historical sending and proceeding of the Spirit in the economy after the incarnation. I am not claiming that eternal generation and eternal procession could not possibly be true, but I see no biblical warrant for such claims.[75] Further, while one might attempt to coherently affirm eternal relations of origin while denying divine timelessness, insofar as eternal relations of origin require strict timelessness (as most suppose), affirming such relations conflicts with what I believe is the biblically warranted conclusion that God is not timeless (see chap. 3).[76]

74. One might argue this view should be adopted on the grounds of the Nicene Creed. However, Craig Keener notes, "Scripture is ultimately more authoritative than creeds and need not be conformed to the creeds (which, like Scripture, may be subject to interpretation)." Keener, "Subordination within the Trinity," 55.

75. Marc Cortez comments, "The eternal generation of the Son and the dual procession of the Spirit are, in my opinion, examples of . . . speculation. Neither of the two doctrines is asserted in Scripture nor do they appear to be necessary (some would say not even justified) inferences from the data." Yet, "this does not mean that they are illegitimate or invalid theological conclusions" (Cortez, "Context and Concept," 95). Paul Helm goes further, "making a plea for the removal from our understanding of the doctrine of the Trinity of certain concepts [eternal generation and procession] which derive not from the New Testament but from pagan philosophy, from Neoplatonism" so that "our understanding of the Trinity may be more faithful to Scripture, and less open to speculative distraction." Helm, "Of God, and of the Holy Trinity," 351, 357.

76. Eternal generation and divine timelessness are typically linked. For example, Augustine writes that the Father "begot him [the Son] timelessly" (Augustine, *Trinity* 15.47 [Hill, 432]). See

238

Eternal Relations of Love

If one denies or doubts eternal relations of origin, however, what might one say regarding how the trinitarian persons are both distinguished and related as one *in se*—that is, apart from the world? In my view, God's oneness and the distinctness of the trinitarian persons might be consistently affirmed in terms of eternal relations of love. From all eternity, the trinitarian persons have been united in essential love relationship *and* distinguished by love relationship in that each person of the Trinity loves the other two persons as an *other* person. "God is love" (1 John 4:8, 16). Yet how could God be love prior to creation when there were no creatures to love? According to Scripture, love relationship existed between trinitarian persons before the world began (John 17:24) such that God has always been in love relationship within the Trinity.[77] Accordingly, prior to and apart from creation, the Father, the Son, and the Spirit could be distinguished in the following way: the Father loves the Son and the Spirit as *other* persons, the Son loves the Spirit and the Father as *other* persons, and the Spirit loves the Father and the Son as *other* persons—a Trinity of love. As T. F. Torrance puts it, "In the Communion of the Holy Trinity the Father is Father in his loving of the Son and the Spirit, the Son is Son in his loving of the Father and the Spirit, and the Spirit is Spirit in his loving of the Father and the Son."[78]

Trinitarian persons might not only be distinguished by eternal relations of love but also be ontologically united thereby.[79] One might affirm God's

---

further Holmes, *Quest for the Trinity*, 112. However, some affirm both divine temporality and eternal generation and procession. See Hasker, *Metaphysics and the Tri-personal God*, 214–25; Swinburne, *Christian God*, 182–85. For criticism of this view, see Mullins, "Hasker on the Divine Processions," 181–216.

77. Some have offered divine love as an argument for why God must be three persons. Specifically, Richard Swinburne argues (while affirming eternal relations of origin) that "perfect love involves there being someone else to whom to be generous; and also that perfect loving involves a third individual, the loving of whom could be shared with the second" such that love is unselfishly directed to a third party (Swinburne, *Christian God*, 190). See also Richard of St. Victor, *On the Trinity*. Swinburne argues further that there "would be something deeply unsatisfactory" about a relationship in which two persons "were concerned solely with each other and did not use their mutual love to bring forth good to others" (Swinburne, *Christian God*, 177–78). See further Swinburne, "Social Theory of the Trinity," 1–19.

78. Torrance, *Christian Doctrine of God*, 166. Torrance himself also affirms that "'Father,' 'Son' and 'Holy Spirit' stand for inexpressible although real relations, 'begetting' and 'proceeding' which are . . . no less ineffable, and should surely be left undefined," but "we cannot but use them if we are not to be altogether silent, but let us use them only with apophatic reserve and reverence" (Torrance, *Christian Doctrine of God*, 193–94). Yet, it seems to me that one could be skeptical of the eternal relations of origin while affirming eternal relations of love. Further, prior to creation, the trinitarian persons could be *proleptically* identified by their economic roles.

79. As Torrance understands it,

The relations in reciprocal loving between the three divine Persons are onto-relations, for they are relations which belong to what they each are hypostatically in themselves

oneness via the biblical concept of mutual indwelling (John 10:30; 14:7–11) of love, sometimes called *perichoresis*.[80] While the term *perichoresis* might be understood variously, I use it here of the concept that the trinitarian persons somehow interpenetrate one another via eternal relations of love and thus coinhere as one and only one God.[81]

This concept of the Trinity of love overlaps with the ongoing debate regarding the nature of triunity, the most prominent views of which are singularity (or Latin) theories and social theories.[82] These views differ over whether the trinitarian persons share one *unitary* faculty of reason, will, and self-consciousness (as singularity theories claim) or whether the three persons each have a distinct faculty of reason, will, and self-consciousness (as social theories claim).[83] Further, singularity theories "attempt to stress the unity of the divine nature, without falling into modalism," and social theories "attempt

---

as divine Persons and to what they are homoousially together in their love for one another, in their self-giving to one another and their receiving from one another. Thus in their Communion in Love with one another they are three Persons, one Being. Their differences from each other as Father, Son and Holy Spirit, instead of separating them from one another involve a "sort of ontological communication" between them, and as such are constitutive of their Unity in Trinity and their Trinity in Unity. (Torrance, *Christian God*, 166)

80. While such texts may not explicitly teach mutual indwelling in the immanent Trinity, they lend themselves to this view (cf. John 14–16).

81. Some protest that we do not have a sufficiently clear concept of what *perichoresis* is. Yet, absent some contradiction, this is no defeater. Christians affirm many things about God without knowing just how they are so. As Oliver Crisp concludes, "What does it mean to say that the three persons of the Trinity interpenetrate one another in their shared life together, whilst remaining, at-one-and-the-same-time one God in three distinct persons? I cannot say because I do not know. This is a divine mystery before which theology must give way to doxology." Crisp, "Problems with Perichoresis," 140.

82. There are other theories, such as the lesser-known relative identity theory (aka "Constitution Trinitarianism") of Jeffrey Brower and Michael Rea based on a medieval strategy, which suggests that "the divine persons may be conceived on analogy with form-matter compounds (such as the difference between lumps and statues)" and argues for "numerical [and essential] sameness without identity" of the persons; "one God, but three persons who are genuinely distinct rather than identical" (McCall, "Relational Trinity," 113–37; McCall, *Which Trinity?*, 131). See Brower and Rea, "Material Constitution and the Trinity," 263–82.

83. These views are often associated with East and West, based on the oft-repeated view that "Western" conceptions of the Trinity (e.g., Augustine) started with oneness and "Eastern" conceptions (e.g., the Cappadocian fathers) started with threeness. However, this thesis has been challenged by many recent scholars. Among others, Holmes has made a case that "the patristic inheritance, East and West, essentially spoke with one voice" regarding the Trinity, affirming the singularity view (Holmes, *Quest for the Trinity*, 144). However, the filioque is a significant point of contention between East and West, and some have interpreted the Cappadocian fathers and others as supporters of a social theory of the Trinity. In this regard, Paul R. Hinlicky warns against "imagin[ing] that a millennium of East-West separation over trinitarian theology was much ado about nothing" and himself sees "the Cappadocians' strong distinction of nature and person as the metaphysic of trinitarianism." Hinlicky, *Divine Simplicity*, 118.

to highlight the diversity or distinctness of the three persons, without falling into polytheism."[84] According to Stephen Holmes (and others), the singularity (aka Latin) theory is the traditional, classical conception, and viewing the Trinity as "three 'persons'" in the sense of three centers of consciousness is "a simple departure from . . . the unified witness of the entire theological tradition."[85] Many disagree, however. McCall contends that such a "robust sense of persons" need not lose "continuity with the tradition."[86] William Hasker argues further, "For the pro-Nicene Fathers, the trinitarian Persons are indeed 'distinct centers of knowledge, will, love, and action'" and, thus, the pro-Nicene Fathers were "also pro-Social trinitarians."[87] Here, again, competent scholars hold competing interpretations of the Christian tradition.

Further, many strict classical theists believe the singularity theory is entailed by strict simplicity, which affirms (among other things) that there are no genuine distinctions in God—all divine "attributes" are identical with God.[88] The only exception, the consistency of which is a point of debate, is that the three persons of the Trinity "are distinguished by eternal relations of origin-begetting and proceeding—and not otherwise."[89] However, there are serious objections to *strict* simplicity.[90] To mention the one most pertinent to the discussion here, McCall worries that *strict* simplicity "truly may be inconsistent with trinitarian theology. If there are no distinctions within God, then the divine persons cannot be distinct. But if the divine persons cannot be distinct, then we do not have any doctrine of the Trinity."[91] McCall discusses other conceptions of simplicity that he believes are compatible with the Trinity doctrine and find support in the patristic tradition (namely, formal simplicity and generic simplicity), but it is beyond my scope to adequately address the

84. T. Morris, *Our Idea of God*, 176–77.

85. Holmes, *Quest for the Trinity*, 195. In Holmes's view, the "persons" of the Trinity do not each possess "self-determination," "volition," "self-awareness," and "cognition" (Holmes, *Quest for the Trinity*, 144). Phillip Cary likewise contends, "According to Nicene orthodoxy there is only one will in God." Cary, "New Evangelical Subordinationism," 6.

86. McCall, *Which Trinity?*, 238. McCall argues that some traditionally categorized as Latin (or singularity) theorists (e.g., Augustine, Richard of St. Victor) make claims consistent with social theories. Indeed, McCall argues that Augustine himself "views the divine persons as distinct agents with will and consciousness." McCall, "Social Trinitarianism," 10.

87. Hasker, *Metaphysics and the Tri-personal God*, 75.

88. See Williams, "Introduction to Classical Theism," 96.

89. Holmes, *Quest for the Trinity*, 200.

90. See the brief discussion of objections to divine simplicity in Peckham, *Doctrine of God*, 227–30. See further Mullins, "Simply Impossible," 181–203.

91. McCall, "Trinity Doctrine," 57. While affirming strict simplicity, James Dolezal himself recognizes, "It is a challenge to understand how there can be a real identity between the essence, which is one, and the divine persons, which are three. *Prima facie* it seems to contravene the law of identity." Dolezal, "Trinity," 88.

technical issues involved here.[92] For my part, while I believe Scripture strongly affirms the essential oneness and unity of God and that nothing is more basic than God, I see no biblical warrant for the *strict* doctrine of divine simplicity. Further, insofar as strict simplicity entails strict timelessness, immutability, and impassibility (as advocates suppose), it conflicts with the conclusions reached in earlier chapters and what I believe Scripture teaches regarding trinitarian relations.[93]

Issues regarding divine simplicity aside, I believe there is biblical warrant for the view that the Father, the Son, and the Spirit each have a distinct faculty of reason, will, and self-consciousness. I thus hold a relational view of the Trinity, which might be (broadly) classified as a social theory but which sharply differs from any social theories with weak views of the ontological unity of the Trinity.[94] Space does not permit me to make a developed case here, so I will simply map out some lines of biblical data that I believe support this view, particularly the way Scripture attributes distinct, unique, and voluntarily undertaken experiences to different trinitarian persons.[95]

For example, the Father gave his beloved Son, but the Son did not. The Son gave *himself* (Eph. 5:2), but the Father did not give *himself* as sin offering and the Spirit did not give *himself* as sin offering. The way Jesus speaks of this distinguishes between his own self-consciousness and will and that of the Father: "For this reason the Father loves me, because I lay down my life in order to take it up again. No one takes it from me, but I lay it down of my own accord. I have power to lay it down, and I have power to take it up again. I have received this command from my Father" (John 10:17–18). This distinguishes between the self-consciousness and will of the Father, who issues the command and loves Christ, and the self-consciousness and will of Christ,

---

92. As McCall defines them, both formal and generic simplicity agree that "there is no composition whereby God is made up of parts or pieces that are ontologically prior to or more basic than God" (McCall, "Trinity Doctrine," 55). McCall identifies John Duns Scotus as an advocate of formal simplicity, which maintains there are no distinctions in God other than formal distinctions, which are neither real distinctions (in the technical sense) nor merely conceptual distinctions. Generic simplicity instead maintains that "the divine attributes are mutually and necessarily coextensive" such that "whatever is properly predicated of the divine nature is a sort of unbreakable package," and thus, while divine attributes are "distinct properties," they are "not, strictly speaking, parts of God" (McCall, "Trinity Doctrine," 50). McCall identifies Gregory of Nyssa as an advocate of this view.

93. Generic simplicity is consistent with covenantal theism, however, and formal simplicity may also be compatible.

94. Cf. McCall, "Relational Trinity," 113–37; McCall, *Which Trinity?*, 236–41.

95. In some sense, however, the operations of the Trinity (*ad extra*) are indivisible—e.g., the Son does nothing of himself (John 5:19). The Father, the Son, and the Spirit create, redeem, etc. However, I believe Scripture teaches that the persons *voluntarily* play distinct roles and that the very distinctness of these voluntary roles indicates three wills in the Trinity.

who receives the command and of *his* "own accord" wills to lay down *his own* life for us (cf. Gal. 1:4).[96] From this (and other data), it seems to follow that the Father, the Son, and the Spirit must hold different *de se* beliefs (i.e., first-person beliefs that no other person could hold). For example, only the Son could hold the *de se* belief "I am laying down my life."[97]

A singularity theorist might attempt to explain this by partitive exegesis—attributing the self-consciousness and will depicted here to *only* Christ's human nature. This move comes at a high cost, however, since it entails that when Jesus here speaks of voluntarily laying down his life, he speaks only of his *human* self-consciousness and will. This not only raises questions for a single-subject Christology but also suggests that texts that teach "Christ loved us and gave himself up for us" (Eph. 5:2; cf. Gal. 2:19; Eph. 5:25) refer only to Christ's human nature such that only relative to Christ's human nature did he give himself up for us. If so, how could Christ's self-giving be the ultimate demonstration of God's love, as Scripture claims (Rom. 5:8)?

Singularity theorists might reply that Christ's divine will is also involved in the sense that the singular will shared by the trinitarian persons willed that Christ give himself for us. Even if so, however, it could still not be true that the divine will made the decision to give *himself* for us—for there would be no distinct, self-conscious self for the divine will to give. It could not be true, then, that any particular *divine* person "loved me and gave *himself* for me" (Gal. 2:20). In this regard, McCall notes that "while it is true that much of the biblical data refers to the economic Trinity, for this distinction to be real in the economy there must be robust distinction within the immanent Trinity. The Son became incarnate—the Logos became human—by humbling himself and taking on himself the form of a servant (Phil. 2:5–11; cf. John 1:1–18). Someone emptied himself and became incarnate, and this someone is the one who was already fully divine and with his Father. He did not become a distinct someone by becoming incarnate; he was already a 'someone' who became incarnate."[98]

96. There is considerable mystery here, and we should tread lightly. But as I (tentatively) understand this, while divinity itself cannot die (at least in the sense of ceasing to exist), the life Christ gave for us is also the life of the *divine* Christ because the Word took on humanity and experienced the "death" of the human nature in whatever way "death" may affect the divine nature.

97. See Mullins, *End of the Timeless God*, 193–94. In this regard, Hasker argues that one must affirm a social view (or something like it) in order to avoid patripassianism (the heretical view that the Father suffered on the cross), for "if it is possible for one Person and not the other to suffer, it must be that, in [Richard] Cross's words, they are distinct 'subjects of mental properties and states'" (Hasker, *Metaphysics and the Tri-personal God*, 71). Cross himself argues that the patristic view is pro-singularity but identifies this as "one powerful argument in favour of a social theory of the Trinity." See Cross, "Two Models of the Trinity?," 275–94.

98. McCall, "Relational Trinity," 119.

Similar issues appear relative to Christ's prayer to the Father in Gethsemane: "Father, if you are willing, remove this cup from me; yet, not my will but yours be done" (Luke 22:42). This explicitly distinguishes the Father's will from the Son's will. Here, again, one might claim that this refers only to Christ's human will. At what cost, however? Are we to believe that only Christ's human will finally decided to give *himself* while Christ's divinity was entirely unaffected? If so, only the human will gave *himself* and Christ's sacrifice affected only his human nature, amounting to a mere human sacrifice.[99]

Even if partitive exegesis could help assuage such problems, and I do not see how it can, how can one know when it is appropriate to apply partitive exegesis? If it is applied whenever revelation about Christ conflicts with one's conception of God, how could the revelation of Christ ever reform one's conception of God? While I believe there is biblical warrant for attributing some things to Christ's divinity (e.g., John 8:58; cf. 1:14; Gal. 4:4) or humanity (e.g., John 4:6; cf. Isa. 40:28) alone, such as when Scripture indicates something cannot apply to divinity or humanity, applying partitive exegesis in the absence of biblically warranted reasons for doing so could undermine Scripture's normative theological authority. Something Christ reveals about God *might* be explained away by predicating it only of Christ's human nature. For my part, I do not see any biblical warrant for attributing Christ's statements in John 10:17–18 and Luke 22:42 to only his human nature; I believe they include Christ's divine will. Christ (qua his divinity and humanity) loved us and gave himself for us (Eph. 5:2; cf. Gal. 2:20) and "for the sake of the joy that was set before him endured the cross" (Heb. 12:2).

Further, Karl Rahner emphasizes that the singularity theory requires that there cannot be any reciprocal love between trinitarian persons. Rahner writes, "The Logos [Word] is not the one who utters, but the one who is uttered. And there is properly no *mutual* love between Father and Son, for this would presuppose two acts."[100] Yet Scripture repeatedly depicts *mutual* love relationship between the Father and the Son; the Father loves the Son (Matt. 3:17; John 3:35; 5:20; 10:17; 15:9–10; 17:23–26), and the Son loves the Father (John 14:31).[101] Indeed, the Father speaks of a person-to-person, I-Thou love

99. Given dyothelitism (a traditional view that attributes a divine will and a human will to Christ), the singularity theorist could posit that the singular divine will of the Trinity timelessly willed that the Son give himself. Yet, if so, only the human will could choose to obey the (so-called) will of the Father as a will other than his own—only the human will could will to "give himself."

100. Rahner, *Trinity*, 106 (emphasis original). Rather, Rahner holds, "The one consciousness [of God] subsists in a threefold way." Rahner, *Trinity*, 107.

101. Because Scripture reveals the Trinity progressively as the persons' roles unfold in salvation history, there is less biblical data on the love of the Spirit, and most information about the

relationship, saying, "You are My beloved Son, in You I am well-pleased" (Mark 1:11 NASB; cf. Luke 3:22). Likewise, Jesus says to the Father, "You loved Me before the foundation of the world" (John 17:24 NASB).[102] Here Christ speaks of an I-Thou love relationship ("you loved me") with the Father *before Christ took on humanity*, an I-Thou love from the *divine* person of the Father to the *divine* person of the Son. In this regard, I agree with McCall's view that "Trinitarian theology should insist on an understanding of persons that is consistent with the New Testament portrayal of the divine persons, that is, as distinct centers of consciousness and will who exist together in loving relationships of mutual dependence."[103]

Some claim that such a view amounts to tritheism, but I disagree.[104] In order to consistently claim that the three distinct persons of Father, Son, and Spirit are one and only one God, one need only affirm that there is some relation between the persons such that the persons together are one and only one God, some "monotheism-securing relation."[105] Eternal relations of love might be

---

Spirit depicts the Spirit's relation to humans. Yet even the Father-Son love relationship is not explicitly revealed until the NT, with most explicit statements in John, among the last books written. Indeed, only one text explicitly says the Son loves the Father (John 14:31). While no texts explicitly say the Spirit loves the Father or the Son, love from the Spirit to the Son may be implied at the baptism of Jesus via "the Spirit of God descending like a dove and alighting on" Jesus as the Father declared, "This is my Son, the Beloved, with whom I am well pleased" (Matt. 3:16–17). Further, given the close association between glory and love that appears in John 17:4–5, 22–26, the Holy Spirit's glorifying the Son (John 16:14) would appear to be an expression of love. More broadly, Paul refers to the "love of the Spirit" (Rom. 15:30; cf. Col. 1:8) and identifies the Holy Spirit as an agent and source of love: "the fruit of the Spirit is love" (Gal. 5:22), "God's love has been poured into our hearts through the Holy Spirit" (Rom. 5:5; cf. 2 Cor. 13:13[14]), and the Spirit bestows love on humans via benevolent actions (e.g., Rom. 8:26–27) in the economy of redemption and via abiding with Christ's followers (John 14:16–17; 1 John 4:12–13, 16; "abiding" is closely associated with love in Johannine writings). In all this (and more, e.g., 1 John 4:8, 16), it is implied that the Holy Spirit is a partner in love relationship—intratrinitarian and divine-human.

102. This understanding complements the idea of the precreation covenant of redemption (*pactum salutis*) within the Trinity, which *implicitly* appears in Scripture in numerous ways. See chap. 4 and Fesko, *Trinity and the Covenant of Redemption*, 51–124, 132–41. While J. V. Fesko argues that the covenant of redemption is consistent with the singularity view, I believe such a covenant involves *distinct* wills of the trinitarian persons.

103. McCall, *Which Trinity?*, 236. As Gijsbert van den Brink notes, in John 14–17 "the Father and the Son are depicted as two distinct persons who mutually address, glorify and coinhere in each other." Van den Brink, "Social Trinitarianism," 342.

104. For one case that at least some "social" or relational conceptions do not entail tritheism, see McCall, "Social Trinitarianism." See further van den Brink, "Social Trinitarianism," 331–50; C. Plantinga, "Social Trinity and Tritheism"; Craig, "Toward a Tenable Social Trinitarianism," 98. Cf. Yandell, "How Many Times," 151–68; Sijuwade, "Functional Monotheism Model."

105. McCall and Rea, "Introduction," 5. Consider McCall's argument that a relative identity approach and a formal simplicity approach avoid tritheism. McCall, "Relational Trinity," 130–31. Further, many scholars have emphasized that Second Temple Judaism sheds light on

monotheism-securing relations, or the trinitarian persons might be ontologically united as one in some other manner. As long as affirming that there is some monotheism-securing relation involves no contradiction, one need not know exactly *how* the trinitarian persons are ontologically united as one in order to coherently affirm *that* this is so.[106] As John Wesley put it, "I believe . . . that God is Three and One. But the *manner how* I do not comprehend." Yet "would it not be absurd . . . to deny the fact [of the Trinity] because I do not understand the manner? That is, to reject *what God has revealed*, because I do not comprehend *what he has not revealed?*"[107]

Some Implications of the Trinity Doctrine

There are a host of important implications of the Trinity doctrine; here I briefly mention only a few. First, the understanding that there is one and only one God and that God is three persons is crucial to the biblical story of redemption, the central point of which is God becoming human in Christ to reconcile humanity to God. Understanding who Christ is and what he accomplishes by the Spirit in the biblical story line of redemption entails a basic conception of the one God who is three persons.

According to Scripture, only God is worthy of worship, and God is the only one to whom we should pray. The proper identification of who God is, then, is crucial to the practice of Christian faith, which involves praying to (Acts 7:60; cf. 1 Cor. 1:2) and worshiping Christ (Matt. 2:11; 14:33; 28:9, 17; Luke 24:52) as the Father himself commanded the angels (Heb. 1:6). As noted earlier, if Christ is not God, it is heresy to address him as God. If Christ is not God, it is heresy to worship him—and it matters a great deal to the God of Scripture whom we worship (cf. Rev. 14:7).[108] If Christ is not God, Christianity is a false religion.

---

this issue. For example, Richard Bauckham makes an impressive case that "the ways in which Second Temple Judaism understood the uniqueness of God" were not incompatible with, and did not prevent, early Christians from "including Jesus in" the "unique divine identity. While this was a radically novel development," it "did not require repudiation of the ways in which Jewish monotheism understood the uniqueness of God" (Bauckham, *God Crucified*, 4). Likewise, Larry Hurtado details how "early Jewish Christians . . . apparently felt thoroughly justified in giving Jesus reverence in terms of divinity *and* at the same time thought of themselves as worshiping *one God.*" Hurtado, *One God, One Lord*, 2.

106. In this regard, Peter Van Inwagen states, "It may be that we cannot understand how God can be three Persons in one Being. It may be that an intellectual grasp of the Trinity is forever beyond us. And why not, really? It is not terribly daring to suppose that reality may contain things whose natures we cannot understand." Van Inwagen, "And Yet There Are Not Three Gods," 243.

107. Wesley, "On the Trinity," in *Works of John Wesley*, 6:220–21 (emphasis original).

108. In Revelation, "the dragon, the sea beast, and the land beast form a competing trinity with the Father, the Son, and the Holy Spirit," usurping worship. Beale, *Revelation*, 729.

If Christ is not God, the crucifixion was merely a human sacrifice, akin to pagan child sacrifice. Yet if Christ (qua divinity) possesses a self-consciousness and will of his own, then Christ (qua divinity) could choose for himself to give *himself* for us (John 10:18; Gal. 2:20), defeating any charge that the atonement is akin to child sacrifice. Moreover, the sacrifice of a mere creature could not be an effective "sacrifice of atonement . . . to show [God's] righteousness" (Rom. 3:25) or to demonstrate God's "love for us" (5:8). If Christ is God, however, then God himself makes atonement at the highest cost to himself; the cross event is God giving *himself* and sacrificing *himself* for us, in the person of Christ. As Fleming Rutledge puts it, God "has not required human sacrifice; he has himself become the human sacrifice."[109] Every Christian, then, must answer for himself or herself the question Jesus puts to Peter in Matthew 16:15: "Who do you say that I am?" Yet Christ's identity and the covenantal plan of redemption itself are inextricably tied to the Trinity doctrine. The Son (qua divinity) willingly gave his life of his "own accord" (John 10:18; cf. Gal. 2:20), in accordance with the covenant of redemption, such that the story of the covenant of redemption is the story of the Trinity of love.

Likewise, the identity of the Holy Spirit is inextricably tied to the Trinity doctrine. The Holy Spirit can only be *another* comforter or advocate (John 14:16) like Christ himself, sent by the Father and the Son to abide with and in Christ's followers wherever they would go (14:16–17; 15:26; cf. 7:38–39; 16:7–16), if the Holy Spirit is one divine person of the one God. Understanding the gravity of this and the many functions of the Holy Spirit in the covenantal plan of redemption is also tied to a basic understanding of the one God who is three persons. Among other activities, the Spirit indwells believers (1 Cor. 6:19–20), convicts of sin (John 16:8), transforms hearts (2 Cor. 3:18; Titus 3:5), is the conduit of God's love poured into our hearts (Rom. 5:5; cf. Gal. 5:22–23), intercedes and translates our prayers (Rom. 8:26–27), gives spiritual gifts to whom he wills (1 Cor. 12:11), and shares the "name" with the Father and the Son in which disciples are to be baptized (Matt. 28:19). In countless ways, understanding who the Spirit is and what the Spirit does is crucial to Christian faith. As Christ warns, "Blasphemy against the Spirit will not be forgiven" and "whoever speaks against the Holy Spirit will not be forgiven, either in this age or in the age to come" (12:31–32; cf. Eph. 4:30).

In this and other ways, the kind of relationships one might have depends on the nature of those involved. I have affection for Brenda, Joel, Lucy, and Bo. However, I have a unique kind of affection and love for Brenda, who is

---

109. Rutledge, *And God Spoke to Abraham*, 302. Kathryn Tanner adds, "God is both the one sacrificing and the one sacrificed. The whole act is God's." Tanner, *Christ the Key*, 268.

my wife, another unique kind of affection and love for Joel, who is my son, and a very different kind of affection for Lucy and Bo, our two cats. Much more so, the trinitarian nature of God massively impacts the way we can and should relate to God and everything else, for if God is Trinity, the Trinity is linked to everything else.

God is love—the eternal Trinity of love. From eternity to eternity, the Father loves the Son and the Spirit as other than himself, the Son loves the Spirit and the Father as other than himself, and the Spirit loves the Father and the Son as other than himself. As Beth Felker Jones puts it, God is "a community of abundant love" and thus "does not need us in order to be in relationship."[110] Nevertheless, God *freely* created the world and is thus worthy

> to receive glory and honor and power,
> for [God] created all things,
> and by [God's] will they existed and were created. (Rev. 4:11)

This same God is supremely worthy of worship and love because he "reconciled us to himself through Christ. . . . In Christ God was reconciling the world to himself" (2 Cor. 5:18–19). In Christ, God's love has been supremely demonstrated (Rom. 5:8). Through the Spirit, the love of God has been poured into human hearts (5:5). And by faith in Christ, anyone can join this fellowship of love and abide in God's love: "For God so loved the world that he gave his only [beloved] Son, so that everyone who believes in him may not perish but may have eternal life" (John 3:16). So who do you say that the Father, the Son, and the Spirit are? This is no mere academic exercise. The trinitarian God is love—the only one to whom and through whom we should pray and the only one worthy of worship. The trinitarian God is the only one who not only loves but also *is* love—the Trinity of love.

Conclusion

While the Trinity doctrine merits book-length treatment all its own, this chapter offered a minimal case regarding the biblical warrant and conceptual coherence of the core Trinity doctrine—there is one and only one God, and God is three distinct (fully) divine persons. This core Trinity doctrine affirms God's perfect oneness and triunity and the distinctness and (full) divinity of the three persons of the Trinity. This involves no contradiction because God is one and three in different respects. God transcends creaturely limitations such

110. Jones, *Practicing Christian Doctrine*, 69.

that the Father, the Son, and the Holy Spirit are ontologically united as one God, ruling out modalism, tritheism, and subordinationism. Regarding other disputed questions about the Trinity, this chapter made a case against eternal subordination within the Trinity and for the view that God is the Trinity of love wherein the Father, the Son, and the Spirit each possess a distinct faculty of reason, will, and self-consciousness whereby from all eternity each trinitarian person loves the other two persons as other than himself (eternal relations of love). This departs from strict simplicity but affirms the unity of God and that there is nothing more basic than God. God is love—the Trinity of love.

Eight

The God
of Covenantal Theism

Who is the God of Christian theism? Who is the God of Scripture? Who is the God whom Christians worship? Who is the covenant-making and covenant-keeping God to whom Christians pray? In previous chapters, I attempted to outline a biblically warranted and systematically coherent conception of God relative to prominent questions such as, Does God change? Does God have emotions? Is God present everywhere? Is God timeless? Does God know the future? Can God do anything and everything? Does God always get what God wants? Is God entirely good and loving? How can God be one and three? Relative to these and other questions, I outlined a case for what I call covenantal theism, which affirms divine aseity and self-sufficiency, qualified immutability and passibility, everlasting eternity, omnipresence, omniscience, omnipotence, sovereign providence, omnibenevolence, and triunity. In this final chapter, after summarizing the basic tenets of covenantal theism as a package, I consider how covenantal theism relates to classical theism, the Christian tradition, perfect being theology, and the issues of worship and prayer.

Covenantal Theism: An Outline

Every conception of God falls far short of perfect correspondence to God. Anyone who thinks about God has a mental image of God—a mosaic of theological ideas—but given our finite and fallible faculties, our theological mosaics never perfectly match the reality. We do not see the entire picture. "We see in a mirror, dimly" and "know only in part" (1 Cor. 13:12). Recognizing this, I have attempted to outline a minimal understanding of some divine attributes that is faithful to the story line and teachings of Scripture while seeking to limit my claims according to the standards of biblical warrant and systematic coherence.

This understanding, which I call covenantal theism, affirms Scripture's depictions of the covenantal God who voluntarily engages in back-and-forth relationship with creatures, including reciprocal love relationships. While God loves all universally prior to any response on the part of creatures, God calls creatures to a special *covenantal* love relationship that is contingent on creaturely response to God's love. Such relationships, however, are not symmetrical. God remains transcendent even as he condescends to be "with us" (immanent). While God is changeless in some respects, God also changes relationally in others, including emotional change. God is repeatedly "moved" by prayer, "relents" in response to human repentance, and responds to creatures in a myriad of other ways. While such relational change is incompatible with pure actuality, covenantal theism affirms divine aseity and self-sufficiency, meaning that God does not need or depend on anything with respect to his existence or his essential nature. Likewise, covenantal theism affirms *qualified* immutability, meaning that God is changeless with respect to his character and essential nature yet changes relationally because he voluntarily engages in back-and-forth relationship with creatures. Further, covenantal theism maintains that God is *voluntarily* passible in relation to the world because God *freely* chose to create this world and *freely* opened himself up to being affected by this world in a way that neither diminishes nor collapses the Creator-creature distinction. The God of Scripture experiences changing emotions, but unlike human emotions, God's emotions are flawless, never irrational, perfectly evaluative, and always in accordance with God's perfect character and will.

While considerable mystery remains regarding the precise manner of divine presence relative to space and time, covenantal theism affirms that God is omnipresent *at least* in the sense that God's knowledge and power extend to all creation, yet God can also be present in a *special* manner in specific locations (special divine presence). However, God is not encompassed by or restricted to any location or physical form. God is Spirit and God is omnipotent such that God cannot be contained by the physical universe that he himself created. God can be genuinely "with us" (immanent) while remaining over and above us (transcendent) as Creator and Lord over all. In this and a host of other ways, the God of Scripture is the God who is near while remaining far and far while remaining near. This understanding of God's relation to the world seeks to avoid the equal and opposite errors of emphasizing God's transcendence to the exclusion of God's genuine immanence ("with us") or emphasizing God's immanence to the exclusion of God's genuine transcendence ("beyond us" and every creaturely category).

With regard to time, covenantal theism affirms that God has no beginning and no end, and yet God is not timeless. God is everlastingly eternal and *analogically* temporal—that is, God (in a manner unique to divinity) experiences succession of time and performs successive actions and reactions but neither is restricted by time nor relates to time in precisely the ways that apply to mere creatures. God is *temporal* in the minimal sense of experiencing temporal succession but relates to and experiences time very differently than creatures, in ways we do not fully understand.

Relative to divine knowledge, covenantal theism affirms divine omniscience and exhaustive definite foreknowledge. God knows all things that can be known and has *certain* knowledge of all future events. Without dogmatically committing to any particular model of just *how* God knows the future, covenantal theism maintains that Scripture teaches God has such foreknowledge. And covenantal theism maintains there is no apparent logical or ontological contradiction involved in affirming both that God has such foreknowledge and that he consistently grants libertarian free will to creatures. At the same time, God knows each creature intimately and in a special way—knowing the first-person perspective of each creature and empathizing with creatures (insofar as is moral and otherwise appropriate) while retaining God's own unique and perfect divine perspective.

Divine omniscience directly relates to questions regarding divine power and providence. Covenantal theism affirms divine omnipotence, meaning that God possesses the power to do anything that is logically possible and consistent with his essential nature. The omnipotent God of Scripture creates all and sustains all, yet he also acts in *special* ways in particular times and places. While God could causally determine history, God chooses instead to consistently grant creatures consequential freedom. I have labeled this view sovereignty indeterminism. Because some creatures exercise their freedom to do otherwise than God ideally desires, God does not always get what he wants. God's ideal desires are often unfulfilled. Yet drawing on his foreknowledge, God takes into account all the *free* decisions of creatures (including the bad ones, which are not up to him) and wills and providentially brings about the most preferable outcome that includes such decisions. I call this God's remedial will. In this way, God sovereignly governs all of creation such that God's

remedial will always comes to pass, but much of what occurs in creation is
not what God ideally desires or actually prefers.

While God possesses the sheer power to determine all events and thus to
determine that there be no evil, the cost of doing so would be to not grant creatures consequential libertarian freedom—that is, freedom to will otherwise
than God ideally desires in ways that impact the world within some consistent
parameters or limits. If, however, the flourishing of love relationship requires
that creatures possess consequential freedom (with nomic regularity—that
is, freedom to act within some "natural order" that "operate[s] by regular
and well-ordered laws of nature,"[1] accounting for the consistent relationship
of causes and effects in the world), then to undermine such freedom would
be to negate love itself. If so, the supreme value of love may be the morally
sufficient reason for God to consistently grant consequential freedom and
thereby permit many evils that result from creatures' evil decisions. However,
it seems God could prevent numerous kinds of evil while consistently granting
creatures consequential freedom. For example, a fatal airplane crash caused
by mechanical failure might be prevented by divine revelation to the pilot
without undermining consequential freedom.

In this regard, covenantal theism maintains that there is more to the story—
a cosmic conflict between God's kingdom and a demonic realm. This conflict
is not one of sheer power (there could be no such conflict with the omnipotent
God), but it is an epistemic conflict revolving around the devil's slanderous allegations against God's goodness, justice, and love. Insofar as God
consistently grants free will (which necessarily includes freedom regarding
one's beliefs), such an epistemic conflict cannot be settled by sheer power but
requires a cosmic demonstration within which Satan and his cohorts might
be afforded the opportunity to make their case. Via the fall, Satan and his
cohorts have been temporarily granted significant jurisdiction on planet Earth,
limited according to some consistent parameters, or "covenantal" rules of
engagement, which are far from ideal as the product of deliberations before
the heavenly council.

Because God is a covenantal God who is perfectly good and holy and always
keeps his promises, God's future actions are *morally* limited by any promise
or commitment he makes and any covenant to which he agrees. Consequently,
any rules of engagement to which God agrees before the heavenly council
morally limit the exercise of God's power to eliminate or mitigate evil that
(temporarily) falls within the enemy's jurisdiction. While God does everything he (morally) can to prevent and eliminate evil, in some cases preventing

---

1. Murray, *Nature Red in Tooth and Claw*, 7.

a particular evil occurrence would (1) impinge on the kind of creaturely free will that is necessary for love, (2) contravene the rules of engagement to which God has committed himself, and/or (3) result in greater evil or less flourishing of love. According to this theodicy of love, God has done everything that could be done for this world without undermining love relationship, and God will finally eradicate evil without compromising love. In the meantime, while creatures suffer immensely due to evil, the voluntarily suffering God of the cross suffers most of all, providing the conclusive demonstration of God's utter love and justice at the cross, thereby defeating the devil's slanderous allegations.

Last but not least, covenantal theism affirms the core Trinity doctrine—there is one and only one God, and God is three distinct (fully) divine persons. This involves no contradiction because God is one and three in different respects. God transcends creaturely limitations such that the Father, the Son, and the Holy Spirit are ontologically united as one God, ruling out modalism, tritheism, and subordinationism. Further, covenantal theism affirms that the Father, the Son, and the Spirit each have a distinct faculty of reason, will, and self-consciousness. From all eternity, the Father loves the Son and the Spirit as persons other than himself, the Son loves the Spirit and the Father as persons other than himself, and the Spirit loves the Father and the Son as persons other than himself—the covenantal Trinity of love who acts in the economy according to the covenant of redemption.

In sum, covenantal theism incorporates Scripture's portrayal of God as dynamically relational and covenantal—the God of steadfast love, passion, compassion, mercy, graciousness, faithfulness, holiness, justice, righteousness, covenant-making and promise-keeping—while affirming the triune God's aseity and self-sufficiency, qualified immutability and passibility, everlasting eternity, omnipresence, omniscience, omnipotence, sovereign providence, and omnibenevolence. The covenantal God of Scripture is the Creator who is always utterly distinct from creation yet voluntarily engages in genuine back-and-forth relationship with creation. Accordingly, throughout Scripture's depiction of God's relationship with the world, there is a crucial juxtaposition of the universal and the particular. God is transcendent and immanent, without contradiction. The God of Scripture reveals himself to all in all times and places (general revelation) yet has specially revealed himself in particular times and places, supremely in the incarnation (special revelation). The God of Scripture is present everywhere (omnipresence) yet is present in special ways at particular times and places (special presence). The covenantal God of Scripture is the omnipotent God who creates *all* and sustains *all* yet also acts in *special* ways at particular times and places (special divine action).

The covenantal God of Scripture knows all things perfectly and exhaustively (omniscience) and also perfectly knows the perspective of every conscious creature while retaining God's own perfect and unique divine perspective. The covenantal God of Scripture loves all creatures universally prior to any response by creatures and calls creatures to *special* covenantal love relationship that is contingent on creaturely response. While God's essential nature is changeless, the covenantal God of Scripture changes relationally because he voluntarily engages in back-and-forth (covenant) relationship with creatures while always remaining the same trinitarian God who was and is and is to come.

Covenantal Theism, Classical Theism, and the Christian Tradition

The way covenantal theism relates to classical theism depends a great deal on how one defines classical theism. Earlier, I distinguished between strict and moderate classical theism. On one hand, moderate classical theism departs from strict classical theism in ways such as affirming that God experiences changing emotions (contra strict impassibility), adopting a qualified conception of immutability (contra strict immutability), and maintaining that God is *analogically* temporal (contra strict timelessness). On the other hand, moderate classical theism affirms what I have called the common core of classical theism—divine perfection, necessity, aseity, self-sufficiency, unity, eternity, immutability, omnipotence, and omniscience. Understood this way, covenantal theism is consistent with moderate classical theism.

A major difference between strict classical theism and moderate classical theism involves whether God can engage in *real* relationship with the world— relationship that is real from God's perspective rather than being merely a relation of reason. Moderate classical theism affirms that God is *really* related to the world but not *essentially* related to the world. God needs no world. As such, moderate classical theism might be described as a kind of relational theism and a kind of classical theism—a kind of *relational classical theism*. This view may be deemed *classical* in that it upholds the tenets of core classical theism, emphasizing an unqualified Creator-creature distinction, in contrast to process and other conceptions wherein God is essentially related to the world. On the other hand, this view is relational in that it affirms that God engages in genuine relationship with the world that makes a difference to God, differentiating it from strict classical theism.

Some, however, reserve the term "classical theism" for *strict* classical theism alone, claiming that strict classical theism is *the* traditional Christian view. However, as seen in part throughout this book, this claim is a matter of considerable dispute. The Christian tradition is not uniform, and traditional voices have been interpreted in various competing ways by competent scholars, including relative to the tenets of strict classical theism.[2] For example, as noted earlier, the patristic view(s) of divine impassibility is a matter of considerable debate. James Dolezal is representative of many who argue that strict impassibility "was the orthodox Christian consensus for nearly two millennia."[3] Conversely, Paul Gavrilyuk is representative of numerous others who argue that there was no single, monolithic patristic view on the question of divine impassibility and that theopaschite language (i.e., language of God suffering) was employed by many church fathers.[4] On his view, the fathers are best understood as qualified impassibilists, but some may be understood in ways that would admit a qualified kind of divine passibility.[5]

This raises significant questions about how various church fathers understood divine immutability and aseity. Regarding immutability, Dolezal claims, "The classical understanding of immutability argues that God's ethical immutability requires his [strict] ontological immutability as its foundation."[6] However, Thomas Oden offers a different understanding of the classical view, maintaining, "It is precisely because God is unchanging in the eternal character of his self-giving love that God is free in responding to changing historical circumstances, and versatile in empathy."[7]

The traditional understanding of God and time is also contested. Many agree with Paul Helm that divine timelessness is "the classical Christian view of God's relation to time."[8] However, Richard Swinburne claims that divine temporality is "the view explicit or implicit in Old and New Testaments and in virtually all the writings of the Fathers of the first three centuries."[9] Related to this, Katherin Rogers claims that the "classic doctrine of [timeless]

2. Andrew K. Gabriel likewise concludes, "Classical theism may not be the near unanimous testimony of the Christian tradition, as some theologians claim." Gabriel, *Lord Is the Spirit*, 10–11.

3. Dolezal, "Still Impassible," 125. So also Weinandy, *Does God Suffer?*, 38n21.

4. Gavrilyuk, *Suffering of the Impassible God*, 89, 127. Gabriel adds, "Clearly disagreement exists regarding the prominence of the doctrine of impassibility within the Christian tradition." Gabriel, *Lord Is the Spirit*, 10.

5. See, e.g., Gavrilyuk, "God's Impassible Suffering," 146. See also Scrutton, *Thinking Through Feeling*, and Jordan Wessling's suggestion that his passibilist conception of God might not be "radically far from patristic teaching on divine impassibility" but "compatible with the patristic spirit" in this regard. Wessling, *Love Divine*.

6. Dolezal, "Still Impassible," 129.

7. Oden, *Classic Christianity*, 68.

8. Helm, "Divine Timeless Eternity," 28.

9. Swinburne, *Christian God*, 138.

eternity" entails "eternalism," the "view that the past and future are as real as the present, as opposed to presentism, the view that only the present actually exists."[10] R. T. Mullins, however, argues that "presentism is the classical Christian position," conflicting with divine timelessness.[11] The debate over God and time holds significant implications for ongoing debates over traditional conceptions of the nature and manner of divine presence, not least with respect to significant debates regarding the incarnation.[12] Indeed, as Mullins puts it, "Many of the early Christological heresies were motivated by the *prima facie* incompatibility of divine timelessness, immutability, impassibility, and the incarnation."[13]

Further, there are differing views within the Christian tradition regarding whether divine foreknowledge is compatible with creaturely free will.[14] Closely related, there is significant debate over the position of numerous traditional figures regarding determinism. For example, according to Eleonore Stump, "Historians of philosophy read Augustine on free will so variously that it is sometimes difficult to believe they are reading the same texts."[15] The position of Thomas Aquinas is similarly contested. However, Swinburne claims, "All Christian theologians of the first four centuries believed in human free will in the libertarian sense, as did all subsequent Eastern Orthodox theologians, and most Western Catholic theologians from Duns Scotus (in the fourteenth century) onwards."[16] Relative to the problem of evil, a host of views (including the free will defense and cosmic conflict) appears in the tradition, hinging on how one interprets traditional voices regarding providence.

There are also competing views of divine simplicity. Some argue the tradition supports strict simplicity, while others point to figures whose views seem to support a weaker concept such as formal or even generic simplicity, which some see as merely a robust commitment to divine unity.[17] This overlaps with considerably differing interpretations of the Christian tradition regarding the Trinity. Some believe there were significant differences between East and West relative to understanding trinitarian relations, and others

10. Rogers, *Perfect Being Theology*, 59.

11. Mullins, *End of the Timeless God*, 75.

12. Some argue the traditional view is that God is aspatial (e.g., Rogers, *Perfect Being Theology*, 59) and others that God is "wholly located in every point or region of space." Mullins, *End of the Timeless God*, 38.

13. Mullins, *End of the Timeless God*, 158. See also Gavrilyuk, "God's Impassible Suffering," 142–43.

14. See chap. 4.

15. Stump, "Augustine on Free Will," 124.

16. Swinburne, *Providence and the Problem of Evil*, 35. See also Wilson, *Augustine's Conversion*, 11–94.

17. See McCall, "Trinity Doctrine," 42–59.

argue East and West held a common understanding.[18] Further, some claim the singularity view is the patristic view, whereas others claim a social or relational theory finds support in the tradition.[19] In this regard, while many claim Augustine as an exemplar of singularity theory, others note that at least some of Augustine's writings might support something like a social conception of the Trinity.[20]

In sum, contemporary scholars hold competing interpretations of the tradition regarding impassibility, immutability, timelessness, omnipresence, determinism, providence, the problem of evil, divine simplicity, and trinitarian relations. Regarding these and other issues, much hinges on what parts of the tradition are closely considered and whose interpretation is favored. As Veli-Matti Kärkkäinen explains, "The leads provided by patristic theologies were developed in more than one way," and different systems "claimed to build on the same biblical and patristic foundations." Further, "Rather than settling doctrinal issues—let alone ending debates—the fathers provided a fertile soil of reflections."[21] It is difficult, then, to see how the kinds of questions addressed in this book could be easily settled by appeal to the Christian tradition. Any such appeal would require numerous decisions regarding *which* parts of the tradition to consider and *whose* interpretation is considered valid.[22] In this regard, one might be able to make a substantive case that some kind of moderate classical theism (perhaps even covenantal theism) is consistent with significant streams of the classical Christian tradition.[23]

According to Gavrilyuk's seminal work, some form of qualified passibility may find support in the tradition, particularly given the (qualified) theopaschite terminology many church fathers employed.[24] Early traditional language of *apatheia* may have been intended to simply deny that God has *irrational* or *evil* passions or that God is restricted to bodily form, like humans and/or the highly anthropomorphic Greek gods. If some form of qualified passibility is admitted, divine immutability cannot be of the strict kind but must be some kind of qualified immutability, such as that which Oden makes a case for

18. See chap. 7. This is not even to mention the recent controversies over (functional) subordination.

19. See Holmes, *Quest for the Trinity*, 195; McCall, *Which Trinity?*, 238.

20. See, e.g., McCall, "Social Trinitarianism," 10.

21. Kärkkäinen, *Doctrine of God*, 57.

22. For further discussion of the methodological issues, see Peckham, *Canonical Theology*, chaps. 4–7.

23. Cf. Oden, *Classic Christianity*.

24. Gavrilyuk, *Suffering of the Impassible God*, 89. Gavrilyuk maintains that even "the orthodox" used "theopaschite expressions" in "reference to Christ's crucifixion as freely as did the Arians" (127).

based on his retrieval of the classical Christian tradition.[25] Such conclusions would be consistent with a view of divine aseity that maintains that God is self-existent, needing nothing relative to his existence or essential nature, yet *freely* engages in real relationship with creatures.

Alongside this, if Swinburne is correct, divine temporality finds strong support in the first three centuries of Christianity.[26] Even if one demurs regarding Swinburne's claim on this issue, however, if Mullins is right that "presentism is the classical Christian position," but presentism and timelessness are incompatible, then to be consistent one must break with the tradition one way or the other.[27] If so, the strict classical theist breaks from the tradition regarding presentism, while the moderate classical theist agrees with the tradition regarding presentism but breaks regarding timelessness. Regarding omnipresence, various views of the manner of divine presence are widely considered to be compatible with the classical Christian tradition.

Further, moderate classical theism affirms, with the majority of Christian theists (past and present), what David Hunt calls "the traditional doctrine" of omniscience, including that "God has complete and infallible foreknowledge of the future."[28] Likewise, moderate classical theism directly affirms divine omnipotence and sovereignty, and covenantal theism more specifically affirms sovereignty indeterminism, for which there is considerable support in various streams of the Christian tradition. Further, moderate classical theism is consistent with various traditional approaches to the problem of evil. Covenantal theism more specifically affirms a free will defense and a cosmic conflict approach, consistent with what Gavrilyuk calls "the common core of patristic theodicy" that the "misuse of angelic and human free will is the cause of evil."[29] Finally, moderate classical theism is consistent with various conceptions of the Trinity, and covenantal theism affirms a relational view of the Trinity, at least the primary features of which are consistent with some prominent interpretations of the Christian tradition.[30]

25. See Oden, *Classic Christianity*, 68.

26. Swinburne, *Christian God*, 138.

27. Mullins, *End of the Timeless God*, 75.

28. Hunt, "Simple-Foreknowledge View," 65. Citing Justin Martyr, Augustine, Boethius, Anselm, Thomas Aquinas, Martin Luther, John Calvin, Jacob Arminius, and John Wesley, Hunt concludes that this is "the overwhelming consensus of the Church's leading thinkers." Hunt, "Simple-Foreknowledge View," 69.

29. Gavrilyuk, "Overview of Patristic Theodicies," 6. Jeffrey Burton Russell adds, "The devil has always been a central Christian doctrine, an integral element in Christian tradition." Russell, *Satan*, 226.

30. See also McCall, *Which Trinity?*, 238; McCall, "Relational Trinity"; Hasker, *Metaphysics and the Tri-personal God*, 75. Likewise, as McCall reads Gregory of Nyssa, generic

I make no claim that the possible interpretations referenced above constitute the best or most likely correct understanding of the Christian tradition.
For one, I do not believe the Christian tradition is monolithic on these issues.
Accordingly, much hinges on which parts of the tradition are closely considered and whose interpretation is adopted. Each issue warrants considerable
treatment all its own based on a close reading of primary sources, tasks far
beyond the scope of this work. Even if one believes that strict classical theism is the view most supported by the classical Christian tradition, however,
considerable issues remain regarding the standard of biblical warrant.

At least as most interpret it, the classical Christian tradition affirms a high
view of Scripture and its authority, consonant with the standard of biblical
warrant. Recall Gregory of Nyssa's commitment that "we make the Holy
Scriptures the rule and measure of every tenet; we necessarily fix our eyes
upon that, and approve that alone which may be made to harmonize with the
intention of those writings" and "we will adopt, as the guide of our reasoning,
the Scripture."[31] Further, Gregory writes, "Let the inspired Scripture, then, be
our umpire, and the vote of truth will surely be given to those whose dogmas
are found to agree with the Divine words."[32]

Similarly, Augustine writes, "As regards our writings, which are not a rule
of faith or practice, but only a help to edification, we may suppose that they
contain some things falling short of the truth." He thus posits "a distinct
boundary line separating all productions subsequent to apostolic times from
the authoritative canonical books of the Old and New Testaments. The authority of these books has come down to us from the apostles through the
successions of bishops and the extension of the Church, and, from a position
of lofty supremacy, claims the submission of every faithful and pious mind."
Thus, "in consequence of the distinctive peculiarity of the sacred writings,
we are bound to receive as true whatever the canon shows to have been said
by even one prophet, or apostle, or evangelist."[33] While extracanonical books
offer "merely a profitable study," one owes "unhesitating assent to nothing but
the canonical Scriptures."[34] The "reasonings" of "Catholics" of "high reputation" are "not to be treated by us in the same way as the canonical Scriptures
are treated. We are at liberty, without doing any violence to the respect which

---

simplicity finds support in the Christian tradition, as does formal simplicity. See McCall, "Trinity Doctrine."

31. Gregory of Nyssa, *On the Soul and the Resurrection* (NPNF 5:439).
32. Gregory of Nyssa, *On the Holy Trinity* (NPNF 5:327).
33. Augustine, *Against Faustus the Manichaean* 11.5 (NPNF 4:180).
34. Augustine, *Against Faustus the Manichaean* 11.8 (NPNF 4:183); Augustine, *Nature and Grace* 71 (NPNF 5:146).

these men deserve, to condemn and reject anything in their writings" if they
are found to be untrue. "I deal thus with the writings of others, and I wish
my intelligent readers to deal thus with mine."[35] Augustine is by no means
alone in the Christian tradition in this regard.[36]

If Augustine is rightly understood to mean that Scripture takes precedence
over any extracanonical teachings of the Christian tradition, then consistency
with the classical Christian tradition itself (at least as represented by Augustine and others) requires that theological conclusions meet the standard
of biblical warrant.[37] Even if the tradition is definitive on some issue, then,
appeal to tradition without biblical warrant would be inconsistent with the
tradition to which it appeals.

Perfect Being Theology, Biblical Warrant, and Systematic Coherence

Alongside issues regarding the Christian tradition, some Christian theists
maintain that the doctrine of God should be determined according to the
methodology of perfect being theology, which operates on the conviction
that God is the greatest conceivable being in every way. As Anselm puts it,
God should be conceived of as "whatever it is better to be than not to be."[38]
Accordingly, perfect being theology attributes to God every good (i.e., great-
making) property to the maximum extent possible (*via eminentiae*) and, in
many versions, denies any property thought to be limiting or less than proper
for perfect being (*via negativa*). Yet perfect being theology takes many forms.
Strict classical theism is perhaps the best-known version, but some versions
of moderate classical theism are forms of perfect being theology. Moreover,
some forms of perfect being theology reject classical theism altogether, such
as Charles Hartshorne's process theology.[39] Such differences stem from the
fact that one theologian may consider some property to be a great-making
property while others consider the same attribute to be a deficiency (e.g., strict
impassibility). Recognizing that "one's value judgments are largely affected
by one's culture" and illustrating this by pointing out that many Germans

---

35. Augustine, *Letters* 148.4.15 (*NPNF* 1:502).
36. See Armstrong, "From the κανὼν τῆς ἀληθείας," 46. Further, Thomas Aquinas writes,
"only the canonical Scriptures are the standard of faith" (*sola canonica scriptura est regula
fidei*). Thomas Aquinas, *Commentary on John*, chap. 21, lectio 6. Cf. Thomas Aquinas, *Summa
Theologiae* I.1.8.
37. On issues regarding deriving theological claims from Scripture and the relationship between Scripture and tradition, consider my treatment of the methodological issues and potential
objections in Peckham, *Canonical Theology* (particularly chaps. 4–10).
38. Anselm, *Proslogion 5*, in *Major Works*, 89.
39. See the discussion in Peckham, *Concept of Divine Love*, 124–27.

once thought Hitler was a great person, T. J. Mawson states, "Is our culture [and individual temperament] even now blinding us to some facet of perfection and thus skewing our use of Perfect Being Theology? It may well be."[40] Kevin Vanhoozer notes, further, "Intuitions about perfection differ, a fact that is arguably the Achilles heel of perfect being theology."[41] The form that perfect being theology takes, then, relies on a host of decisions regarding what is worthy of divinity and what is not, regarding which there are many protracted debates.[42]

I fully agree that God is the greatest conceivable being and is thus the perfect being, uniquely worthy of worship and praise. There is "no one greater" (Heb. 6:13), and no one could be greater than the living God. However, I also believe that God is greater than how we conceive of him, and accordingly, I am not at all confident that, absent special revelation, humans are in a position to know *in every case* just what properties are worthy of divinity and which are not. I thus look to Scripture as the uniquely normative guide to what God—*the perfect being*—is actually like, at least to the extent that God has revealed such things. Accordingly, without claiming that my view is the only possible view that might meet such standards, throughout this book I have made a case that covenantal theism is both biblically warranted and systematically coherent and thus meets the two standards that I believe warrant methodological priority.

Relative to the standard of biblical warrant, I will not rehearse the biblical material surveyed in previous chapters, which is only a sample of the canonical investigation I conducted to write this book. All the biblical passages surveyed in this book warrant further discussion, and there is much more to say about the interpretation of individual texts and passages, theologically and otherwise. Recognizing that my interpretations and theological judgments are fallible, I hope those who may disagree with my conclusions will set forth their own views with special attention to showing how their views meet the standard of biblical warrant.

For my part, I have outlined a proposal that covenantal theism is most consistent with the portrayals and claims about God that Scripture affirms, including the repeated testimony that God

---

40. Mawson, *Divine Attributes*, 11.
41. Vanhoozer, *Remythologizing Theology*, 96.
42. In order to know which properties to predicate or deny of God, one must know which properties are worthy of divinity. While obvious deficiencies might be easy to address, what one deems worthy of divinity may sometimes come down to subjective value judgments, affected by one's social location. One who has been a victim of abuse of power might see unbridled power rather differently than one in a position of power.

creates, sustains, and creates anew;

speaks, hears, and responds;

sees, provides, delivers/saves, and rules;

knows, plans, wills, calls, and chooses but has unfulfilled desires;

judges, acts justly, *and* mercifully and graciously forgives;

loves compassionately, passionately, and steadfastly;

grieves, suffers, laments, and relents;

promises, covenants, and engages in covenant relationship;

engages in court proceedings and defeats evil; and

dwells with us and makes holy.

I believe the above actions should be interpreted as real, historical actions of God and that metaphysical and theological commitments should be normed by, and sometimes reformed by, Scripture. Therefore, I believe there is biblical warrant for affirming that God is (among other things) self-existent and self-sufficient, eternal and analogically temporal, immutable relative to essential nature and character while experiencing relational change, passible in the qualified sense of voluntarily entering into affective relationship with creatures, omnipresent, omniscient, omnipotent, omnibenevolent, and a relational Trinity of love.

Relative to the standard of systematic coherence, I believe the tenets of covenantal theism are internally consistent and consistent with one another. If God experiences changing emotions responsive to creatures, as covenantal theism affirms, it follows that God is passible. If God is passible in this way, it follows that God experiences at least some kinds of (relational) change. This is consistent with qualified immutability—God changes relationally but is changeless with respect to his essential nature and character. This also coheres with the view that God is self-existent (aseity) and self-sufficient—God does not depend on any world relative to his existence or essential nature but freely created the world (the Creator-creature distinction). This is complemented by understanding God as the Trinity of love—affirming that the trinitarian persons enjoy eternal love relationship, and thus, prior to and apart from creation, God is love. If God *freely* created the world, it follows that divine passibility relative to creation is voluntary rather than essential, as qualified passibility maintains.

Since change requires the passing of time, for God to experience any change—emotional or otherwise—temporal succession is required, consistent with analogical temporality. This conception of divine eternity is consistent with the view that God can be present in a special way at particular locations (special divine presence) while remaining omnipresent. Omnipresence entails *at least* that God's knowledge and power extend to the entire universe and thus complements and is complemented by divine omnipotence and omniscience.

God can be omnipotent yet affected by creation if God grants creatures consequential freedom to affect him. Likewise, God can be sovereign while consistently granting creatures consequential freedom because God retains his power to finally defeat evil and, as omniscient, knows the future exhaustively in a way that does not causally determine the decisions of creatures. God knows the future free decisions of creatures such that God can plan just how he will bring about the most preferable outcome given the free decisions of creatures, including the bad ones that are not up to God and which God does not want, ensuring that God can and will keep his promises while respecting the kind of freedom necessary for the flourishing of love. Understanding that God grants creatures (both humans and celestial creatures such as angels and demons) consequential freedom for the sake of love provides an avenue (namely, the free will defense and a cosmic conflict framework) for reconciling God's omnipotence, omniscience, and omnibenevolence with the fact that there is so much evil in this world.[43]

The Covenantal God of Scripture Is Worthy of Worship

In what remains of this final chapter, rather than attempting to argue that the understanding of God set forth in covenantal theism is preferable relative to the standard of perfect being theology, I will simply highlight numerous ways covenantal theism matches the characteristics that Scripture identifies as worthy of worship and praise.

Scripture identifies God as worthy "to receive glory and honor and power" because he freely "created all things," and "by [God's] will they existed and were created" (Rev. 4:11). In contrast to false gods, the God of Scripture is praiseworthy because he "made the world and everything in it"; God is "Lord of heaven and earth" who needs nothing but "himself gives to all mortals life and breath and all things" (Acts 17:24–25; cf. Ps. 50:8–15; Isa. 42:5; Rom. 11:33–36). Indeed, he "sustains all things" (Heb. 1:3), and "from him and through him and to him are all things. To him be the glory forever" (Rom. 11:36). So Revelation 14:7 exhorts, "Worship him who made heaven and earth, the sea and the springs of water."

43. See Peckham, *Theodicy of Love.*

God alone is to be worshiped and "exalted" as the uniquely transcendent Creator, the "most high over all the earth" (Ps. 97:9; cf. Isa. 40:22), the holy one and source of all holiness. God declares, "My glory I give to no other, / nor my praise to idols" (Isa. 42:8). Creatures are to "give thanks to his holy name" (Ps. 30:4; cf. 96:9; 99:3; 1 Chron. 16:35), for there is none "like" YHWH "among the gods"; there is none "like" YHWH, "majestic in holiness, / awesome in splendor, doing wonders" (Exod. 15:11).

Yet God is also praiseworthy as the God who is present wherever we may go (omnipresent; see Ps. 139:7–10) and, in a special way, "with us" (Gen. 26:24; Matt. 18:20; 28:20), the one who even condescends to "dwell among" humans (Exod. 25:8; Rev. 21:3) and "is not far from each one of us" (Acts 17:27). Thus, the psalmist says, "I shall again praise Him / For the help of His presence" (Ps. 42:5 NASB). If God is with us, we do not need to be afraid (Isa. 41:10). Because God is everlasting, he can love us with an "everlasting love" (Jer. 31:3) and bestow on others the eternal life he possesses in and from himself (John 5:25–26; Rev. 21:6). As Psalm 41:13 declares, "Blessed be the LORD, the God of Israel, / from everlasting to everlasting" (cf. 106:48).

Scripture repeatedly praises God as the great deliverer and savior (1 Chron. 16:35; Ps. 106:47; Jer. 20:13; Zeph. 3:19). In Christ, God "became flesh and lived among us" (John 1:14), the supreme example of "God with us" (Matt. 1:23 NASB), providing the ultimate deliverance for which God is praised (Luke 1:68; Eph. 1:5–8). The salvation of all who believe could only be accomplished by the trinitarian God at unfathomable cost—the ultimate price. Only given the relationally trinitarian nature of God could the Father give the Son out of love (John 3:16), the Son give himself out of love (Gal. 2:20; Eph. 5:2, 25), and the Holy Spirit be "given to us" to (among other things) pour God's love into our hearts (Rom. 5:5) and give spiritual gifts "to each one individually just as the Spirit chooses" (1 Cor. 12:11).

Scripture also consistently praises God for his awesome power. As Psalm 21:13 proclaims, "Be exalted, O LORD, in your strength! / We will sing and praise your power" (cf. Jer. 32:17). Revelation 11:17 adds,

> We give you thanks, Lord God Almighty,
>   who are and who were,
> for you have taken your great power
>   and begun to reign. (cf. 19:6)

The God of Scripture is repeatedly praised for the perfectly wise, righteous, and loving way he exercises his power and providentially governs the universe. As the victorious multitude in Revelation 15:3–4 sings,

> Great and amazing are your deeds,
>   Lord God the Almighty!
> Just and true are your ways,
>   King of the nations!
> Lord, who will not fear
>   and glorify your name?
> For you alone are holy.
>   All nations will come
>   and worship before you,
> for your [righteous] judgments have been revealed.

Later, in Revelation 16:7, it is proclaimed, "Yes, O Lord God, the Almighty, your judgments are true and just!" Far earlier, Daniel proclaims, "Blessed be the name of God from age to age, for wisdom and power are his" (2:20).

Because God knows and declares "the end from the beginning" and accomplishes his good purpose (Isa. 46:9–10; cf. Eph. 1:9–11), we can have confidence that his promises are sure and his plans can be trusted as perfectly wise. He always takes the most preferable available course, without compromising his holiness, love, or justice. We can thus be sure that God will finally eradicate evil; God will make all things new, and evil will never rise again (Rev. 21:4–5). Moreover, the God who knows the end from the beginning foreknows each individual and has a good and loving plan for every person. Thus, Paul speaks of "the only wise God, through Jesus Christ, to whom be the glory forever!" (Rom. 16:27).

Because God's righteous acts have been revealed—supremely in Christ's ultimate demonstration of God's righteousness and love (Rom. 3:25–26; 5:8)— we can have confidence and praise God for his utter and complete goodness. Even when we do not understand why some things happen as they do, the God of the cross can be trusted and is worthy of all praise:

> Worthy is the Lamb that was slaughtered
> to receive power and wealth and wisdom and might
> and honor and glory and blessing! (Rev. 5:12)

God is to be worshiped and praised for his perfect and changeless character of steadfast love, faithfulness, truth, and justice. As Psalm 136:1 declares, "O give thanks to the LORD, for he is good, for his steadfast love endures forever" (cf. Isa. 63:7). Psalm 89:5 likewise proclaims, "Let the heavens praise your wonders, O LORD, your faithfulness in the assembly of the holy ones" (cf. 117:2). Deuteronomy 32:3–4 adds, ascribe greatness to our God!

The Rock, his work is perfect,
and all his ways are just.
A faithful God, without deceit,
just and upright is he.

Because God's essential nature and character are changeless (Ps. 102:25–27), we can trust that (among other things) God always has the power to save, always has the wisdom to know just what to do, is always with us, and is always and only good and loving (cf. Mal. 3:6). God gives only good gifts because with him "there is no variation or shadow due to change" (James 1:17). Because God never lies (Titus 1:2) and "remains faithful—for he cannot deny himself" (2 Tim. 2:13), we can be sure that God will always keep his promises and covenants (Deut. 7:9; Neh. 9:32; Dan. 9:4). The God of Scripture is praiseworthy not only for always keeping his promises and covenants but also for repeatedly maintaining covenant relationship with humans even after humans have forfeited any right to such relationship (cf. Exod. 33:12–34:7).

In this regard, God is repeatedly praised for his mercy, grace, and compassion as the one who is moved to grief and sorrow and otherwise changes in relation to creatures. In compassionate love, God freely bestows grace far beyond any reasonable expectations. "Blessed be the God and Father of our Lord Jesus Christ, the Father of mercies and the God of all consolation, who consoles us in all our affliction" (2 Cor. 1:3–4; cf. 1 Pet. 1:3). Indeed, Psalm 103 exhorts, "Bless the LORD" for "The LORD is compassionate and gracious / Slow to anger and abounding in lovingkindness." "Just as a father has compassion on his children, / So the LORD has compassion on those who fear Him" (vv. 1, 8, 13 NASB; cf. Exod. 34:6; Pss. 116:5; 145:8–9; Isa. 49:15–16; Jer. 31:20)

When we pray, the God of mercy and compassion hears us. It makes sense to offer petitionary prayer to the God of covenantal theism, for this God deeply cares for us, can be affected by and genuinely *respond* to our prayers, has the wisdom and power to appropriately respond to any prayer, and relates to the world in a way that petitionary prayer might make a significant difference relative to God's own actions in the world. For this, Scripture repeatedly praises God. "Blessed be the LORD, for he has heard the sound of my pleadings" (Ps. 28:6). Psalm 66:20 adds,

Blessed be God,
because he has not rejected my prayer
or removed his steadfast love from me.

In these and many other ways, the God of Scripture is the holy one who is uniquely and supremely worthy of worship. The God of Scripture is the compassionate hearer to whom it makes sense to pray. The God of Scripture is the most loving but also the most lovable—God is love. The God of Scripture is the self-existent one in whom is life and to whom we owe everything; he owes us nothing, but he freely and extravagantly bestows his love on creation. The God of Scripture, who lovingly makes and keeps covenants and to whom Christians are to "pray without ceasing" (1 Thess. 5:17), is uniquely worthy of worship and unceasing gratitude, obedience, and praise. So let all who know him pray to him, love him, obey him, worship him, and praise him with all their heart, soul, strength, and mind—now and forevermore.

> Holy, holy, holy,
> the Lord God the Almighty,
>   who was and is and is to come. (Rev. 4:8)
>
> You are worthy, our Lord and God,
>   to receive glory and honor and power,
> for you created all things,
>   and by your will they existed and were created. (4:11)

Bibliography

Abraham, William. *Divine Agency and Divine Action*. 4 vols. Oxford: Oxford University Press, 2017–.

Achtemeier, Elizabeth. *Nahum-Malachi*. Interpretation. Atlanta: John Knox Press, 1986.

Acolatse, Esther E. *Powers, Principalities, and the Spirit: Biblical Realism in Africa and the West*. Grand Rapids: Eerdmans, 2018.

Adams, Robert M. "Must God Create the Best?" In Rowe, *God and the Problem of Evil*, 24–37.

Albright, W. F., and C. S. Mann. *Matthew*. The Anchor Bible 26. New Haven: Yale University Press, 2008.

Alden, Robert L. *Job*. New American Commentary 11. Nashville: Broadman & Holman, 1993.

Allen, Leslie. *Psalms 101–150*. Word Biblical Commentary 21. Dallas: Word, 2002.

Allen, Michael. "Exodus 3 after the Hellenization Thesis." *Journal of Theological Interpretation* 3, no. 2 (2009): 179–96.

Alston, William. *Divine Nature and Human Language*. Ithaca, NY: Cornell University Press, 1989.

Anatolios, Khaled. *Retrieving Nicaea: The Development and Meaning of Trinitarian Doctrine*. Grand Rapids: Baker Academic, 2011.

Andersen, Frances. *Job*. Nottingham: Inter-Varsity, 1976.

Anizor, Uche. *How to Read Theology: Engaging Doctrine Critically and Charitably*. Grand Rapids: Baker Academic, 2018.

Anselm of Canterbury. *The Major Works*. Edited by Brian Davies and G. R. Evans. New York: Oxford University Press, 1998.

Arcadi, James. *An Incarnational Model of the Eucharist*. Cambridge: Cambridge University Press, 2018.

Arminius, Jacob. *The Works of James Arminius*. Vol. 2. Translated by James Nichols. Reprint, Grand Rapids: Baker, 1991.

Armstrong, Jonathan J. "From the κανὼν τῆς ἀληθείας to the κανὼν τῶν γραφῶν: The Role of the Rule of Faith in the Formation of the New Testament Canon." In *Tradition and the Rule of Faith in the Early Church*, edited by Ronnie J. Rombs and Alexander Y. Hwang, 30–47. Washington, DC: Catholic University of America Press, 2010.

Arnold, Clinton. *Powers of Darkness: Principalities and Powers in Paul's Letters*. Downers Grove, IL: IVP Academic, 1992.

Augustine. *On Free Choice of the Will*. Translated by Thomas Williams. Indianapolis: Hackett, 1993.

———. *The Trinity*. Translated by Edmund Hill. Brooklyn: New City, 1991.

Aune, David E. *Revelation 1–5*. Word Biblical Commentary 52A. Dallas: Word, 1998.

Ayres, Lewis. *Nicaea and Its Legacy: An Approach to Fourth-Century Trinitarian Theology*. Oxford: Oxford University Press, 2006.

Baelz, Peter. *Prayer and Providence: A Background Study*. London: SCM, 1968.

Baer, D. A., and R. P. Gordon. "חֶסֶד." *NIDOTTE* 2:211–218.

Baggett, David, and Jerry Walls. *Good God: The Theistic Foundations of Morality*. New York: Oxford University Press, 2011.

Baker, David W. "רָעַע." *NIDOTTE* 3:1154–58.

Baloian, Bruce. "Anger." *NIDOTTE* 4:377–85.

Barr, James. *Biblical Words for Time*. London: SCM, 1969.

Barth, Karl. *Das Evangelium in der Gegenwart*. Theologische Existenz heute 25. Munich: C. Kaiser, 1935.

Barth, Markus. *Ephesians 1–3*. The Anchor Bible 34. Garden City, NY: Doubleday, 1974.

Bartholomew, Craig. *Introducing Biblical Hermeneutics: A Comprehensive Framework for Hearing God in Scripture*. Grand Rapids: Baker Academic, 2015.

Basinger, David. *The Case for Freewill Theism: A Philosophical Assessment*. Downers Grove, IL: InterVarsity, 1996.

———. *Divine Power in Process Theism: A Philosophical Critique*. Albany: State University of New York Press, 1988.

Bauckham, Richard. *God Crucified: Monotheism and Christology in the New Testament*. Grand Rapids: Eerdmans, 1998.

———. "In Defence of *The Crucified God*." In Cameron, *Power and Weakness of God*, 93–118.

———. *Jude, 2 Peter*. Word Biblical Commentary 50. Dallas: Word, 2002.

———. *The Theology of the Book of Revelation.* Cambridge: Cambridge University Press, 1993.

Beale, G. K. *Revelation.* New International Greek Testament Commentary. Grand Rapids: Eerdmans, 1999.

Beasley-Murray, George. *John.* Word Biblical Commentary 36. Dallas: Word, 2002.

Beilby, James K., and Paul R. Eddy, eds. *Divine Foreknowledge: Four Views.* Downers Grove, IL: InterVarsity, 2001.

Bergmann, Michael, and Daniel Howard-Snyder. "Reply to Rowe." In Rowe, *God and the Problem of Evil,* 137–40.

Bietenhard, H. "Satan, Beelzebul, Devil, Exorcism." *NIDNTT* 3:468–72.

Block, Daniel I. *The Book of Ezekiel: Chapters 1–24.* New International Commentary on the Old Testament. Grand Rapids: Eerdmans, 1997.

———. *The Gods of the Nations.* 2nd ed. Grand Rapids: Baker Academic, 2000.

———. *Judges, Ruth.* New American Commentary 6. Nashville: Broadman & Holman, 1999.

Bloesch, Donald. *God the Almighty.* Downers Grove, IL: InterVarsity, 1995.

Blomberg, Craig. *Matthew.* New American Commentary 22. Nashville: Broadman & Holman, 2001.

Blount, Douglas K. "On the Incarnation of a Timeless God." In Ganssle and Woodruff, *God and Time,* 236–48.

Boethius. *The Consolation of Philosophy.* Translated by H. F. Stewart, E. K. Rand, and S. J. Tester. Loeb Classical Library. Cambridge, MA: Harvard University Press, 1973.

Bonhoeffer, Dietrich. *Letters and Papers from Prison.* Dietrich Bonhoeffer Works 8. Fortress: Minneapolis, 2009.

Borchert, Gerald L. *John 1–11.* New American Commentary 25A. Nashville: Broadman & Holman, 2001.

Bovon, François. *Luke 1:1–9:50.* Hermeneia. Minneapolis: Fortress, 2002.

Bowling, Andrew. "זָכַר." *TWOT* 1:241–43.

Boyd, Gregory. *God at War: The Bible and Spiritual Conflict.* Downers Grove, IL: IVP Academic, 1997.

———. "The Open-Theism View." In Beilby and Eddy, *Divine Foreknowledge,* 13–47.

———. "Open-Theist Response to Craig." In Jowers, *Four Views on Divine Providence,* 123–40.

———. "Open-Theist Response to Helm." In Beilby and Eddy, *Divine Foreknowledge,* 190–94.

———. *Satan and the Problem of Evil.* Downers Grove, IL: InterVarsity, 2001.

Bray, Gerald. "Has the Christian Doctrine of God Been Corrupted by Greek Philosophy?" In *God Under Fire,* edited by Douglas S. Huffman and Eric L. Johnson, 105–18. Grand Rapids: Zondervan, 2002.

Brower, Jeffrey E., and Michael C. Rea. "Material Constitution and the Trinity." In McCall and Rea, *Philosophical and Theological Essays on the Trinity*, 263–82.

Bruce, F. F. *The Epistles to the Colossians, to Philemon, and to the Ephesians*. New International Commentary on the New Testament. Grand Rapids: Eerdmans, 1984.

Brueggemann, Walter. "The Book of Exodus: Introduction, Commentary, and Reflections." *NIB* 1:675–982.

Brümmer, Vincent. *The Model of Love: A Study in Philosophical Theology*. Cambridge: Cambridge University Press, 1993.

Brunner, Emil. *The Christian Doctrine of God*. Translated by Olive Wyon. Philadelphia: Westminster, 1950.

Burnett, Richard E. *Karl Barth's Theological Exegesis: The Hermeneutical Principles of the Romerbrief Period*. Grand Rapids: Eerdmans, 1979.

Burns, Charlene P. E. *Christian Understandings of Evil: The Historical Trajectory*. Minneapolis: Fortress, 2016.

Butterworth, Mike. "רחם." *NIDOTTE* 3:1093–1095.

Byerly, T. Ryan. *The Mechanics of Divine Foreknowledge and Providence: A Time-Ordering Account*. New York: Bloomsbury Academic, 2014.

Callender, Craig, ed. *The Oxford Handbook on the Philosophy of Time*. New York: Oxford University Press, 2011.

Calvin, John. *Calvin's Calvinism: Treatises on the Eternal Predestination of God and the Secret Providence of God*. Translated by Henry Cole. 2 vols. London: Wertheim and Macintosh, 1856–57.

———. *Commentaries on the Catholic Epistles*. Grand Rapids: Eerdmans, 1948.

———. *Commentary on the Epistles of Paul the Apostle to the Corinthians*. Translated by John Pringle. 2 vols. Edinburgh: Calvin Translation Society, 1849.

———. *Institutes of the Christian Religion*. Translated by Ford Lewis Battles. Edited by John T. McNeill. Philadelphia: Westminster, 1960.

Cameron, Nigel M. de S., ed. *The Power and Weakness of God: Impassibility and Orthodoxy*. Edinburgh: Rutherford, 1990.

Campbell, Ronnie, Jr. *Worldviews and the Problem of Evil: A Comparative Approach*. Bellingham, WA: Lexham, 2019.

Campbell, William S. "The Freedom and Faithfulness of God in Relation to Israel." *JSNT* 13 (1981): 27–45.

Canale, Fernando L. *Back to Revelation-Inspiration: Searching for the Cognitive Foundation of Christian Theology in a Postmodern World*. Lanham, MD: University Press of America, 2001.

———. *Basic Elements of Christian Theology*. Berrien Springs, MI: Andrews University Lithotech, 2005.

———. *A Criticism of Theological Reason: Time and Timelessness as Primordial Presuppositions*. Berrien Springs, MI: Andrews University Press, 1987.

———. "Doctrine of God." In *Handbook of Seventh-Day Adventist Theology*, edited by Raoul Dederen, 105–57. Hagerstown, MD: Review and Herald, 2000.

Capes, David. *The Divine Christ: Paul, the Lord Jesus, and the Scriptures of Israel*. Grand Rapids: Baker Academic, 2018.

Carson, D. A. *The Difficult Doctrine of the Love of God*. Wheaton: Crossway, 2000.

———. *The Gospel According to John*. Pillar New Testament Commentary. Grand Rapids: Eerdmans, 1991.

Carter, Craig A. *Interpreting Scripture with the Great Tradition: Recovering the Genius of Premodern Exegesis*. Grand Rapids: Baker Academic, 2018.

Cary, Phillip. "The New Evangelical Subordinationism: Reading Inequality into the Trinity." In Jowers and House, *New Evangelical Subordinationism*, 1–12.

Castelo, Daniel. *Apathetic God: Exploring the Contemporary Relevance of Divine Impassibility*. Paternoster Theological Monographs. Colorado Springs: Paternoster, 2009.

———. "Qualified Impassibility." In Matz and Thornhill, *Divine Impassibility*, 53–74.

Chalamet, Christophe. "No Timelessness in God: On Differing Interpretations of Karl Barth's Theology of Eternity, Time, and Election." *Zeitschrift für Dialektische Theologie* 4 (2010): 21–37.

Cherbonnier, Edmond La Beaume. "Is There a Biblical Metaphysic?" *Theology Today* 15, no. 4 (1959): 454–69.

Chesterton, G. K. *The Man Who Was Thursday: A Nightmare*. New York: Dodd, Mead, 1912.

Childs, Brevard S. *Biblical Theology in Crisis*. Philadelphia: Westminster, 1970.

———. *The Book of Exodus*. Old Testament Library. Philadelphia: Westminster, 1974.

Chisholm, Robert B., Jr. "Does God 'Change His Mind'?" *BSac* 152, no. 608 (2007): 387–99.

Christensen, Duane L. *Deuteronomy 21:10–34:12*. Word Biblical Commentary 6A. Dallas: Word, 2002.

Clements, Ronald E. "Deuteronomy." *NIB* 2:269–539.

Coenen, L. "καλέω." *NIDNTT* 1:536–42.

Cole, Graham. *Against the Darkness: The Doctrine of Angels, Satan, and Demons*. Wheaton: Crossway, 2019.

———. *He Who Gives Life: The Doctrine of the Holy Spirit*. Wheaton: Crossway, 2007.

Cone, James. *God of the Oppressed*. New York: Seabury, 1975.

Conrad, J. "נדב." *TDOT* 9:219–26.

Cooper, John W. *Panentheism, the Other God of the Philosophers*. Grand Rapids: Baker Academic, 2006.

Cooper, Lamar Eugene, Sr. *Ezekiel*. New American Commentary 17. Nashville: Broadman & Holman, 1994.

Copan, Paul. *Loving Wisdom: A Guide to Philosophy and Christian Faith*. 2nd ed. Grand Rapids: Eerdmans, 2020.

Cortez, Marc. "Context and Concept: Contextual Theology and the Nature of Theological Discourse." *Westminster Journal of Theology* 67 (2005): 85–102.

Couenhoven, Jesse. "Augusine of Hippo." In Timpe, Griffith, and Levy, *Routledge Companion to Free Will*, 247–57.

Cowan, Steven B., and James S. Spiegel. *The Love of Wisdom: A Christian Introduction to Philosophy*. Nashville: B&H, 2009.

Craig, William Lane. "Divine Eternity." In Flint and Rea, *Oxford Handbook of Philosophical Theology*, 145–66.

———. "Ducking Friendly Fire: Davison on the Grounding Objection." *Philosophia Christi* 8, no. 1 (2006): 161–66.

———. "A Middle-Knowledge Response [to Boyd]." In Beilby and Eddy, *Divine Foreknowledge*, 55–60.

———. "A Middle-Knowledge Response [to Helm]." In Beilby and Eddy, *Divine Foreknowledge*, 202–6.

———. "A Middle-Knowledge Response [to Hunt]." In Beilby and Eddy, *Divine Foreknowledge*, 109–13.

———. "The Middle-Knowledge View." In Beilby and Eddy, *Divine Foreknowledge*, 119–43.

———. "Middle Knowledge, Truth-Makers, and the 'Grounding Objection.'" In Rea, *Oxford Readings in Philosophical Theology*, 2:68–83.

———. *The Only Wise God: The Compatibility of Divine Foreknowledge and Human Freedom*. Grand Rapids: Baker, 1987.

———. "Timelessness and Omnitemporality." In Ganssle, *God and Time*, 129–60.

———. "Toward a Tenable Social Trinitarianism." In McCall and Rea, *Philosophical and Theological Essays on the Trinity*, 89–99.

Craigie, Peter C. *The Book of Deuteronomy*. New International Commentary on the Old Testament. Grand Rapids: Eerdmans, 1976.

Creegan, Nicola Hoggard. *Animal Suffering and the Problem of Evil*. New York: Oxford University Press, 2013.

Creel, Richard. *Divine Impassibility: An Essay in Philosophical Theology*. Cambridge: Cambridge University Press, 1986.

Cremer, Hermann. *The Christian Doctrine of Divine Attributes*. Translated by Robert B. Price. Eugene, OR: Pickwick, 2016.

Crisp, Oliver. "Desiderata for Models of the Hypostatic Union." In *Christology: Ancient and Modern*, edited by Oliver D. Crisp and Fred Sanders, 19–41. Grand Rapids: Zondervan, 2013.

———. "Problems with Perichoresis." *Tyndale Bulletin* 56, no. 1 (2005): 119–40.

Cross, Richard. "The Incarnation." In Flint and Rea, *Oxford Handbook of Philosophical Theology*, 452–75.

———. "Two Models of the Trinity?" *Heythrop Journal* 43 (2002): 275–94.

Crump, David. *Knocking on Heaven's Door: A New Testament Theology of Petitionary Prayer*. Grand Rapids: Baker Academic, 2006.

Cyril of Alexandria. *On the Unity of Christ*. Translated by J. A. McGuckin. Crestwood, NY: St. Vladimir's Seminary Press, 1995.

Davids, Peter H. *The Letters of 2 Peter and Jude*. Pillar New Testament Commentaries. Grand Rapids: Eerdmans, 2006.

Davidson, Jo Ann. *Toward a Theology of Beauty: A Biblical Perspective*. Lanham, MD: University Press of America, 2008.

Davidson, Richard M. "The Divine Covenant Lawsuit Motif in Canonical Perspective." *JATS* 21, nos. 1–2 (2010): 45–84.

———. *Typology in Scripture: A Study of Hermeneutical Typos Structures*. Berrien Springs, MI: Andrews University Press, 1981.

Davies, Oliver. *A Theology of Compassion: Metaphysics of Difference and the Renewal of Tradition*. Grand Rapids: Eerdmans, 2001.

Davies, W. D., and Dale C. Allison. *Matthew 8–18*. International Critical Commentary. New York: T&T Clark, 1991.

Davis, Stephen T., ed. *Encountering Evil: Live Options in Theodicy*. Louisville: Westminster John Knox, 2001.

———. "Free Will and Evil." In Davis, *Encountering Evil*, 73–89.

———. *Logic and the Nature of God*. Grand Rapids: Eerdmans, 1983.

Davison, Scott A. "Craig on the Grounding Objection to Middle Knowledge." *Faith and Philosophy* 21, no. 3 (2004): 365–69.

———. *Petitionary Prayer: A Philosophical Investigation*. Oxford: Oxford University Press, 2017.

DeWeese, Garrett. "Atemporal, Sempiternal, or Omnitemporal: God's Temporal Mode of Being." In Ganssle and Woodruff, *God and Time*, 49–61.

———. *God and the Nature of Time*. Burlington, VT: Ashgate, 2004.

———. "Natural Evil: A 'Free Process' Defense." In *God and Evil: The Case for God in a World Filled with Pain*, edited by Chad Meister and James K. Dew Jr., 53–64. Downers Grove, IL: InterVarsity, 2013.

Diller, Kevin. "Are Sin and Evil Necessary for a Really Good World?" In *The Problem of Evil: Selected Readings*, edited by Michael L. Peterson, 390–409. Notre Dame, IN: University of Notre Dame Press, 2017.

Dolezal, James E. "Still Impassible: Confessing God without Passions." *Journal of the Institute of Reformed Baptist Studies* 1 (2014): 125–51.

———. "Strong Impassibility." In Matz and Thornhill, *Divine Impassibility*, 13–37.

———. "A Strong Impassibility Response." In Matz and Thornhill, *Divine Impassibility*, 114–16.

———. "Trinity, Simplicity and the Status of God's Personal Relations." *IJST* 16, no. 1 (2014): 79–98.

Duby, Steven J. *Divine Simplicity: A Dogmatic Account*. London: Bloomsbury T&T Clark, 2016.

Dunn, James D. G. *The Epistle to the Colossians and to Philemon*. New International Greek Testament Commentary. Grand Rapids: Eerdmans, 1996.

———. *Romans 9–16*. Word Biblical Commentary 38B. Dallas: Word, 1998.

Durham, John I. *Exodus*. Word Biblical Commentary 3. Dallas: Word, 1987.

Durst, Roderick K. *Reordering the Trinity: Six Movements of God in the New Testament*. Grand Rapids: Kregel, 2015.

Duvall, J. Scott, and J. Daniel Hays. *God's Relational Presence: The Cohesive Center of Biblical Theology*. Grand Rapids: Baker Academic, 2019.

Eckert, J. "ἐκλεκτός." *EDNT* 4:416–17.

Ellingsworth, Paul. *The Epistle to the Hebrews*. New International Greek Testament Commentary. Grand Rapids: Eerdmans, 1993.

Erickson, Millard. *Christian Theology*. 3rd ed. Grand Rapids: Baker Academic, 2013.

———. *Who's Tampering with the Trinity?* Grand Rapids: Kregel, 2009.

Esser, H. H. "ἔλεος." *NIDNTT* 2:593–98.

Fee, Gordon D. *The First Epistle to the Corinthians*. New International Commentary on the New Testament. Grand Rapids: Eerdmans, 1987.

———. *Paul's Letter to the Philippians*. New International Commentary on the New Testament. Grand Rapids: Eerdmans, 1995.

Feinberg, John S. *No One Like Him: The Doctrine of God*. Wheaton: Crossway, 2001.

Ferdinando, Keith. *The Triumph of Christ in African Perspective: A Study of Demonology and Redemption in the African Context*. Carlisle, UK: Paternoster, 1999.

Fesko, J. V. *The Trinity and the Covenant of Redemption*. Fearn: Mentor, 2016.

Fitzmyer, Joseph A. *Romans*. The Anchor Bible 31. New York: Doubleday, 1993.

Flint, Thomas P. "Divine Providence." In Flint and Rea, *Oxford Handbook of Philosophical Theology*, 262–85.

———. *Divine Providence: The Molinist Account*. Ithaca, NY: Cornell University Press, 1998.

Flint, Thomas P., and Michael C. Rea, eds. *The Oxford Handbook of Philosophical Theology*. New York: Oxford University Press, 2008.

Frame, John. *The Doctrine of God*. Phillipsburg, NJ: P&R, 2002.

France, R. T. *The Gospel of Matthew*. New International Commentary on the New Testament. Grand Rapids: Eerdmans, 2007.

Freedman, David Noel. "The Name of the God of Moses." *JBL* 79 (1960): 151–56.

Fretheim, Terence E. *Exodus*. Interpretation. Louisville: John Knox, 1991.

———. "The Repentance of God: A Key to Evaluating Old Testament God-Talk." *HBT* 10, no. 1 (1988): 47–70.

———. *The Suffering of God: An Old Testament Perspective*. Minneapolis: Fortress, 1984.

Fuchs, Erich, and Pierre Reymond. *La deuxième Épitre de Saint Pierre. L'épitre de Saint Jude*. Neuchatel: Delachaux & Niestle, 1980.

Gabriel, Andrew K. *The Lord Is the Spirit: The Holy Spirit and the Divine Attributes*. Eugene, OR: Pickwick, 2011.

Ganssle, Gregory E., ed. *God and Time: Four Views*. Downers Grove, IL: InterVarsity, 2001.

Ganssle, Gregory E., and David M. Woodruff, eds. *God and Time: Essays on the Divine Nature*. New York: Oxford University Press, 2002.

Garrigou-Lagrange, Reginald. *God, His Existence and Nature*. 2 vols. 5th ed. Translated by Dom Bede Rose. St. Louis: Herder, 1936.

Gasser, Georg. "God's Omnipresence in the World: On Possible Meanings of 'en' in Panentheism." *International Journal for Philosophy of Religion* 85 (2019): 43–62.

Gatumu, Kabiro wa. *The Pauline Concept of Supernatural Powers: A Reading from the African Worldview*. Paternoster Biblical Monographs. Milton Keynes: Paternoster, 2008.

Gavrilyuk, Paul L. "God's Impassible Suffering in the Flesh: The Promise of Paradoxical Christology." In Keating and White, *Divine Impassibility and the Mystery of Human Suffering*, 127–49.

———. "An Overview of Patristic Theodicies." In *Suffering and Evil in Early Christian Thought*, edited by Nonna Verna Harrison and David G. Hunter, 1–6. Grand Rapids: Baker Academic, 2016.

———. *The Suffering of the Impassible God: The Dialectics of Patristic Thought*. New York: Oxford University Press, 2006.

Geach, P. T. "Omnipotence." In *Contemporary Philosophy of Religion*, edited by Steven M. Cahn and David Shatz, 46–60. New York: Oxford University Press, 1982.

Giles, Kevin. "The Trinity without Tiers." In Jowers and House, *New Evangelical Subordinationism*, 262–87.

Gilmore, George W., and Walter Caspari. "Renunciation of the Devil in the Baptismal Rite." In *The New Schaff-Herzog Encyclopedia of Religious Knowledge*, edited by Samuel Macauley Jackson, 9:488–89. Grand Rapids: Baker, 1953.

Goldingay, John. *Daniel*. Word Biblical Commentary 30. Dallas: Word, 1989.

———. *Old Testament Theology*. Vol. 1, *Israel's Gospel*. Downers Grove, IL: IVP Academic, 2003.

————. *Old Testament Theology*. Vol. 2, *Israel's Faith*. Downers Grove, IL: IVP Academic, 2006.

González, Justo L. *Essential Theological Terms*. Louisville: Westminster John Knox, 2005.

————. *Mañana: Christian Theology from a Hispanic Perspective*. Nashville: Abingdon, 1990.

Gowan, Donald E. *From Eden to Babel: A Commentary on the Book of Genesis 1–11*. International Theological Commentary. Grand Rapids: Eerdmans, 1988.

Green, Joel B. *The Gospel of Luke*. New International Commentary on the New Testament. Grand Rapids: Eerdmans, 1997.

Gregg, Brian Han. *What Does the Bible Say about Suffering?* Downers Grove, IL: IVP Academic, 2016.

Griffin, David Ray. "Creation out of Nothing, Creation of Chaos, and the Problem of Evil." In Davis, *Encountering Evil*, 108–25.

————. "Critique of a Theodicy of Protest." In Davis, *Encountering Evil*, 25–28.

————. "Critique of the Free Will Defense." In Davis, *Encountering Evil*, 93–97.

Griffin, David Ray, John B. Cobb Jr., and Clark H. Pinnock, eds. *Searching for an Adequate God: A Dialogue between Process and Free Will Theists*. Grand Rapids: Eerdmans, 2000.

Griffin, Jeffery D. "An Investigation of Idiomatic Expressions in the Hebrew Bible with a Case Study of Anatomical Idioms." PhD diss., Mid-America Baptist Theological Seminary, 1999.

Grössl, Johannes and Leigh Vicens. "Closing the Door on Limited-Risk Open Theism." *Faith and Philosophy* 31, no. 4 (2014): 475–85.

Gulley, Norman. *Systematic Theology: God as Trinity*. Berrien Springs, MI: Andrews University Press, 2011.

Gunton, Colin E. *The Barth Lectures*. Edited by P. H. Brazier. London: T&T Clark, 2007.

Gupta, Nijay K. "What 'Mercies of God'? *Oiktirmos* in Romans 12:1 against Its Septuagintal Background." *BBR* 22, no. 1 (2012): 81–96.

Guthrie, Shandon L. *Gods of This World: A Philosophical Discussion and Defense of Christian Demonology*. Eugene, OR: Pickwick, 2019.

Haak, Robert D. "A Study and New Interpretation of *Qsr Nps*." *JBL* 101, no. 2 (1982): 161–67.

Hagner, Donald A. *Matthew 14–28*. Word Biblical Commentary 33b. Dallas: Word, 2002.

Hahn, Scott W. *Kinship by Covenant: A Canonical Approach to the Fulfillment of God's Saving Promises*. New Haven: Yale University Press, 2009.

Hall, Christopher, and John Sanders. *Does God Have a Future? A Debate on Divine Providence*. Grand Rapids: Baker Academic, 2003.

Hamilton, Victor P. *The Book of Genesis: Chapters 1–17*. New International Commentary on the Old Testament. Grand Rapids: Eerdmans, 1990.

———. "Satan." *ABD* 5:985–89.

Hanson, Paul D. *Isaiah 40–66*. Interpretation. Louisville: John Knox, 1995.

Harris, Murray J. *Jesus as God: The New Testament Use of* Theos *in Reference to Jesus*. Grand Rapids: Baker, 1998.

Hartley, John E. *The Book of Job*. New International Commentary on the Old Testament. Grand Rapids: Eerdmans, 1988.

Hartman, Louis F., and Alexander A. Di Lella. *Daniel*. The Anchor Bible 23. New Haven: Yale University Press, 2008.

Hartshorne, Charles. *The Divine Relativity: A Social Conception of God*. New Haven: Yale University Press, 1964.

———. *Man's Vision of God and the Logic of Theism*. Hamden, CT: Archon, 1964.

———. *Omnipotence and Other Theological Mistakes*. Albany: State University of New York, 1984.

Harwood, Adam. "Did the Incarnation Introduce Change among the Persons of the Trinity?" *JBTM* 16, no. 2 (2019): 37–46.

Hasker, William. *God, Time, and Knowledge*. Ithaca, NY: Cornell University Press, 1989.

———. *Metaphysics and the Tri-personal God*. Oxford: Oxford University Press, 2013.

———. *The Triumph of God over Evil: Theodicy for a World of Suffering*. Downers Grove, IL: IVP Academic, 2008.

Heiser, Michael S. "Deuteronomy 32:8 and the Sons of God." *BSac* 158 (2001): 52–74.

———. "Divine Council." In *The Lexham Bible Dictionary*, edited by John D. Barry et al. Bellingham, WA: Lexham, 2016 (electronic edition).

———. *The Unseen Realm: Recovering the Supernatural Worldview of the Bible*. Bellingham, WA: Lexham, 2015.

Helm, Paul. "The Augustinian-Calvinist View." In Beilby and Eddy, *Divine Foreknowledge*, 161–89.

———. "Divine Timeless Eternity." In Ganssle, *God and Time*, 28–60.

———. *Eternal God: A Study of God without Time*. New York: Oxford University Press, 1998.

———. "God, Compatibilism, and the Authorship of Sin." *Religious Studies* 46, no. 1 (2010): 115–24.

———. "The Impossibility of Divine Passibility." In Cameron, *Power and Weakness of God*, 119–40.

———. "Of God, and of the Holy Trinity: A Response to Dr. Beckwith." *Churchman* 115, no. 4 (2001): 350–57.

Helseth, Paul Kjoss. "God Causes All Things." In Jowers, *Four Views on Divine Providence*, 25–52.

———. "Response to Boyd." In Jowers, *Four Views on Divine Providence*, 209–23.

Heschel, Abraham. *The Prophets*. New York: Perennial, 2001.

Hess, Elijah. "Has Molina Collapsed the Neo-Molinist Square? A Rejoinder to Kirk MacGregor. *Philosophia Christi* 21, no. 2 (2019): 195–206.

———. "The Open Future Square of Opposition: A Defense." *Sophia* 56, no. 4 (2017): 573–87.

Hick, John. *Evil and the God of Love*. London: Macmillan, 1966.

Hinlicky, Paul R. *Divine Simplicity: Christ the Crisis of Metaphysics*. Grand Rapids: Baker Academic, 2016.

Hoffman, Joshua, and Gary S. Rosenkratz. *The Divine Attributes*. Malden, MA: Blackwell, 2002.

Holmes, Stephen R. *The Quest for the Trinity: The Doctrine of God in Scripture, History and Modernity*. Downers Grove, IL: IVP Academic, 2012.

Horton, Michael. *The Christian Faith: A Systematic Theology for Pilgrims on the Way*. Grand Rapids: Zondervan, 2011.

———. *Lord and Servant: A Covenant Christology*. Louisville: Westminster John Knox, 2005.

Howell, Brian C. *In the Eyes of God: A Metaphorical Approach to Biblical Anthropomorphic Language*. Cambridge: James Clarke and Co., 2014.

Hudson, Hud. "Omnipresence." In Flint and Rea, *Oxford Handbook of Philosophical Theology*, 119–216.

Hume, David. *Dialogues Concerning Natural Religion*. Edinburgh: Blackwood and Sons, 1907.

Hunt, David. "A Simple-Foreknowledge Response [to Boyd]." In Beilby and Eddy, *Divine Foreknowledge*, 48–54.

———. "A Simple-Foreknowledge Response [to Helm]." In Beilby and Eddy, *Divine Foreknowledge*, 195–201.

———. "The Simple-Foreknowledge View." In Beilby and Eddy, *Divine Foreknowledge*, 65–103.

Hurtado, Larry. *One God, One Lord: Early Christian Devotion and Ancient Jewish Monotheism*. 3rd ed. London: T&T Clark, 2015.

Inman, Ross D. "Divine Immensity and Omnipresence." In *The T&T Clark Companion to Analytic Theology*, edited by James M. Arcadi and James T. Turner Jr. London: T&T Clark, forthcoming.

———. "Omnipresence and the Location of the Immaterial." In *Oxford Studies in Philosophy of Religion*, edited by Jonathan Kvanvig, 8:168–206. Oxford: Oxford University Press, 2018.

Janzen, J. Gerald. *Exodus.* Westminster Bible Companion. Louisville: Westminster John Knox, 1997.

Jenson, Robert. "Ipse Pater Non Est Impassibilis." In Keating and White, *Divine Impassibility and the Mystery of Human Suffering,* 117–26.

———. *Systematic Theology.* 2 vols. New York: Oxford University Press, 1997.

Jepsen, Alfred. "אָמַן." *TDOT* 1:292–323.

Johnson, Daniel M. "Calvinism and the Problem of Evil: A Map of the Territory." In *Calvinism and the Problem of Evil,* edited by David E. Alexander and Daniel M. Johnson, 19–55. Eugene, OR: Pickwick, 2016.

Jones, Beth Felker. *Practicing Christian Doctrine: An Introduction to Thinking and Living Theologically.* Grand Rapids: Baker Academic, 2014.

Jowers, Dennis W., ed. *Four Views on Divine Providence.* Grand Rapids: Zondervan, 2011.

Jowers, Dennis W., and H. Wayne House, eds. *The New Evangelical Subordinationism? Perspectives on the Equality of God the Father and God the Son.* Eugene, OR: Pickwick, 2012.

Jüngel, Eberhard. *God as the Mystery of the World.* Translated by Darrell L. Guder. Grand Rapids: Eerdmans, 1983.

Kane, Robert, ed. *The Oxford Handbook of Free Will.* 2nd ed. Oxford: Oxford University Press, 2011.

Kärkkäinen, Veli-Matti. *The Doctrine of God: A Global Introduction.* 2nd ed. Grand Rapids: Baker Academic, 2017.

Keathley, Kenneth. *Salvation and Sovereignty: A Molinist Approach.* Nashville: B&H Academic, 2010.

Keating, James, and Thomas Joseph White, eds. *Divine Impassibility and the Mystery of Human Suffering.* Grand Rapids: Eerdmans, 2009.

Keener, Craig. *Romans.* New Covenant Commentary. Eugene, OR: Cascade, 2009.

———. "Subordination within the Trinity: John 5:18 and 1 Corinthians 15:28." In Jowers and House, *New Evangelical Subordinationism,* 39–58.

Kenny, Anthony. *The God of the Philosophers.* Oxford: Clarendon, 1979.

Kinghorn, Kevin S., with Steven Travis. *But What about God's Wrath? The Compelling Love Story of Divine Anger.* Downers Grove, IL: IVP Academic, 2019.

Kitamori, Kazoh. *Theology of the Pain of God.* Richmond, VA: John Knox, 1965.

Kreider, Glenn R. *God with Us: Exploring God's Personal Interactions with His People throughout the Bible.* Phillipsburg, NJ: P&R, 2014.

Kretzmann, Norman. "Omniscience and Immutability." *Journal of Philosophy* 63 (1966): 409–21.

Kugel, James L. *The God of Old: Inside the Lost World of the Bible.* New York: Free Press, 2004.

Kvanvig, Jonathan. *Destiny and Deliberation.* New York: Oxford University Press, 2011.

Laing, John. *Middle Knowledge: Human Freedom in Divine Sovereignty.* Grand Rapids: Kregel Academic, 2019.

Leftow, Brian. "God, Concepts of." In *The Routledge Encyclopedia of Philosophy.* London: Taylor and Francis, 1998. https://www.rep.routledge.com/articles/thematic /god-concepts-of/v-1/sections/classical-theism.

———. "Omnipotence." In Flint and Rea, *Oxford Handbook of Philosophical Theology,* 167–98.

Leibniz, Gottfried. *Theodicy.* Translated by E. M. Huggard. Chicago: Open Court, 1990.

Lenski, R. C. H. *The Interpretation of St. Paul's Epistle to the Romans.* Columbus, OH: Wartburg, 1945.

Lewis, C. S. "Christianity and Culture." In *Christian Reflections,* edited by Walter Hooper, 12–36. Grand Rapids: Eerdmans, 1967.

———. *The Lion, the Witch, and the Wardrobe.* New York: Scholastic, 1987.

———. *Mere Christianity.* New York: HarperOne, 2001.

———. *The Problem of Pain.* New York: HarperOne, 2001.

Lister, J. Ryan. *The Presence of God.* Wheaton: Crossway, 2015.

Lister, Rob. *God Is Impassible and Impassioned: Toward a Theology of Divine Emotion.* Wheaton: Crossway, 2013.

Lloyd, Michael. "The Fallenness of Nature: Three Nonhuman Suspects." In *Finding Ourselves after Darwin: Conversations on the Image of God, Original Sin, and the Problem of Evil,* edited by Stanley P. Rosenberg, 262–79. Grand Rapids: Baker Academic, 2018.

Loke, Andrew. "Divine Omnipotence and Moral Perfection." *Religious Studies* 46, no. 4 (2010): 525–38.

———. *A Kryptic Model of the Incarnation.* New York: Routledge, 2014.

———. "On the Coherence of the Incarnation: The Divine Preconscious Model." *Neue Zeitschrift für Systematische Theologie und Religionsphilosophie* 51, no. 1 (2009): 50–63.

Longman, Tremper, III. *Daniel.* NIV Application Commentary. Grand Rapids: Zondervan, 1999.

MacDonald, Neil B. *Metaphysics and the God of Israel.* Grand Rapids: Baker Academic, 2006.

MacGregor, Kirk R. *Luis de Molina: The Life and Theology of the Founder of Middle Knowledge.* Grand Rapids: Zondervan, 2015.

———. "The Neo-Molinist Square Collapses: A Molinist Response to Elijah Hess." *Philosophia Christi* 18, no. 1 (2016): 195–206.

Mackie, J. L. "Evil and Omnipotence." *Mind* 64, no. 254 (1955): 200–212.

Manis, R. Zachary. "Could God Do Something Evil? A Molinist Solution to the Problem of Divine Freedom." *Faith and Philosophy* 28, no. 2 (2011): 209–23.

Markschies, Christoph. *God's Body: Jewish, Christian, and Pagan Images of God.* Translated by Alexander Johannes Edmonds. Waco: Baylor University Press, 2019.

Marshall, I. Howard. *The Epistles of John.* Grand Rapids: Eerdmans, 1978.

———. "The New Testament Does Not Teach Universal Salvation." In *Universal Salvation? The Current Debate*, edited by Robin A. Parry and Christopher H. Partridge, 55–76. Grand Rapids: Eerdmans, 2003.

Martens, Peter W. "Embodiment, Heresy, and the Hellenization of Christianity: The Descent of the Soul in Plato and Origen." *HTR* 108, no. 4 (2015): 594–620.

Mason, Rex. *The Books of Haggai, Zechariah, and Malachi.* New York: Cambridge University Press, 1977.

Mathews, Kenneth A. *Genesis 1–11:26.* New American Commentary 1A. Nashville: Broadman & Holman, 1995.

Matz, Robert, and A. Chadwick Thornhill, eds. *Divine Impassibility: Four Views.* Downers Grove, IL: IVP Academic, 2019.

Mavrodes, George. "Some Puzzles Concerning Omnipotence." *Philosophical Review* 72 (1963): 221–23.

Mawson, T. J. *The Divine Attributes.* Cambridge: Cambridge University Press, 2019.

McBrayer, Justin P., and Daniel Howard-Snyder, eds. *The Blackwell Companion to the Problem of Evil.* Malden, MA: Wiley-Blackwell, 2013.

McCall, Thomas H. *Against God and Nature: The Doctrine of Sin.* Wheaton: Crossway, 2019.

———. "Relational Trinity: Creedal Perspective." In *Two Views on the Doctrine of the Trinity*, edited by Jason S. Sexton, 113–37. Grand Rapids: Zondervan, 2014.

———. "Social Trinitarianism and Tritheism Again: A Response to Brian Leftow." *Philosophia Christi* 5, no. 2 (2003): 405–30.

———. "Trinity Doctrine, Plain and Simple." In *Advancing Trinitarian Theology: Explorations in Constructive Dogmatics*, edited by Oliver D. Crisp and Fred Sanders, 42–59. Grand Rapids: Zondervan, 2014.

———. *Which Trinity? Whose Monotheism? Philosophical and Systematic Theologians on the Metaphysics of Trinitarian Theology.* Grand Rapids: Eerdmans, 2010.

McCall, Thomas, and Michael C. Rea. "Introduction." In McCall and Rea, *Philosophical and Theological Essays on the Trinity*, 1–15.

———, eds. *Philosophical and Theological Essays on the Trinity.* New York: Oxford University Press, 2009.

McCann, Hugh J. "The God beyond Time." In Rea and Pojman, *Philosophy of Religion*, 90–103.

McCaulley, Esau. *Reading While Black: African American Biblical Interpretation as an Exercise in Hope.* Downers Grove, IL: IVP Academic, 2020.

McComiskey, Thomas E. "קָדֵשׁ." *TWOT* 2:786–89.

McCormack, Bruce L. "The Actuality of God: Karl Barth in Conversation with Open Theism." In *Engaging the Doctrine of God: Contemporary Protestant Perspectives*, edited by Bruce L. McCormack, 185–243. Grand Rapids: Baker Academic, 2008.

McFague, Sallie. *The Body of God: An Ecological Theology.* Minneapolis: Fortress, 1993.

Meyer, B. F. "Many [= All] Are Called, but Few [= Not All] Are Chosen." *NTS* 36 (1990): 89–97.

Miller, Patrick D. *Deuteronomy.* Interpretation. Louisville: John Knox, 1990.

Miyahira, Nozumu. *Towards a Theology of the Concord of God: A Japanese Perspective on the Trinity.* Carlisle, UK: Paternoster, 2000.

Moffit, David. *Atonement and the Logic of Resurrection in the Epistle to the Hebrews.* Leiden: Brill, 2011.

Molina, Luis de. *On Divine Foreknowledge: Part IV of the Concordia.* Translated by Alfred J. Freddoso. Ithaca, NY: Cornell University Press, 1988.

Moltmann, Jürgen. *The Crucified God: The Cross of Christ as the Foundation and Criticism of Christian Theology.* Translated by R. A. Wilson and John Bowden. New York: Harper & Row, 1974.

———. *The Trinity and the Kingdom.* Translated by Margaret Kohl. Minneapolis: Fortress, 1993.

Moo, Douglas J. *The Epistle to the Romans.* New International Commentary on the New Testament. Grand Rapids: Eerdmans, 1996.

———. *2 Peter and Jude.* NIV Application Commentary. Grand Rapids: Zondervan, 1996.

Moo, Douglas J., and Jonathan A. Moo. *Creation Care: A Biblical Theology of the Natural World.* Grand Rapids: Zondervan, 2018.

Mooney, Justin. "How God Knows Counterfactuals of Freedom." Faith and Philosophy 37, no. 2 (2020): 220–29.

Moreland, J. P., and William Lane Craig. *Philosophical Foundations for a Christian Worldview.* Downers Grove, IL: IVP Academic, 2003.

Morris, Leon. *The Epistle to the Romans.* Pillar New Testament Commentary. Grand Rapids: Eerdmans, 1988.

———. *The Gospel According to John.* Revised Edition. New International Commentary on the New Testament. Grand Rapids: Eerdmans, 1995.

———. *The Gospel According to Matthew.* Pillar New Testament Commentary. Grand Rapids: Eerdmans, 1992.

Morris, Thomas V. *Our Idea of God: An Introduction to Philosophical Theology.* Notre Dame, IN: University of Notre Dame Press, 1991.

Motyer, J. Alec. *Isaiah: An Introduction and Commentary.* Downers Grove, IL: InterVarsity, 1999.

———. *The Prophecy of Isaiah: An Introduction and Commentary*. Downers Grove, IL: InterVarsity, 1993.

Mounce, Robert H. *Romans*. New American Commentary 27. Nashville: Broadman & Holman, 1995.

Mullen, E. T., Jr. "Divine Assembly." *ABD* 2:214–17.

Müller, D. "βούλομαι." *NIDNTT* 3:1015–18.

———. "θέλω." *NIDNTT* 3:1018–23.

Muller, Richard. *God, Creation and Providence in the Thought of Jacob Arminius*. Grand Rapids: Baker, 1991.

Mullins, R. T. "Divine Temporality, the Trinity, and the Charge of Arianism." *Journal of Analytic Theology* 4 (2016): 267–90.

———. *The End of the Timeless God*. New York: Oxford University Press, 2016.

———. "Four-Dimensionalism, Evil, and Christian Belief." *Philosophia Christi* 16, no. 1 (2014): 117–37.

———. *God and Emotions*. Cambridge: Cambridge University Press, forthcoming.

———. "Hasker on the Divine Processions of the Trinitarian Persons." *European Journal for Philosophy of Religion* 9, no. 4 (2017): 181–216.

———. "Simply Impossible: A Case Against Divine Simplicity." *Journal of Reformed Theology* 7 (2013): 181–203.

———. "Why Can't the Impassible God Suffer? Analytic Reflections on Divine Blessedness." *Theologica* 2, no. 1 (2018): 3–22.

Murray, Michael. *Nature Red in Tooth and Claw: Theism and the Problem of Animal Suffering*. New York: Oxford University Press, 2008.

Nash, Ronald. *The Concept of God: An Exploration of Contemporary Difficulties with the Attributes of God*. Grand Rapids: Zondervan, 1983.

Nicholls, Jason. "Openness and Inerrancy: Can They Be Compatible?" *JETS* 45, no. 4 (2002): 629–49.

Nnamani, Amaluche G. *The Paradox of a Suffering God*. New York: Peter Lang, 1995.

Noll, Stephen F. "Angels, Doctrine of." In *Dictionary for Theological Interpretation of the Bible*, edited by Kevin J. Vanhoozer et al., 45–48. Grand Rapids: Baker Academic, 2005.

———. *Angels of Light, Powers of Darkness: Thinking Biblically about Angels, Satan, and Principalities*. Downers Grove, IL: InterVarsity, 1998.

Nolland, John. *The Gospel of Matthew*. New International Greek Testament Commentary. Grand Rapids: Eerdmans, 2005.

Ockham, William. *Predestination, God's Foreknowledge, and Future Contingents*. 2nd ed. Translated by Marilyn McCord Adams and Norman Kretzmann. Indianapolis: Hackett, 1983.

O'Connor, Timothy. "The Impossibility of Middle Knowledge." In Rea, *Oxford Readings in Philosophical Theology*, 2:45–67.

Oden, Thomas C. *Classic Christianity: A Systematic Theology*. San Francisco: HarperOne, 2009.

Ogden, G. S. "Idem Per Idem: Its Use and Meaning." *JSOT* 17, no. 53 (1992): 107–20.

Olson, Dennis T. "The Book of Judges." *NIB* 2:721–888.

Olson, Roger. *The Essentials of Christian Thought*. Grand Rapids: Zondervan, 2017.

———. *The Story of Christian Theology*. Downers Grove, IL: InterVarsity, 1999.

Oord, Thomas Jay. *The Uncontrolling Love of God: An Open and Relational Account of Providence*. Downers Grove, IL: IVP Academic, 2015.

Origen. *Homilies 1–14 on Ezekiel*. Translated by Thomas P. Scheck. Ancient Christian Writers 62. New York: Newman, 2010.

Ortlund, Gavin. "On the Fall of Angels and the Fallenness of Nature: An Evangelical Hypothesis Regarding Natural Evil." *Evangelical Quarterly* 87, no. 2 (2015): 114–36.

Osborne, Grant R. *Matthew*. Zondervan Exegetical Commentary on the New Testament 1. Grand Rapids: Zondervan, 2010.

Oswalt, John N. *The Book of Isaiah: Chapters 40–66*. New International Commentary on the Old Testament. Grand Rapids: Eerdmans, 1998.

The Oxford Dictionary of the Christian Church, edited by Frank L. Cross and E. A. Livingstone, s.v. "Impassibility of God," 828. 3rd rev. ed. New York: Oxford University Press, 2005.

Padgett, Alan. "Eternity as Relative Timelessness." In Ganssle, *God and Time*, 92–110.

———. *God, Eternity, and the Nature of Time*. Eugene, OR: Wipf & Stock, 2000.

———. "Response to Wolterstorff." In *God and Time: Four Views*, edited by Gregory Ganssle, 219–21. Downers Grove, IL: InterVarsity, 2001.

Page, Sydney H. T. *Powers of Evil: A Biblical Study of Satan and Demons*. Grand Rapids: Baker, 1995.

Pannenberg, Wolfhart. "The Appropriation of the Philosophical Concept of God as a Dogmatic Problem of Early Christian Theology." In *Basic Questions in Theology*, 2:119–83. Translated by George H. Kehm. London: SCM, 1971.

———. *Systematic Theology*. 3 vols. Grand Rapids: Eerdmans, 1991–94.

Parunak, H. Van Dyke. "A Semantic Survey of NHM." *Biblica* 56 (1975): 512–32.

Pasnau, Robert. "On Existing All at Once." In *God, Eternity, and Time*, edited by Christian Tapp and Edmund Runggaldier, 11–28. Farnham: Ashgate, 2011.

Peckham, John C. *Canonical Theology: The Biblical Canon, Sola Scriptura, and Theological Method*. Grand Rapids: Eerdmans, 2016.

———. *The Concept of Divine Love in the Context of the God-World Relationship*. Studies in Biblical Literature 159. New York: Peter Lang, 2014.

———. *The Doctrine of God: Introducing the Big Questions.* London: T&T Clark, 2019.

———. "The Influence Aim Problem of Petitionary Prayer." *Journal of Analytic Theology* 8 (2020): 412–32.

———. *The Love of God: A Canonical Model.* Downers Grove, IL: IVP Academic, 2015.

———. "The Passible Potter and the Contingent Clay: A Theological Study of Jeremiah 18:1–10." *JATS* 18, no. 1 (2007): 130–50.

———. "Qualified Passibility." In Matz and Thornhill, *Divine Impassibility*, 87–113.

———. "The Rationale for Canonical Theology: An Approach to Systematic Theology after Modernism." *AUSS* 55, no. 1 (2017): 83–105.

———. *Theodicy of Love: Cosmic Conflict and the Problem of Evil.* Grand Rapids: Baker Academic, 2018.

Pelikan, Jaroslav. *The Emergence of the Catholic Tradition: 100–600.* Chicago: University of Chicago Press, 1971.

Perszyk, Ken, ed. *Molinism: The Contemporary Debate.* New York: Oxford University Press, 2011.

Pike, Nelson. "Divine Omniscience and Voluntary Action." *Philosophical Review* 74 (1965): 27–46.

———. *God and Timelessness.* London: Routledge & Kegan Paul, 1970.

Pinnock, Clark. *Most Moved Mover.* Grand Rapids: Baker Academic, 2001.

———. "Systematic Theology." In Pinnock et al., *Openness of God*, 101–25.

Pinnock, Clark, Richard Rice, John Sanders, William Hasker, and David Basinger. *The Openness of God: A Biblical Challenge to the Traditional Understanding of God.* Downers Grove, IL: InterVarsity, 1994.

Piper, John. "Are There Two Wills in God?" In *Still Sovereign: Contemporary Perspectives on Election, Foreknowledge, and Grace*, edited by Thomas R. Schreiner and Bruce A. Ware, 107–32. Grand Rapids: Baker Books, 2000.

———. "How Does a Sovereign God Love? Reply to Thomas Talbott." *Reformed Journal* 33, no. 4 (1983): 9–13.

Plantinga, Alvin. *God, Freedom, and Evil.* Grand Rapids: Eerdmans, 1977.

———. *The Nature of Necessity.* Oxford: Clarendon, 1974.

———. "On Ockham's Way Out." *Faith and Philosophy* 3 (1986): 235–69.

———. "Self-Profile." In *Alvin Plantinga*, edited by James E. Tomberlin and Peter van Inwagen, 3–97. Dordrecht: Riedel, 1985.

———. "Supralapsarianism or 'O Felix Culpa.'" In *Christian Faith and the Problem of Evil*, edited by Peter van Inwagen, 1–25. Grand Rapids: Eerdmans, 2004.

———. *Warranted Christian Belief.* New York: Oxford University Press, 2000.

———. *Where the Conflict Really Lies: Science, Religion, and Naturalism.* Oxford: Oxford University Press, 2011.

Plantinga, Cornelius, Jr. "Social Trinity and Tritheism." In *Trinity, Incarnation, and Atonement: Philosophical and Theological Essays*, edited by Ronald J. Feenstra and Cornelius Plantinga Jr., 21–47. Notre Dame, IN: University of Notre Dame Press, 1989.

Plantinga, Richard J., Thomas R. Thompson, and Matthew D. Lundberg. *An Introduction to Christian Theology*. Cambridge: Cambridge University Press, 2010.

Polhill, John. *Acts*. New American Commentary 26. Nashville: Broadman, 1992.

Pomplun, Trent. "Impassibility in St. Hilary of Poitiers's *De Trinitate*." In Keating and White, *Divine Impassibility and the Mystery of Human Suffering*, 187–213.

Prior, Arthur. "The Formalities of Omniscience." *Philosophy* 37, no. 140 (1962): 114–29.

Rahner, Karl. *Theological Investigations*. Vol.18, *God and Revelation*. New York: Crossroad, 1983.

———. *The Trinity*. New York: Herder & Herder, 1970.

Rasmussen, Joshua. "The Great Story Theodicy." In *Is God the Best Explanation of Things? A Dialogue*, by Joshua Rasmussen and Felipe Leon, 223–42. Cham, Switzerland: Palgrave Macmillan, 2019.

Rea, Michael C., ed. *Oxford Readings in Philosophical Theology*. 2 vols. New York: Oxford University Press, 2009.

Rea, Michael, and Louis P. Pojman. "The Concept of God." In Rea and Pojman, *Philosophy of Religion*, 1–5.

———, eds. *Philosophy of Religion: An Anthology*. 7th ed. Stamford, CT: Cengage, 2015.

Reese, David George. "Demons: New Testament." *ABD* 2:140–42.

Reibsamen, Jonathan. "Divine Goodness and the Efficacy of Petitionary Prayer." *Religious Studies* 55 (2019): 131–44.

Reichenbach, Bruce. *Divine Providence: God's Love and Human Freedom*. Eugene, OR: Cascade, 2016.

———. *Evil and a Good God*. New York: Fordham University Press, 1982.

Reuter, E. "קָנָא." *TDOT* 13:47–58.

Rice, Richard. *The Openness of God: The Relationship of Divine Foreknowledge and Human Free Will*. Nashville: Review and Herald, 1980.

———. *Suffering and the Search for Meaning*. Downers Grove, IL: IVP Academic, 2014.

Richard of St. Victor. *On the Trinity*. Translated by Ruben Angelici. Cambridge: James Clark, 2012.

Richards, Jay Wesley. *The Untamed God: A Philosophical Exploration of Divine Perfection, Simplicity, and Immutability*. Downers Grove, IL: InterVarsity, 2003.

Ridderbos, J. *Isaiah*. Grand Rapids: Regency, 1985.

Ritz, H. J. "Βουλή." *EDNT* 1:224–25.

Roberts, R. L. "The Rendering 'Only Begotten' in John 3:16." *ResQ* 16 (1973): 2–22.

Rodrigues, Adriani Milli. *Toward a Priestly Christology: A Hermeneutical Study of Christ's Priesthood.* Lanham, MD: Lexington Books/Fortress Academic, 2018.

Rogers, Katherin A. *Perfect Being Theology.* Edinburgh: Edinburgh University Press, 2000.

Roth, John K. "A Theodicy of Protest." In Davis, *Encountering Evil*, 1–20.

Rowe, William L., ed. *God and the Problem of Evil.* Malden, MA: Blackwell, 2001.

———. "Introduction to Part II: The Logical Problem of Evil." In Rowe, *God and the Problem of Evil*, 75–76.

———. *Philosophy of Religion: An Introduction.* 4th ed. Belmont, CA: Wadsworth, 2007.

Russell, Jeffrey Burton. *Satan: The Early Christian Tradition.* Ithaca, NY: Cornell University Press, 1981.

Rutledge, Fleming. *And God Spoke to Abraham: Preaching from the Old Testament.* Grand Rapids: Eerdmans, 2011.

Sakenfeld, Katharine D. "Love in the OT." *ABD* 4:375–81.

Sanders, Fred. *The Triune God.* Grand Rapids: Zondervan, 2016.

Sanders, Fred, and Scott R. Swain, eds. *Retrieving Eternal Generation.* Grand Rapids: Zondervan, 2017.

Sanders, John. *The God Who Risks: A Theology of Providence.* Downers Grove, IL: InterVarsity, 1998.

———. "Historical Considerations." In Pinnock et al., *Openness of God*, 59–91.

Sanou, Boubakar, and John C. Peckham. "Canonical Theology, Social Location, and the Search for Global Theological Method" (forthcoming).

Sarna, Nahum M. *Exodus.* JPS Commentary. Philadelphia: Jewish Publication Society, 1991.

———. *Genesis.* JPS Commentary. Philadelphia: Jewish Publication Society, 1989.

Sauer, G. "קָנָא." *TLOT* 3:1145–47.

Schafer, A. Rahel. "'You, YHWH, Save Humans and Animals': God's Response to the Vocalized Needs of Non-human Animals as Portrayed in the Old Testament." PhD diss., Wheaton College, 2015.

Schaff, Philip, ed. *The Creeds of Christendom.* 3 vols. New York: Harper & Brothers, 1890.

Schleiermacher, Friedrich. *The Christian Faith.* Translated by H. R. Mackintosh. Edinburgh: T&T Clark, 1948.

Schreiner, Thomas R. *1, 2 Peter, Jude.* New American Commentary 37. Nashville: B&H, 2007.

———. *The Epistle to the Romans.* Baker Exegetical Commentary on the New Testament. Grand Rapids: Baker, 1998.

Schrenk, Gottlob. "εκλεγομαι, εκλογη, εκλεκτος." *TDNT* 4:181–92.

Schunck, K. D. "חָמָה." *TDOT* 4:462–65.

Scrutton, Anastasia Philippa. *Thinking Through Feeling: God, Emotion, and Passibility*. London: Continuum, 2011.

Sijuwade, Joshua R. "The Functional Monotheism Model and the Tri-Theism Objection." PhD diss., University of York, 2020.

Simian-Yofre, H. "פָּנִים." *TDOT* 11:589–615.

Solivan, Samuel. *The Spirit, Pathos, and Liberation: Toward an Hispanic Pentecostal Theology*. Sheffield, UK: Sheffield Academic Press, 1998.

Sommer, Benjamin D. *The Bodies of God and the World of Ancient Israel*. Cambridge: Cambridge University Press, 2009.

Sonderegger, Katherine. *Systematic Theology: The Doctrine of God*. Minneapolis: Fortress, 2015.

Spicq, Ceslas. "σπλάγχνα, σπλαγχνίζομαι." *TLNT* 3:273–75.

Stanglin, Kenneth D., and Thomas H. McCall. *Jacob Arminius: Theologian of Grace*. New York: Oxford University Press, 2012.

Staudinger, F. "ἔλεος." *EDNT* 1:429–31.

Stein, Robert H. *Luke*. New American Commentary 24. Nashville: Broadman & Holman, 2001.

Stoebe, H. J. "נגם." *TLOT* 2:734–39.

———. "רחם." *TLOT* 3:1225–30.

Stott, John R. W. *The Cross of Christ*. Downers Grove, IL: InterVarsity, 2006.

Stuart, Douglas. *Exodus*. New American Commentary 2. Nashville: B&H, 2006.

Stump, Eleonore. "Augustine on Free Will." In *The Cambridge Companion to Augustine*, edited by Eleonore Stump and Norman Kretzmann, 124–47. Cambridge: Cambridge University Press, 2006.

———. *The God of the Bible and the God of the Philosophers*. Milwaukee: Marquette University Press, 2016.

———. *Wandering in the Darkness: Narrative and the Problem of Suffering*. New York: Oxford University Press, 2010.

Swinburne, Richard. *The Christian God*. Oxford: Clarendon, 1994.

———. *The Coherence of Theism*. Rev. ed. Oxford: Clarendon, 1993.

———. *Providence and the Problem of Evil*. Oxford: Clarendon, 1998.

———. "The Social Theory of the Trinity." *Religious Studies* 54, no. 3 (2018): 1–19.

———. "Some Major Strands of Theodicy." In Rowe, *God and the Problem of Evil*, 240–64.

Swoboda, A. J. *Subversive Sabbath: The Surprising Power of Rest in a Nonstop World*. Grand Rapids: Brazos, 2018.

Taliaferro, Charles. *Consciousness and the Mind of God*. New York: Cambridge University Press, 1994.

Talley, David. "חָפֵץ." *NIDOTTE* 2:231–34.

Tanner, Kathryn. *Christ the Key*. New York: Cambridge University Press, 2010.

Thomas Aquinas, *Commentary on John*. Translated by Fabian R. Larcher. Revised and edited by The Aquinas Institute, 2020. https://aquinas.cc/la/en/~Ioan.

———. *Summa Contra Gentiles*. Translated by the English Dominican Fathers. London: Burns Oates & Washbourne, 1924.

———. *Summa Theologiae*. Translated by the English Dominican Fathers. London: Burns Oates & Washbourne, 1920.

———. *Truth*. Volume 1. Translated by Robert W. Mulligan. Indianapolis: Hackett, 1994.

Thompson, J. A. *Deuteronomy*. Nottingham: Inter-Varsity, 1974.

———. *Jeremiah*. New International Commentary on the Old Testament. Grand Rapids: Eerdmans, 1980.

Thornhill, A. Chadwick. *The Chosen People: Election, Paul and Second Temple Judaism*. Downers Grove, IL: IVP Academic, 2015.

Thurman, Howard. *Jesus and the Disinherited*. New York: Abingdon-Cokesbury, 1949.

Tigay, Jeffrey. *Deuteronomy*. JPS Commentary. Philadelphia: Jewish Publication Society, 1996.

Timpe, Kevin. *Free Will in Philosophical Theology*. New York: Bloomsbury Academic, 2014.

———. *Free Will: Sourcehood and Its Alternatives*. 2nd ed. New York: Bloomsbury Academic, 2013.

———. "Leeway vs. Sourcehood Conceptions of Free Will." In Timpe, Griffith, and Levy, *Routledge Companion to Free Will*, 213–24.

Timpe, Kevin, Meghan Griffith, and Neil Levy, eds. *The Routledge Companion to Free Will*. New York: Routledge, 2017.

Tinkham, Matthew L., Jr. "Neo-subordinationism: The Alien Argumentation in the Gender Debate." *AUSS* 55, no. 2 (2017): 269–73.

Tonstad, Sigve. *The Lost Meaning of the Seventh Day*. Berrien Springs, MI: Andrews University Press, 2009.

———. "Theodicy and the Theme of Cosmic Conflict in the Early Church." *AUSS* 42, no. 1 (2004): 169–202.

Torrance, Thomas F. *The Christian Doctrine of God: One Being Three Persons*. London: T&T Clark, 2016.

———. *Divine and Contingent Order*. Edinburgh: T&T Clark, 1998.

Towner, Philip H. *The Letters to Timothy and Titus*. New International Commentary on the New Testament. Grand Rapids: Eerdmans, 2006.

Tozer, A. W. *The Knowledge of the Holy: The Attributes of God*. San Francisco: Harper & Row, 1961.

Treier, Daniel J. *Introducing Theological Interpretation of Scripture: Recovering a Christian Practice*. Grand Rapids: Baker Academic, 2008.

Trible, Phyllis. *God and the Rhetoric of Sexuality*. Philadelphia: Fortress, 1978.

van den Brink, Gijsbert. "Social Trinitarianism: A Discussion of Some Recent Theological Criticisms." *IJST* 16, no. 3 (2014): 331–50.

van der Woude, A. S. "פָּנִים." *TLOT* 2:995–1014.

van Driel, Edwin Chr. *Incarnation Anyway: Arguments for a Supralapsarian Christology*. New York: Oxford University Press, 2008.

Vanhoozer, Kevin J. *The Drama of Doctrine: A Canonical-Linguistic Approach to Christian Theology*. Louisville: Westminster John Knox, 2005.

———. *Faith Speaking Understanding*. Louisville: Westminster John Knox, 2014.

———. *Remythologizing Theology: Divine Action, Passion, and Authorship*. New York: Cambridge University Press, 2010.

Van Inwagen, Peter. "And Yet There Are Not Three Gods but One God." In *Philosophy and the Christian Faith*, edited by Thomas V. Morris, 241–77. Notre Dame, IN: University of Notre Dame Press, 1988.

Verhoef, Pieter. *The Books of Haggai and Malachi*. New International Commentary on the Old Testament. Grand Rapids: Eerdmans, 1987.

Vögtle, Anton. *Der Judasbrief, der Zweite Petrusbrief*. Evangelisch-Katholischer Kommentar zum Neuen Testament. Düsseldorf: Benziger, 1994.

Volf, Miroslav. *Free of Charge: Giving and Forgiving in a Culture Stripped of Grace*. Grand Rapids: Zondervan, 2006.

von Balthasar, Hans Urs. *Theo-Drama: Theological Dramatic Theory*. Vol. 4, *The Action*. San Francisco: Ignatius, 1994.

Voss, Hank. "From 'Grammatical-Historical Exegesis' to 'Theological Exegesis': Five Essential Practices." *ERT* 37, no. 2 (2013): 140–52.

Walls, Jerry L. "One Hell of a Problem for Christian Compatibilists." In *Free Will and Theism*, edited by Kevin Timpe and Daniel Speak, 79–98. Oxford: Oxford University Press, 2016.

Waltke, Bruce K. *The Book of Proverbs: Chapters 1–15*. New International Commentary on the Old Testament. Grand Rapids: Eerdmans, 2004.

Walton, John. *Covenant: God's Purpose, God's Plan*. Grand Rapids: Zondervan, 1994.

Ware, Bruce. "An Evangelical Reexamination of the Doctrine of the Immutability of God." PhD diss., Fuller Theological Seminary, 1984.

———. *God's Greater Glory: The Exalted God of Scripture and the Christian Faith*. Wheaton: Crossway, 2004.

———. "A Modified Calvinist Doctrine of God." In *Perspectives on the Doctrine of God: Four Views*, edited by Bruce Ware, 76–120. Nashville: B&H, 2008.

Watson, D. C. K. *My God Is Real*. London: Falcon, 1970.

Webb, Stephen H. *Jesus Christ, Eternal God: Heavenly Flesh and the Metaphysics of Matter*. Oxford: Oxford University Press, 2012.

Webster, John. *God without Measure: Working Papers in Christian Theology*. Vol. 1, *God and the Works of God*. New York: T&T Clark, 2016.

Weinandy, Thomas. *Does God Suffer?* Notre Dame, IN: University of Notre Dame Press, 2000.

Wenham, Gordon. *Genesis 1–15*. Word Biblical Commentary 1. Dallas: Word, 1987.

Wesley, John. *The Works of John Wesley*. 14 vols. Albany, OR: Ages, 1997.

Wessling, Jordan. *Love Divine: A Systematic Account of God's Love for Humanity*. Oxford: Oxford University Press, forthcoming.

Westermann, Claus. *Genesis 1–11*. Continental Commentaries. Minneapolis: Fortress, 1994.

Whitehead, Alfred North. *Process and Reality: An Essay in Cosmology*. Cambridge: Cambridge University Press, 1929.

Wierenga, Edward. "Omnipresence." In *The Stanford Encyclopedia of Philosophy*, edited by Edward N. Zalta. Summer 2019 Edition. https://plato.stanford.edu/archives/sum2019/entries/omnipresence.

————. "Omniscience." In Flint and Rea, *Oxford Handbook of Philosophical Theology*, 129–44.

Williams, Thomas. "Introduction to Classical Theism." In *Models of God and Alternative Ultimate Realities*, edited by Jeanine Diller and Asa Kasher, 95–100. New York: Springer, 2013.

Williamson, Dorena. "Botham Jean's Brother's Offer of Forgiveness Went Viral. His Mother's Calls for Justice Should Too." *Christianity Today*, October 4, 2019. https://www.christianitytoday.com/ct/2019/october-web-only/botham-jean-forgiveness-amber-guyger.html.

Willis, John T. "The 'Repentance' of God in the Books of Samuel, Jeremiah, and Jonah." *HBT* 16 (1994): 156–75.

Wilson, Kenneth M. *Augustine's Conversion from Traditional Free Choice to "Non-free Free Will": A Comprehensive Methodology*. Tübingen: Mohr Siebeck, 2018.

Wilson, Lindsay. *Job*. Two Horizons Old Testament Commentary. Grand Rapids: Eerdmans, 2015.

Wink, Walter. *Walter Wink: Collected Readings*. Edited by Henry French. Minneapolis: Fortress, 2013.

Witherington, Ben, III. *The Acts of the Apostles: A Socio-rhetorical Commentary*. Grand Rapids: Eerdmans, 1998.

Wolterstorff, Nicholas. *Inquiring about God: Selected Essays*. Vol. 1. Cambridge: Cambridge University Press, 2010.

————. "Response to Craig." In Ganssle, *God and Time*, 170–74.

———. "Response to Critics." In Ganssle, *God and Time*, 225–38.

Wood, Jeff, and E. J. Irish. *Secrets of the Kingdom*. Chapel Records, 1983, vinyl.

Wright, N. T. *Matthew for Everyone, Part 1: Chapters 1–15*. London: SPCK, 2004.

———. *Paul and the Faithfulness of God*. Minneapolis: Fortress, 2013.

Wykstra, Stephen J. "Rowe's Noseeum Arguments from Evil." In *The Evidential Argument from Evil*, edited by Daniel Howard-Snyder, 126–50. Bloomington: Indiana University Press, 1996.

Wynkoop, Mildred Bangs. *A Theology of Love: The Dynamic of Wesleyanism*. Kansas City, MO: Beacon Hill, 1972.

Yandell, Keith. "Divine Necessity and Divine Goodness." In *Divine and Human Action: Essays in the Metaphysics of Theism*, edited by Thomas V. Morris, 313–44. Ithaca, NY: Cornell University Press, 1988.

———. "How Many Times Does Three Go into One?" In McCall and Rea, *Philosophical and Theological Essays on the Trinity*, 151–68.

Yeago, David. "The Bible: The Spirit, the Church, and the Scriptures." In *Knowing the Triune God*, edited by David Yeago and James Buckley, 49–93. Grand Rapids: Eerdmans, 2001.

Yong, Amos. *Spirit of Love: A Trinitarian Theology of Grace*. Waco: Baylor University Press, 2012.

Zagzebski, Linda. *The Dilemma of Freedom and Foreknowledge*. New York: Oxford University Press, 1991.

———. "Omnisubjectivity." In *Oxford Studies in Philosophy of Religion*, edited by Jonathan Kvanvig, 1:231–47. Oxford: Oxford University Press, 2008.

———. *Omnisubjectivity: A Defense of a Divine Attribute*. Milwaukee: Marquette University Press, 2013.

Zimmerman, Dean. "God inside Time and before Creation." In Ganssle and Woodruff, *God and Time*, 75–94.

Zobel, Hans-Jürgen. "חֶסֶד." *TDOT* 5:44–64.

Scripture Index

Name Index

Subject Index